HOLL

CARBURETORS & MANIFOLDS

By Mike Urich & Bill Fisher

HPBooks

Drawings by Erwin Acuntius
Photos by Mike Urich, Bill Fisher and Howard Fisher unless otherwise noted
Cover photo by Bill Keller

The cooperation of Holley Carburetor Division, Colt Industries Operating Corporation is gratefully acknowledged.
However, this publication is a wholly independent production of Price Stern Sloan, Inc.

Library of Congress Cataloging-in-Publication Data

Urich, Mike.
Holley carburetors & manifolds.

  Includes index.
  1. Holley carburetors. I. Fisher, Bill.
II. Title. III. Title: Holley carburetors and manifolds.
TL212.U74   1987   629.2'533   87-11952
ISBN 0-89586-433-9

Published by HPBooks
A division of Price Stern Sloan, Inc.
11150 Olympic Boulevard, Sixth Floor
Los Angeles, California 90064
© 1987 Price Stern Sloan, Inc.
Revised edition
12 11 10 9 8

NOTICE: The information in this book is true and complete to the best of our knowledge. All recommendations on parts and procedures are made without any guarantees on the part of the author or Price Stern Sloan. Author and publisher disclaim all liability incurred in connection with the use of this information.

CONTENTS

INTRODUCTION

Holley's low-cost performance team for small-block Chevrolet is 0-1850 Model 4160 carburetor on low-profile 300-38 intake manifold.

WHY A BOOK ON HOLLEY CARBURETORS & MANIFOLDS?

First—When we printed the first edition of this book in 1972, no such book was available. The automotive enthusiast needs accurate and tested information on using Holley high-performance carburetors.

Automotive textbooks have carburetion sections. And, entire books are devoted to carburetor design. But neither type of book really helps the enthusiast because there's usually not enough practical information among the theory and mathematics.

While there's some carburetor information in auto shop manuals, it is usually about repairs on a *normal* car—not one being tuned for *high-performance, racing* or *economy*.

Second—Holley Engineering is constantly developing a lot of good information. But to use it you need a basic understanding of the various systems within the carburetor and how they are interrelated.

So, it was a case of Holley not being able to explain important details unless the listener or reader knew how a carburetor works. Details without the necessary underlying knowledge and understanding can be misleading. They can even cause problems for the user unless he understands the systems relationships—which are not that obvious.

Third—Holleys are the most widely used high-performance carburetors in the world. So it was important to create a book describing the important ones in detail and telling how to get the most out of them.

Finally—The past 25 years or so have seen a continuously increasing emphasis on emission controls. Because the carburetor has been one of the main controls, understanding its relationship to other systems and components in the automobile has become essential. Everyone needs to know more about how the various systems work—and the role played by the carburetor in meeting emission standards.

Photos and illustrations have been used copiously to describe construction features and operation. Some show how to use standard or special parts to get improved performance.

Factory service and overhaul manuals are not often available, so we've included how-to photo sequences on disassembly and assembly of the most commonly used Holley carburetors.

You will find a lot of tips on high-performance carburetors. We incorporated answers to all of the questions enthusiasts ask again and again at technical seminars and at the racetracks. We have dispelled many rumors, myths and half-truths that are part of the romance of using Holley carburetors.

Because Holley continually improves their replacement, high-performance and economy carburetors, changes are to be expected. There is no way to capture more than a snapshot of development and parts availability at that final moment when the printing presses roll.

So, keep track of what is happening in high-

Model NH Holley was original equipment for countless Model Ts.

George Holley in a replica of his 1897 three-wheeler. He built it at age 19!

performance carburetion by staying tuned to the availability of new parts and pieces from Holley. Make sure you always have a copy of the latest Holley High-Performance catalog.

HOLLEY HISTORY
ORIGIN

Holley Carburetor Company combined an intense interest in racing with a dedication to engineering excellence from its beginning. Founded in 1902 by the Holley brothers of Bradford, Pennsylvania, the company grew out of their experiments with the infant horseless carriage.

George M. Holley designed and built his first car at 19. It was a single-cylinder three-wheeler capable of 30 mph (miles per hour). Fascination with speed and things mechanical soon led George into motorcycle racing. He made a name for himself in national competition. With his brother Earl, he formed Holley Brothers to

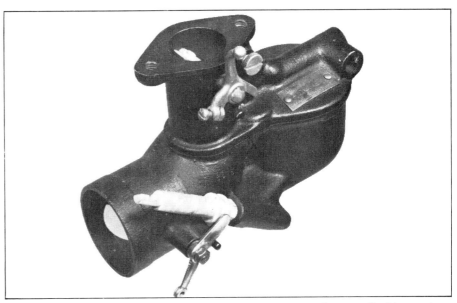

Holley's Model 390 for Model A Ford. Several million were made. Because Zenith was also a supplier, Holley carburetors had a cast "H" or Zenith "Z" on outside, or "Holley" cast in small letters inside bowl.

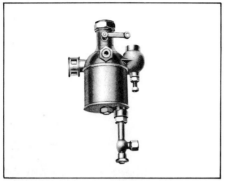

"Iron Pot" carburetor made by Holley Brothers for 1904 curved-dash Oldsmobile started their specialization into carburetor manufacturing. Early customers also included Buick, Pierce-Arrow and Winton.

$100 per horsepower! Holley "Motorette" Runabout cost $550 with 5-1/2 HP engine. This 64-in. wheelbase car weighed 600 pounds. Features included sight-feed lubrication, planetary-drive transmission and tilting steering wheel with lock. Carburetion? A single-barrel Holley, of course. 600 were made in 1903—05.

HOLLY CARBURETOR

For Ford Cars

This carburetor is the present standard equipment of all Ford cars, possessing all the latest features of automatic carburetor construction; especially adapted for the Model T Ford car. Fits manifold and operating rods without any extra fittings. Shipping weight, 5 lbs.

L122—Each... 3.75

1926 Western Auto Catalog advertised a new Holley at a low price! They're worth more than that today. Carburetor is Model NH for Model T Ford.

build motorcycle engines when they were not racing. Later, they built complete motorcycles.

Their combination of talents led to still another vehicle (long since disappeared from the auto scene) the Holley *Motorette*. This fully equipped, jaunty little red sports model was introduced in 1903 and sold for $550. More than 600 of the 5.5-HP vehicles were built over three years. Only three survive; one is in Holley's lobby in Warren, Michigan.

As the fledgling auto industry was taking shape, the first hint of industrial specialization began to emerge. Sensing this trend, the Holley brothers concentrated on designing and building carburetors and ignition components. They left building basic vehicles to their customers and became original equipment suppliers to Pierce-Arrow, Winton, Buick and Ford.

FIRST CARBURETOR

Their first original carburetor, called the *iron pot,* appeared on the curved-dash Oldsmobile in 1904. Over the years, Holley carburetors were installed on AMC, Chrysler, Ford, General Motors, International Harvester, Mack, Diamond Reo and other vehicles. They were often used as original equipment on high-performance cars such as the Corvette LT-1 and the Camaro Z-28. Holley ignition distributors were standard equipment on thousands of vehicles built by International Harvester, Ford and other makers.

Holley makes hundreds of different carburetors for replacement applications. Should you want more fuel flow or decide to alter your basic induction system, they probably produce the parts to do so.

COMPLETE INDUCTION SYSTEMS

Holley carburetors have long been front runners in performance applications, including these models: The original three-barrel, the NASCAR 4500, and a family of large two-barrels, double-pumpers and the Model 4165 small/large spread-bore for good emissions with performance.

In 1976, Economaster economy carburetors and a line of Dominator Street and Strip manifolds joined the Holley Induction Team. Holley is the only carburetor manufacturer in the world making the entire system: fuel pumps, fuel lines, fuel filters, carburetors, air cleaners and intake manifolds. Other items in the Holley line include high-performance electric fuel pumps, ignition kits, valve covers and electrical components.

The transition from carburetors to fuel injection on new cars began in earnest in the '80s. Holley has responded to this change by supplying fuel injection equipment for new car manufacturers and for aftermarket fuel injection rebuilders.

In the aftermarket, Holley offers remanufactured fuel injection systems, individual components and new direct-replacement units. Holley's complete packages offer performance gains over original equipment.

High performance was the cornerstone on which Holley began. It remains an important element of Holley Carburetor and Holley Replacement Parts Divisions of Colt Industries.

ENGINE REQUIREMENTS

Determine your engine's fuel and air requirements before selecting a carb/manifold combination. Double-pumper 850-cfm 4150 0-8162 on Strip Contender 300-25 manifold is a typical drag-race setup.

This chapter concentrates on explaining some of the variables that affect the air/fuel (A/F) requirements of an engine. The objective is to understand these requirements so you can then apply a carburetor that satisfies them.

Don't worry about following complicated formulas because we've distilled carburetion theory into some fundamental concepts. We'll leave the complex calculations to the Holley design engineers.

AIRFLOW REQUIREMENTS

Because the air an engine consumes has to come in through the carburetor, knowing how much air the engine *can* effectively consume will help you select the correct carburetor size.

How big should the carburetor be? Two variables plugged into a simple formula can help

determine the correct carburetor for an engine.

Remember, 1000 cubic centimeters (cc) = 1 liter = 61 CID. Or divide engine displacements specified in cc by 16.4 to convert metric displacement values to CID. For example a 2-liter engine equals 122 CID (2 X 61 = 122) or 2000cc divided by 16.4 equals 122 CID. **Maximum rpm**—the peak rpm that the engine will achieve. Be realistic with this value. An inflated figure will cause you to buy too large a carburetor, which will cause problems discussed throughout this book.

Let's assume your engine has perfect "breathing" or 100% *volumetric efficiency* (VE) and apply our values to calculate the air-flow requirement for the engine in cubic feet per minute *(cfm)*.

For 2-Cycle Engines

$$\frac{CID \times rpm \times Volumetric\ Efficiency}{1728} = cfm$$

For 4-Cycle Engines

$$\frac{CID}{2} \times \frac{rpm}{1728} \times Volumetric\ Efficiency = cfm$$

Example: 350 cubic inch engine
8000 rpm maximum
Assume volumetric efficiency
of 1 (100%)

$$\frac{350\ CID}{2} \times \frac{8000\ rpm}{1728} \times 1 = 811\ cfm$$

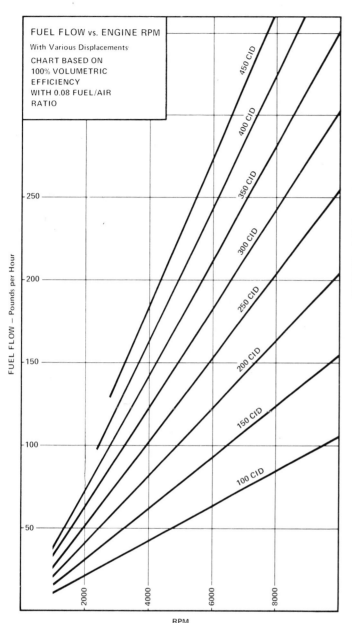

FUEL FLOW vs. ENGINE RPM
With Various Displacements
CHART BASED ON 100% VOLUMETRIC EFFICIENCY WITH 0.08 FUEL/AIR RATIO

To estimate fuel flow, multiply rpm by VE you expect from engine. Chart is based on full-power F/A ratio of 0.08 (A/F = 12.5:1), which is suitable for nearly all engines.

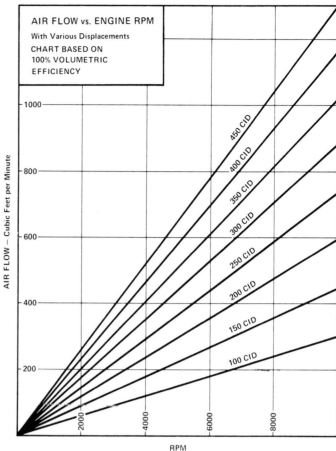

AIR FLOW vs. ENGINE RPM
With Various Displacements
CHART BASED ON 100% VOLUMETRIC EFFICIENCY

To find engine's airflow requirement, select maximum rpm, CID and note cfm at left. Multiply this value by VE you expect from engine (i.e., 0.80). Use carburetor with airflow rating equal to or slightly smaller than this airflow requirement.

STANDARD TEMPERATURE & PRESSURE

High air temperature and high altitude reduce engine performance because both reduce air density. When air is less dense, an engine gets less usable air into the cylinders and makes less power.

Automotive test engineers eliminate air temperature and pressure as design variables by correcting all airflow and engine power readings to what they would be at a *standard temperature and pressure.*

Standard temperature is 59F (15C). Standard pressure is air pressure at sea level, 14.7 pounds per square inch (psi). Carburetor engineers measure air pressure in inches of mercury (in.Hg) instead of psi. Standard air pressure is 29.92 in.Hg. One in.Hg is approximately 0.5 psi.

A VE of 100% or 1.00 is usually not attainable with a naturally aspirated (unsupercharged) engine. There are losses in the induction system and air pumping capability of the engine that must be accounted for. Thus, our example engine won't flow 810 cfm of air (at standard temperature and pressure). Let's talk about volumetric efficiency and how it affects airflow requirement.

VOLUMETRIC EFFICIENCY (VE)

This value, signified by the Greek letter *eta* (η), is a measure of how well an engine breathes. The better the breathing ability, the higher the VE. VE is really an incorrect description of what is measured. But, the term's usage is established, so it's futile to try to change it to the correct term, *mass efficiency*.

VE is the ratio of the *actual* mass (weight) of air taken into the engine, to the mass the engine displacement would *theoretically* consume *if there were no losses*. The ratio is expressed as a percentage.

$$VE = \frac{\text{Actual mass of air taken in}}{\text{Theoretical mass of air that could be taken in}}$$

VE is quite low at idle and low speeds because the engine is being throttled. It reaches a maximum at a speed close to the point where maximum torque at wide-open throttle (WOT) occurs, then falls off as engine speed is increased to peak rpm. A VE curve closely follows the torque curve of an engine.

Effect of VE—After calculating the airflow requirement for an engine with 100% VE, you'll *reduce* the cfm value according to the actual VE you expect out of the engine. What percentage VE can you expect?

An ordinary low-performance engine has a VE of about 75% at maximum speed; about 80% at maximum torque. A high-performance engine has a VE of about 80% at maximum speed; about 85% at maximum torque. An all-out racing engine has a VE of about 90% at maximum speed; about 95% at maximum torque.

A highly tuned intake and exhaust system with efficient cylinder-head porting, and a camshaft ground to take full advantage of the engine's other equipment, can provide such complete cylinder filling that a VE of 100% (or slightly higher) is obtained *at the speed for which the system is tuned.*

Our example 350-CID engine was calculated as requiring 810 cfm of air at 100% VE. If this is a high-performance engine with a maximum of 85% VE, then the actual airflow requirement becomes 810 cfm x 0.85 = 688 cfm (at standard temperature and pressure).

AIR MASS & DENSITY

Because the mass of air taken in is directly related to air density, VE (η) can be expressed as a ratio of the density achieved in the cylinder (γ cyl) to the inlet air density (γ inlet), or

$$\eta = \gamma \text{ cyl} / \gamma_i$$

Ideal mass flow for a 4-cycle engine is calculated by multiplying:

$$\frac{rpm}{2} \times CID \times \gamma_i$$

where γ_i is the inlet air density.

Air density varies directly with pressure. The lower the pressure, the less dense the air. At altitudes above sea level, pressure drops, reducing power because the density is reduced.

Tables that relate air density to pressure (corrected barometer) and temperature are available. Or, you can use this formula:

$$\gamma = \frac{1.326P}{t + 459.6}$$

where:

γ = density in lb/cubic feet

P = absolute pressure in inches of mercury (Hg) read directly off of barometer (corrected)

t = temperature in degrees Fahrenheit at induction-system inlet

Actual mass flow into an engine can be measured as the engine is running with a laminar-flow unit or other gas-measuring device. A calibrated orifice or a pitot tube can also be used.

This actual mass flow is usually lower than ideal in a naturally aspirated engine because air becomes less dense as it is heated in the intake manifold. Absolute pressure (and density) also drop as the mixture travels from the carburetor inlet into the combustion chamber. This further reduces the mass of the charge reaching the cylinder.

The greater the pressure drop across or through the carburetor, the lower the density can be inside of the manifold and in the combustion chamber. If the carburetor is too small, pressure drop at WOT will be greater than the desired 1.0 in.Hg for high performance. Power will be reduced because the mixture won't be as dense as it needs to be for full power.

Carburetor flow capacity is one way to state equivalent size. It is the quantity of airflow through the carburetor (at standard temperature and pressure) at a given pressure drop: Usually 1.5 in.Hg for four-barrel carburetors and 3.0 in.Hg for one- and two-barrel carburetors. The higher the flow rating, the bigger the carburetor. Or, the bigger the carburetor, the lower the pressure drop across it at any given airflow.

To keep VE as high as possible, we would like to use a large carburetor, thereby keeping the pressure drop down. *The size limitations are at the other end of the flow curve.* Will the carburetor meter fuel correctly at low airflows? Will it work OK at the engine's frequent speed range?

MORE AIR, MORE HP

If you're unfamiliar with thinking about the density of the combustion charge as it enters during the intake stroke, all this talk of mass flow, pressure drop, and VE probably becomes confusing. Here is an engine model to ponder which can make these concepts clearer.

The engine is an air pump—it ingests air and compresses it. It's often assumed the reason air enters cylinders is because the pistons draw it in—they create a vacuum and that pulls in the air. But, atmospheric pressure (about 15 psi) will push air into a void, provided its passage is non-restrictive.

When a carburetor is large and its throttle is wide open, atmospheric pressure helps fill the lower-pressure area above a piston on an intake stroke. Close the throttle to a small opening and atmospheric pressure forces a partial charge of air past the restriction. The result is less-dense air in the consuming cylinder—so, less power.

Consequently, a small venturi and throttle blade opening restrict the amount of air atmospheric pressure can push into the cylinder. For most street and highway driving a small venturi carburetor is most efficient. If your goal is maximum power, and low- and mid-range economy, driveability and torque are secondary, then think big.

Think big all the way. Bigger intake ports, higher lift cam with longer duration, bigger intake valves and an efficient exhaust system to discharge burned mixture properly. Restrictions anywhere in the induction path keep atmospheric pressure from driving in a full air charge and the engine won't perform to full potential.

The more air atmospheric pressure can force into the combustion chamber, the more HP.

9

On this test stand airflow is measured by critical flow orifices; fuel flow is measured electronically. Here, airflow is being measured on Holley's Model 3739 throttle-body injection unit. Test stand is used for carburetors or injection throttle bodies.

EQUIVALENT RATIO TABLE

A/F (Air/Fuel)	F/A (Fuel/Air)	A/F (Air/Fuel)	F/A (Fuel/Air)
22:1	0.0455	13:1	0.0769
21:1	0.0476	12:1	0.0833
20:1	0.0500	11:1	0.0909
19:1	0.0526	10:1	0.1000
18:1	0.0556	9:1	0.1111
17:1	0.0588	8:1	0.1250
16:1	0.0625	7:1	0.1429
15:1	0.0667	6:1	0.1667
14:1	0.0714	5:1	0.2000

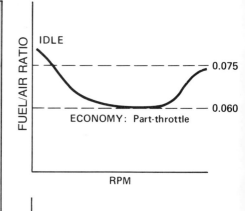

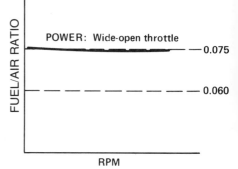

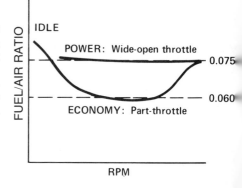

FUEL REQUIREMENTS

Fuel requirements relate to the airflow requirement because fuel is consumed in proportion to the air used by the engine. Fuel flow is stated in pounds per hour (lb per hr) and sometimes in pounds per HP hour (lb per HP hr), termed *specific fuel consumption* because it states how much fuel is used for *each* horsepower in one hour.

The relationship between the amount of fuel and the amount of air which flow together into an engine is called the *fuel/air (F/A) ratio*. This is pounds of fuel divided by pounds of air. An engine uses a lot more air than fuel, so fuel/air ratios are always small numbers such as 0.08, which equals 1 pound of fuel divided by 12 pounds of air.

Some people find this easier to understand if the ratio (0.08) is turned upside down to become an *air/fuel (A/F) ratio*. This gives a number like 12.5:1, meaning the engine uses 12.5 pounds of air for each pound of fuel (or 1.0 divided by 0.08). Obviously, calculations can be made either way because these ratios are just two different ways to state the same unit.

First, let's look at the WOT full-power fuel requirement for our example 350-CID engine that needed 810 cfm of air at 8000 rpm with 100% VE.

To convert airflow into lb per hr:

cfm x 4.38 = Air Flow lb/hr

Where 4.38 is a factor for 60F at one atmosphere pressure (14.7 psi).

Multiply by the F/A ratio, which we will assume to be a typical full-power ratio of 0.077 F/A or A/F ratio of 13:1.

cfm x 4.38 x F/A = Fuel Flow lb/hr

or

811 x 4.38 x 0.077 = 273 lb/hr at 8000 rpm

This is the maximum fuel the engine could consume with 810-cfm airflow. This fuel flow will rarely be reached because—like airflow—fuel flow must be reduced by VE; assume 0.85 VE in this example:

Assuming η = 0.85

cfm x 4.38 x F/A x η = Fuel Flow lb/hr

or

811 x 4.38 x 0.077 x 0.85 = 232 lb/hr at 8000 rpm

Fuel flow is less when the engine is running slower. For instance, 232 lb per hr at 8000 rpm drops to 1/2 or 116 lb per hr at 4000 rpm and 58 lb per hr at 2000 rpm. These consumption measurements assume WOT and the same F/A ratio in each instance.

The chart on page 8 shows fuel flow for various engine sizes over typical rpm ranges. If this book isn't handy when you need to estimate fuel requirements for fuel pump and fuel line selection, here is a rule of thumb.

WOT typically requires 0.5 lb of fuel per HP every hour. Thus, a 300-HP engine needs 300 X 0.5 = 150 lb per hr, or 25 gallons per hr because gasoline weighs 6 pounds per gallon (150 lb per hr divided by 6 lb per gallon equals 25 gallons per hr).

These calculations are for the maximum fuel consumption rate of an engine under full-power, WOT conditions. This knowledge will help you select the fuel line sizes, fuel pump capacity and tank capacity required for your driving application.

Stoichiometric Mixture—This is the ideal fuel mixture—proportioned so all of the fuel burns with all of the air—the exhaust has only carbon monoxide (CO), water vapor (H_2O) and nitrogen (N_2).

$$Fuel + Air \rightarrow CO_2 + H_2O + N_2$$

Stoichiometric mixture is achieved at an F/A ratio of approximately 0.068, or an A/F ratio of 14.7:1.

The actual ratio at which this occurs with an ideal set of conditions varies with the fuel's molecular structure. Gasolines vary somewhat in structure, but not significantly. Fuels other than gasoline require different ratios for the stoichiometric condition.

Alcohol has a lower heat content (calorific value) than gasoline and requires a 0.14 F/A ratio (7.15:1 A/F) for its ideal burning condition. This is so much more fuel volume than required for gasoline that most carburetors can't be used with alcohol, except when highly modified. Passages in the carburetor are actually too small to allow correct fuel flow and metering. See the chapter on alcohol and carburetion, page 200, for more details.

Maximum Power—Maximum power requires excess fuel to make sure all of the oxygen in the air is consumed. The reasons for more fuel: mixture distribution to the various cylinders and fuel/air mixing are seldom perfect. Imperfect combustion leads to the formation of oxides of nitrogen (NO_X) and carbon monoxide (CO). See page 132 for details on mixture and emission control.

When all of the air enters into the combustion process, more heat is generated and heat means pressure the engine can convert to work. A typical combustion reaction looks like this:

$$Fuel + Air \rightarrow CO_2 + H_2O + CO + HC + N_2$$

where:

CO_2	=	carbon dioxide
H_2O	=	water
CO	=	carbon monoxide
HC	=	unburned hydrocarbons (gasoline)
N_2	=	nitrogen

The fuel excess usually amounts to 10%—15%, giving F/A ratios of 0.075—0.080 (13.3:1—12.5:1 A/F ratios). Sometimes, an excess of fuel beyond that for producing maximum power is used for internal cooling of the engine. This is done to reduce or prevent knock and detonation. But from a pollution stand-

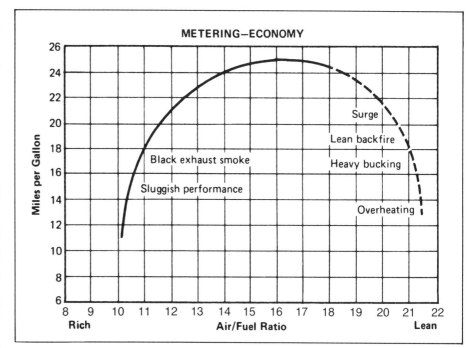

Best fuel economy is achieved at A/F ratio of about 16:1.

Thermocouples in headers (arrows) measure exhaust temperatures for each cylinder to assess distribution characteristics of manifold/carburetor combination. Holley engineers strive to keep all EGTs within 100F (38C) spread.

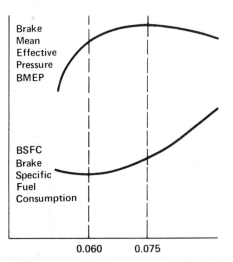

Brake mean effective pressure (BMEP) of engine operating with perfect distribution, showing relationship of F/A ratio supplied by carburetor. For maximum power, 0.075—0.080 F/A yields lowest possible fuel consumption for that output. For maximum economy, 0.060 F/A gives lowest possible fuel consumption consistent with a lower, best-economy output.

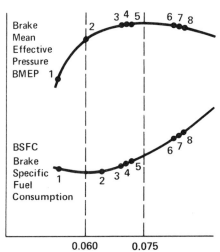

Same curve as at left with numbers representing cylinders receiving various F/A ratios at maximum power output with non-perfect distribution. Cylinders 6, 7, 8 with too-rich F/A produce less power and consume excess fuel; 3, 4, 5 receive correct F/A for best power and consume least fuel for that output; 1, 2 have lean F/A ratio. Richer mixture would have to be supplied to ALL cylinders to bring 1 & 2 to the flat part of curve to avoid detonation. Net result: Only cylinders 1 & 2 will operate at peak power with minimum fuel consumption for that output.

point, unburned HC and CO are undesirable byproducts of this excess.

Maximum Economy—Maximum economy requires excess air to ensure that all of the fuel is consumed. A typical F/A ratio is 0.06 (A/F = 16:1). The combustion reaction looks like this:

$$Fuel + Air \rightarrow CO_2 + H_2O + N_2$$
$$+ \text{ small amounts of}$$
$$CO + HC + O_2$$

Under heavy loads, any mixture leaner than stoichiometric burns with sufficient heat to cause any free oxygen to combine with the remaining nitrogen to produce oxides of nitrogen (NO_x). This is another undesirable emission product.

At high engine speeds and low loads, mixtures as lean as 0.055 F/A (A/F = 18:1) are sometimes approached when seeking peak economy. This mixture is on the borderline where it begins to become unstable in its ability to burn in normal engines.

Idle—At idle, the problem of exhaust dilution appears. Intake charge dilution is caused by the high manifold vacuum and by opening the intake valve before the piston reaches top center. When the intake valve opens, some exhaust gases are forced into the intake manifold by the pressure difference, assisted by the still-upward-rising piston.

The exhaust gases dilute and effectively lean the charge. Also, some exhaust gas stays in the cylinder clearance volume. When the piston descends on the intake stroke, the initial charge consists largely of exhaust gas, with a small portion of fresh fuel/air mixture. As the piston completes its intake stroke, the percentage of fresh fuel/air mixture is usually somewhat higher and this portion of the inlet charge burns well enough to supply power for idling the engine.

In the dilution process, some fuel molecules combine (or line up, as the chemists say) with the exhaust molecules and some fuel molecules line up with oxygen in the air. To make sure the mixture is combustible, the mixture has to be made 10%—20% richer than stoichiometric to offset that part of the fuel which combines with the exhaust gas. The richer mixture also helps to offset distribution problems. It also creates additional emission problems because rich idle mixtures generate large amounts of CO.

Cold Starting—Starting a cold engine requires the richest mixture of all. Slow cranking speeds create air velocity too low for much fuel vaporization to occur. And, because both the fuel and the manifold are cold, fuel vaporizes poorly.

Vaporization is necessary for combustion, so a lot of excess fuel is required for starting. Typical F/A ratios are 1.0—2.0. The F/A ratio being supplied isn't what actually gets to the cylinders. Distribution problems and liquid fuel depositing on the manifold walls and on the cylinder-head ports all rob fuel from the mixture. The mixture actually reaching the cylinders in a vaporized form is probably in the 0.06—0.10 F/A range (16:1—10:1 A/F).

Once the engine fires, rpm goes up and velocity through the carburetor increases. There is better vaporization and liquid fuel on the manifold walls vaporizes. As this happens, the mixture gradually leans out to 0.12—0.14 F/A (8:1—7:1 A/F). When the engine warms up, normal operating mixtures can be used.

UNIFORM DISTRIBUTION

We have looked at the engine's fuel and air requirements. Now let's consider another important engine requirement: Uniform (or equal) fuel and air mixture distribution to the cylinders. Uniform distribution helps every phase of engine operation. Non-uniform (unequal) distribution causes a loss of power and efficiency, and may increase emissions.

Uniform distribution relies on a number of factors. Good atomization of the fuel by the carburetor, use of fuel with the correct volatility for seasonal temperature variations, using appropriate techniques to ensure vaporization of the fuel, and correct manifold design. Manifold design is detailed in a separate chapter. We will discuss the other items after we have established the importance of uniform distribution to the cylinders.

Uniform Distribution at Idle—As discussed in the preceding section, idle F/A is typically 10%—20% richer than ideal to offset dilution by exhaust gas. Idle mixtures with less than 1% CO (a common emission setting) require that all cylinders receive approximately the same idle mixture.

If distribution is not good, getting a reasonably smooth idle may require idle mixture settings that are too rich. This can give CO emissions too high to meet emission regulations.

Uniform Distribution for Economy—Maximum economy, as previously discussed, requires a F/A ratio of approximately 0.06 (16:1 A/F). If one cylinder receives a lean charge due to a mixture-distribution problem, this can increase the amount of fuel required for a given power output. To avoid misfiring in the lean cylinder, the other cylinders must be operated at mixtures richer than the desired 0.06 F/A to bring the lean one up to the 0.06 figure.

All cylinders should be operating at the same F/A because lean cylinders produce more NO_x if they are still firing. And, if they are so lean that misfiring occurs, unburned HC is emitted. Rich-running cylinders produce excess CO and unburned HC. In either case, undesirable

Pontiac 4-cylinder, 2.5-liter "Iron Duke" engine on engine dynamometer. Exhaust-manifold probes measure temperature of exhaust gases as they exit port to determine cylinder-to-cylinder distribution of fuel/air mixture.

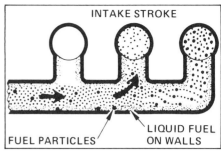

If mixture is partially vaporized, liquid particles clinging to manifold walls (or avoiding sharp turns into cylinder), may cause some cylinders to run lean and some rich. Here, center cylinder tends to run lean and end cylinder tends to receive a rich mixture. When possible, it's best to divide mixture before a change in direction occurs. Liquid particles are relatively heavier than the rest of the mixture and tend to continue in one direction. A fully vaporized mixture promotes good distribution in every instance.

effects include decreased economy and increased emissions.

Uniform Distribution for Power—F/A ratios of approximately 0.075 (13.3:1 A/F) are needed to produce maximum power. If one cylinder runs lean, an excessively rich mixture must be supplied to the other cylinders to bring the lean cylinder up to the correct ratio so it won't run into detonation.

Rich cylinders will waste a lot of fuel and fuel consumption will be increased to maintain a specified power level. Running some cylinders rich reduces their power output. All cylinders must have the same F/A to get the best possible power.

Unequal distribution not only affects fuel consumption and power, it also means ignition timing can only be a rough approximation or compromise of what could be used if all cylinders received equal F/A mixtures. Usable spark advance is directly related to the F/A available in the cylinder.

Timing advance is typically limited so it won't produce knock in the leanest cylinder. This limits the power that can be developed from those cylinders that have been richened to compensate for unequal distribution.

Checking for Correct Distribution—Automobile engine designers (and carburetion designers too) use several methods to check whether the various cylinders in an engine are receiving a uniform mixture. All methods require using a chassis or engine dynamometer.

Generally speaking, these methods aren't used by individual tuners because of the cost and complexity of the equipment. In many instances combinations of methods are used.

Distribution is checked by:

• Chemically analyzing exhaust gas (combustion products) samples from the individual cylinders at various operating modes: Idle, cruise, acceleration, maximum power and maximum economy.

There is a definite relationship between F/A and the chemical components in the exhaust gas. By using the accurate analytical equipment developed for emission studies, exact determinations of F/A ratio are obtained to check distribution. The availability of such equipment has made chemical analysis the preferred method automotive engineers use for distribution studies.

• Measuring exhaust gas temperature (EGT) with thermocouples inserted into the exhaust manifold or header at each cylinder's exhaust port. The designer looks for EGT peaks as various main-jet sizes are tried.

If all cylinders were brought to the same temperature, one (or more) cylinder(s) might be 200F (93C) below its peak (and therefore below its peak output). This occurs because all cylinders don't produce the same EGT due to differences in cooling, valves, porting and ring sealing. Perfect distribution would place all cylinders at their peak EGTs with the same jet. *This ideal is rarely achieved.*

• Studying specific fuel consumption to determine how closely the F/A delivered by a particular carburetor and manifold match ideal F/A ratios at various operating conditions. Any great variance is cause for suspecting a distribution problem.

• Observing combustion temperatures at various operating conditions.

WHAT AFFECTS DISTRIBUTION?

Atomization & Vaporization—Before gasoline can be burned, it must be vaporized. Vaporization changes the liquid to a gas state and this change only occurs when the liquid absorbs enough heat to boil. For example, a tea kettle changes water to water vapor (steam) by transferring heat into the water until the boiling temperature is reached. At this point, additional heat must be added to change the water into steam. Steam enters the atmosphere as water vapor (a gas, really). This extra heat is called the *heat of vaporization*.

Pressure controls the boiling point of any liquid. In the case of water, 212F (100C) is the sea-level boiling point. At higher altitudes, due to lowered atmospheric pressure, water boils at lower temperatures. Remember this relationship. It is important in understanding what happens in the carburetor and manifold.

In most passenger car engines, heat is applied to the intake manifold to raise the temperature of the incoming mixture.

The higher the temperature, the better the va-

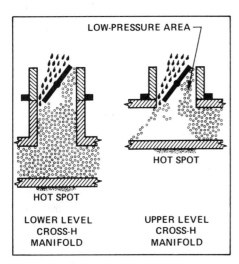

LOW-PRESSURE AREA

HOT SPOT

HOT SPOT

LOWER LEVEL
CROSS-H
MANIFOLD

UPPER LEVEL
CROSS-H
MANIFOLD

Cross section through V8 engine manifold of Cross-H or dual-plane, two-level type shows how riser height affects distribution. Throttle in this position causes worst distribution.

Holley high-rise manifold for Chevrolet small block. Two distinct levels below carb-mounting pad identify this as a cross-H or dual-plane design. Ribs in manifold floor help distribution; they direct mixture and aid in controlling liquid fuel when vaporization is not perfect.

porization. There is some sacrifice in top-end power when the mixture is heated sufficiently to ensure vaporizing most of the fuel.

This power loss is because charge density is reduced when the mixture is heated to this point. In most passenger car engines, the loss is more than offset by the smoother running gained at part throttle. No manifold heat is used in a racing engine because a cold, dense mixture produces more power.

Not only is it necessary to vaporize fuel before it can be expected to burn, it is essential to vaporize it to aid distribution. It is much easier to distribute vaporized fuel in a fuel/air mixture than it is to distribute liquid fuel. Some liquid fuel is nearly always present on the manifold surfaces. The only time manifold surfaces are "dry" is during high-manifold-vacuum conditions that promote vaporization.

The carburetor discharges gasoline into the air stream as a spray atomized (torn or sheared into fine droplets) into a mist. At this point it should become vaporized. Pressure in the intake manifold will be much lower than atmospheric (except at WOT) and this considerably lowers the boiling point of the gasoline. At the reduced pressure, some fuel particles vaporize as they absorb heat from the surrounding air. And, some fuel particles vaporize when they contact or pass close by the manifold hot spot.

Imperfect Vaporization—This may occur if the mixture velocity is too low, if the manifold or incoming air is cold, if manifold vacuum is low (higher pressure), and if fuel volatility is too low for the ambient temperature. Vaporization is also affected by manifold design and the carburetor size (flow capacity). With the same engine speed, a large carburetor has less veloc-

ity through its venturi (air passage). So, there is less pressure drop and a greater tendency for the fuel to come out of the discharge nozzle in liquid blobs or large drops that are not easily vaporized.

Manifold design also influences vaporization because the passage size affects mixture velocity and heating. If the mixture travels slowly, some liquid fuel particles may deposit onto the manifold walls before they have a chance to vaporize. The hot-spot size and location and the surface area inside the manifold influence vaporization.

When vaporization is poor, an excess of liquid fuel gets into the cylinders. Because it does not completely burn due to the lack of time available for evaporation and burning, it is expelled as unburned hydrocarbons. In some cases, excess fuel washes oil off of the cylinder walls to cause rapid wear. A portion of this liquid fuel also drains past the rings into the crankcase where it dilutes the oil.

Exhaust-Heated Hot Spots—These spots are typically small areas just under the area fed by the carburetor. Manifold ends are not usually heated. The hot spot is kept as small as possible, consistent with the needs for flexible operating and smooth running. Because the spot is small, the manifold automatically cools as rpm is increased. The large amount of fuel being vaporized at high speed extracts heat from the

manifold, often making it so cold that water condenses on its exterior surfaces.

Although most passenger car manifolds heat the mixture with an exhaust-heated spot, some are water-heated by engine coolant. Cars equipped with emission controls often heat the incoming air by passing it over the exhaust manifold on its way to the air cleaner inlet.

Intake Manifolds—Excepting racing intake systems, intake manifolds are compromises. Their shape, cross-sectional areas and heating arrangements accomplish the necessary compromises between good mixture distribution and VE over the range of speeds at which the engine will be used.

If only maximum or near-maximum rpm is being used, high mixture velocity through the manifold helps to ensure good distribution. This helps to vaporize the fuel, or at least hold the smaller particles of fuel in suspension in the mixture. At slower speeds, using manifold heat is essential to ensure vaporizing the fuel. If heat is not used, the engine will run roughly at slower speeds and distribution problems will be worsened.

Fuel Composition—The more volatile the fuel, the better it will vaporize. All fuels are blends of hydrocarbon compounds and additives. Blending is typically accomplished to match the fuel to ambient temperature and altitude conditions.

Thus, fuel supplied in the summertime has a higher boiling point than fuel available in winter. Fuel volatility is rated by a number known as *Reid Vapor Pressure*. The higher the number, the greater the volatility or tendency to go from the liquid to a gaseous state. In Detroit, for example, the Reid number varies from 8.5 in the summer to 15 in winter.

Fuel blending at the refinery is a compromise made on the basis of estimates of what the temperature will be when the gasoline is used at the pump. A sudden temperature change, such as a warm day in winter, usually causes a rash of vapor-lock and hot-starting problems.

Carburetor Placement—Location of the carburetor on the manifold in relation to the internal passages can drastically affect distribution. If the geometric layout of the manifold places the carburetor closer to one or more cylinders, this can create problems. Carburetor location is especially important with multiple carburetors.

The engine designer checks power, economy and mixture distribution with the carburetor, air cleaner and manifold installed. Sometimes the physical positioning of the air cleaner or a connecting elbow atop the carburetor is so critical that turning it to a different position can create distribution problems.

Throttle-Plate Angle—A directional effect is given to the fuel when the throttle is partially open. This effect becomes especially apparent when there is little or no riser between the carburetor and the manifold passages. A *riser* is the vertical passage conducting mixture from the carburetor into the intake manifold.

On a V8 engine, throttle-plate angle affects distribution in the upper level of a cross-H, dual-plane or two-level manifold more than it does the lower level. The longer riser into the lower level has a straightening effect on the mixture.

This leads to one of the advantages of high-riser designs that allow better straightening of the mixture flow with less directional effects at all throttle openings. High-riser designs typically offer better cylinder-to-cylinder mixture distribution. Riser height is usually limited by hood clearance. Holley tests have shown definite improvements in part-throttle distribution with risers designed to 1-1/2—2-in. high before opening into the manifold branches.

Mixture Speed & Turbulence—Mixture velocities and turbulence within the manifold affect vaporization and consequently distribution. More details on these affects are on page 91. Turbulence in the combustion chamber helps to prevent stratification of the fuel and promotes rapid flame travel.

Time—Volatility of the fuel and heat available to assist in vaporization are especially important when you consider the tiny amount of time available to vaporize the atomized fuel supplied by the carburetor. Unlike water in a tea kettle, which can be left on the stove until it boils, fuel must be changed to the vapor state in about 0.003 second in a 12-in. long manifold passage at a mixture velocity of 300 feet per second.

DISTRIBUTION SUMMARY

To summarize the factors that can aid distribution:

● Vaporize as much fuel as possible in the manifold so a minimum of liquid fuel gets into the cylinders.

● Use fuels with the correct volatility for ambient-temperature and altitude conditions.

● Use the smallest passages consistent with the desired VE to ensure high velocities in the manifold and cylinder head.

● Carefully select venturi size (carburetor flow capacity) to have good atomization in the carburetor.

● Avoid manifold construction that causes fuel to separate out of the mixture due to sharp turns and severe changes in cross-sectional area.

● Have sufficient turbulence in the manifold to ensure fuel and air are kept well mixed as they travel to the cylinder.

● Supply manifold heating and heating of the incoming air to ensure that fuel is well vaporized.

Not all of these factors can be controlled by an individual. But, they point out a few important considerations, such as avoiding carburetors that are too large for the engine. Use fuel that is correct for the season; don't try to race with fuel you bought in a different season or another locality. And, for engines being operated on the street, use a heated manifold with the smallest passages consistent with desired performance.

Dual-lung float on Model 5200 has bumper spring (white arrow). Spring-loaded inlet valve hooks to lever so valve opens positively when float drops (outline arrow). Brass wire-mesh filter (in hand) catches dirt that could cause inlet-valve malfunction. Large tube is fuel inlet. Smaller tube returns fuel to tank to purge vapors from fuel line; helps cool fuel to avoid vapor lock. Float setting requires 0.010—0.025-in. clearance between float tang and bumper spring with cover inverted and float resting against spring-loaded needle as shown.

barrels built into a single unit. It's essential to learn the basics of a one-barrel before trying to comprehend more complex carburetors. So, read this chapter first to establish a solid background before tackling those carburetors.

A carburetor:

- Controls engine input and therefore controls power output.
- Mixes fuel and air in correct proportions for engine operation.
- Atomizes and vaporizes the fuel/air mixture to put it in a state for combustion.

Let's look at a carburetor's basic systems one at a time and see what parts do each job.

INLET SYSTEM

The inlet system has three primary components:

- Fuel bowl.
- Float.
- Inlet valve (needle and seat).

Fuel for the basic metering systems is stored in the *fuel bowl*. The inlet system maintains the specified fuel level in the bowl. Basic fuel metering systems are calibrated to deliver the correct mixture only when the fuel is at this level. Correct fuel level also greatly affects *fuel handling,* which is the carburetor's ability to withstand maneuvering—accelerations, turns, and stops.

The amount of fuel entering the bowl through the fuel-inlet valve is determined by the space between the movable needle and its fixed seat *(flow area),* and by pump pressure. Needle movement in relation to the seat is controlled by the float, which rises and falls with fuel level. As fuel level drops, the float drops to open the needle valve, allowing fuel to enter the bowl. When the engine is running with constant load, the float moves the needle to a position where it restricts the flow of fuel. Only enough fuel is admitted to replace that being used. Any slight fuel level change causes a corresponding float movement. Opening or closing the fuel-inlet valve restores or maintains the correct fuel level.

DESIGN FEATURES

Fuel Bowl—The fuel bowl or float chamber is a reservoir supplying all fuel in the carburetor.

Two- and four-barrel staged carburetors have primary venturis that are opened first, and secondary barrels that are opened to airflow later when higher engine power is required. Primary and secondary venturis (throttle bores) may have separate float bowls.

Fuel height in the bowl is controlled by the float and inlet valve. An air passage or vent

Understanding how your carburetor works is the key to extracting top performance from your engine/carburetor combination. It's a quick way to get more performance with less work. You'll understand its internals and then do precise tuning without wasting time. Tuning by trial and error can wreck a carburetor, leave an engine in a worse state of tune and cost you money.

You can confidently chose the right carburetor for your driving application once you understand their design and function. You won't have to rely on guesswork, self-proclaimed experts or rumors about the current "hot setup."

There's really nothing tricky about how a

carburetor works. No black magic makes one work differently from another. Whether you have a one-, two- or four-barrel carburetor, all operate essentially the same. Their minor differences relate to the way the same systems are built into a particular carburetor.

A four-barrel double-pumper looks impressive and complex, but it works exactly like a one-barrel. Its functions are no harder to understand. Just as you can learn about an engine by examining the operation of one cylinder, we'll start learning by examining a one-barrel carburetor.

After you've become familiar with the one-barrel, then we'll proceed to two- and four-barrel units. Think of them as several one-

connects the float bowl to the carburetor's air inlet passage.

Venting the fuel bowl to outside air means the fuel is no longer pressurized by the fuel pump. It is pressurized up to the float valve. Once it is in the fuel bowl, it is at *vented pressure*, approximately the same as outside air.

The bowl acts as a vapor separator. Vapors entrapped in the fuel as it was pumped from the tank escape through this vent so pressure does not build in the bowl.

Connecting the vent to the inlet air horn vents the fuel bowl to clean air obtained through the air cleaner. Because the vent "sees" the same pressure as the carburetor inlet, a dirty air cleaner does not change the F/A ratio. Dirty air cleaners restrict airflow, create lower absolute pressure to the carburetor, and cause a power loss. If the fuel bowl is not vented to the inlet air horn, a dirty air cleaner will enrich the mixture.

The preferred vent location is near the center of the fuel bowl. It must be high enough so fuel will not slosh into the air horn during hard stops or maneuvering. Cars from 1970 and later have an additional vent connecting the float bowl to a charcoal canister when the engine is turned off.

This emission control unit collects escaping fuel vapors boiled off when heat from the engine block warms gasoline in the carburetor. The same canister may also collect fuel tank vapors. Vapors stored in the canister are drawn into the intake manifold when the engine is running. Pre-emission-control models often had a mechanical vent valve on the fuel bowl. At curb idle or when the engine was stopped, this external vent released fuel vapors into the engine compartment.

The fuel bowl may be an integral part of the main body casting, or it can be a separate casting attached to the carburetor body with screws. Holley uses both designs and each has a replaceable screw-in inlet valve.

Bowl capacity is important. It must contain sufficient fuel to allow good response when accelerating from a stop after a hot engine has been idling or stopped (called a *hot soak)*. Under these conditions the fuel pump may deliver spurts of liquid fuel and pockets of fuel vapor intermittently.

Thus the bowl must be large enough to supply fuel to the metering systems until the pump is purged of vapor and able to deliver liquid fuel. Holley carburetors typically have large capacity fuel bowls.

Float—A float on a hinged lever operates the inlet valve so fuel enters the bowl when the fuel level is below the desired reference height. It shuts off fuel when the desired height is reached.

A float may have one or two buoyant ele-

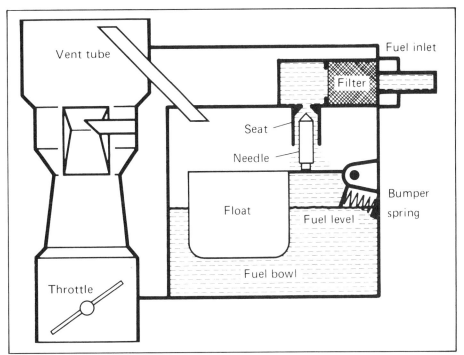

Inlet system schematic. Float hasn't reached desired level, so inlet valve is admitting fuel to bowl. Fuel flow shuts off when float rises to close inlet valve needle against seat.

Three Holley removable fuel bowls. Left is *center-hung*, *center-pivot* or *center-inlet* "race" type. It can be tapped for fuel entry on either or both sides. Center is *side-hung* bowl. Both bowls have externally adjustable inlet valves to set float and fuel level. Adjusting nut positions inlet valve; lock screw holds the adjustment. *Nose* bowl at right is available for restorations of older Shelby Mustangs and real Cobras. These are supplied as the Le Mans Fuel Bowl Conversion Kit 34-14.

ments, called *lungs*. Their shape is often similar to the human lung. Some floats are made from brass stampings soldered into an air-tight assembly, or they are made from a closed-cell material not affected by gasoline, alcohol or any other commonly used fuel or fuel additive. In 1987, Holley began using a molded hollow plastic float in many carburetors.

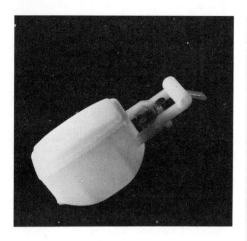

In 1987 Holley introduced hollow plastic floats as direct replacements for many brass and nitrophyl floats.

Examples of brass and nitrophyl floats.

The float is designed with buoyancy to positively shut the inlet valve when the desired fuel level has been reached. The buoyant portion is usually mounted on a lever to multiply the buoyancy effects of the float itself. The lever is also a surface for operating the inlet valve.

Float vibration is caused by engine or vehicle vibration or bouncing—or both. It causes wide fuel level variations because a vibrating float allows the inlet valve to admit fuel when it is not needed. A float spring is sometimes added under the float or on a tang to minimize float vibration. These are called *float bumper springs.* Some carburetors use a tiny spring inside the inlet valve instead of, or in addition to, a spring under the float. Such springs are especially helpful in dirt-track, off-road and marine applications.

Float shape and mounting *(pivot orientation)* may be dictated by bowl size and carburetor use. The float has to provide enough buoyancy to close the inlet valve. Sometimes this requires making an odd shape float to get enough volume for the required buoyancy.

Float lever length determines the mechanical advantage float buoyancy (and float spring, if used) can apply to close the inlet valve at a given fuel level.

Every carburetor has a published *float setting.* The setting is the float location that closes the inlet valve when the required fuel level in the bowl is reached.

In some Holley carburetors, a threaded inlet valve assembly can be adjusted to set fuel level without taking the carburetor apart. A sight plug in the fuel bowl is removed to observe fuel level. Other float settings are established by measuring float position, usually in relation to a gasket surface, while the carburetor is dis-

Side-hung float in secondary fuel bowl shows (1) float, (2) adjustable inlet-valve assembly, (3) adjusting nut, (4) lock screw, (5) plastic baffle to direct inlet fuel and contain froth, (6) float-bumper spring, (7) sight plug for fuel-level checking, (8) hole for transfer tube, and (9) fuel-inlet fitting. Transfer tube directs fuel from the primary to the secondary bowl. When correctly set up, half-round float is adequate for all but the most-severe cornering loads such as may be generated on a flat asphalt track, road racing or autocrossing.

assembled.

A fuel level for a particular carburetor is established by the designer and test engineer so the carburetor will operate without problems. Fast starts and stops and maneuvers ordinarily encountered in the particular vehicle must be considered. The level is set so there will be no fuel spillage when a passenger car is parked or operated facing up, down, or sideways on a hill with 32% grade (18°).

A military vehicle specification requires cor-

rect operation when parked or operated at 60% (31°) up/down and/or a 40% (22°) side slope.

For best operation in high-speed cornering, bowls are equipped with *center-pivoted floats.* The pivot axis is parallel with the car axles. Effects of acceleration and braking are best resisted by *side-hung floats* with pivots perpendicular to the axles.

Fuel tends to slosh over as it moves toward the carburetor throttle bores on hard stops. To offset this, fuel levels in rear bowls are typical-

EFFECTS OF INLET–SYSTEM CHANGES

Change	Effect
High float level	Raises fuel level in bowl. Speeds up main system start-up because less *depression*—reduction of pressure—is required at venturi to extract fuel from bowl. Start of flow from the bowl via the nozzle is sometimes called *pullover*. Increases fuel consumption. May cause fuel to spill through discharge nozzles and vent into carburetor air inlet on abrupt stops or turns to cause over-rich air/fuel mixture. Engine then runs erratically or stalls. This spillage affects low rpm emissions. Increases chances for the carburetor to *percolate* and *boil over*. This is a condition in which fuel is pushed by rising vapor bubbled out of the discharge from the main well when it is hot. Also, when the vehicle is parked on a hill or side slope, high float level may cause fuel spillage through the vent or main system.
Low float level	Lowers fuel level in bowl. Delays main system start-up because more vacuum is required at venturi to start fuel flow. This delay may cause flat spots or *holes* in power output. May expose main jets in hard maneuvering, causing *turn cutout*—misfire from lean air/fuel mixture. Can lessen maximum fuel flow at wide-open throttle—WOT.
Float assist spring too strong	Causes low fuel level. Inlet valve closes prematurely because of added force of spring.
Assist spring too weak	Causes high fuel level. Inlet valve closes after correct fuel level is reached because more float movement is required to compensate for weak spring.
High fuel pressure	Raises fuel level approximately 0.020-in. for each psi—pounds per square inch—fuel pressure increase. This factor varies with bouyancy, leverage, and needle-orifice size. Don't exceed 9 psi.
Low fuel pressure	Lowers fuel level
Larger inlet-valve seat	Raises fuel level.
Smaller inlet-valve	Lowers fuel level.

NOTE: Changing almost any part in fuel-inlet system requires resetting float to maintain correct fuel level.

ly set 1/16- to 1/8-in. lower than the forward or primary bowls. This lower fuel level makes the fuel rise higher before it can spill over through the main discharge nozzle or vents. The carburetor is then more tolerant of hard stops.

Inlet Valve—The needle's rounded end rests against the float lever arm or is connected to it by a hook. The tapered end closes against an inlet-valve seat as the float rises.

Some inlet needles are hollow. They may contain a tiny damper spring and pin to help cushion the needle valve against road shocks and vehicle vibrations.

Inlet-valve needles are usually steel with a tapered seating surface. Viton-tipped needles are extremely resistant to dirt and conform to the seat for good sealing with low closing forces. Plain-steel needles should be used with fuels such as alcohol and nitromethane.

Inlet valves are supplied with various seat openings. Each inlet valve assembly (if the needle is an integral part) and each inlet-valve seat is stamped with a number. This number indicates seat opening in thousandths of an inch. A valve assembly marked 110S has a 0.110-in. diameter seat opening and a Viton-tipped needle; a 110 is the same seat opening with a steel needle.

Seat diameter is an indication of how much fuel flow occurs at a given fuel pressure. A smaller opening flows less fuel; a larger opening more. The chart on page 20 shows fuel flow with a 0.110-in. inlet seat at various fuel

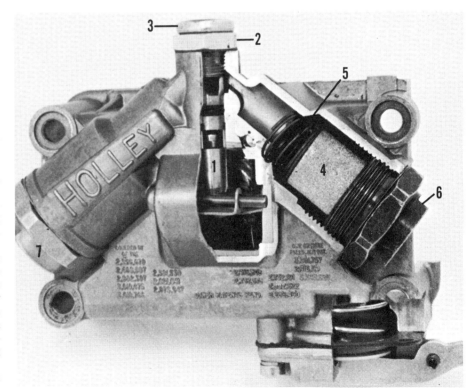

Cutaway center-inlet dual-feed "race" bowl shows (1) adjustable inlet-valve assembly, (2) adjusting nut, and (3) lock screw. Sintered-bronze filter (4) in inlet has spring (5) to allow fuel bypass if filter plugs up. Fuel-inlet nut (6) can be swapped with plug (7) to allow plumbing opposite side.

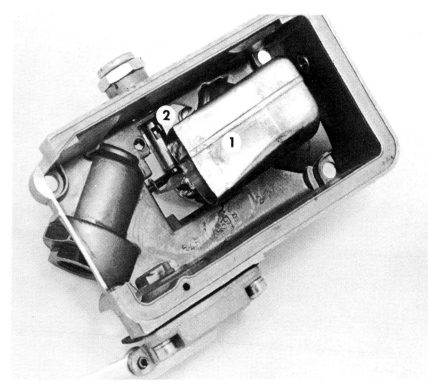

Cutaway side view of dual-feed "race" bowl shows shows half of float (1) and segment of mounting bracket (2).

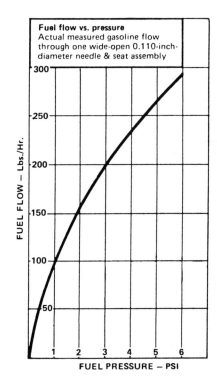

Measured gasoline flow through one wide-open 0.110-in.-diameter window-type inlet-valve assembly. Float held at bottom of bowl.

Three inlet-valve assemblies (left to right): Pointed needle with Viton tip, pointed-tip steel needle, and ball-tip needle with float hook. Viton tips may be any color.

Two spring-loaded inlet-valve assemblies. Spring cushions needle when float bounces needle up against seat. Hooked needle has spring and ball end in a hollow needle.

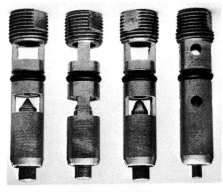

Round-hole inlet-valve (right) is used for low-flow applications. *Picture-window* assemblies (to left) are common where higher fuel flow is required. O-ring on stems seals inlet side from fuel bowl. Threaded portion at top allows fuel-level adjustment.

pressures with the needle fully open (float dropped all the way down)

Seat size is selected to allow reasonably quick bowl filling to handle quick accelerations after standing parked with a hot engine. Minimum restriction is also needed for high fuel demands such as WOT at high rpm.

Larger seats provide better vapor purging from the fuel lines. A small needle seat has the best hot-fuel control because vapor pressure in the fuel line acts against less area to force the needle off of its seat. A too-large needle seat is a hindrance for off-road and other types of racing. Because a small needle seat aids fuel

control, always use the smallest possible inlet valve that will work with the engine. Any needle-seat change requires resetting the float to the float height specification.

Fuel Filter—A fuel filter or screen may be included in the carburetor body, fuel bowl or cover as part of the fuel inlet system. The filter

Viton-tip needle is captured in seat by cap at left so needle/seat can be replaced as assembly.

FUEL FLOW vs. FUEL PRESSURE FOR VARIOUS SIZE
NEEDLES & SEATS

Dia. of Needle Seat	Type	Fuel Flow @ 2 P.S.I lbs./hr.	Fuel Flow @ 4 P.S.I. lbs./hr.	Fuel Flow @ 6 P.S.I. lbs./hr.
0.082''	Holes	106	153	204
0.097''	Holes	121	174	225
0.101''	Holes	138	194	254
0.110''	Holes	153	230	275
0.110''	Windows	160	232	295
0.120	Windows	167	236	305

NOTE: Checked with needle & seat assembly installed with float held at bottom of bowl.

Holley Tests
October, 1971

is placed between the fuel pump and the inlet valve to trap dirt that could cause inlet-valve-seating problems. Fuel-line fuel filters are discussed on page 139.

MAIN SYSTEM

The main metering system supplies fuel/air mixture to the engine for cruising speeds and above. Fuel is fed by the *idle* and *accelerating pump* systems until engine speed or airflow increases to a point where the main metering system begins to operate. When the engine must produce full power under high-load conditions, added fuel comes from the *power system*. These other carburetor systems are explained elsewhere in this chapter.

Throttle—Many people believe the throttle controls the *volume* of fuel/air mixture being pumped into the engine. Not so! Piston displacement never changes, so the *volume* of air pulled into the engine is constant for any given speed.

The throttle controls the *density* or *mass flow* of the air pumped into the engine by piston action: *Least* charge density is available at idle, *highest* density is at WOT. A dense charge has more air mass, therefore higher compression and burning pressures can be developed for higher power output. So, the throttle controls engine speed and power output by varying the *charge density* supplied to the engine.

Venturi—This is the one simple part that really makes a carburetor function. It is important to understand how the venturi operates before looking further into how the main metering system works.

The venturi and its principle of operation are named after G. B. Venturi, an Italian physicist (1746—1822). He discovered when fluid flows through a constricted tube, flow is fastest and pressure lowest at the point of maximum constriction in the tube.

In the internal-combustion engine, a partial vacuum is created in the cylinders by the pistons' downward strokes. Because atmospheric pressure (14.7 psi at sea level) is higher than the reduced pressure in the cylinders, air rushes through the carburetor and into the cylinders to fill the vacuum. On its way to the cylinders, air passes through the venturi.

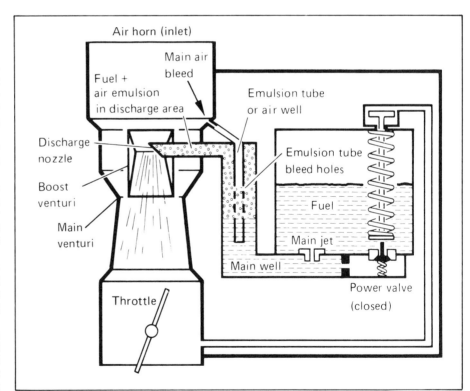

Main venturi's reduced diameter speeds up airflow. Reduced pressure in venturi area allows air stream to pick up fuel from bowl through passages. Main jet in fuel path limits fuel flow.

The venturi is a smooth-surface restriction in the path of the incoming air. It constricts or "necks-down" the inrushing air column, then allows it to widen back to the throttle-bore diameter. Air is rushing in with a certain pres-sure. To get through the venturi, it must speed up, which reduces pressure inside the venturi. A gentle diverging section is used to recover as much of the pressure as possible.

The venturi is the controlling factor in the

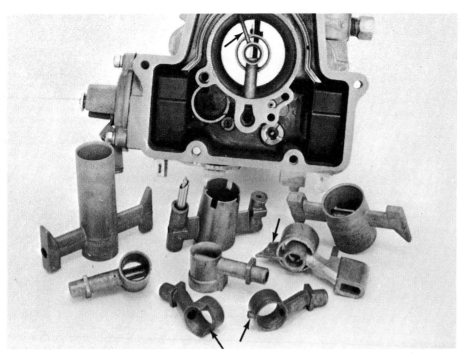

Boost venturis may have wings or tabs (arrows) to make carburetor work with specific engine/manifold combination. Picture how these work by touching the edge of water streaming from a faucet. Mixture is deflected in the same way.

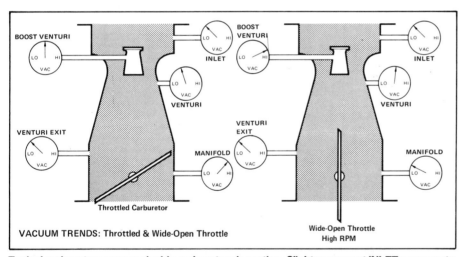

VACUUM TRENDS: Throttled & Wide-Open Throttle

Wide-Open Throttle High RPM

Typical carburetor vacuums inside carburetor air section. Slight vacuum at INLET represents pressure drop across air cleaner. Gage at large VENTURI throat shows higher vacuum because air is still at relatively high velocity. Vacuum returns almost to inlet value just before throttle plate at VENTURI EXIT. Throttled carburetor shows very high manifold vacuum because a large pressure drop occurs across the partially-opened throttle. Wide-open throttle (WOT) low MANIFOLD vacuum indicates a heavy-load/dense-charge condition. In both cases, highest carburetor vacuum is at BOOST VENTURI throat that supplies signal to main system.

carburetor because fuel discharges into the venturi at the point of lowest pressure (greatest vacuum). This minimum-pressure point applies a *signal* to the main metering system.

The pressure drop or vacuum signal is measured at the discharge nozzle in the venturi. Because the fuel bowl is maintained near atmospheric pressure by the vent system, fuel flows through the main jet and into the low pressure or vacuum area in the venturi.

Pressure drop (vacuum) at the venturi varies with engine speed and throttle position, increasing with engine rpm. WOT and peak rpm give the highest fuel flow and the highest pressure difference between the fuel bowl and a discharge nozzle in the venturi. Pressure difference (ΔP) as engine speed changes is approximately proportional to the difference in velocity squared (ΔV^2), $\Delta P \sim \Delta V^2$.

Pressure drop in the venturi also depends on venturi size. A small venturi provides a higher pressure drop at any given rpm and throttle opening than a large venturi. The Design Features portion of this section explains more about this important consideration and how it relates to performance.

No fuel issues from the discharge nozzle until flow through the venturi and hence, pressure drop, is sufficient to offset the level or "head" difference between the discharge nozzle and the lower level of fuel in the bowl.

Main Jet—Once main system flow starts, fuel is metered (measured) through a main jet in the fuel bowl. From the main jet, fuel passes into a main well. As fuel passes up through this main well, air from a main air or "high speed" bleed is added. This pre-atomizes or emulsifies the fuel into a light, frothy fuel/air mixture that issues from the discharge nozzle into the air stream flowing through the venturi. The discharge nozzle is often located in a small boost venturi centered in the main venturi.

Liquid fuel is converted into a fuel/air emulsion for two reasons. First, it vaporizes much easier when discharged into the air flowing through the venturi. Second, the emulsion has a lighter viscosity than liquid fuel and responds faster to any change in the venturi vacuum (signal from the venturi applied through the discharge nozzle). It will start to flow sooner and quicker than liquid fuel.

Main Air Bleed—The strong signal from the discharge nozzle is bled off or reduced by the main air bleed so there is less effective pressure difference to cause fuel flow. The mixture becomes leaner as bleed size is increased. Decreasing bleed size increases pressure drop across the main jet. More fuel is pulled through the main system, giving a richer mixture.

Main air bleed changes affect the entire range of main metering system operation. Holley establishes main air bleed size for each carburetor to work correctly over that carburetor's airflow range. Changes in these sizes are rarely necessary or advisable. Calibration changes are easy to make by changing main metering jets.

The main air bleed also acts as an anti-siphon or siphon-breaker so fuel does not continue to dribble into the venturi after airflow is reduced or stopped.

DESIGN FEATURES
Throttle—The throttle shaft is offset slightly (about 0.020 in. on primaries and about 0.060 in. on secondaries) in the throttle bore. So, one side of the throttle has a larger area to cause self-closing.

Air from main air bleed can be introduced into main well in several ways. Sometimes it is brought in through the center of an *emulsion tube*. Separate emulsion tubes are from a Holley 2110 Bug Spray (right) and a 5200 (left). In carburetors with removable metering blocks (plates, bodies), bleed air is often introduced through tiny holes in an air well paralleling the main well. This well is on the surface assembled toward carburetor body. Arrows indicate bleed holes that are necked down to about 0.026-in. diameter.

There are two reasons for this design. First, idle-return consistency is greatly aided by the sizable closing force generated when manifold vacuum is high—as at idle. Second, it is a safety measure to guard against overspeeding an engine started without installing the linkage or throttle return spring. Airflow past the throttles will tend to close them.

Throttles seldom close tightly against the throttle bore; they are factory-set against a stop. The factory setting provides a closed-throttle airflow specified for that particular carburetor.

Venturi—The most efficient (or *ideal*) venturi that creates maximum pressure drop with minimum flow loss requires a 20° entry angle and a diverging section with a 7°—11° included angle on the "tail." This ideal venturi won't always fit into a carburetor short enough to fit under the hood of the average automobile.

Holley uses a radiused entry to the venturi because it is less affected by production variations. Designers try to keep as close as possible to the ideal venturi entry and exit angles within the limitations imposed by engine position and hood heights.

Although the theoretical low-pressure point and point of highest-velocity would be expected at the venturi's minimum diameter, fluid friction causes the point to occur about 0.030 in. below the smallest diameter. This low-pressure, high-velocity point is called the *vena contracta*. The center of the discharge nozzle or the *tail* of the boost venturi is placed at this point.

A venturi allows a much greater metering signal than a straight tube and has a minimum airflow loss. This is because the venturi's trailing edge conforms to the normal air stream. It recovers most of the pressure drop so a greater mass of air is available for the engine. It is a very efficient air metering structure because of the high signal levels it supplies with minimum pressure loss.

The venturi supplies fuel in the correct proportion to the mass of air rushing into the engine. Its size affects the pressure drop available to operate the main metering system. The *smaller* the venturi, the *greater* the pressure drop, the *sooner* the main system will be brought into operation, and the *better* the mixing of fuel with air. The rpm at which main system spill-over or *pull over* starts is affected by the size of the engine that is pulling air through the carburetor.

With any given engine size, a larger carburetor requires a higher rpm to bring the main system into operation; a smaller carburetor, a lower rpm. But venturi size also controls the amount of air available at WOT.

If the venturi is too small, top-end HP will be reduced, even though the carburetor provides very good fuel/air mixing at cruising speeds. For this reason automobile manufacturers typically compromise.

They use carburetors with smaller-than-optimum (maximum power) airflow capacities. And for very good reasons. Good fuel atomization and vaporization promotes good distribution and improves running and economy at around-town and cruising speeds.

Manufacturers offering more performance typically supply a carburetor with a secondary system. This retains the advantages of a small primary venturi with the capability of higher airflow for top-end power.

Boost Venturi—These act the same as the larger venturi, but supply a stronger signal to the discharge nozzle because boost-venturi velocity is higher than that in the main venturi. Boost venturis are *signal amplifiers*.

By increasing the available signal for main system operation, the boost venturi allows the carburetor to work well at lower speeds, and therefore lower airflows. This is especially helpful in a performance carburetor because the boost venturi does not seriously affect the carburetor's airflow capacity.

The boost venturi tail discharges at the low-pressure point *(vena contracta)* in the main venturi. Consequently, boost venturi airflow is accelerated to a higher velocity because it "sees" a greater pressure differential than the

Look-alike main jets. Only the markings indicate a difference. The 50 is a standard jet. Two-digit (50) series jets had 3% possible variation between any two jets with the same marking. Sizes are available from 40—100. Order 122-XX (jet number). Close-limit series 501, 502, 503 have only 1.5% flow difference (maximum) between any jet with the same marking. Close-limit main-jet sizes from 352—742 are available. Order 122-XXX. Jets with numbers ending in 1 or 3 are used by the factory during calibration. Metric jets used in 4360 and 5200 series carburetors use a 124-XXX number.

main venturi.

Air and fuel emerging from the boost venturi are traveling faster than the surrounding air. A shearing effect between the two airstreams improves fuel atomization.

Boost venturis also aid fuel distribution because the ring of air flowing between the two venturis directs the charge to the center of the airstream. This helps keep some of the wet fuel/air mixture off of the carburetor wall below the venturi so more of it reaches the manifold hot spot for improved vaporization.

Tabs, bars, wings and other devices may be used to provide correct directional effects for good cylinder-to-cylinder distribution with a particular manifold. All such development work is accomplished on the dynamometer during design and development of the carburetor and manifold combination.

Boost venturis allow using a much shorter main venturi so the carburetor can be made short enough to fit under the hood. Carburetor designers could achieve essentially the same results with a long (ideal) venturi as they can with one or more boost venturis stacked in the main venturi. But it is tough to build a carburetor that allows the 20° entry to the venturi and a 7°—11° tail, and at the same time get venturi size down to the required diameter for adequate signal. Some Holley carburetors, especially very short ones, use as many as two booster venturis to get adequate signal for main system operation.

Main Jets—These metering orifices control fuel flow into the metering system. They are rated in flow capacity and are removable for calibration purposes.

Main jets are not selected solely by trial and error. For a given venturi size, a small range of

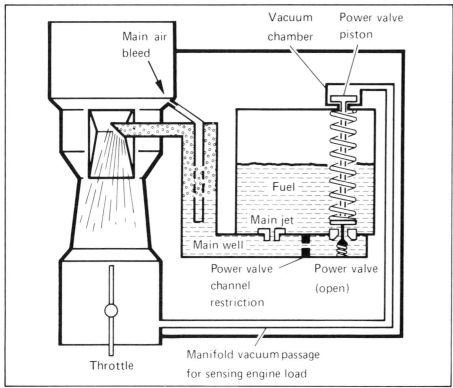

Power system schematic.

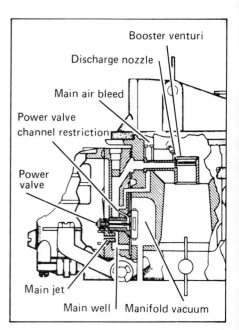

Typical vacuum and fuel-passage routing used in Holleys with removable fuel bowls. These are *diaphragm-type* power valves. Using a power valve on secondary side allows using smaller main jet to improve fuel handling during deceleration and braking.

main jets will cover all conditions. Nevertheless, final selection of the correct jet for the application has to be done by testing. Design and operational variations (climate, altitude and temperature) affect jet size requirements.

There's a basic misconception about jets: that size alone determines flow characteristics. Actually, the shape of the jet entry and exit, as well as the finish, affect flow. Holley checks each jet on a flow tester and later grades it according to flow. This flow rate is compared to a master chart. A number is stamped on the jet to indicate its flow.

The tolerance range for each size explains why a 66 jet may not seem to give a richer mixture than 65. If the 65 is on the high side of its allowable tolerance and the 66 is on its low side of its tolerance limit, then the two jets may flow very close to the same amount of fuel. The 65 tolerance range is from 351.5—362.0 cubic centimeters (cc) per minute at a specified head with a given test fuel. The 66 ranges from 368.5—379.5cc per minute.

In each case, there is a 3% flow range within a jet size, and about 4.5% difference in flow between average jets in the two sizes. In 1975 Holley developed a new *close-limit* series of main jets in the standard size range of 30 to 74. This new series was developed so flow could be closely tailored to fit emission requirements.

These jets use the first two numbers, such as 65 or 66, with a third number indicating whether the jet flows lean (651) in the middle

(652), or rich (653). There is approximately 1.5% difference in flow between each of the three jets, or a flow range of 4.5%. There can only be a 1.5% difference in flow between two jets with the same flow marking. Jets with the same markings in the old two-digit numbering system could have up up to 3% flow difference. The new jet series has the same brass or aluminum color used previously.

Holley offers close-limit jets in mean sizes only, that is, 352, 262, and so on. You may have a carburetor with a 351 or a 353 in it, but these jets are only available in the assembly plant where the carburetor is made and flow-checked.

Close-limit jets offer a good way to accomplish fine tuning, provided you can use jets ranging from 35 to 74 (352 through 742). Order these jets as 122-XX2.

Some jets used in the Models 5200 and 5210 are marked to indicate jet opening or inside diameter in millimeters (mm): 130 = 1.3mm. In 1976, a system of jet marking relating directly to the flow in cc per minute was adopted for use in Models 5200, 5210, 2280, 2360 and 4360 carburetors.

These jets were dyed green to identify that they are marked according to flow. A jet marked 357 has a tolerance ranging from 354.3—359.7cc, or 1.5% maximum difference between two jets with the same markings. The flow rating is made at 50-centimeters head. Order these jets as 124-XXX. Consult the cur-

rent Holley Performance Parts Catalog for available sizes.

Don't drill jets to change their size. This always destroys the entry and exit features. It may introduce a swirl pattern, even if the drill is held in a pin vise and turned by hand. You can't be sure of the flow characteristics of a jet that is modified by drilling.

Main Air Bleed—All Holley carburetors, except some Model 5200 and 5210s, are equipped with built-in fixed-dimension air bleeds. Some *"feedback"* or *closed-loop control* carburetors (those with metering adjusted by electronics) have variable air bleeds. A flat surface in the inlet horn is used for mounting these bleeds. They see total pressure and are not affected by airflow variations.

POWER SYSTEM

When the engine is called upon to produce power in excess of normal cruising requirements, the carburetor has to provide a richer mixture. Added fuel for power operation is supplied by the power system controlled by manifold vacuum.

Manifold vacuum accurately indicates engine load. Vacuum is usually strongest at idle. As load increases, the throttle valve must be opened wider to maintain a given speed. This offers less restriction to air entering the intake manifold and reduces manifold vacuum.

A vacuum passage in the carburetor applies manifold vacuum to a power-valve piston or

Power valve at right discharges through *windows* for increased flow and cross-sectional strength. It is less likely to break off in installation or removal than *drilled* type at left. Window type can be used as a replacement with gasket without protrusions on inside diameter. Window valve is offered in two sizes: 125-XX for carburetors with two power-valve-channel restrictions (PVCR) up to 0.095-in.; 125-165 and 125-1005 for larger PVCR.

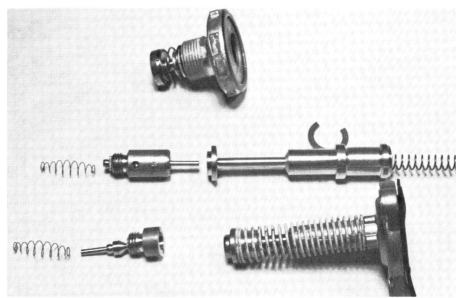

Three Holley power valves. Top is single-stage screw-in type used on Model 2300, 2305, 4150/60/75, 4500 and 3150. Center is a gradient power valve used on Model 2245 and 1945. *Gradient* valve operates over a wide range of manifold vacuum and meters fuel proportionally with a tapered valve. Piston and spring are retained in the air horn by clip. Valve, seat and spring screw into the main body. Valve at bottom is from Models 5200 and 5210. Diaphragm and spring assembly attach to air horn by three screws. Seat, valve and spring are in main body.

diaphragm. At idle or normal cruising conditions, manifold vacuum acting against a spring holds the valve closed. As high power demands load the engine, manifold vacuum drops.

Below a preset point, usually about 6 inches of mercury (in.Hg), the power-valve spring overcomes manifold vacuum and opens the power valve. Fuel flows through the power valve and through a power-valve restriction to join fuel already flowing through the main metering system from the main jet. The mixture is richened.

Consider the power valve as a "switch" operated by manifold vacuum. It is designed to operate (add more fuel) at a given load. It turns on extra fuel to change from an economical cruising fuel/air mixture to a power mixture. The power-valve channel restriction (PVCR) controls the amount of enrichment.

When engine power demands are reduced, increasing manifold vacuum acts on the diaphragm or piston to overcome power-valve-spring tension, closing the power valve and shutting off the added fuel supply.

DESIGN FEATURES

Power Valves—Holley high-performance carburetors usually have single-stage power valves. Carburetors for street use, especially on 1973 and later engines with exhaust gas recirculation (EGR), have two-stage power valves. Two-stage power valves are discussed on page 26.

Single-stage power valves are used in the 2300, 4150, 4160, 4165, 4175 and 4500 series. These screw-in type valves are available with different flow areas and opening points. The

Numbers stamped onto screw-in power valves indicate manifold vacuum at which valve opens. These show 50, 65, 75 and 85, specifying 5.0, 6.5, 7.5 and 8.5 in.Hg, respectively. Large rectangular holes (two) on each valve ensure it doesn't become a restriction. Only time metering is done in valve is in first stage of two-stage valves. PVCR is sized to supply added fuel needed for power enrichment.

flow area used must always be larger than the combined area of the PVCR.

Opening points are available in increments from 2.5—10.5 in.Hg. The last digits in the part number indicate the opening point in in.Hg for that single-stage power valve when a decimal point is placed ahead of the last digit. This number is also stamped on the valve. Examples:

125-105 opens at 10.5 in.Hg

125-25 opens at 2.5 in.Hg

Power-valve opening point is another variable the carburetor designer uses to arrive at the best compromise between economy, exhaust emissions and driveability. On normal replacement carburetors, the valve may be opened quite late to allow a particular engine to meet emission requirements, as well as maintain a broad economy range.

Three power valves. Piston rod operates valve at left. Center is two-stage for 4150/60/80, 4165/75 and 2300 models. Valve at right fits same carburetors, but is "inverted." Normally open valve closes when manifold drops. This type of valve is useful where severe high-rpm pulsing increases main-system fuel flow. A four-cylinder engine is a good application.

Racing engines, on the other hand, have substantial manifold-vacuum fluctuations at idle and low speeds. The tuner must install a power valve that won't open and close in response to variations caused by valve timing instead of throttle position or engine load. Selecting power valves to meet these special requirements is explained on page 119.

Most Holley two- and four-barrel performance carburetors use *picture-window* power valves with flow capacity sufficient for two 0.095-in. PVCRs. Older Holley power valves used 4 or 6 drilled holes in place of the picture window. No longer available as service parts,

they may be factory-installed in some carburetors. Current two-stage power valves use the drilled-hole construction.

Screw-in power valves may be stamped with additional numbers, such as A5. This manufacturing code indicates the month and year the valve was made. A is January and 5 is 1985. C6 indicates March, 1986. Of course, the year could be off in increments of 10 years, so it is helpful to have some idea of when the carburetor was made.

Two-stage power valves are used on replacement carburetors to allow a particular engine to pass emission tests. Staged power valves open

partially at one vacuum level, then open fully when manifold vacuum falls to a lower level. The first stage in these valves open a metering orifice smaller than the PVCR.

Holley offers two-stage power valves as replacement parts. These valves improve driveability in vehicles with relatively low power-to-weight ratios. Two-stage power valves for Models 2300, 4150/40/80 are identified with numbers. Deciphering the numbers requires looking at a Holley catalog.

Two power valves, 125-165 and 125-1005, open at 6.5 and 10.5 in.Hg, respectively. These flow adequate fuel to handle two 0.128-in. PVCRs. Because of its size, the valve stem cannot be piloted and the power valve can be damaged by dirt in the fuel. Don't use them unless you have a real need.

Holley cannot guarantee economy improvements, but some benefit should be realized if two-stage power valves are applied as follows:

● Don't use the valves in any vehicle that will be used on the drag strip. Two-stage valves are restrictive and could cause leaning out at high rpm.

● Best economy improvement will be realized in recreational vehicles equipped with the 0-6619, 0-6909 and similar carburetors, and in some station wagons and heavy sedans using Model 4165 spreadbore carburetors. Use the valve only on the primary side in the Model 4165. Best results are obtained in stop-and-go driving, or driving in rolling or mountainous terrain.

● Some fuel economy may be lost in other applications. Typical two-stage power valves operate as follows. The 125-206 opens the lst stage at 12.5 in.Hg and the 2nd stage at 5.5 in.Hg. For applications above 4000 ft., the

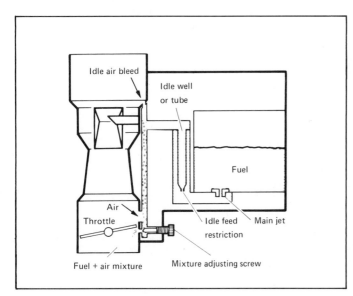

Idle system operates like main system, only on smaller scale.

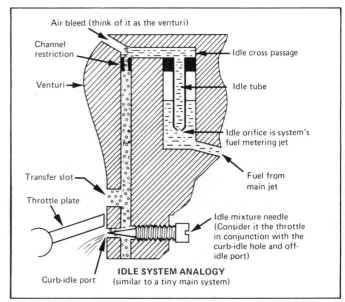

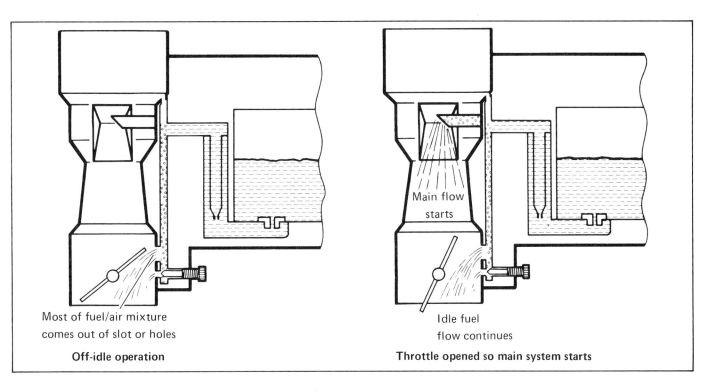

Most of fuel/air mixture
comes out of slot or holes

Off-idle operation

Main flow
starts

Idle fuel
flow continues

Throttle opened so main system starts

125-207 opens the lst stage at 10.5 in.Hg and the 2nd at 5 in.Hg.

Piston-type power valves are used in Models 1940, 1945, 1946, 2210, 2245, 2280, 2360 and 4360. Spring force is factory-set to open at a specified manifold vacuum. This setting can be changed by adding or deleting shims from the spring at the foot of the piston stem. The greater the number of shims, the higher the manifold vacuum at which the valve opens. If the spring is shortened or shims removed, the valve opens at a lower manifold vacuum.

IDLE SYSTEM

Idling requires richer mixtures than part-throttle operation. Unless the idle mixture is richer, slow and irregular combustion will occur. This is due to the high dilution of the charge by residual exhaust gases that exist at idle vacuums.

The idle system supplies fuel at idle and low speeds. It has to keep the engine running, even when accessory loads are applied to the engine. These include the alternator, air-conditioning compressor and power-steering pump. The idle system also has to keep the engine running against the load imposed by an automatic transmission in one of the operating ranges (Low, Drive, Reverse).

At idle and low speeds, not enough air is drawn through the venturi to cause the main metering system to operate. Intake-manifold vacuum is high because of the great restriction to the airflow by the nearly closed throttle

valve. This high vacuum provides the pressure differential for idle-system operation.

Perhaps the easiest way to understand how the idle system works is to look at it as a tiny main metering system. Because air enters the idle system through the idle air bleed, think of the bleed as the venturi. Flow through this system depends on transfer-slot and discharge-hole area exposed by the main throttle plate and idle-mixture screw position. Consider the discharge hole or slot and the idle screw as forming the "idle-system throttle."

Backing out the idle screw or opening the throttle to expose more of the slot to manifold vacuum opens the idle system "throttle" so more air flows through the system. Pressure drop across the idle air bleed increases, bringing more fuel from the idle well so the mixture stays at the desired fuel/air ratio. Fuel flows through the main jet, then into a vertical idle well, past the idle-feed restriction. It then mixes with air from the idle air bleed.

Sometimes the idle restriction is at the bottom of the idle well. The mixture is lifted up and across to another vertical passage. Fuel-air mixture flows down this second vertical passage and branches in two directions: through the idle-discharge passage into the throttle bore *below* the throttle valve, and to an idle-transfer slot (or holes) just *above* the throttle valve.

When the throttle valve is opened and engine speed increases, airflow through the venturi increases so the main metering system begins discharging fuel through the discharge nozzle

in the booster venturi. Flow from the idle system tapers off as the main system starts to discharge fuel. The two systems are designed to provide a smooth gradual transition from idle to cruising speeds *when carburetor capacity is correctly matched to engine displacement.*

When driving, flow swings quickly back and forth between idle and main operation as the vehicle is accelerated, slowed by closing the throttle, idled at stop, and then reaccelerated.

When the throttle is closed, high vacuum below the throttle plate draws air and fuel through the idle system and out the idle-discharge port. When the throttle is partially open, vacuum below the throttle plate is reduced and flow through the idle system is reduced. Some flow is out the idle port and some is out the idle-transfer port.

When the throttle is fully open, there is not enough vacuum at the idle port to draw any fuel-air mixture through the idle system. Idle system flow gradually ceases as the throttle is moved from idle to cruising. Naturally, flow through the main-metering system increases as idle flow decreases, so the transition is smooth—if the right carburetor is chosen for the engine.

DESIGN FEATURES

Throttle Stop—The throttle lever is seated against a stop instead of closing the throttle against the throttle bore. This ensures against the throttle sticking in the bore. It also makes the idle system less sensitive to mixture adjust-

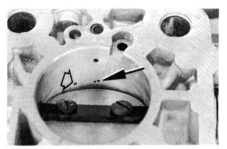

Some idle-transfer circuits (also called *progression* or *off-idle*) use a slot (top). Others use a series of holes (bottom). Curb idle is always hole nearest the flange. Outline arrows indicate spark ports.

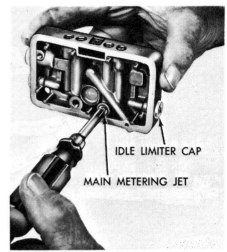

Idle limiters on idle-adjustment screws hold adjustments within a narrow band. This ensures specification emission levels for a given engine/carburetor combination. Limiter caps cover screw access openings or fit on adjustment screw. In either case, further adjustments require mutilating the cap.

ments. Holley carburetors are factory-set to an idle airflow specification. They should not be readjusted to seat the throttle in the bore (especially diaphragm-operated secondaries).

Idle-Air-Bleed Size—Increasing idle-air-bleed size reduces pressure drop across the bleed, decreasing the amount of fuel pulled over from the idle well. Increasing idle-air-bleed size leans the idle mixture, even if the idle-feed restriction is left constant. Conversely, decreasing idle-air-bleed size increases pressure drop in the system and richens the idle mixture.

Idle-Speed Setting—Before emission-control requirements became important, idle setting was typically the slowest speed at which the engine would keep running smoothly. Emission requirements make higher idle speeds necessary. A higher idle speed reduces exhaust-gas dilution that occurs at lower idle speeds so leaner idle mixtures can be used without misfiring.

Engines designed to pass emission requirements are typically set for lean best idle at a specified rpm and a subsequent reduction in idle speed by leaning the mixture still further—as stated on a label in the engine compartment.

Manufacturers have correlated this lean best idle and subsequent idle drop-off to provide the required carbon monoxide percentage (CO%) to pass the emission requirement. From this lean-best-idle point, and at this specified rpm figure, each of the idle-mixture-adjustment

screws are turned in to provide a specified rpm drop-off. Where there are two screws, each is adjusted to provide 1/2 of the specified idle drop-off. CO levels are usually stated for use when an analyzer is available.

Older non-emission-controlled cars and racing cars typically set for the desired idle rpm and best manifold vacuum. This is not a minimum-emission setting.

Idle Limiter—An idle-limiter cap limits idle-mixture-screw adjustment to approximately 3/4 turn. Applied after the desired idle mixture has been set, this limiter prevents easy tampering with the idle-mixture adjustment. This factory setting is made when the carburetor is flow-checked. The limiter is constructed so removing it requires destroying the cap, thereby showing that the carburetor has been readjusted and may not be providing required emission performance.

Beginning in the late '70s, idle-mixture-adjustment capability was virtually eliminated. Idle adjustment is trapped in a fixed setting by a limiter cap. Or, the idle-adjustment needle is hidden beneath a plug.

Intermediate Idle System—In five of the largest Holley high-performance carburetors (Model 4500), an intermediate idle system discharges through a tube into the venturi's trailing edge. This extra idle system provides additional transfer fuel between idle and main system operation. Opening the throttle past the usual idle system transfer slot greatly reduces the manifold vacuum that was being applied to the idle system. In these large-venturi carburetors, velocity through the venturi is not sufficient to establish main-system flow at this time. A giant flat spot would occur without this

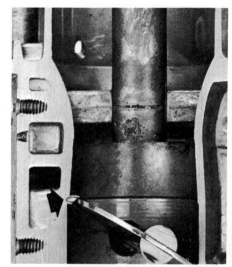

Cutaway Model 4500 shows intermediate idle-system discharge tube (arrow). System is fed from its own restriction in fuel bowl.

intermediate idle system.

The discharge tube for the intermediate idle system is above the transfer slot at the main venturi tail. Operation of the intermediate system starts as the throttle moves past the intermediate discharge. The system flows continuously beyond this point.

The intermediate idle system has its own air idle-air bleed and idle-feed restriction. There are no adjustments. Nevertheless, the bowl-fed system continues feeding fuel after the main system starts because the discharge tube is at a lower pressure than the fuel bowl.

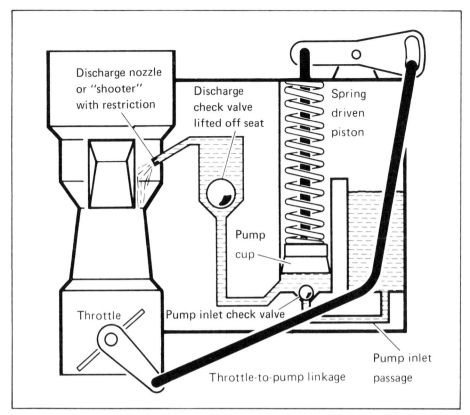

Here partially open throttle causes accelerator pump to move to bottom of its well. Pump-inlet check ball (valve) is forced onto its seat and discharge-check ball has lifted off its seat. Fuel sprays into carburetor throat through *shooter* nozzle. In many carburetors, pump cup serves as the inlet valve when the pump moves upward to refill.

Two pump-inlet-valve types. Inlet valve at bottom is a rubber umbrella-shape valve. It seats instantly for best tip-in performance. Hanging-ball type at top requires an instant to seat before pump shot can be delivered. A tiny part of the shot is wasted into the bowl as pump pressure seats the ball. There's a clearance of 0.011—0.013 in. between ball and retainer (arrow) when bowl is inverted.

Auxiliary Air Bleeds—These are sometimes used in the idle system. Although these usually add air to the idle system downstream from the traditional idle air bleed, they act in parallel with the idle air bleed.

ACCELERATOR PUMP

The accelerator pump:

● Makes up for fuel that condenses onto manifold surfaces when the throttle is opened suddenly.

● Makes up for the lag in fuel delivery when the throttle is opened suddenly, which allows more air to rush in.

● Acts as a mechanical injection system to supply fuel before the main system starts.

High manifold vacuum tends to keep the mixture well vaporized. As the throttle is opened quickly, intake-manifold vacuum instantly drops, moving the pressure toward atmospheric. As pressure in the manifold rises toward atmospheric, some of the fuel drops out of the vapor and becomes liquid. It condenses into puddles and spots on the walls and floor of the manifold. Consequenlty, only a lean mixture is now available for the cylinders.

The engine hesitates or stumbles unless more fuel is immediately added to replace that which fell out of the mixture. This additional fuel is especially important with big-port and large-plenum manifolds because there is more surface area for fuel to condense onto.

Making up for condensed fuel loss onto the manifold and taking care of fuel-delivery lagging behind increasing airflow are both important. But the relative importance of the two has not been established.

The accelerator pump supplies fuel when the throttle is quickly opened past the point where the idle-transfer system would have supplied fuel until the main system could begin its normal operation. Here, it supplies the required fuel until the main system starts flowing. During the low-flow, low-vacuum period, the accelerator pump injects fuel under pressure into the throttle bore. Duration of accelerator-pump operation must be carefully engineered to provide a "cover up" of sufficient length to allow main-system flow to be established so good vaporization will be ensured and correct fuel/air ratio reestablished.

The accelerator pump operates when the pump-operating lever is actuated by throttle movement. As the throttle opens, the pump linkage operates a *pump diaphragm* or plunger. Pressure in the pump forces the *pump-inlet ball* or valve onto its seat so fuel won't escape from the pump into the fuel bowl. And the pressure also raises the *discharge needle* or ball off its seat so fuel discharges through a *shooter* into the venturi.

As the throttle is moved toward the closed position, the linkage returns to its original position. The pump-inlet ball or valve moves off its seat to allow the pump to refill from the bowl. The piston or diaphragm is positively pulled back to the at-rest position. This creates a vacuum in the pump cavity to ensure quick refilling of the pump. As pump pressure is relieved, the discharge check needle or ball reseats so there is a closed check valve to refuel the pump.

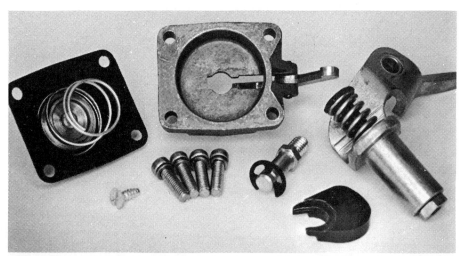

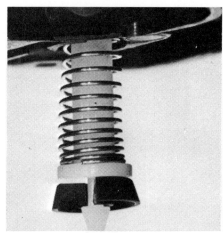

High-capacity (50cc per 10 strokes) accelerator pump Kit 20-11 is often added when large secondaries are to be opened quickly. It is also helpful when there is a wild camshaft or when the carburetor is a long way from the intake ports. Pump is sometimes called a *REO Pump* because similar ones were used on REO trucks. Installation may require raising carburetor with a spacer so pump lever will clear manifold.

Spring-driven accelerator pumps fill through center of pump cap. Cup has been cut away to show it fits loosely on stem to allow filling when closing throttle linkage cocks pump against spring. Cup seals against plastic pump piston face during delivery stroke.

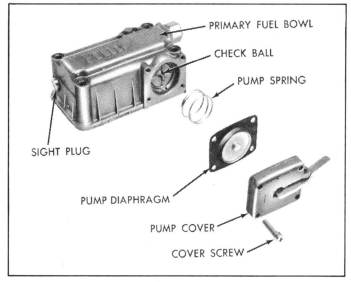

Diaphragm pump in removable fuel bowl showing components. Check ball is used as inlet valve in this example. Some use rubber-type inlet valves. Pump is actuated by a separate lever that rides against a cam on the throttle shaft.

The weight of the discharge-check valve keeps it closed against the signal created by air passing by the pump shooters so fuel is not pulled out of the pump system. In some carburetors the discharge check is a lightweight ball at the bottom of the pump passage.

In this instance, fuel is stored in the passage between the check and the nozzle (shooter). An anti-pullover discharge nozzle is used in such systems so air passing by the shooter won't pull fuel out of the pump passage. Because the discharge check is a lightweight ball, excess vapors in the pump can easily escape into the passage to the shooter.

This is helpful when a diaphragm-type pump is equipped with a rubber-type inlet valve because these valves seal so vapors cannot escape back to the fuel bowl. Vapors can only be purged from the pump when the pump is operated or when pressure becomes sufficient to raise the discharge ball or needle off its seat.

Clearance around the hanging-ball-type inlet check in a diaphragm pump allows excess vapors to escape to the fuel bowl. Pump-stem clearance in a piston-type pump is used for a vapor-escape path.

Remember, the pump's function is to replace fuel that dropped out of suspension and to compensate for fuel inertia or delay.

DESIGN FEATURES

Accelerator-Pump Inlet Valves—The synthetic-rubber-type valve provides an immediate pump shot with very little throttle movement. This is called *tip-in* capability. Because it is normally closed, no time delay or fuel flow is required to close it. This type valve also requires the least pressure difference to fill the pump. A rubber valve doesn't allow vapors generated in the pump to escape. And, it cannot be used with exotic fuels.

A ball-type valve is not as good for tip-in because of the delay required to force the ball against its seat by part of the pump shot escaping past it. Advantages include good purging of vapors generated in the pump. Vapors escape through the clearance between the ball and the seat. Exotic fuels do not affect the steel-ball valve.

Two Pump Types—Holley replacement carburetors use both piston- and diaphragm-type accelerator pumps.

All Holley high-performance carburetors use diaphragm-type accelerator pumps because they have the most positive action. These pumps have maximum capacities of 30cc and 50cc. Capacity is selected to fit application requirements. Accelerator pump capacity is measured by collecting the output of 10 full strokes of the pump. Thus, a 30cc pump delivers 3cc per pump shot at maximum stroke. Pump capacity and delivery rate are controlled by the pump cam and linkage settings.

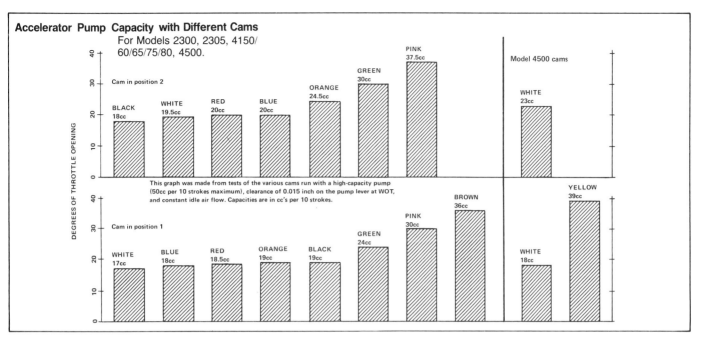

Accelerator Pump Capacity with Different Cams
For Models 2300, 2305, 4150/60/65/75/80, 4500.

Cam in position 2

| BLACK 18cc | WHITE 19.5cc | RED 20cc | BLUE 20cc | ORANGE 24.5cc | GREEN 30cc | PINK 37.5cc |
Model 4500 cams: WHITE 23cc

This graph was made from tests of the various cams run with a high-capacity pump (50cc per 10 strokes maximum), clearance of 0.015 inch on the pump lever at WOT, and constant idle air flow. Capacities are in cc's per 10 strokes.

Cam in position 1

WHITE 17cc | BLUE 18cc | RED 18.5cc | ORANGE 19cc | BLACK 19cc | GREEN 24cc | PINK 30cc | BROWN 36cc
Model 4500 cams: WHITE 18cc, YELLOW 39cc

DEGREES OF THROTTLE OPENING

Pump Cams—High-performance carburetors use a nylon cam on the throttle lever to operate the pump lever. A "white" cam is typically supplied on the carburetor. Cam shape affects pump action. First, total lift of the cam affects the stroke and therefore the capacity available from the pump. Cam profile or shape controls the phasing of the pump system.

Cams are color-coded to identify each profile. See the accompanying chart for pump capacities with various cams.

A sharp-nose pump cam gives a quicker pressure rise and causes strong pump action to begin immediately as the pump is activated. A gentle-ramp cam gives the opposite effect.

The pump cam is one more tool the tuner can use to make the carburetor perform well in a particular application. Several cams have been developed for specific applications. All pumps have adjustments on either the cam or the pump linkage.

Pump Discharge Nozzles (Shooters)—The pump discharges through a *shooter*. Hole size governs the rate of discharge. A larger hole allows pump contents to be discharged quicker and with less pressure than a small discharge hole.

Discharge-hole size in thousandths is stamped on removable shooters. A 25 marking indicates 0.025-in. holes. Sizes range from 0.021—0.052 in.

Removable pump shooters are used in all Holley high-performance carburetors. Several shooter types are used. They are not interchangeable between carburetor models.

The shooter is usually aimed or targeted so fuel hits the booster venturi (if one is used).

Accelerator-pump discharge nozzles are targeted so pump shot *breaks* against booster venturi. Photo shows how shot is pulled toward lower edge of booster venturi by air streaming into carburetor. Bubbly fuel flow from main discharge nozzle issuing from tail of booster indicates air is already mixing with fuel. Carburetor was placed on a Holley Engineering air box for this photo.

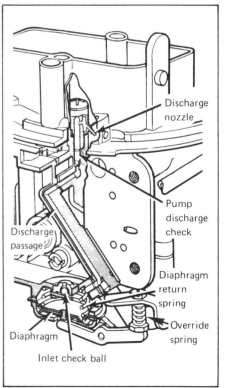

Typical pump-passage routing in carburetor with removable fuel bowls and metering blocks.

Discharge nozzle · Pump discharge check · Diaphragm return spring · Override spring · Diaphragm · Discharge passage · Inlet check ball

31

Accelerator-pump discharge nozzles or shooters are marked to indicate hole diameter in thousandths of an inch. Three types shown here include anti-pullover design used in 4165 and other models with lightweight pump-discharge-check valves. Two shooters at right are used with heavier check valves immediately under the shooter.

Pump discharge nozzle screw Kit 26-12 includes screw with smaller shank to allow increased fuel flow to shooter. Use one of these screws with any shooter larger than 0.040 in., as it ensures the nozzle will be the limiting restriction. This is for Models 2300, 2305, 4150/60/80, 4165/75 and 4500.

This breaks up the fuel so it is more nearly vaporized as it enters the engine. Some shooters are aimed toward the throttle plate or against the bore.

Pump Override Spring—A pump override spring is used in piston and diaphragm-type pumps. It controls fuel pressure in the accelerator pump system and pump-shot duration during WOT "punches" or "slams." When the cam or link has lifted or pushed the pump linkage to its maximum lift point, the override spring takes up the full lift travel and continues to apply pressure to operate the piston or diaphragm. Without the override spring, something would have to give or break. Because fuel is not compressible, tremendous forces would be built up instantaneously.

Pump Selection and Timing—More details on pumps, cams and shooters are on page 118.

CHOKE SYSTEM

The choke system supplies the rich mixture required to start and operate a cold engine. Cranking speeds for a cold engine are often around 50—75 rpm. These speeds are low compared to engine operating speeds, so little manifold vacuum is created to operate the idle system. A closed choke valve creates a vacuum below it so fuel is pulled out of both the idle. The main-metering systems during cranking.

This surplus fuel creates an extremely rich mixture: approximately half fuel and half air. The super-rich mixture is needed because there is not much manifold vacuum to help vaporize the fuel. Because the manifold is cold, most fuel immediately recondenses and puddles onto the manifold surfaces. The fuel is cold too and not volatile. And, the fuel from the main metering system is largely liquid because there is no air velocity to assist in atomizing it. Liquid fuel cannot be evenly distributed to the cylinders. When it arrives there, it will not burn well. During starting, only a small portion of the fuel ever reaches the cylinders as vapor.

Once the engine starts, off-center mounting of the choke plate shaft allows airflow to open the choke slightly against a spring to start leaning out the mixture.

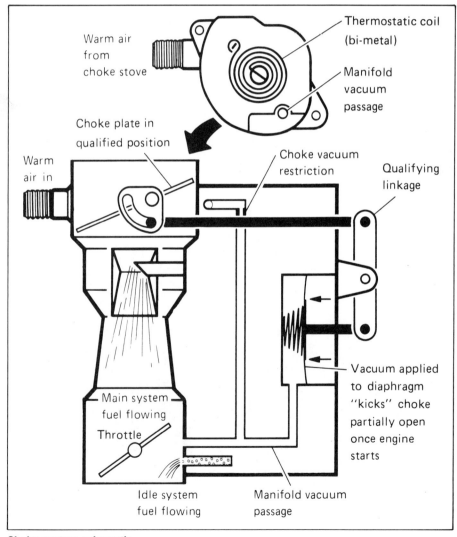

Choke system schematic.

In the case of the automatic choke, a vacuum *qualifying diaphragm* pulls the choke valve to a preset opening once the engine starts. In some cases a temperature-modulated diaphragm varies this preset opening with ambient temperature. When the choke assumes the qualifying position it is still providing a 20%—50% richer than normal operating mixture as the engine warms up and the choke "comes off" or opens.

This richer mixture is required because fuel won't vaporize well until the exhaust hot spot in the manifold warms sufficiently to ensure good vaporization. So long as the choke is "on," the engine idles quite fast: 800—1100 rpm or higher with a cold engine. This higher speed results because the choke linkage also includes a fast-idle cam to keep the engine running fast to aid in vaporizing fuel and overcoming cold-engine friction loads.

As the engine warms up, the choke is opened fully by the bimetal spring in an automatic choke, or by the operator if the choke is a manual one. This action also reduces the idle speed to a normal "curb idle."

DESIGN FEATURES
Automatic Chokes—There are two types of automatic chokes: integral and divorced.

The *integral* choke uses a tube to connect heated air from the exhaust manifold or exhaust-heat crossover to the bimetal spring inside a housing on the carburetor. Some integral chokes use engine coolant or electricity to heat the bimetal.

An integral choke may close because there is no flow of heated air past the bimetal spring when the engine is not running. So, the integral choke can close while the engine is still hot, even though a choke-supplied rich mixture and fast idle are not needed to start the engine and keep it running.

The *divorced* choke uses a bimetal spring mounted on the intake manifold or in a pocket in the exhaust-heat passage of the intake manifold. A mechanical linkage from the bimetal spring operates the choke lever on the carburetor. Divorced chokes accurately respond to engine requirements because the choke only operates when the engine is cold.

Divorced choke is actuated by remotely mounted bimetal (arrow). It is often placed in an exhaust-heated pocket in the intake manifold. Divorced chokes are subject to greater production tolerances than integral types.

Electric choke caps. Top one uses nichrome-wire resistance heating element to warm bimetal and open choke. Lower unit uses a solid-state heating device. Power is supplied from vehicle's 12-volt source.

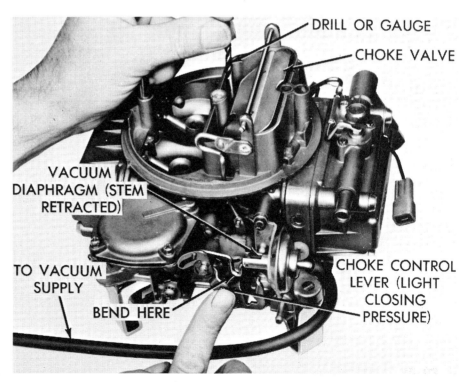

DRILL OR GAUGE
CHOKE VALVE
VACUUM DIAPHRAGM (STEM RETRACTED)
TO VACUUM SUPPLY
BEND HERE
CHOKE CONTROL LEVER (LIGHT CLOSING PRESSURE)

Vacuum qualification setting is detailed in repair kit instructions and tune-up specifications. In some cases check is made on down side of choke plate (as here); in others, on the up side.

Examples from left to right: *Manual* choke (arrows indicate cable-housing and lever clamps); *Integral* choke with bimetal and housing removed to show built-in vacuum qualifier piston (arrow); *Divorced* choke with vacuum-qualifier diaphragm (arrow) attached to carburetor body.

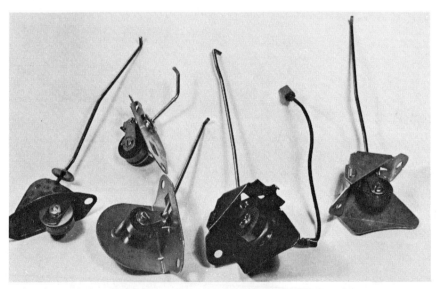

Collection of remote or divorced chokes from GM and Chrysler vehicles. Some have been made with Calrod heaters next to bimetal to program choke come-off to meet emission standards. Pre-'72 units sometimes had adjustable bimetal to allow changing preload.

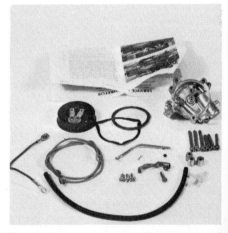

Electric-choke conversion Kit 45-224 uses external air supply. Fits 0-4412, 0-4776-2 through 0-4781-2, 0-6299, 0-6708, and 0-6709.

Electric Choke—Chokes can be operated by a bimetal spring heated by a solid-state heating unit (used in current carburetors) or an electric resistor nichrome-wire (no longer used by Holley). Either heater increases temperature similarly to that of the engine as it warms up. The choke operates as if the bimetal spring were sensing temperature supplied by the engine.

The advantage of an electric choke is simple hook up without plumbing and other attachments to the engine. Only a single wire is needed, usually from the ignition switch. Disadvantages of an electric choke are:

• Current is taken from the battery when power demands are high.

• A quick come-back-on activates the choke whenever the engine is turned off, even if the engine stays warm.

• Unless the engine is immediately started when the ignition is turned on, the choke opens, even though the engine is still cold. This prob-

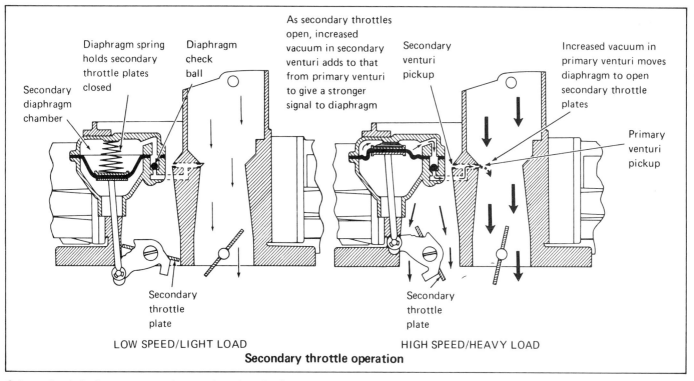

Diaphragm spring holds secondary throttle plates closed

Diaphragm check ball

Secondary diaphragm chamber

As secondary throttles open, increased vacuum in secondary venturi adds to that from primary venturi to give a stronger signal to diaphragm

Secondary venturi pickup

Increased vacuum in primary venturi moves diaphragm to open secondary throttle plates

Primary venturi pickup

Secondary throttle plate

Secondary throttle plate

LOW SPEED/LIGHT LOAD

HIGH SPEED/HEAVY LOAD

Secondary throttle operation

Schematic of diaphragm-operated secondary throttle. Signal from primary venturi is augmented by an increasing signal from secondary venturi as secondary throttle starts opening. Closing primary throttle closes secondary by mechanical override linkage. As signal from venturi ports decreases (pressure goes closer to atmospheric) check valve blows off seat to remove vacuum from diaphragm chamber. Secondary opening rate is controlled by spring behind diaphragm and size of restriction through which vacuum is applied.

WHAT'S A BIMETAL?

It is two different metals bonded into a strip and formed into a coil. Because the metals have unequal thermal expansion characteristics, the coil unwraps when heated and wraps up again when cooled.

The outer or "free" end of the coil attached to the choke linkage holds the choke closed. Or, it loads the choke plate so it closes when the throttle is opened.

When the bimetal is heated, the choke opens. Warming it is done by exhaust-gas-heated air, jacket water or an electric heating element. Bimetal temperature response characteristics are built-in according to the metals used. Most choke bimetals wrap up (the choke is just closed) at 65F—70F (18C—21C).

Electric-choke conversion Kit 45-223 converts carburetors with an internal vacuum supply. Fits 0-1850, 0-3310, 0-6425 and 0-7448.

Choke index can serve as guide when changing choke settings. Limit such changes to one mark RICH or LEAN as noted on choke housing. Three screws must be loosened to allow adjustment.

lem can be fixed by powering the choke from the alternator circuit so the choke only gets power when the engine is operating. Switch 12-810 can be used for this with wires connected to the C and NO terminals.

• The choke can come off while the engine is still cold.

Choke Index—Automatic chokes have index marks. The factory setting causes the choke to close (on a new carburetor) when the choke

bimetal is approximately 70F (21C). Tapping the carburetor lightly overcomes any shaft friction so the choke seeks the position being set by the bimetal.

If less choke is desired at this temperature,

move the choke index one mark. An arrow on the housing shows the direction to move the index to change the choke operating characteristic (either lean or rich). A choke mixture change rarely requires more than one index

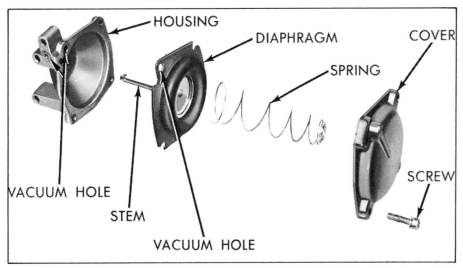

Exploded view of secondary-throttle diaphragm. Spring is only item to vary when tuning for a different opening point for secondary throttles.

Mechanically actuated secondary throttles operate progressively as shown here. Primaries (at top) open 40° or so before secondary opening begins. Linkage opens secondaries fully as primary throttles reach full-open.

Diaphragm-operated secondary opens as engine needs added airflow. This type of secondary operation is forgiving in terms of size selection. A too-large carburetor (airflow capacity) can often be used without spoiling low-end performance and driveability. Arrow indicates secondary-throttle stop.

mark change from the factory setting

Unloader—If the engine doesn't start quickly, extra fuel fed by the choke to the engine will create an overrich mixture that can't be burned. This must be cleared (or purged) from the manifold with air. Crank the engine while holding the throttle wide open (push accelerator pedal to floorboard) and open the choke so additional fuel is not drawn in. With an automatic choke, opening the throttle wide causes a tang on the throttle lever to contact the fast-idle cam. This opens (unloads) the choke plate sufficiently to

clear excess fuel from the manifold.

SECONDARY SYSTEM

For many years U.S. carburetors were single-stage carburetors; V8 engines were equipped with a two-barrel. It was merely a single casting containing two one-barrel carburetors side by side. One was used for each level of the traditional two-level cross-H manifold. So consider the usual two-barrel as a single-stage carburetor.

The late '40s saw an increased emphasis on

vehicle performance. Because more airflow means more power, single-stage carburetors became bigger and better—with accompanying driveability problems.

The large venturis required higher rpm or greater airflows to start main-system flow. Under some conditions, the idle system could be made to cover up the late entry of the main system. But, because the idle system was controlled by manifold vacuum, a great deficiency was felt at low manifold vacuum and low airflows. For example, when driving in a high-load, low-rpm condition.

In addition, the low venturi velocities at low rpm resulted in poor fuel vaporization and poor fuel/air mixing. Cylinder-to-cylinder distribution problems and erratic operation of the engines at lower airflows were the norm.

The metering range of the single- or two-barrel carburetor was too narrow to satisfy all driving requirements. The answer was obvious: use a staged carburetor to stretch the metering range. This allowed using venturis small enough to get the main systems flowing at low rpm. The design supplied good vaporization and the required capacity for high-rpm operation when it was needed.

Six-cylinder engines of medium displacement remained the economy workhorses. The first staged two-barrel on a U.S. car was on the 1970 Pinto. Such systems had long been used on European and Japanese cars. There costs were outweighed by the need to get maximum economy and maximum performance from small displacement engines.

In the early '50s, a whole host of four-barrel carburetors were introduced for V8s. The primary side of these carburetors was just like the older single-stage carburetors. Primary-venturi size was smaller than it had been on the single-stagers, returning all of the benefits provided by small venturis. These include early start of the main system, good vaporization and fuel/air mixing, and good distribution. Primary carburetor barrels were used for cruising loads and light accelerations encountered in normal traffic. Flexibility of operation and economy were regained.

Coupled to the primary carburetor barrels were two secondary carburetor barrels. These operated when maximum airflow was required for more power. The carburetor's metering range was essentially doubled. Consequently, good part-throttle operation was combined with relatively unrestricted flow for maximum-power conditions.

The secondary side is simply another carburetor. It usually opens later than the primary. Secondaries always have their own main metering system. Most have an idle system, which gives better mixture distribution and idle stability. The result is improved emissions performance because leaner idle settings can be used. The idle system also keeps the fuel level from

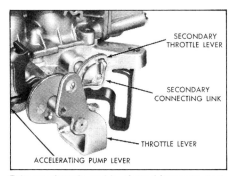

SECONDARY THROTTLE LEVER

SECONDARY CONNECTING LINK

THROTTLE LEVER

ACCELERATING PUMP LEVER

Primary throttle rod in slotted lever on secondary shaft won't allow secondary-throttle opening beyond an equivalent primary-throttle opening. Even though primaries may be opened wide, secondaries won't start to open until there is sufficient airflow through primary venturis to cause the diaphragm to actuate secondary throttles.

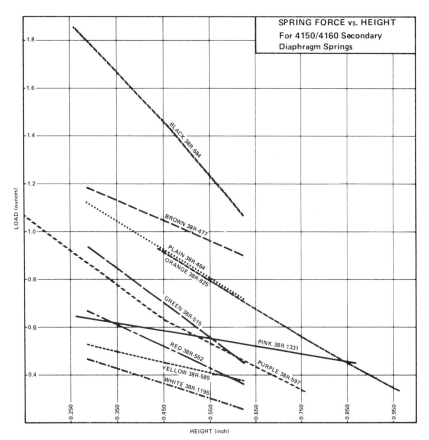

SPRING FORCE vs. HEIGHT
For 4150/4160 Secondary
Diaphragm Springs

LOAD (ounces)

BLACK 38R-684
BROWN 38R-477
PLAIN 38R-464
ORANGE 38R-825
GREEN 38R-515
RED 38R-552
PINK 38R-1331
PURPLE 38R-597
YELLOW 38R-585
WHITE 38R-1195

HEIGHT (inch)

rising in the secondary bowl when the needle and seat leak slightly, or open due to float bouncing. A secondary idle system also ensures fresh fuel in the secondary bowl.

In 1967 Holley began building some carburetors with accelerator pumps for both primary *and* secondary barrels. Some carburetors have power systems in the secondary side.

Secondary operation can be activated in several ways:

- Mechanical only.
- Diaphragm.
- Mechanical with velocity valve.
- Mechanical with air valve.

Holley carburetors use the first two methods.

Mechanically actuated secondaries are simple in operation. Secondary throttles are opened by a direct link from the primaries, usually progressively. Secondary opening is delayed until primaries have reached approximately 40% of opening. Secondary-throttle closing is positive because of the return spring, because throttles are offset on their shaft so airflow aids closing, and because a return link from the primary throttle pulls them closed.

Holley pioneered the use of separate accelerator pumps on mechanically actuated secondaries. This is now considered an essential feature for high-performance applications. The secondary pump ensures adequate fuel to carry the engine through any period when the driver opens the throttles quickly.

This is important when they are opened at an rpm too low to generate sufficient signal for main system flow on both the primary and secondary sides of the carburetor. The pumps actually supply mechanical fuel injection during the time the signal is being reestablished.

Diaphragm-operated secondaries have also been highly refined by Holley. These carburetors use a diaphragm to open the secondary

SECONDARY THROTTLE OPERATION RANGES
Diaphragm Secondary Springs From 85BP-3185 Used
in Model 4150, List 3310-1 Carburetor

Spring Color	350 CID Engine		402 CID Engine	
	RPM to Open	RPM at Full Open	RPM to Open	RPM at Full Open
Yellow (short spring)	1620	5680	1410	4960
Yellow	1635	5750	1420	5020
Purple	1915	6950	1680	6050
Plain (Std. Spring)	2240	8160	1960	7130
Brown	2710	8750	2380	7650
Black	2720	Not fully open at maximum air flow	2390	Not fully open at maximum air flow

NOTE:
All data taken without air cleaner. An air cleaner would cause earlier opening in all cases. Values subject to change due to cleaner restrictions.

Formula

$$CFM = \frac{RPM \times CID}{2 \times 1728} \times \eta$$

Where η = Volumetric Eff. = .9

Holley Tests
November, 1971

Chart and table clearly indicate relationship of secondary diaphragm springs and opening points for each with two popular engine displacements. Note how displacement affects opening point. Larger engine opens secondaries earlier. Bottom spring (white) is a clear or plain steel spring. Line slope indicates secondary-opening rate. Shallow slope opens more quickly. Springs toward bottom of graph open secondaries sooner. Yellow 38R-585 is fastest-opening spring in Secondary-Diaphragm Spring Kit 20-13. Black spring delays secondary opening longest and opens them at the slowest rate.

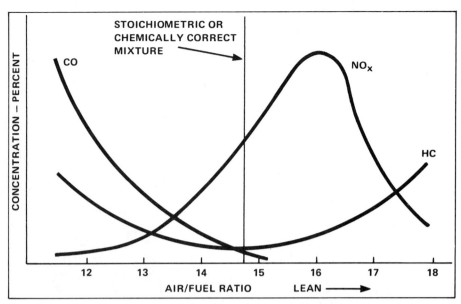

Approximate relationship between CO, HC, and NO_x as air/fuel ratio changes. Closed-loop control is designed to keep the ratio close to stoichiometric, 14.7:1.

Bosch Lambda sensor (oxygen sensor) is mounted in exhaust system upstream of catalytic converter. Its 0—1 volt output is sent to ECU at right.

throttles. Vacuum for the diaphragm is obtained from one of the primary venturis. Part of this signal is usually bled off through an opening or bleed into one of the secondary venturis. As the engine is operated at increasingly higher rpm, velocity through the primary venturi creates a vacuum signal.

The amount of secondary opening depends initially on airflow through the primary barrel.

As the secondary throttles begin to open and flow is established in the secondary barrel, the vacuum signal from the primary is augmented by vacuum from one of the secondary barrels through the bleed opening.

The secondary throttles are fully open at maximum speed. If the carburetor is too large for the engine, the diaphragm automatically *sizes* the carburetor. The diaphragm partially opens the secondary throttles to supply only the needed amount of mixture. Secondaries remain closed when the primary throttles are opened wide at low rpm. This eliminates small bogs and allows using the carburetor with a wide range of engine displacements, gear ratios, car weights and so forth.

A ball check in the vacuum passage to the diaphragm applies vacuum at a controlled rate through a bleed (a groove in the check-ball seat). When rpm is reduced so secondary airflow is not needed, the ball check instantly releases vacuum from the diaphragm so the throttles are closed by the return spring behind the diaphragm and by airflow acting against the throttles, which are offset on their shaft. The mechanical link positively closes the secondaries when the primaries are closed.

The diaphragm-operated secondary has an especially low opening effort or pedal "feel" because the throttle linkage only has to open the primaries and only actuates one accelerator pump. Secondaries are opened by the diaphragm without any assistance from the driver.

FEEDBACK CARBURETION

In general, gasoline engines produce three harmful emissions: hydrocarbons (HC), carbon monoxide (CO) and oxides of nitrogen (NO_X). The amount of each emitted by a vehicle under controlled test conditions is limited by law.

Emission standards have become more and more stringent over the years. Car manufacturing has become further complicated by the Corporate Average Fuel Economy (CAFE) standards. Changes made to satisfy one set of standards may adversely affect the other.

Catalytic Converters—In 1975 we saw the introduction of an exhaust catalyst as a method of handing HC and CO. The original catalytic converters are *oxidizing* catalysts; they encourage both compounds to take on more oxygen. Carbon monoxide is changed to carbon dioxide (CO_2) which is harmless, and hydrocarbons are converted to water (H_2O) and carbon dioxide.

Oxides of nitrogen (NO_X) were lowered by engine modifications that lowered combustion temperatures. Most of the improvement was accomplished through lowered compression ratios and exhaust gas recirculation (EGR). EGR dilutes the intake charge with exhaust gas.

Closed-Loop Control—Further reductions of NO_X require more advanced technology (including superior catalytic converters and microprocessors), which brings us to the *feedback* or *closed-loop* system. The fuel/air mixture is now controlled by engine demand conditions, not just by the amount of air flowing through the carburetor.

If the concentrations of HC, CO and NO_X can be held in proper balance, they can all be treated by a single catalyst or what is called a *three-way catalyst*. It uses palladium and/or rhodium as agents to reduce NO_X to harmless nitrogen and oxygen.

What happens in practice is straighforward. Oxygen released from NO_X combines with HC and and CO. NO_X becomes free nitrogen (N_2—an inert gas under normal conditions) and HC and CO become water and carbon dioxide.

The design challenge is in maintaining the correct balance. The ideal combination occurs near the chemically correct or *stoichiometric* air/fuel ratio, approximately 14.7:1.

Maintaining the emissions balance is the major reason for the closed-loop or feedback system. It is a system of engine sensors supplying data to a controlling microprocessor that manipulates a mixture adjuster in the carburetor.

The fuel/air ratio is monitored from an exhaust gas sample via an *oxygen sensor*. This typically sends a voltage output for interpretation by an *electronic control unit* (ECU, a microprocessor). It, in turn, alters the fuel/air mixture in the carburetor with a *solenoid-controlled valve* (also called a *duty-cycle solenoid*) to maintain the emissions balance.

If the the air/fuel ratio is kept close to 14.7:1, the three-way converter's efficiency is high for all three exhaust products. A lean mixture lessens the converter's efficient handling of NO_X. A rich mixture causes an efficiency drop for CO and HC.

Oxygen Sensor—In addition to the three pollutants mentioned, oxygen concentration also varies with fuel/air ratio in a predictable manner. Consequently, the amount of oxygen in the exhaust can be used as a guide to adjust the mixture.

The oxygen sensor is placed in the exhaust upstream of the catalyst. The sensor puts out a low-voltage signal to the ECU. As oxygen content increases—lean mixture—the voltage output drops. As it decreases—rich mixture—the voltage output increases. These outputs are used by the ECU to adjust the fuel/air ratio accordingly.

The sensor's total output ranges from 0—1000 millivolts (mv) (1.0 volt = 1000 mv). A lean mixture would typically be indicated by a reading of 100—200 mv. Rich mixtures are found at 700—900 mv. A defective sensor doesn't change voltage as the fuel/air mixture is altered, or its voltage output changes *very* slowly as oxygen content increases or decreases.

A correctly operating sensor will send minute fluctuating voltages, i.e, 910, 920, 900, 930 mv as it monitors oxygen content in the exhaust. A sensor's effective life is usually rated at 30,000 miles.

The current disadvantage to closed-loop control is that the oxygen sensor must be at 600F (315C) to supply reliable data to the ECU for adjusting the mixture. Consequently, during cold starts, closed-loop control reverts to open-loop control of the mixture.

Open-Loop Control—During warmup and heavy throttle applications, richer mixtures are required. These richer driving cycles are called *open-loop* because the oxygen sensor in the exhaust stream isn't supplying data to the ECU for controlling the fuel/air mixture.

Mixture control at cold starting is regulated by programmed instructions stored in the ECU's memory. When the oxygen sensor operating temperature is reached, 600F (315C), and coolant temperature has risen, the ECU accepts data from the oxygen sensor; closed-loop control begins.

Two sensors usually supply the necessary input to the ECU for WOT mixture control. A *vacuum sensor* (manifold pressure) and *throttle position sensor*. When these indicate heavy throttle application, the system goes open-loop (rich mixture supplied). When this requirement is stopped, the ECU switches back to closed-loop control and relies on the oxygen sensor for data to alter the solenoid-controlled valve's activity.

Vacuum Feedback System—On a vacuum feedback system, using the Holley 6500 as an example, the low voltage signal from the oxygen sensor signal is fed through an amplifier to a switch. This switch controls a valve that channels manifold vacuum to a special diaphragm on the carburetor. The diaphragm mechanically controls a bleed to a revised power valve.

The vacuum-feedback system (Holley 6500) was introduced on the 1978 Ford 2.3-liter engines for California. Application was extended nationwide on the same engine in 1981.

Electronic Feedback System—A new version of the feedback carburetor was introduced in the 1980 model year for Chevette (Holley 6510) and Omni/Horizon (Holley 6520), for California only. Application was extended nationwide for 1981. Since then, the principle has been extended to other models.

In this feedback method, the voltage signal originates at the oxygen sensor and the ECU generates a 10-hertz (10 cycles per second) output. This is sent to a solenoid-controlled valve in the carburetor.

This *duty-cycle solenoid* opens and closes at the same frequency sent by the ECU. The percentage of time the valve remains closed (the duty cycle) during each cycle varies, depending on the output from the ECU.

For example, under certain conditions the valve might be open 6 milliseconds (ms) (1.0 second = 1000 milliseconds), closed 4 ms, open 6 ms, closed 4 ms and so on. If the oxygen sensor indicates this is causing too rich a mixture, the valve's timing could be altered by the ECU to open only 4 ms and close 6 ms. Either way, each total cycle, (open *and* closed together) is 10 ms.

On some carburetors this solenoid-controlled valve only operates on the main system by opening and closing a restriction to supplement the main jet. Other carburetors have valves that also open and close an auxiliary air bleed affecting the idle mixture as well.

Mixture is controlled by the length of time the valve is held open or closed. The ECU's output to the valve is constantly altered as it monitors the different drivetrain sensors, oxygen, throttle position, manifold pressure, coolant temperature and so on that specify engine demand.

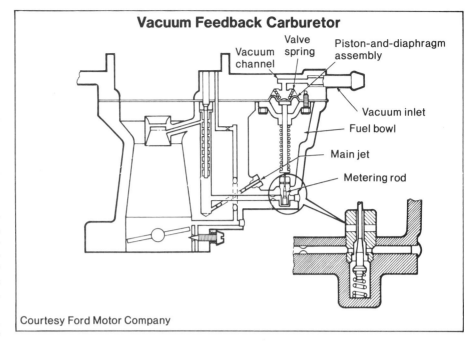

Vacuum Feedback Carburetor

Valve spring · Vacuum channel · Piston-and-diaphragm assembly · Vacuum inlet · Fuel bowl · Main jet · Metering rod

Courtesy Ford Motor Company

Duty-cycle removed from carburetor. Actual fuel-control valve is at bottom. Two O-rings (arrows) keep fuel from flowing around valve.

Model 6510 for 1981 Chevette. Duty-cycle solenoid is connected to electrical lead at left. Throttle-position sensor (arrow) supplies input to ECU.

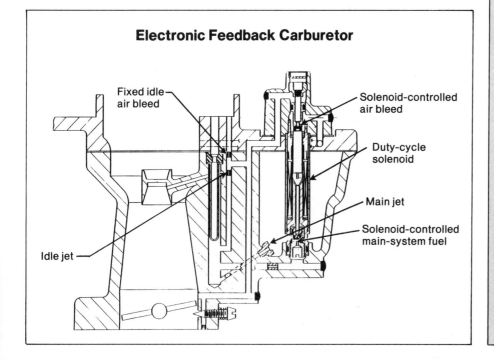

Electronic Feedback Carburetor

Fixed idle air bleed

Solenoid-controlled air bleed

Duty-cycle solenoid

Main jet

Solenoid-controlled main-system fuel

Idle jet

Driver Control of Mixture—The technology used in the closed-loop system can be used to improve fuel economy. With this in mind, Holley introduced a driver-controlled open-loop system: the Quarter Mile Dial.

In this system, the feedback control is replaced by a driver-controlled switch/mixture-control box, which is a signal generator. The solenoid-controlled air bleed is eliminated, so the duty-cycle solenoid affects *only* fuel flow.

The solenoid is controlled from an 11-position switch that changes the duty cycle (the percentage of time the solenoid is closed) from maximum rich to maximum lean. You can electronically adjust in a range of about five jet

Quarter Mile Dial schematic: (1) duty-cycle solenoid, (2) auxiliary jet, and (3) screw-in jet. Solenoid is adjusted by driver for optimum fuel flow through main system under different operating conditions.

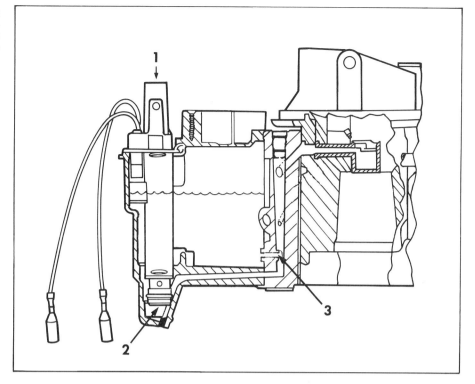

sizes. Every switch position is one-half jet size or about 2%.

You can set the system for maximum economy on the street or tune for the best F/A ratio for maximum power. This can be done for any combination of engine components and existing atmospheric conditions. Holley markets this equipment as Quarter Mile Dial.

Let's look first at the equipment to adapt to the popular Model 2300 and 4150/4160 carburetor families. Extra fuel is introduced downstream of the power-valve restriction to control both part-throttle and WOT mixtures.

Kits or complete systems are available. Kits contain the mixture-control box, one or two metering blocks, one or two fuel bowls, gaskets and a wiring harness. Systems contain a complete carburetor equipped with a duty-cycle solenoid, plus the mixture-control box and wiring harness.

If you already have one of the adaptable carburetors, you can use a kit. If not, buy a complete system for your application.

Although the Quarter Mile Dial allows controlling fuel economy, its primary use is for dialing in the best power under prevailing conditions. This is accomplished without removing the fuel bowl or changing main jets. You can use a stop watch to time acceleration, but sophisticated drag-strip timing is the ultimate. Racing associations have ruled these systems as legal bolt-on equipment.

Quarter Mile Dial systems are a useful tool for anyone doing dynamometer test work and setting best fuel at every load point. The system provides a 20% fuel adjustment range. Changing the main jets moves the range of control up or down as desired.

Kits and systems for various applications are listed in the Holley Performance Parts Catalog.

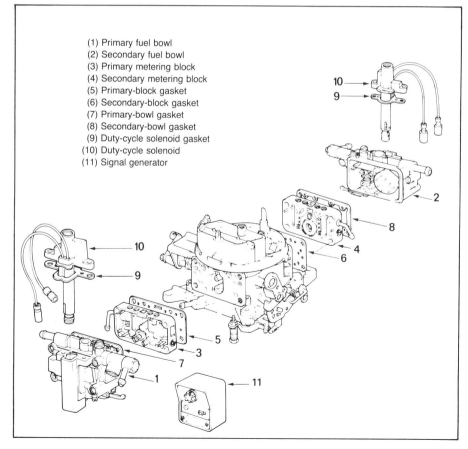

(1) Primary fuel bowl
(2) Secondary fuel bowl
(3) Primary metering block
(4) Secondary metering block
(5) Primary-block gasket
(6) Secondary-block gasket
(7) Primary-bowl gasket
(8) Secondary-bowl gasket
(9) Duty-cycle solenoid gasket
(10) Duty-cycle solenoid
(11) Signal generator

Quarter Mile Dial for 4150. Some systems have a solenoid just in primary bowl.

Holley 4500s on Pro Stock engine: the definition of high-performance carburetion.

HOLLEY NUMBERS

A complete Holley assembly, such as a carburetor, can be referred to by three different numbers: model number, engineering part or list number, and sales number.

Model Number—This describes the class, type and general features of products with that group. For example, Model 4150 describes a basic four-barrel configuration. Many different calibrations and individual features exist on various part/list numbers within the same model grouping.

Model numbers have meaning. The first digit usually designates the number of barrels (throttle bores). For example: Models 2210,

2300 and 2360 all start with 2 and all are two-barrels. The other digits indicate variations making one different from the other. The 4150 and 4160 are similar four barrels with different secondary metering and throttle actuation.

As with any numbering system, there are exceptions. For instance, models 1901 and 5200 are two-barrels. Numbers beginning with 6 are usually "closed-loop" or "feedback" carburetors. Here too, these are exceptions.

Engineering Part Number—This is assigned to a carburetor or other assembly in strict numerical sequence without regard for any other factor. If a two-barrel carburetor, a fuel pump and a four-barrel carburetor were initiated in

that succession, the part numbers will follow that order. These numbers are then assigned to their model groupings. Engineering numbers were originally set up with an R- prefix for the assembly number and on group numbers of components. Example: Part 0-4776 double-pumper high-performance carburetor has also been shown as List R-4776 AAA and List R-4776-lAAA.

The prefix letter may be changed to assist identification, such as P- for fuel pumps. Performance carburetors now use a 0- prefix.

The part number is stamped on the carburetor. On the 2300 and 4150/4160 it is on the air-horn extension supporting the choke shaft.

Sales Number—This number is assigned in numerical sequence for popular replacement carburetors and service items. For example: needle/seat, pump piston, pump diaphragm, repair kits, gasket kits, and so forth.

Sales numbers include a prefix number, a dash and a suffix number. Prefix 1- identifies carburetors, with the suffix identifying an individual carburetor. For example, 1-108 completely identifies a particular replacement carburetor. The number is used for merchandising and computer data processing. It doesn't appear on the carburetor, even though it may be used on the carton and in price sheets. Economaster carburetors use a 2- prefix. Performance carburetors use a 0- prefix.

Carburetor service components are also identified by product categories or groups. Prefix numbers are assigned to screws, gaskets, throttle plates, and other like pieces. Suffix numbers identify the particular parts.

PERFORMANCE CARBURETORS

MODEL 2300

These carburetors have been used on vehicles ranging from Jeeps to muscle cars. It was used for years on Ford passenger cars and trucks, Chevrolet trucks, International Harvester vehicles, American Motors vehicles, White Motors, Reo, and Willys Jeep.

Performance enthusiasts will remember that 2300s were used on three-carburetor Chevrolets and Dodge/Plymouth "Six-Packs." Racers who compete in drag or circle-track classes allowing only single two-barrels are quite familiar with List 0-4412, the 500-cfm version.

Venturi sizes on the Model 2300 have ranged from 1- to 1-7/16-in. diameter with air flows from 210 to 600 cfm. The largest 2300 current-

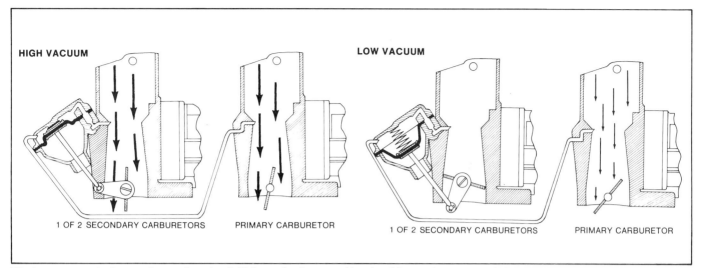

HIGH VACUUM

LOW VACUUM

1 OF 2 SECONDARY CARBURETORS   PRIMARY CARBURETOR

1 OF 2 SECONDARY CARBURETORS   PRIMARY CARBURETOR

Diaphragm-operated secondary carburetor. Initial opening is caused by signal from primary venturi. As secondaries start opening, vacuum from primary venturi is augmented by increasing signal from secondary venturi. Opening rate of secondary carburetors is controlled by spring behind diaphragm and size of restriction through which vacuum is applied. Closing primary throttle closes secondary by mechanical override linkage. As signal from venturi ports "dies" (pressure moves toward atmospheric) check ball blows off seat to remove vacuum from diaphragm chamber. The 3 x 2 diaphragm-operated carburetors work on same principle as a diaphragm-operated four-barrel carburetor. Center carburetor acts as the primaries and outboard carburetors as secondaries. Hoses connect secondary vaccum passages.

ly made flows 500 cfm.

Chevrolet and Chrysler muscle-car triple manifolds used diaphragm-operated 2300s as the end or outboard units. These have no chokes or accelerator pumps and use metering plates like the Model 4160. The center 2300 has a choke, accelerator pump, and a metering block with screw-in main jets and a power valve. These are available as replacement units for restoration projects.

Description of Operation—Because the 2300 is literally the front half of a 4150/4160 carburetor, operation is just like that described for a Model 4150 on page 46.

Some 2300s have a "reverse" idle adjustment as described and illustrated in the 4150 section. The adjustment *screws in* to *richen* the mixture and *backs out* to *lean* it, just the opposite of what has always been done in the past. A metering-block label identifies this idle system.

List 0-4412, 500-cfm —The 0-4412 Model 2300 is of special interest to racers and mechanics who need the utmost performance from a two-barrel. This 500-cfm version was first introduced in 1969.

The 4412 became an instant success among engine builders and tuners preparing engines to race in classes limited to one two-barrel carburetor. Two 1-3/8-in. venturis are fed by 73 main jets. The power valve is a 5.0-in. unit. A high-capacity (50cc per 10 strokes) accelerator pump is used. The center-pivot-float, race-type bowl has a sight plug and externally adjustable needle-and-seat assembly.

REAR OUTBOARD CARBURETOR
THROTTLE CONTROL VACUUM DIAPHRAGM
VACUUM DIAPHRAGM SUPPLY TUBE
CENTER CARBURETOR
FRONT OUTBOARD CARBURETOR
THROTTLE CONTROL VACUUM DIAPHRAGM
DISTRIBUTOR VACUUM ADVANCE TUBE
BOWL VENT TUBE
VACUUM DIAPHRAGM SUPPLY TUBE
CRANKCASE VENT TUBE

Diaphragm-operated outboard carburetors on 3 x 2 Chrysler manifolds are opened by vacuum signal from center carburetor as engine requires extra airflow. Only center carburetor has accelerator pump. Careful installation is needed to ensure that bases aren't distorted and throttle shafts must work freely. Holley's high-performance catalog lists replacement carburetors for 1969—'71 440-CID and for 1970—'71 340-CID engines. Holley also offers 500-cfm outboard carburetors (Part 0-4783) with accelerator pumps. They are used with progressive mechanical linkage and 350-cfm center carburetor. Center unit, Part 0-4782, has an accelerator pump and automatic choke. Manual linkage that operates all carburetors simultaneously is *not* recommended.

Part 0-4412 Model 2300 has center-pivot race bowl with adjustable needle/seat and sight plug for externally setting fuel level. High-capacity accelerator pump (50cc per 10 strokes) is used. Hand choke linkage is standard. The carburetor base fits Ford 2-bbl manifolds. An adapter is required for use on other engines. This performance carburetor is designed for modified engines. It isn't suitable for street use on stock 289- or 302-CID engines.

Holes in 0-4412 throttle plates (solid arrows) keep correct relation of throttles to idle-transfer slots immediately opposite the holes. Holes are on same side of throttle shaft as transfer slots. This modification can be helpful when using a modified camshaft.

Front view of obsolete List 6425 shows hand choke linkage and high-capacity accelerator pump. Accessory velocity stacks improved airflow. Stacks, Part 85R-4235 won't fit other 2300s without modification.

Discharge holes around edge of venturis are used in 6425 instead of usual booster-venturi/discharge nozzle combination. Accelerator-pump discharge nozzle is anti-pullover design with ball-check valve in lower portion of metering block.

Hose connections in the carburetor base are for timed and vacuum spark advance and for a PCV valve. The timed port can also be used to purge charcoal canisters. An SAE 1-1/2-in. spread-bore pattern (3-1/2-in. x 5-1/2-in. hole spacing) fits Ford two-barrel 289—390-CID engines without automatic transmissions.

The linkage is universal. It fits the carburetor to GM and Ford applications, including Ford automatic-transmission units with kickdown lever (except automatic overdrive). A throttle-lever extension, Part 20-7, adapts the 0-4412 to Chrysler applications.

Non-Ford engines require an adapter to mate the bolt pattern and 1-11/16-in. throttle bores to the manifold flange. Adapter 17-19 fits the SAE 1-1/2-in. 2V pattern used on some late Chevrolets. Chrysler products (318 CID) and some early Chevrolets have a SAE 1-1/4-in. 2V pattern that works with adapter 17-3.

The 0-4412 and its little brother, the 350-cfm 0-7448 (B) can be equipped for driver control

Two Model 2305 Primary Plus carburetors are 500-cfm 0-80095 (left) and 0-80120 350-cfm (right). 500-cfm is identifiable by additional struts cast under airhorn extension. Features include annular boosters on primary barrels, side-pivot fuel bowl with swivel (banjo) input and staged progressive linkage.

Staged progressive linkage operation is shown here. Note how primary leads secondary opening. This improves driveability.

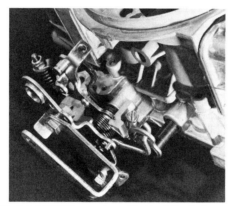

Universal throttle linkage supplied on some Model 4150/60s works with Ford (including automatics with kickdown lever), Chrysler and Chevrolet. Left is Ford with A/T kickdown lever (note spring and bracket), center is Chrysler with outrigger lever bolted to throttle arm, and Chevrolet is at right. Some carbs, such as Model 2300 0-4412 and Model 4160 0-1850 and 0-3310, fit Chevy as supplied. But they can be adapted for Ford with a "Throttle Shaft Kit" with Ford A/T Kickdown Lever and for Chrysler with a "Throttle Lever Extension."

of the fuel mixture. Quarter Mile Dial Kit 34-103 allows electronic adjustment within a range of about five jet sizes. Details of the kit are on page 40.

Racers will be interested in 0-9647, a 500-cfm model 2300 calibrated for use with methanol fuel. More details on running methanol in carburetors are found in Chapter 12.

List 6425—This carburetor flowed 600 cfm and was available with velocity stacks. While it is obsolete, service parts are available. If you own one, hang on to it! These true collector's items bring big bucks. A special feature was annular discharge of the fuel through the main-venturi walls. There was no booster. Universal linkage allowed installation on Chrysler, Ford or GM vehicles. A center-pivot fuel bowl was sight-plug equipped. These had 1-3/4-in. throttle bores and 1-7/16-in. venturis.

MODEL 2305

As interest developed in trying to obtain performance from 4-cylinder engines, it became apparent that the 270 cfm provided by Holley's 5200 was not enough airflow capacity. In 1986 Holley introduced the Model 2305 in 350- and 500-cfm versions. It uses a lot of Model 2300 parts: from the throttle body up, it is essentially the same carburetor. A few exceptions are noted later.

The 2305 is a staged carburetor. Mechanical linkage starts opening the secondaries as the primaries reach approximately 40° of angular travel. Primary and secondary bores have individual throttle shafts positioned 90° from the 2300's single shaft. Throttle linkage is opposite the fuel bowl.

Throttle bores are 1-11/16-in. (43mm) in both versions. Airflow is controlled by venturi size: 1-3/16-in. in the 350 cfm, 0-80120; 1-3/8-in. in the 500 cfm, 0-80095. Throttle bore and stud spacing are the same as the Model 2300.

Model 4150 0-9381 is competition unit with annular-discharge booster venturis. This 830 cfm carb has dual-inlet center-pivot fuel bowls, double accelerator pumps and adjustable secondary idle mixture screws. The choke is removed.

WARNING:
Model 2300 throttle bores ARE NOT CENTERED. They are offset toward the rear of the carburetor base. If you're careless when installing the gasket, it can prevent correct throttle operation. The engine may start and run, but the throttles may snag in the gasket and not close. Check the throttle action before starting the engine.

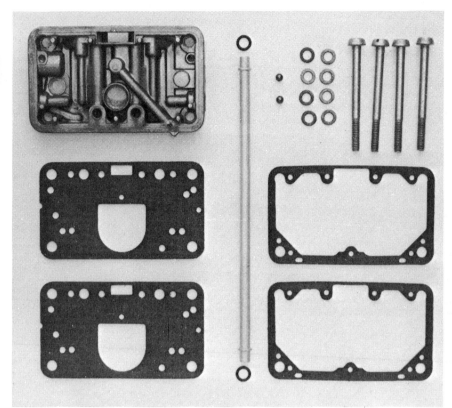

Kit 34-6 converts 4160s to 4150 secondary metering block configuration with replaceable main jets. Longer bowl screws, metering block, gaskets and a longer fuel-transfer tube are included. Lead balls are included to close holes left when balance tube is removed. Note that a power valve can't be installed in metering block.

The accelerator pump is actuated by the primary shaft. Pump nozzles discharge simultaneously into the primary and secondary sides.

The 350-cfm version, intended primarily for street performance, is equipped with a manual choke. Kit 45-385 converts it to an electric choke and 45-836 is a hot-air choke conversion. The 500-cfm edition is intended for competition and has no choke.

Both versions use annular-discharge booster venturis to improve low-end signal. Side-hung fuel bowls have sight plugs and externally adjustable needle-and-seat assembly. Bowls are equipped with a 5/16-in. fuel-hose fitting. A center-hung float bowl, Kit 34-15, is also available.

Manifold adapters are available for Ford, Chrysler, Datsun, Pontiac and Toyota 4-cylinder engines.

A big advantage of the Model 2300 family is that most service parts are interchangeable and readily available: power valve, main jets, pump nozzles and so forth. Even the Quarter Mile Dial performance kits will fit.

These carburetors are *not bolt-on replacements* by any stretch of the imagination. If you want to use one, consult the Holley Standard Replacement Catalog. These carburetors are for enthusiasts and racers whose engines need more airflow. Expect to do a little "cobbling" or improvising when installing a 2305.

MODELS 4150, 4160 & 4180

Current Holley four-barrel carburetors fall into three basic families: 4150, 4160 and 4180 are described here. The now-obsolete 3150 and 3160 three-barrels have similar construction and operation. The 4165/4175, and 4500 versions are separately described because of important construction and operation differences.

Holley 4150 carburetors were first introduced in 1975 on Ford 312-CID engines. And, while we like to think of these units as strictly high-performance devices, they have seen widespread use on regular passenger cars and trucks. Some even have governors!

4150 Features—These carburetors have some interesting design features.

Center-pivot fuel bowls as used in current Holley carburetors were developed for Chevrolet applications. Conversion kits are now available to replace side-hung bowls with the center-pivot type: Kit 34-2 converts 4150/60 carburetors.

The original center-pivot float bowls were a *snout-type,* first used on Ford and Chrysler NASCAR racing engines in 1964. They were also used on Shelby Mustangs and Cobras. Ford performance and restoration enthusiasts can buy the Le Mans Fuel Bowl Conversion, Kit 34-14. These bowls don't work with double-pumpers.

Externally adjustable floats with sight plugs, first used on 1957 Ford Model 4150s. External adjustment is available on both side-hung and center-pivot float bowls.

Bowl vent plastic "whistles," first used in carburetors supplied for 1966 Fords.

Double accelerator pumps, first used on List 4296, 4150s for 1967 Chevrolet big-block applications.

Mechanical secondary linkage, first used for Chrysler in 1959, List 1970.

Center-mounted accelerator pump discharge nozzle, designed for plenum-type tunnel-ram manifolds and first used in 1967, List 4224.

Annular-discharge boosters, first used on Model 4180 on 1979 Ford trucks.

Numerous 4150 carburetors have been used as original equipment by the big-three auto-

Secondary metering plate on 4160/80 is flat steel plate with holes, a gasket, and a die casting with cast-in fuel and air channels. Main metering is through drilled holes in bottom of casting. Attachment is by clutch-head screws.

Model 4180 is a much-modified Model 4160. Significant changes in main and idle systems improve fuel metering, calibration and control. Sealed idle-mixture screws are in throttle body instead of metering block. Primary boosters are annular-discharge type. This carburetor has been used as original equipment on Ford trucks and on high-output 302-CID engines in Mustangs and Capris.

mobile manufacturers. And, a range of 4150-type carburetors is offered for aftermarket use. Vacuum-secondary types are available in 390—850 cfm in stair-step sizes to fit almost any requirement. Double-pumper types with mechanical-secondary actuation are available in 50-cfm increments from 600—850 cfm. There is also a 390-cfm double-pumper for NASCAR racing.

4150 & 4160—These carburetors are very similar. They are absolutely alike in operation. Except for the secondary *metering block,* their construction is identical. A 4150 secondary metering block has the same physical dimensions as the primary metering block. It is sandwiched between the secondary fuel bowl and the carburetor body—as is the primary metering block.

4160—This carburetor has a secondary metering *plate* with built-in orifices. It is screw-attached to the carburetor main body. This metering plate requires less drilling, no plugging or tapping, and has no screw-in main jets or power valves.

It has vacuum-operated (diaphragm) secondaries. The 0-4224 is an exception. This 660-cfm "center squirter" has mechanical linkage and is used with tunnel-ram manifolds. All have single accelerator pumps. Any of three fuel bowls may be used, depending on requirements: side-hung, side-hung with external adjustment for level setting, or center-pivot with an inlet at each fuel bowl.

This model has been used by American Motors, Chevrolet, Chrysler and Ford as original equipment. They are just as high-performance oriented as any 4150. A 4160 can be converted to a 4150 with Kit 34-6. This includes a secondary metering block with gaskets, a longer fuel-transfer tube and matching fuel-bowl screws. Other items, such as bowl vents and high-capacity accelerator-pump kits can also be installed.

Why produce the 4160? Well, if you're making automobiles by the thousands and can buy Holley performance for several dollars less per carburetor, the savings can be substantial. The 4160 was engineered to be manufactured at lower cost than the 4150. In some instances, this lower cost, coupled with Holley's performance image, allowed car makers to put a Holley 4160 on high-performance engines.

In an all-out racing application, two of the shorter 4160s can fit onto a 2 x 4 manifold. Holley offers a Secondary Vacuum Balance Kit, Part 20-28 to adapt 4160s for 2 x 4 manifold applications.

If you need an aftermarket carburetor for your vehicle, you can buy a 4160 at a lower price than a 4150.

4180—The 4180, a 4160 look-alike, is an emissions-oriented carburetor. But it incorporates substantial changes to improve fuel metering, calibration and control. The most-obvious change is the use of *annular-discharge boosters.*

The 4180's primary metering block is substantially changed. To ensure idle quality, idle and main-well passages are drilled into the metering block. They are not formed in cavities between the metering block and the main body gasket. Because of larger drilled wells, accelerator-pump passage routing had to be changed. Then the primary main jets had to be angled into the metering block.

A brass orifice on the fuel-bowl side of the accelerator-pump passage allows pump vapors to bleed off into the bowl, keeping the pump filled. While this causes a minor loss of pump shot, it tends to eliminate pump "sag" after a hot soak. You can adjust the idle speed, but you won't find any idle-mixture-adjustment screws on the primary metering block. They are factory-set and sealed under plugs in the throttle body.

The secondaries are vacuum-actuated and a metering plate is screwed onto the back of the main casting like a 4160.

First use of the 4180 was as original equipment on the 1979 Ford 460-CID trucks and on the 1983—'85 Ford/Mercury Mustang/Capri 302-CID.

Description of Operation—The following descriptions are applicable to all 3150/60, 4150/60/80, 4165/75, 4500 (except for the intermediate system described in that section) and 2300 carburetors. The basic functions of these carburetors' systems are fully covered in How Your Carburetor Works.

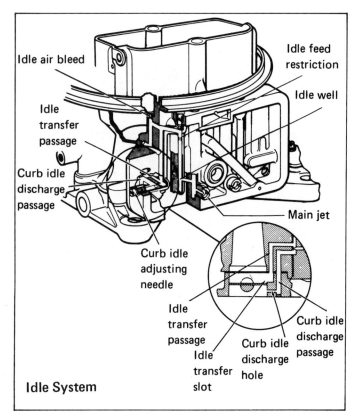

Idle System

Idle air bleed

Idle feed restriction

Idle well

Idle transfer passage

Curb idle discharge passage

Main jet

Curb idle adjusting needle

Idle transfer passage

Idle transfer slot

Curb idle discharge hole

Curb idle discharge passage

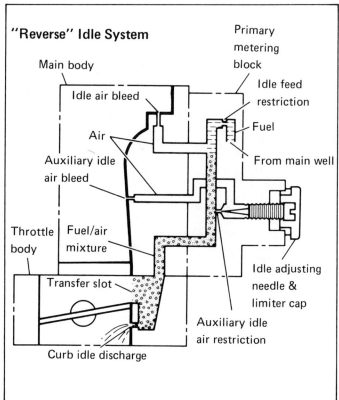

"Reverse" Idle System

Main body

Primary metering block

Idle air bleed

Idle feed restriction

Air

Fuel

Auxiliary idle air bleed

From main well

Throttle body

Fuel/air mixture

Idle adjusting needle & limiter cap

Transfer slot

Auxiliary idle air restriction

Curb idle discharge

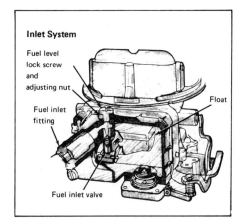

Inlet System

Fuel level lock screw and adjusting nut

Fuel inlet fitting

Float

Fuel inlet valve

Fuel Inlet—Fuel enters the primary fuel bowl through a screen or filter and passes through the inlet needle-and-seat assembly into the fuel bowl. Where there is only one fuel inlet for the carburetor, fuel reaches the secondary needle and seat through a transfer tube that is O-ring-sealed to each fuel bowl. If there are two fuel inlets, a fuel line must be plumbed to each. Holley's universal fuel line, Part 34-1, makes this easy.

Idle—An idle system is provided for each barrel. The primary side is adjustable on all four-barrel units except the 4180, which has sealed idle adjustments. It is adjustable on the secondary side on competition carburetors and on a few others. Except for adjustability, primary and secondary idle systems are essentially identical in construction and operation.

At idle, fuel flows from the bowl through the main jet and into the main well. From the main well, a passage connects to the idle well. Fuel flows through an idle-feed restriction into the idle well, up the idle well and is mixed with air from the air bleed as it flows down another vertical passage. At the bottom of this passage, idle fuel branches. One leg goes to the transfer slot above the throttle. The other goes past the adjustment needle (if used) to a discharge hole below the throttle plate. At curb idle, idle fuel is primarily supplied through the hole below the throttle.

Some 2300 and 4150/60 carburetors have a *reverse* idle adjustment. Turn the screws *in* to *richen* the mixture and *back them out* to *lean* the mixture. These actions are the opposite of what has always been done. Labels indicate the adjustment change. This difference came as part of a development program to improve idle quality with the lean idle mixtures needed to pass emission requirements.

The idle system was changed as shown in the accompanying drawing. Note the adjustable second air bleed in this new idle circuit. The mixture screw varies inlet-air area through a second air bleed connected to the throttle bore just below the venturi.

Idle improvement is so great that this system has been incorporated in other carburetors. It is used in 4160 and 2300 aftermarket carburetors for late Ford automobiles. It is also in most 4165, 4175 and in the emission/performance 4150 double-pumpers.

Main Metering—At cruising speeds, fuel flows from the fuel bowl, through the main jet into the bottom of the main well. Fuel moves up the well past air-bleed holes in the side of the well. These air-bleed holes are supplied with filtered air from the main air-bleed openings in

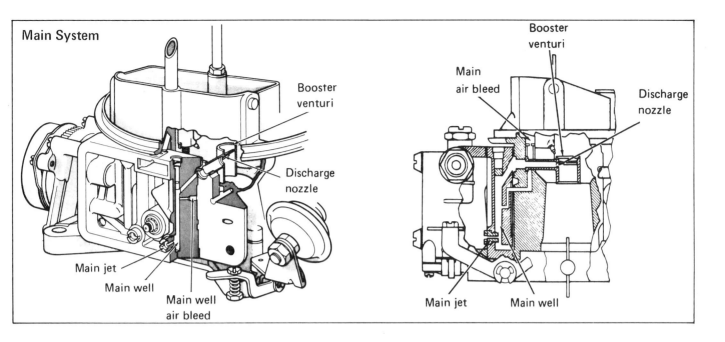

Main System

Booster venturi
Discharge nozzle
Main jet
Main well
Main well air bleed

Booster venturi
Main air bleed
Discharge nozzle
Main jet
Main well

"Reverse" idle system is labeled. Adjustment is leaned by turning counter-clockwise, admitting more air, as shown in accompanying drawing.

Annular booster shown with its two component parts. Top section containing *annular track* and *discharge holes* is pressed into larger ring section. Larger section contains *fuel discharge channel* from main well. Assembly is spun into place in main body just like conventional booster is installed.

Typical installation of annular boosters is seen in 0-9381, a 830 cfm competition carburetor.

the carburetor air inlet. The fuel/air mixture moves up the main well and across to the discharge nozzle in the booster venturi.

Power System—During high-speed operation or any driving condition when manifold vacuum is low (near atmospheric), the carburetor adds fuel for power operation. A vacuum passage in the throttle body transmits manifold vacuum to the power-valve chamber in the main body. Vacuum applied to a dia-

phragm in the power valve holds the valve closed at idle and normal loads. When manifold vacuum drops, a spring inside the power valve opens the valve to admit extra fuel. Fuel flows through the power valve via the power-valve restriction and into the main well where it joins fuel flow in the main metering system to enrich the mixture.

As engine power demands are reduced, manifold vacuum increases. Power-valve-spring

tension is overcome and the valve closes, stopping the extra fuel flow.

Some 4150/4160s have two power valves, one for the primary and another for the secondary side.

WARNING: Power valves can be damaged by an engine backfire. Backfire-caused pressure can rupture the diaphragm. The result is an excessively rich mixture at all speeds.

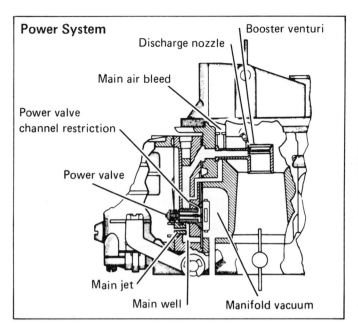

Power System

- Booster venturi
- Discharge nozzle
- Main air bleed
- Power valve channel restriction
- Power valve
- Main jet
- Main well
- Manifold vacuum

Screw-in power valves with their respective gaskets. Window-type (left) uses plain gasket without protrusions. Power valves with drilled holes use protrusions on gasket ID to center gasket.

This 0-9834 is 600-cfm 4160 non-emission, street-performance carburetor for later model (through '79) non-EGR passenger car and RV applications. It has electric choke, single inlet for ease of plumbing, adjustable needle-and-seat assemblies in side-hung fuel bowls. Vacuum secondaries and emissions hook-ups combine with universal throttle linkage for Ford's A/T kickdown linkage.

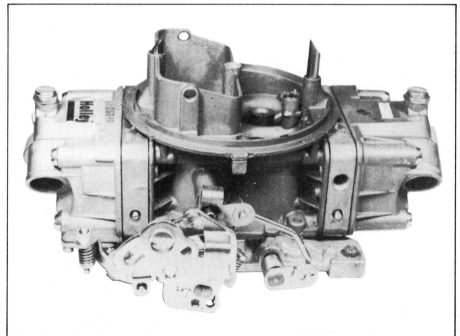

0-8156 and 0-8162 are 750- and 850-cfm carburetors designed and calibrated for single four-barrel competition. Features include dual-inlet center-pivot fuel bowls, double accelerator pumps and no choke. Secondary idle screws are included for improved idle control and throttle response. 0-8162 provides increased closed-throttle airflow to compensate for modern racing-camshaft profiles.

Accelerator Pump—The pump is a diaphragm type in the bottom of the primary fuel bowl. There is also a pump in the bottom of the secondary fuel bowl on double-pumpers. The pump functions when the throttle linkage actuates the pump lever. Pressure forces the pump-inlet check valve onto its seat, preventing fuel from flowing back into the fuel bowl. Fuel from the pump is pushed through a diagonal passage in the metering block to the main body. Fuel under pressure raises a discharge check needle off its seat and fuel sprays into the venturi through the discharge nozzle.

As the throttle returns to a more-closed position, the pump linkage returns to its original position. The diaphragm spring forces the diaphragm down. The pump-inlet valve falls off

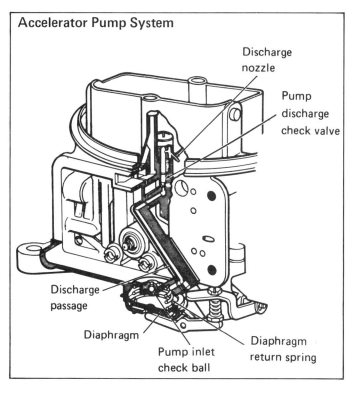

Accelerator Pump System

Discharge nozzle

Pump discharge check valve

Discharge passage

Diaphragm

Pump inlet check ball

Diaphragm return spring

O-ring-sealed accelerator-pump transfer tubes were used on Holley four barrels for several years, starting in 1975. This construction is also used on the 4180. Note how gasket is cut away to clear tube. Any attempt to use non-tube metering block with this style gasket will draw fuel from accelerator-pump system. A very rich mixture results.

its seat and the pump refills. As pressure is relieved from the pump passage, the discharge check needle reseats. Air flowing past the discharge nozzles then can't pull fuel out of the pump passages.

Secondary System—Secondary systems are operated by a vacuum diaphragm or by a mechanical linkage to the primary throttles.

The secondary side has a fuel-inlet system, an idle system (usually non-adjustable) and a main metering system. Double-pumpers also have an accelerator-pump system. These systems operate exactly like those on the primary side in nearly all instances.

Some secondary systems have a power valve, others do not. Although no longer used, a balance tube was sometimes included to connect primary and secondary bowls. This equalized fuel levels when one inlet valve supplied more fuel than the other.

Mechanical Secondary—There are various linkage types. Most use a direct link between the primary and secondary. A slot in the secondary lever provides progressive action. Through 1975, a slotted primary lever with a roller/lever transmitted opening motion through a rod to the secondary throttles. This method of secondary actuation has been retained on some competition carburetors, such as the 0-8156 and 0-8162.

Mechanical secondary opening is controlled entirely by primary-throttle position. On some competition carburetors, the linkage is direct or 1:1. The primary and secondary throttles open

Second-design double-pumper mechanism has direct action. Slot in secondary lever takes up link travel during early primary opening and delays secondary opening. Secondary lever moves faster once it starts due to a smaller radius.

equally at the same time.

When progressive action is used, the primary throttles open approximately 40° before the secondaries start to open. Both primary and secondary throttles reach wide-open at the same time.

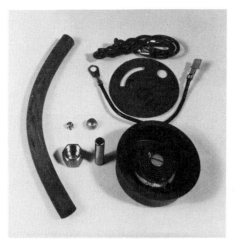

Electric choke Kit 45-226 converts integral choke Holley carburetors to electric operation for use on engines with headers or without exhaust heat. Solid-state heating element is used instead of formerly used nichrome-wire heater.

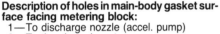

Description of holes in main-body gasket surface facing metering block:
1—To discharge nozzle (accel. pump)
2—To timed-spark port
3—To curb-idle discharge
4—To curb-idle transfer slot
5—Used only with auxiliary idle air bleed
6—To idle air bleed
7—To main discharge nozzle
8—To main air bleed
9—Dowel locators for metering block
10—Not used
11—To bowl vent (pitot tube)

Description of holes and passages in metering block. Center photo shows side that mates to main-body gasket. Lower photo is fuel bowl side of metering block.
1—Accelerator-pump discharge passage
2—Timed-spark passage (see 12)
3—Curb idle discharge
4—Idle-transfer fuel connects to main body and to curb idle-adjust screw
6—Idle bleed air enters from main body
7—Main passage to discharge nozzle
8—Main bleed air enters from main body
9—Dowels to position bowl and gasket
11—Bowl vent passage
12—Timed spark tube boss
13—Idle-mixture-adjustment needle
14—Main jet
15—Power valve threaded opening
16—Power valve
17—Power valve channel restriction (connects to main well 21)
18—Manifold vacuum chamber (for power valve operation)
19—Idle down well
20—Idle well
21—Main well
22—Air bleed holes into main well
23—Main air well
24—Idle fuel from main well
25—Idle feed restriction to idle well
26—Fuel entry from accelerator pump in fuel bowl

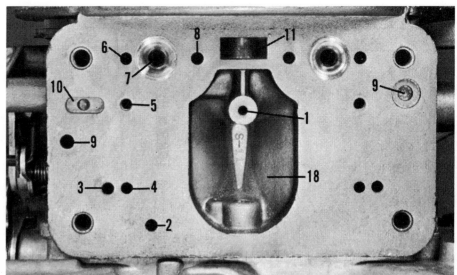

Holley's most popular carburetor is Model 4160, List 0-1850. This 600-cfm street/competition, non-emission carburetor features vacuum secondaries, hand choke, single fuel inlet with side-hung fuel bowls. Don't adapt this carburetor onto a spread-bore manifold. See text.

0-1850 converted to driver-adjustable mixture control with a 34-105 Quarter Mile Dial.

Choke System—Both integral and divorced choke mechanisms have been supplied on 4150/60/80 carburetors. Some have manual chokes. Conversion Kit 45-225 converts integral automatic chokes to manual operation. Some carburetors are factory-equipped with electric chokes. Kits 45-223 and 45-224 can be used to convert to this type of choke actuation. Kit 45-226 converts hot-air integral chokes to electric operation.

Quarter Mile Dial—Driver control of the fuel mixture is a reality. You can electronically adjust within a range of about five jet sizes.

Model 4150 and 4160 carburetors with all the specially designed Quarter Mile Dial components and circuitry installed are referred to as *systems*. Quarter Mile Dial Kits include all of the required components to convert Holley 4150/4160 carburetors to the electronically adjustable configuration.

NOTE: As fuel injection becomes the norm for late-1980s cars, Holley will continue to consolidate part numbers so fewer carburetors will fit more applications. It is always a good idea to check what is currently being supplied on a carburetor, rather than relying on information that may have become out of date through manufacturing changes.

0-1850—The lowest-cost four barrel 0-1850 is Holley's most-popular seller. This 600-cfm 4160 is designed for street/competition use. It is not designed to pass emissions tests. Vacuum secondaries provide only the airflow that the engine requires, allowing successful use on 300-CID and larger engines.

The throttle linkage works with GM and Ford engines, except Ford automatics. Kit 20-48 converts the carburetor for Ford automatic transmissions with the kickdown lever (except automatic overdrive). A throttle-lever extension, Part 20-7, adapts the 0-1850 to Chrysler applications.

Cost-engineering at Holley has eliminated all non-essential parts to reduce cost without sacrificing performance. Some throttle linkage adapting or other modifications may be needed when using a 0-1850, which would not be required with a Holley bolt-on carburetor designed for specific applications.

Because the 0-1850 calibration is universal, some tuning of variables such as jets, power valve, secondary diaphragm spring, and so forth may also be needed.

Fuel-line connection is simple. Install a 26-42 fitting and screw in a flared fitting. Or, use a swivel (banjo) fitting such as Holley's 26-25 with a 5/16-in. hose.

A hand choke with fast-idle adjustment can be replaced with an electric choke by using Kit 45-223.

Kit 34-105 converts your 0-1850 carburetor for use with the Holley Quarter Mile Dial System. This system allows you to change the fuel/air mixture from a dashboard-mounted control. The 34-1850 is a 0-1850 carburetor incorporating all of the specially designed components and circuitry of the Holley Quarter Mile Dial System.

0-3310—Another very popular four barrel is the 0-3310, a 750-cfm carburetor for 350-CID and larger engines.

Originally introduced in 1966 on Chevrolet's 425-HP Corvettes and the 375-HP Chevelles with 396-CID engines, the carburetor has also seen original-equipment use on 302- and 350-CID Z-28 Camaros.

Chevrolet versions of the carburetor have different numbers. Also, in 3310-1 form, it was a 4150. As the 3310-2, it was changed to a 4160 to reduce cost. Earlier versions flowed 780 cfm instead of the current 750-cfm rating.

Perhaps the reason for the 0-3310's popularity is due to its high-performance image. And, it installs easily on a variety of cars with good assurance of working well on almost any 300- to 455-CID engine. Its flexibility of application stems from diaphragm-operated secondaries that allow the carburetor to operate effectively over a varying of airflow requirements.

This 750-cfm 4160 is designed for street/competition use. It is not designed to pass emissions tests. The throttle linkage was originally universal. Currently, the throttle linkage works with GM and Ford engines, except Ford automatic transmissions. Kit 20-49 converts the carburetor for Ford automatic transmissions with kickdown lever (except automatic overdrive). Throttle-lever extension, Part 20-7, adapts it to Chrysler applications.

If your application is for a Ford and you can use a 600-cfm carburetor, consider the 0-9834 instead. It includes an electric choke, Ford automatic-transmission kickdown linkage and a swivel (banjo) fuel-inlet fitting.

Model 4160 0-3310 is performance-oriented street/competition, non-emission carburetor. It has vacuum secondaries, dual-inlet center-pivot fuel bowls, universal throttle linkage and flows 750 cfm.

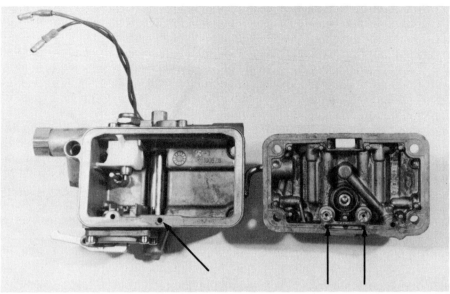

Quarter Mile Dial float bowl with solenoid (float removed for clarity). Fuel is fed from bowl through solenoid jet via hole (arrow) to metering block. Metering-block slot distributes fuel through holes (arrows) to main wells.

Small primary/large secondary throttle-bore design is generally the best plan for staged carburetors, whether high-performance or not. Holley's 4165 series was first spread-bore design combining high-performance with specification emission performance at same time. Note two accelerator pumps and mechanical secondary linkage. These carburetors are designed as bolt-on replacements for GM cars.

Holley has eliminated all non-essential parts to reduce cost without sacrificing performance. It is not a bolt-on replacement carburetor. Because the 0-3310 calibration is universal, some tuning of variables such as jets, power valve, secondary diaphragm spring, and so forth may be needed.

Fuel-line connection is simple. Just use a Holley 34-1 Fuel Line Kit to plumb fuel to the two inlet fittings.

A hand choke with fast-idle adjustment can be replaced with an electric choke by using Kit 45-223.

Kit 34-104 converts the 0-3310 for use with the Holley Quarter Mile Dial System. This system allows you to change the fuel/air mixture from a dashboard-mounted control. The 34-3310 is a 0-3310 carburetor that incorporates all of the specially designed components and circuitry of the Holley Quarter Mile Dial System.

Adapters & Manifolds—It is always best to install a carburetor that fits the manifold directly. The 4150/60/80 units have a 5-3/16 x 5-5/8-in. bolt-hole pattern, sometimes referred to as a "square" pattern. A single four-barrel intake manifold with the same pattern should be installed on the car. Otherwise, an adapter is required.

Unfortunately, adapters are "thieves." They steal airflow capacity and may cause uneven fuel/air distribution. As an example, a 750-cfm 0-3310 flows only 640 cfm when adapted to a spread-bore manifold.

If your engine was originally equipped with a spread-bore carburetor (1-3/8-in. primaries and

Model 4175. Diaphragm-operated secondary throttles make this carburetor ideal for spread-bore applications where heavy loads occur at low speeds, as with trucks and RVs.

2-1/4-in. secondaries), choose a Holley 4165, 4175 or 4360. These fit without an adapter. And, the fuel distribution is considerably better than can be expected when a square-bore carburetor is adapted to a spread-bore manifold.

If one of these is not offered for your car, consider changing to a manifold with the square-bore pattern. Adapting a carburetor is no easy task because there are so many connections and linkages to consider.

MODELS 4165 & 4175

Model 4165—Holley's spread-bore 4165 carburetors were introduced in 1971. These bolt-on replacements found favor among owners of cars equipped with Rochester QuadraJet (Q-Jet) and Carter Thermo-Quad carburetors.

A true "bolt-on" accessory or part is rare in the automotive business, as you know if you have done much wrenching. Holley designed a carburetor that bolts to the manifold and retains all stock equipment, including air cleaner, linkage and *all* emission-control connections.

Initial development was done on Chevrolets. The 650-cfm unit was calibrated on a 350-CID engine and the 800-cfm unit was developed from tests on both 402- and 454-CID engines.

Under actual driving conditions, the Model 4165 outperformed the original carburetor in traffic accelerations, hot starting, hot-idle con-

ditions, vapor-lock prevention and general driving. In basic WOT acceleration tests on a 1971 350-CID automatic transmission Impala, the Model 4165 was 0.85 second and 5.4 mph faster over a 1/4-mile drag strip. Dynamometer testing showed 14-HP performance improvements on both small and big-block Chevys. Emission levels were similar to the original equipment.

Although the first 4165s were designed specifically for Chevrolets, Holley supplies units for Buick, Oldsmobile and Pontiac. Chrysler 340- and 400-CID versions replace the Carter Thermo-Quad on 1971 and later vehicles.

A 650-cfm 4175 model is similar to the 4165 except it has vacuum-operated secondaries. This unit has side-hung fuel bowls and a single accelerator pump.

Design Features—At first glance the carburetor looks like any other Holley four-barrel of the 4150/4160 double-pumper class. Take our word for it—it's not! Nearly every part on the 4165 is special or unique. Little is the same on the 4165, except for jets, power valves, bowl vent "whistles," needle and seat assemblies and floats. Gaskets, accelerator pumps, metering blocks, pump-discharge nozzles (shooters) and fuel bowls are all different. They can't be interchanged with other Holley parts.

Let's look at the 4165 very carefully to see

how it is made and why it is different. First of all, the bolt holes are on a 4-1/4-in. x 5-5/8-in. spacing to fit spread-bore manifolds. Next, depending on the List number, the carburetor has the appropriate connections for emission equipment and the correct linkage to fit the specific automobile using that List number. Some 4165s for street/competition/off-road use where emission controls are not needed may not allow hooking up all emission devices.

Primary & Secondary Venturis—One important difference between the 4165 and original-equipment carburetors is the use of fixed-size secondary venturis and main jets. Primary 1-5/32-in. diameter venturis provide good response during part-throttle operation and allow a broad range of vehicle speeds and load conditions without operating the secondaries. Keeping "out of the secondaries" achieves greater fuel economy.

Primary venturis are smaller than the secondaries to allow meeting emissions requirements. A small (20cc per 10 strokes) accelerator pump on the primaries matches primary-venturi airflow requirements.

Secondary venturis are either 1-3/8-in. or 1-23/32-in. diameter, depending on if the carburetor is a 650- or an 800-cfm unit. Secondaries are mechanically operated and use a high-capacity (50cc per 10 strokes) accelerator pump.

Accelerator-Pump Circuits—These are different on the 4165. This difference makes the 4165 bowl gaskets, metering blocks, fuel bowls and pump inlets and discharge nozzles unlike some other Holley carburetors. Pump circuits are the same for primary and secondary sides of the carburetor. Rubber type inlet/check valves are used. A steel-ball inlet/check was used on the secondary side of some early 4165s.

This difference in pumps between the 4165 and other Holley four barrels resulted from the extensive testing program required to get good hot-fuel handling. When the carburetor and fuel are hot, there is always the possibility that there will be an off-idle bog because the pump has "dried out."

All pumps have a problem of fuel boiling in the pump cavity (quite close to the engine and subject to a lot of heat) during a hot soak. Several features were incorporated in the design to enhance hot-start driveway capabilities. Both pumps (primary and secondary) are self-filling so they always fill immediately after the pumps have been used. It is very important for the primary pump to provide an instant shot of fuel at the slightest throttle movement. Because the usual hanging-ball-inlet/check valve requires an instant to seat before the pump can deliver its shot, Holley chose the rubber-type inlet/check valve.

With this pump, the inlet/check valve seals instantly as the pump is operated by only a very

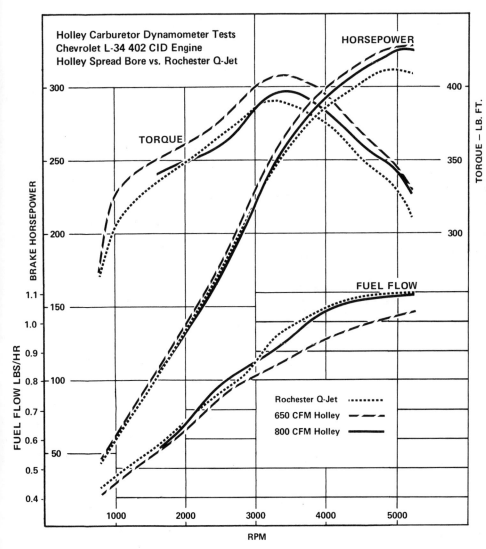

Holley Carburetor Dynamometer Tests
Chevrolet L-34 402 CID Engine
Holley Spread Bore vs. Rochester Q-Jet

HORSEPOWER

TORQUE

FUEL FLOW

Rochester Q-Jet ·········
650 CFM Holley — — —
800 CFM Holley ————

BRAKE HORSEPOWER

FUEL FLOW LBS/HR

TORQUE – LB. FT.

RPM

Economy and performance seldom come in same package, but spread-bore Holley may be an exception according to these dyno charts. The 650 cfm put out more peak HP and torque—on less fuel, but above 5000 rpm the picture will change. One of these carbs will drop right onto your Q-Jet or Thermo-Quad manifold.

Comparing 4165 metering block (also 4175 primary) at bottom with 4150 block shows housing for accelerator-pump discharge check ball as indicated by pen. 4165 block has two aluminum plugs on underside.

Pipe plug in hose fitting must be removed before installing line from gulp valve on Chevrolets through 1970 models. Those 4165s without a hose fitting have a manifold-vacuum port in this location for power-brake line.

small movement of the throttle lever. The discharge check is a steel ball near the bottom of the pump passage. This check valve, in conjunction with an anti-pullover discharge nozzle (which prevents fuel in the passage connected to the nozzle from being pulled into the airstream), tends to keep the passage to the "shooter" (nozzle) filled with liquid fuel.

As the throttle is moved back toward a closed position, the ball discharge check seats instantly to create a partial vacuum in the pump cavity which further ensures filling the pump quickly. The lightweight ball provides another

advantage. It allows vapors to escape from the pump cavity during hot-soak conditions caused by the carburetor heating up when the engine is stopped or idling for a long period. As in many of the other Holley carburetors, discharge nozzles are targeted so the pump shot "breaks" against the lower edge of the booster venturis. This ensures at least partially vaporized fuel entering the engine.

Reverse Idle—Some 4165s have "reverse" idle adjustment as described and illustrated in the 4150/4160 section. The adjustment screws in to richen the mixture and backs out to lean

it—just opposite of what has always been done in the past. Labels identify carburetors with this changed idle system.

Standard & High-Performance Types—There are two versions of 4165 carburetors: Standard and high-performance. "Standard," "normal-replacement," or "emission-design/ street-performance" 4165 carburetors are really "high-performance" in so many respects that it seems strange to give them a name that sounds "low-performance." These carburetors automatically give a performance increase while holding emissions at legal levels. Mechanical secondaries and double accelerator pumps are included in the same package.

Standard units have a single fuel inlet on the front float bowl. Side-hung float bowls are connected by a fuel-transfer tube that is O-ring-sealed where it enters each fuel bowl. Float settings for these units are accomplished by removing the fuel bowls and bending a tab on each float, if resetting is required.

A brass baffle on the metering block in the primary bowl reduces fuel slosh through the vent into the carburetor on acceleration. Fuel bowls on the standard carburetors are designed to accept stock non-high-performance air cleaners. If the air cleaner has to be rotated slightly for installation, the air-cleaner-base locating tabs may have to be modified slightly.

Automatic chokes are provided on standard 4165s. Buick, Chevrolet and Pontiac units through 1972 use the stock divorced-choke actuating mechanism. The 1973 and later Pontiac and Oldsmobile units use an integral choke with an accessory stove and connecting tubing installed on the intake manifold heat riser on some models. Chrysler units also work with the stock divorced-choke equipment.

High-performance or "Street/competition/off-road/non-emission" 4165s are exactly like the standard units in every respect except the fuel bowls are the center-pivot-float type with externally adjustable inlet valves and sight plugs on the side of the bowls for setting fuel level.

Two other differences are in the use of "whistle" type bowl vents in both primary and secondary bowls and a manual choke linkage. If you buy a high-performance version you may have to replace the stock air cleaner with a high-performance unit to clear the center-pivot "race" bowls. An accessory fuel line is needed to plumb fuel to both bowls and you must hook up a manual choke to complete the installation. Linkage on these carburetors fits the cars for which each carburetor is designed.

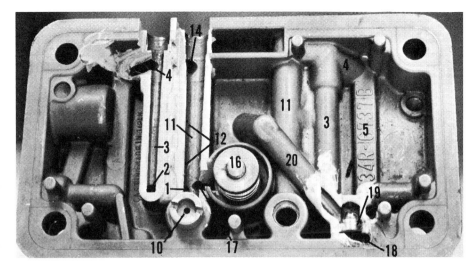

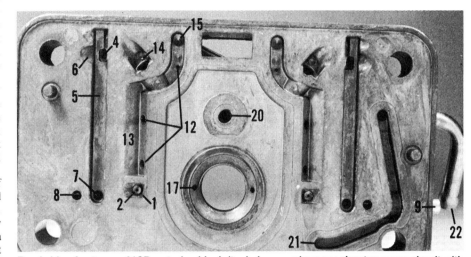

Bowl side of cutaway 4165 metering block (top) shows unique accelerator-pump circuit with ball check at bottom of pump-discharge passage. Ball has its own pressed-in brass seat. Two aluminum plugs and check-valve housing are a quick identity check for these unique blocks, which can't be used on other Holleys. System routing can be understood by comparing passages in cutaway block at top and block at bottom. Top view is from bowl side, bottom view is from the side that fits against main body.

IDLE SYSTEM
1—Idle feed from main well
2—Idle-feed restriction to idle well
3—Idle well
4—Idle cross-channel
5—Idle down well
6—Idle air bleed from main body enters at this point
7—Idle-transfer fuel is fed to main body from this point. Also feeds curb idle through screw-adjustable needle
8—Curb-idle discharge passage to main body

9—Curb-idle mixture-adjustment screw

MAIN SYSTEM
10—Main jet
11—Main well
12—Air-bleed holes from main air well
13—Main air well
14—Discharge nozzle passage
15—Air bleed from main body enters at this point

POWER SYSTEM
16—Power valve

17—Power valve channel restriction (connects to main well 11)

ACCELERATOR-PUMP SYSTEM
18—Discharge passage connection from pump in fuel bowl
19—Pump discharge check ball & seat
20—Pump discharge to nozzles in main body

TIMED SPARK
21—Connects to main body at this point
22—Timed spark tube

Model 4175 0-80073 is a 650-cfm direct replacement for Rochester Q-Jet on 1982—'83 Chevrolet Z-28 and Pontiac Trans-Am with 305-CID engines. It has vacuum secondaries, full emissions provisions and direct computer hookup. Feedback solenoid is at front of primary bowl.

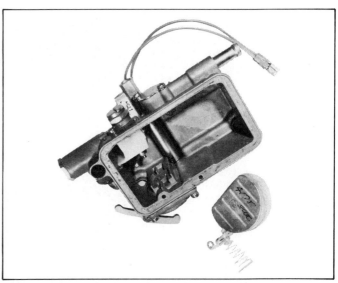

Inside primary bowl of closed-loop 4175 shows solenoid assembly at front of bowl, fuel inlet baffle, needle and seat adjustment and float with its bumper spring.

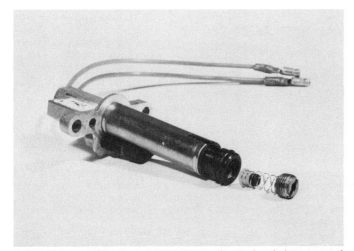

Solenoid from 4175 with poppet valve, spring and main jet removed to show construction. Main jet and poppet are not serviced separately. Jet size is factory-selected so carburetor will meet emission requirements.

Primary metering block of closed-loop Model 4175 has slot with three holes under main jets. This area is fed supplementary fuel under electronic control via solenoid valve in primary fuel bowl.

The 650-cfm versions are recommended for all normal-replacement applications from 327- through 402-CID engines. The same carburetors also work very well on low-performance "smog" version 427- and 454-CID engines. The 800-cfm units are recommended for standard replacement on high-performance 396-, 402-, 427- and 454-CID engines. They can also be used on racing-type small-block engines with a real need for this much airflow.

MODEL 4175

In 1974 Holley introduced the Model 4175. It was designed specifically for pick-up trucks, campers, race-car tow vehicles and other applications on 340-CID and larger engines where low-speed "lugging" makes mechanical secondaries undesirable.

Flow capacity is 650 cfm. Divorced and integral chokes are supplied so the carburetor works with the stock equipment on Chevrolet, Oldsmobile, Pontiac and Chrysler applications. It is constructed the same as the Model 4165 except it has diaphragm-operated secondaries and there is no accelerator pump on the secondary side. A metering plate is used on the secondary side.

"Feedback" Control—The basics of feedback or *closed loop* design and operation are explained in How Your Carburetor Works. In 1981 GM introduced a closed loop model of the Q-Jet for most V8 passenger cars. Mixture control is accomplished with a duty-cycle solenoid

Three members of Model 4500 family: 0-7320, 0-8082 and 0-8896 (left to right). Airflow capacity is 1150, 1050 and 1050 cfm, respectively. Two others, 0-9375 and 0-9377 offer 1050 and 1150 cfm airflow, respectively, and feature annular-discharge boosters.

almost identical to the one used in the Holley "open-loop" carburetors and kits.

The Model 4175 utilizes the same duty-cycle solenoid and related hardware. But instead of the driver controlling the duty-cycle manually, it is wired directly to the GM Electronic Control Unit (ECU).

The 4175 is totally compatible with the GM systems. Metering specifications were calibrated to suit. A few physical characteristics and mechanical hook-ups were modified to work with various GM cars. At this writing, P/N 1-629 handles the Chevrolet 305-CID engines for 1983—'85. P/N 1-602 covers the Olds 307 CID for the same years.

These carburetors come close to being direct bolt-on replacements. Just follow the installation instructions. In some cases the original air cleaner can be used. Several applications require using a performance air cleaner because of space limitations. Holley has designed a replacement carburetor compatible with GM's on-board electronics. And, that good response and "feel" for which Holley is so well known, has been retained.

MODEL 4500

The first Holley 4500 was designed for Ford in 1969 as a single four barrel on NASCAR Stock Car engines. This expanded four barrel mated a sand-cast carburetor body to the basic Holley metering blocks and fuel bowls. Base stud spacings allowed 2-in.-diameter throttle bores and 1150-cfm airflow capacity. An accelerator pump on each fuel bowl made these some of the first "double-pumpers." The carburetors were made exclusively for Ford, using temporary tooling.

In 1970, Holley made the Model 4500 in production as a single four barrel, List 4575. In converting from handmade units to production items, some airflow was lost. The 1-11/16-in. venturi versions of the carburetor flow approximately 1050 cfm, depending on die castings, trim dies and other production variations.

MODELS 4165/4175 ARE DIFFERENT

Don't try swapping parts between 4165/4175 and 4150/4160 or 2300 carburetors, even though their removable fuel bowls make them look similar. We have covered most of the differences in the accompanying text, but let's review to make sure it is all completely clear.

Fuel Bowls—4165/4175 accelerator pump delivery holes mate with the unique metering blocks containing the accelerator-pump discharge valve near the bottom of the block. Side- or center-hung bowls from other models cannot be interchanged. 4165s are available with side-hung bowls that work with a stock air cleaner, and with race-type bowls that require using a performance-type air cleaner.

Model 4175s come with side-hung bowls only. Race-type dual-inlet center-pivot-float bowl kits are available for 4165/4175s. Use Kit 34-5 for Chrysler or Kit 34-4 for GM applications.

Bowl Gaskets—4165/4175 bowl gaskets match the accelerator-pump-delivery holes in the mating metering blocks. Other gaskets don't fit gasket-locators on 4165 metering blocks (and primary metering block of 4175) and will block the pump-delivery passage.

Hand Choke—If a hand choke is required, buy a 4165 already equipped that way because 4165s with automatic integral or divorced chokes don't easily convert to hand-choke operation. 4175s are all equipped for automatic-choke operation.

Interchangeable Parts—The Carburetor Numerical Listing and Parts Guide in the Holley Performance Parts Catalog shows that some metering-block-to-main-body gaskets, main jets, power valves and inlet needle/seat assemblies are interchangeable between the 4165/4175, and the 4150/4160 and 2300 carburetors.

End view of 0-7320 shows 50cc per 10 strokes accelerator pump used on both bowls of all current production Model 4500s. Center-hung race bowl with externally adjustable needle/seat has dual inlets for plumbing fuel lines from either side. These fuel bowls are on all 4500s.

This 4500 is original sand-cast version made specifically for Ford's use in NASCAR racing. Machined venturis were held in place by boost-venturi supports. Note accelerator-pump shooters were part of main body casting.

Saw a 4500 in half and you'll see a rugged linkage. It is fully enclosed once carburetor is bolted to manifold. This is the 1:1 linkage on a 6214. Black arrows indicate accelerator-pump discharge passages. Outline arrows point to vent-tube bosses for bowl venting through main body.

List 4575 continued to be used on NASCAR engines. For a couple of years restrictor rings pressed into the carburetor bores below the throttle plates reduced air flow, thereby "controlling" power and top speeds. Knurled on the outside, the rings had a 1-11/16-in. inside diameter. Later, special restrictor plates between the carburetor and manifold served the same purpose.

The 4500 carburetor should only be used on a manifold designed with 5.380-in.-square stud spacing pattern. Any adapter to fit it onto a smaller manifold seriously reduces airflow capability.

Applications—In 1971 Holley released two additional versions of the 4500. List 6214 was an isolated/individual runner (IR) carburetor with 1-13/16-in. venturis and long boost venturis. IR manifolding supplies each engine cylinder with its own single-barrel carburetor, in this case, one barrel of a Model 4500. Some of the first 4500s supplied to Ford were used in an IR configuration on Ford 302 Trans Am engines during the 1969 season.

An IR system allows ram tuning of the intake system, see page 108. No Model 4500 carburetor was ever large enough for true IR use on any U.S.-made small-block or big-block V8. Plenum manifolds are now used almost exclusively for drag racing. List 0-6214, 0-6464 and 0-9377 can be modified for use on plenum manifolds. Kit 34-8 contains two metering blocks that can be used with power valves.

The 0-6214 and 0-9377 are not designed for use on *any* single four-barrel manifold. They arc not for use on street-driven vehicles. The 0-6214 has also been retired and the 0-9377 with annular-discharge boosters has taken its place.

List 6464 had 1-11/16-in. venturis and was optimized for 2 x 4 use on plenum-type race manifolds. List 7320 had 1150-cfm airflow. It was designed for Pro-Stock and modified-production, as well as single four-barrel applications such as NHRA Econo-rail and some AHRA Super-Stock Classes. List 8082 has 1050-cfm airflow and is used for applications similar to 0-7320.

List 0-8896 is for modified-production and Pro-Stock use on small-block Chevrolet and Chrysler engines used on Holley Pro-Contender 2 x 4 manifolds.

List 0-9375 has annular-discharge boosters and is for the same applications as 0-8896.

Design Features—Several versions are separately described in this section, but some features are common throughout. All have 2.00-in. throttle bores and a 5.380-in. square stud pattern. Dual-inlet, center-pivot-float fuel bowls are tapped on both sides to allow fuel line connections to either side. Plastic bowl vents are provided in all fuel bowls.

Reduced-section 1/2-in. throttle shafts are used for improved airflow. The "blind end" of

Many Pro-Stock engines are based on venerable Chevrolet big block, no matter what they may be called. Most engine builders make their own manifolds, as seen in left photo. Right photo shows Ford with cast tunnel-ram manifold.

MODEL 4500 COMPARISON CHART

	Application	Flow	Venturi (in.)	MJ	P.V.	Idle	Linkage[2]	Inter. Idle System	Choke	Accel. Pump	Booster[3]	Cam
4575[1]	General	1050	1-11/16	84	6.5	Prim. only	Prog.	No	Yes	50cc	Short	Yellow
6214[1]	I.R.	1150	1-13/16	95	NA[4]	4	1:1	Yes	No	30cc	Long	White
6464[1]	Pro-Stock Plenum ram 2x4	1050	1-11/16	88	NA[4]	4	1:1	Yes	No	50cc	Short	Yellow
0-7320	Plenum ram 2x4 or single 4-bbl.	1150	1-13/16	95	Plugs[5]	4	Prog.	No	No	50cc	Short	Yellow
0-8082	Same as 0-7320	1050	1-11/16	84	6.5[5]	4	Prog.	No	No	50cc	Short	Yellow
0-8896	Modified prod. Pro-stock small blocks	1050	1-11/16	88	Plugs	4	Soft-Prog.	Yes	No	50cc	Short	Yellow
0-9375	Same as 0-8896	1050	1-11/16	86	None	4	Soft-Prog.	Yes	No	50cc	Annular discharge	Yellow
0-9377	I.R.	1150	1-13/16	94	None[4]	4	Soft-Prog.	Yes	No	50cc	Annular discharge	Yellow

Notes:

[1] Obsolete part number, no longer made.

[2] Replacement linkage cams are available for 1:1, soft progressive and progressive operation, See Holley Performance Parts Catalog.

[3] Kit 34-9 Conversion Kit has annular-discharge booster venturis, retainer sleeves and all parts necessary to update any model 4500.

[4] Kit 34-8 includes metering blocks to convert 0-6214, 0-6464 and 0-9377 to use power valves in primary and secondary.

[5] PV restriction passages are machined. Supplied with PV plugs. If larger than 100 main jets required, remove plugs and install a power valve. Then reduce main-jet size.

each shaft is sealed with an expansion plug. The lever end is sealed with an O-ring. Linkage between primary and secondary throttle shafts is enclosed inside the carburetor body to protect it from dirt.

Each of the rugged 0.150-in.-thick throttle shaft levers has a plastic cam to actuate an accelerator pump. Accelerator pumps give 30cc per 10 strokes on the 0-6214 IR version; 50cc per 10 strokes on all the other 4500s. Both accelerator pumps fill through rubber-type inlet valves. These valves seal immediately when the pumps are operated. They give an instant pump shot when there is the slightest throttle movement.

In 1983 Holley removed the choke towers from all 4500s. Most racers machined them off anyway. Because they are not designed for the

Underside of 4500 shows rugged enclosed linkage connecting primary and secondary throttles. Accelerator pumps are actuated by levers operationg on cams at back of throttle lever and on the secondary shaft (arrows).

Velocity stacks, Part 17-16, add 3-in. rams to Model 4500. Center *keeper* holds stacks in place and locks securing capscrew.

Accelerator pump uses umbrella-type inlet valve to ensure quick pump shot when throttle is actuated.

Holes (arrows) feed fuel from bowl for intermediate-idle system. Whistle-type vent is standard on 4500s.

Slot and discharge nozzle for intermediate-idle system (arrows).

street, the choke wasn't necessary.

A superb air cleaner for the 7-1/4-in. mounting pad of the 4500 is made by K & N Engineering, Box 1329, Riverside, California 92502.

Three-inch velocity stacks are offered. These chrome stacks are typically used on the 0-6214 and 0-9377 to contain fuel standoff and for their good looks. A slot must be cut in the base of each stack to allow fitting over the booster-nozzle assembly and to provide a passage for fuel from the pump shooter into the venturi. Stacks are held by a long bolt with a metal safety tab. Velocity stacks can be in-

stalled after removing any choke.

Dynamometer tests showed approximately 3% torque gain with 3-in. stacks on a 0-6214 mounted on an IR manifold, even though airbox tests showed no flow gain. Current Pro Stock racers don't use the stacks.

Description of Operation—Because these are essentially "stretched" versions of the 4150/4160 carburetor, look at that section for a description of operation. Only the intermediate-idle system is different. It is explained in the idle system portion of How Your Carburetor Works, page 28.

NOTE: Adjustment and repair of these carburetors is similar to that described for Model 4150s, beginning on page 153.

MODEL 4500

Holley Typical View 42–1

NOTE: General view is useful for visualizing relationship of various parts in carburetor. Specific details will vary with Part Numbers because each carburetor is made to fit a particular application. Current production 4500s don't have chokes and air horns don't protude as in this drawing.

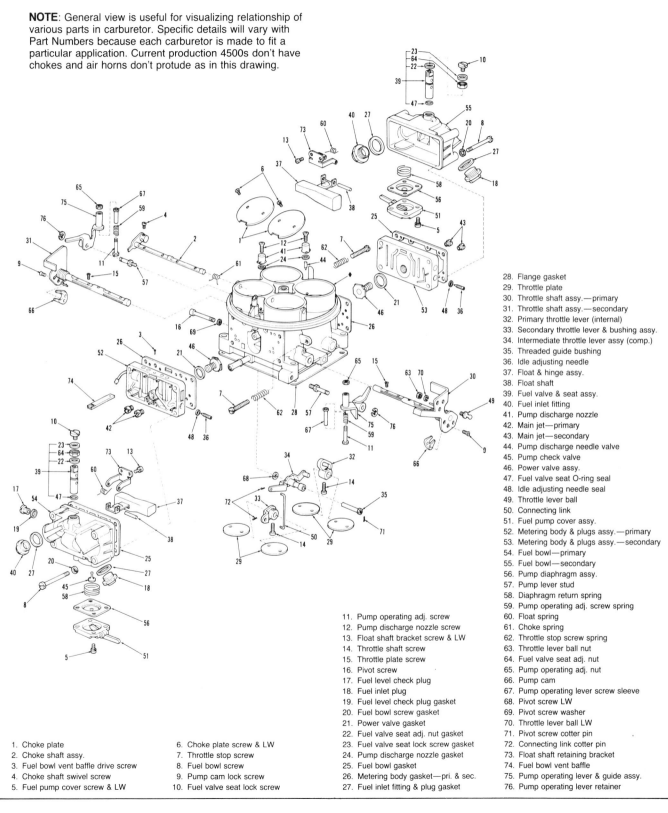

28. Flange gasket
29. Throttle plate
30. Throttle shaft assy.—primary
31. Throttle shaft assy.—secondary
32. Primary throttle lever (internal)
33. Secondary throttle lever & bushing assy.
34. Intermediate throttle lever assy (comp.)
35. Threaded guide bushing
36. Idle adjusting needle
37. Float & hinge assy.
38. Float shaft
39. Fuel valve & seat assy.
40. Fuel inlet fitting
41. Pump discharge nozzle
42. Main jet—primary
43. Main jet—secondary
44. Pump discharge needle valve
45. Pump check valve
46. Power valve assy.
47. Fuel valve seat O-ring seal
48. Idle adjusting needle seal
49. Throttle lever ball
50. Connecting link
51. Fuel pump cover assy.
52. Metering body & plugs assy.—primary
53. Metering body & plugs assy.—secondary
54. Fuel bowl—primary
55. Fuel bowl—secondary
56. Pump diaphragm assy.
57. Pump lever stud
58. Diaphragm return spring
59. Pump operating adj. screw spring
60. Float spring
61. Choke spring
62. Throttle stop screw spring
63. Throttle lever ball nut
64. Fuel valve seat adj. nut
65. Pump operating adj. nut
66. Pump cam
67. Pump operating lever screw sleeve
68. Pivot screw LW
69. Pivot screw washer
70. Throttle lever ball LW
71. Pivot screw cotter pin
72. Connecting link cotter pin
73. Float shaft retaining bracket
74. Fuel bowl vent baffle
75. Pump operating lever & guide assy.
76. Pump operating lever retainer

11. Pump operating adj. screw
12. Pump discharge nozzle screw
13. Float shaft bracket screw & LW
14. Throttle shaft screw
15. Throttle plate screw
16. Pivot screw
17. Fuel level check plug
18. Fuel inlet plug
19. Fuel level check plug gasket
20. Fuel bowl screw gasket
21. Power valve gasket
22. Fuel valve seat adj. nut gasket
23. Fuel valve seat lock screw gasket
24. Pump discharge nozzle gasket
25. Fuel bowl gasket
26. Metering body gasket—pri. & sec.
27. Fuel inlet fitting & plug gasket

1. Choke plate
2. Choke shaft assy.
3. Fuel bowl vent baffle drive screw
4. Choke shaft swivel screw
5. Fuel pump cover screw & LW
6. Choke plate screw & LW
7. Throttle stop screw
8. Fuel bowl screw
9. Pump cam lock screw
10. Fuel valve seat lock screw

ANNULAR-DISCHARGE BOOSTERS

In 1980 Holley introduced a booster design never before used in performance carburetors: annular discharge.

These boosters have higher air velocity close to the venturi surface where the discharge holes are located. This increases the metering signal and gets the main system flowing at lower airflows.

The stronger signal, together with equally spaced radial location of the discharge holes, improves atomization and cylinder-to-cylinder distribution. The higher signal reduces main-jet requirement by 4—5 sizes. With annular-discharge boosters there is less dependence on accelerator pumps to cover up hesitation or bogs.

Note the photo in the previous 4150 section of this chapter. It shows the booster's two-piece construction. The top section contains the annular track and discharge holes. It is pressed into the large ring section containing the fuel-discharge channel from the main well. The assembly is spun into place just like a conventional booster.

Annular-discharge boosters are used in the Model 4180 and 4150 competition carburetors 0-9379 (750cfm), 0-9381 (830 cfm) and 0-9380 (850 cfm). Annular-discharge boosters are also used in two of the Model 4500s and a conversion kit allows converting any 4500 to this type of booster.

Annular-booster Kit 34-9 converts any Model 4500 to annular-booster configuration. Brass inserts are inserted from metering-block gasket surfaces to lock boosters in place.

REPLACEMENT CARBURETORS

MODEL 4360

This compact, lightweight spread-bore carburetor was introduced in 1976 as a cost-competitive replacement for the Rochester Q-Jet on 1965—82 GM cars. It also replaces Thermo-Quad carburetors on 1975 and later Chrysler products. And, Holley has calibrated the Model 4360 in combination with many of its 4-, 6- and 8-cylinder intake manifolds. The Holley Performance Parts Catalog contains specific recommendations.

There have been 123 different versions of this model, each with a physical and/or specification variation. It all came to an end with the 1982 car model year. Beginning with the 1981 car model year, emission considerations forced GM to convert the Q-Jet to a feedback (closed-loop) carburetor. Because there is no feedback version of the Model 4360, Holley's Model 4175 can be used for 1982 and later applications.

One design objective was to provide a carburetor fitting the trend toward lower-power smaller engines, as in GM's 260-, 262-, and 305-CID V8s and GM V6s. Here the Model 4360 serves as an excellent *performance* carburetor because its small primaries give excellent throttle response and feel in the low- and mid-rpm ranges.

The combination of small venturis and a good delivery system yields excellent atomization and strong signals even at low airflows. These provide good driveability and fuel economy and low exhaust emissions.

Model 4360 is bolt-on replacement for Rochester Q-Jet. Small primaries provide higher air velocity at a given air speed, promoting improved throttle response. It features 450-cfm capacity, all-aluminum construction, changeable main jets and mechanical secondaries. Choke actuation is designed for specific application. This unit has integral choke.

Universal throttle lever works with all Chevrolet and Pontiac applications. Primary lever moves alone for 40° until tang (arrow) meets tang on intermediate free-floating lever to actuate secondary lever.

Looking into fuel bowl and throttle bores with airhorn removed. Float pivots on combination hinge pin and retainer. Bowl capacity is about 90cc. Primary boosters are inserted, secondary boosters are cast-in.

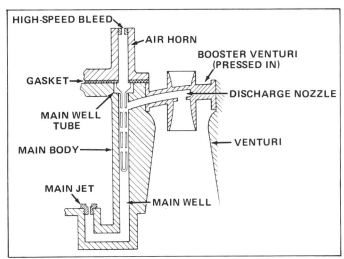

Primary main system schematic. Fuel enters main well through main jet. Air enters main well through high-speed bleed and holes in well tube. Air and fuel mix to form an emulsion that is discharged into the air section through booster venturi.

Mechanical secondaries are available for acceleration or top power output when required. The carburetor is a fine normal-driving replacement for big-block engines.

Design Features—Primary bore size is 1-3/8-in.; secondary is 1-7/16-in. This combination yields 450-cfm airflow tested at WOT with a 1.5-in.Hg pressure drop. About 40% of the flow comes through the primary side. At first glance 450 cfm seems small, especially if you are used to high-flow carburetors. But when tested (flowed) at 3 in.Hg., as two-barrel carburetors are, it flows 630 cfm. This represents a 60% gain over the largest original-equipment two-barrel. And is 30 cfm larger than Holley's 6425 giant two-barrel (no longer made).

A single fuel bowl integral with the main body nestles between the venturis. To accomplish this, secondary-bore centers were widened 0.36-in. from the Q-Jet. This was possible because the smaller secondary bores, even with the offset, fit well within the manifold's 2-1/4-in. bores. This unique arrangement is the key to the 4360's compact design. Primary bore centers and all stud spacings are identical to the Q-Jet.

The 90cc fuel bowl has proven more than adequate under severe temperature conditions. A brass float is mounted at the front of the fuel bowl. Fuel enters from the front through a single 0.110-in. inlet valve with a Viton needle. Level adjustment is accomplished by bending a float-hinge tab.

The primary main metering system is similar to that used in the Models 5200 and 5210.

The secondary main system is a diagonal-well type formed inside and adjacent to a cast-in booster venturi. This efficient system helps

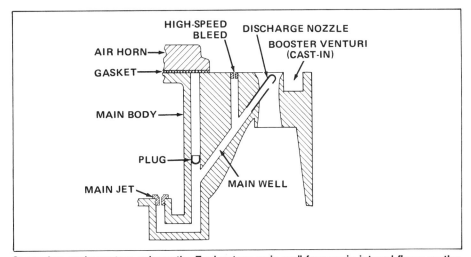

Secondary main system schematic. Fuel enters main well from main jet and flows up the diagonal well where it meets air entering through high-speed bleed. The emulsion is discharged through booster-venturi nozzle.

to get the main system flowing at very low airflows. This, combined with the small venturis, allows the use of mechanical secondaries without adding a pump to the secondary side. Secondaries begin opening when primary throttles are about 40° open.

Idle systems are conventional. While both primaries and secondaries have idle systems, only the primary side is adjustable. This adjust-

ment is right at the discharge where there is maximum velocity to help vaporization and cylinder-to-cylinder fuel/air distribution. Adjustment is conventional: lean is clockwise and rich, counterclockwise.

All metering restrictions, other than the main jets and power valves, are pressed in. Main jets with metric threads are similar to those in the Models 5200 and 5210.

Three principal castings and their assemblies: air horn, main body and throttle body.

Primary idle air bleeds (1), primary high-speed bleeds (2) and secondary idle air bleeds (3).

Idle-mixture screw (1) and idle-speed screw (2). 4360s have plastic limiter cap on idle-mixture screw.

Pressed-in primary nozzle or booster venturi (1). Primary idle-feed restriction is at (2). Idle fuel meets idle-air bleed in matching pocket in air horn. The emulsion travels through track (3) and down a diagonal passage to the discharge. Idle-channel restriction is at (4).

The three-piece construction has separate aluminum castings for the air horn, main body and throttle body. Aluminum is lighter than zinc and more stable at higher temperatures, making for tighter sealing. Aluminum is also easy to machine. This construction allows using heat-insulating gaskets between the castings. The complete assembly weighs only 6.4 lbs. as compared with 8.8 lbs. for the Q-Jet. It is only 0.5 pound heavier than a Rochester two-barrel.

The spring-driven, piston-type accelerator pump has a synthetic-rubber cup. Three adjustment positions are provided.

When this design was started, many emissions features, such as the EGR signal system, evaporative vent valve, throttle-control solenoids and others were already defined. These were incorporated in the original package. All necessary vacuum tubes and ports are provided so this carburetor is a true bolt-on replacement.

The choke on the early Chevrolet and Pontiac types is either remote or divorced and with a diaphragm-type qualifying system. The original choke rod and sensing unit can be used. Because GM has been using a 100% integral choke since the mid-'70s, integral choke 4360s are provided to fit other applications.

4360 Performance—Performance tests were run at Holley on an engine dynamometer. The chart (page 68) shows Holley dynamometer data from a new 1975 Chevrolet LM-1 350-CID engine. It illustrates a torque and horsepower comparison between the Holley 4360 and the OEM two-barrel, and the OEM four-barrel Q-Jet. All data were obtained within two days on the same engine with an intake-manifold change to run the two-barrel.

Peak torque with the Model 4360 occurred at 2800 rpm and exceeded the other carburetors. At the high end, the 4360's torque and horsepower curves fall between the two-barrel and Q-Jet. This is what you would expect when comparing airflow capacity. Note how very close it is to the much larger Q-Jet. Uniformity of the fuel/air mixture between cylinders was within ± 9% across all the cylinders at all WOT points (within one F/A ratio).

The 4360 was designed to fulfill the need for a small carburetor that drives well and performs better than the much larger Q-Jet. In addition, it offers a performance option for those who wish

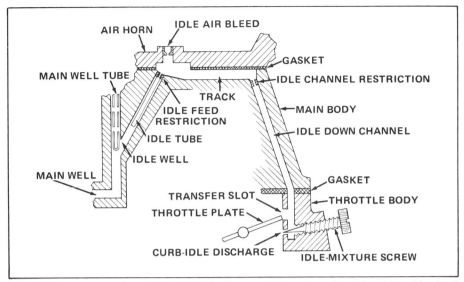

Choke lever hooks to original choke rod. Hole (1) is for units that pull to close. Hole (2) is for those that push to close.

Primary idle system schematic. Idle fuel is drawn out of main well and is metered by feed restriction at top of idle tube. Air enters at idle-air bleed just above feed restriction. Emulsion moves along a track in top of main body, then through a channel restriction, and finally down channel to a mating passage in throttle body. The throttle body contains both an adjustable discharge and a transfer slot. Idle mixture control is conventional: clockwise to lean and counterclockwise to richen.

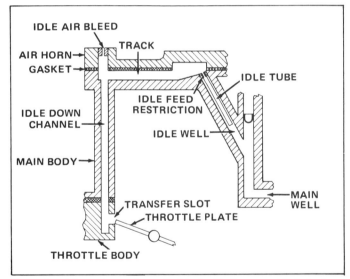

Secondary idle system schematic. Idle fuel is drawn up idle tube from main well and metered by restriction at top. Metered fuel travels along track in top of main body, joining air from idle air bleed at top of vertical channel. Emulsion travels down channel and discharges out transfer slot in throttle body. The emulsion also discharges through a non-adjustable discharge port below the throttle plate.

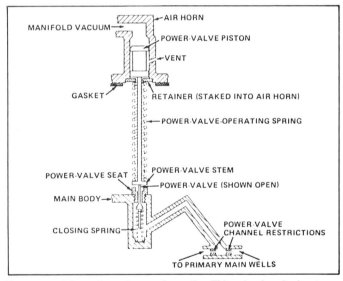

Power enrichment system schematic. This simple single-stage enrichment system is shown in rich or "on" position. Manifold vacuum acts to pull power-valve piston up. Manifold vacuum acts counter to operating-spring tension that is pulling power-valve piston down. When manifold vacuum drops to a given value, spring forces piston and stem down. This opens power valve in bottom of fuel bowl. Fuel flows through valve and through power-valve-channel restrictions. It's there fuel is metered before entering each primary main well.

to convert their two-barrel installation to a four-barrel. Many owners do this to make today's smaller and more congested engines run better.

Driveability is a very subjective trait and it's hard to put a number on it. But the little Holley four-barrel offers a plus in almost every area.

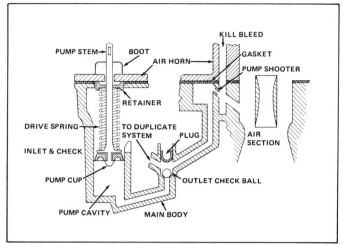

Accelerator pump system schematic. Fuel is drawn into pump well through floating cup. Cup moves up as throttle closes. While this happens, the outlet check seals and prevents air from entering well. As throttle opens, drive spring forces piston down. Fuel is forced past outlet check and through shooters into primary air section. A kill-bleed arrangement prevents fuel pull-over at high air velocities.

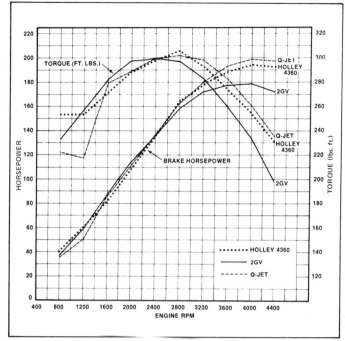

WOT data obtained from new 1975 Chevrolet LM-1 350-CID engine compares Holley 4360 power and torque with that from Rochester Q-Jet and 2GV.

Here are the two kinds of 5200/10 main jets. Brass ones on left were used through 1975; they are marked for diameter. Green-dyed ones on right are marked for flow.

5200 MAIN JETS

In 1975 Holley began using a new series of main jets in Model 5200/5210s. These jets are sized and marked according to average flow. They are dyed green to avoid confusion with the pre-'75 brass-color jets, which are marked to indicate approximate diameter of the opening.

For example, a 22R-130A-325 (marked 325) flows approximately 325 cubic centimeters per minute with a supply head of 50 centimeters. The nearby chart shows the relation of flow-rated jets to the diameter-marked jets.

This 5200 has fuel inlet with plug (1) in fuel-return opening, deceleration valve tube (2) (used with external deceleration valve on some Pintos and other Fords), diaphragm accelerator pump (3) and water connections for automatic choke (4).

Metric Main Jets—With the introduction of the Model 4360 in 1976, Holley started using main jets with tighter flow tolerances. The stamped number relates to average flow range. Example: 124-203 (stamped 203) flows approximately 203cc per minute with a 50cc

Model 5210 for 1977 and later Pontiac Astre and Sunbird four-cylinder engines. Note electric choke and solenoid-assisted bowl vent with tube for canister connection.

Vacuum-controlled bowl vent is closed to canister while engine is running and open when it's off. Small solenoid in vent cover ensures vent doesn't open under low-vacuum, heavy-load conditions. This feature isn't found on all 5200/5210 carbs. Don't put diaphragm or solenoid in harsh carb cleaners.

head. These same jets are used on the Models 2360 and 2280 two-barrel carburetors.

MODELS 5200, 5210 & 5220

These are carburetors for small engines. The 5200 is used on Ford products including Pinto, Capri, Mustang II, Fairmont, Zephyr and Cortina. The 5220 is used on VW/Audi engines used in AMC Gremlins, Chrysler Omni and Horizon.

Model 5210 is used on the Vega L-11 engine and on the Pontiac 151-CID four-cylinder engine. Major differences between these carburetors are in the throttle-lever and fuel-inlet areas. Also, the 5210 and 5220 do not have the 5200's deceleration system. Other differences exist, but the same description can be used for all three.

Design Features—These 270-cfm, (flow at 3.0 in.Hg) staged two-barrels have a mechanically actuated secondary throttle. Venturi sizes are different, as is common for progressive-secondary carburetors used on emission-controlled engines.

The primary venturi is 26mm (1-1/32-in.) and the secondary is 27mm (1-1/16-in.). Throttle bores are 32mm (1.25-in.) and 36mm (1.40-in.) diameter, spaced 1.7-in. apart on a metric 2V flange. The rectangular stud pattern measures 1.84-in. x 3.66-in.

A diaphragm-type accelerator pump is used. Hose connections are provided for jacket water to the thermostatically operated choke, the fuel inlet and return, timed and vacuum spark and for a PCV valve. A connection is provided for the deceleration valve used on some Fords.

If you have been servicing U.S.-designed carburetors, the 5200's screw-in main air-bleed, main-metering, and idle-metering restrictions (jets) may seem unusual. The Vega 5210 carburetor changed to a pressed-in idle-metering restriction in 1976. Pontiac's 5210 has an idle tube with the restriction at the bottom.

Description of Operation—This description is applicable to all Model 5200s. No attempt has been made to explain the overall systems functioning of the carburetor because, except as noted, these operate as described in How Your Carburetor Works.

HOLLEY 5200 & 5210 JET CHART

Green Main Jets	Brass-Color Main Jets	High Speed Air Bleeds	Idle Jets
124-227	22R-103-130	123-150	123-45
124-239	22R-103-132	123-160	123-50
124-243	22R-103-133	123-170	123-55
124-255	22R-103-135	123-175	123-60
124-263	22R-103-137	123-180	123-65
124-275	22R-103-140	123-185	123-70
124-283	22R-103-142	123-190	123-80
124-299	22R-103-145		
124-311	22R-103-147		
124-325	22R-103-150		
124-346	22R-103-155		
124-357	22R-103-157		
124-374	22R-103-160		
124-404	22R-103-165		
124-423	22R-103-170		
124-455	22R-103-175		
124-477	22R-103-180		
124-524	22R-103-185		

Brass-color jets use old numbering system and metric sizing: 130 = 1.3mm.

Green jets listed in first column are the same flow capacity as the early brass jets shown in second column. For example, a 124-227 has the same flow rating as a 22R-103-130.

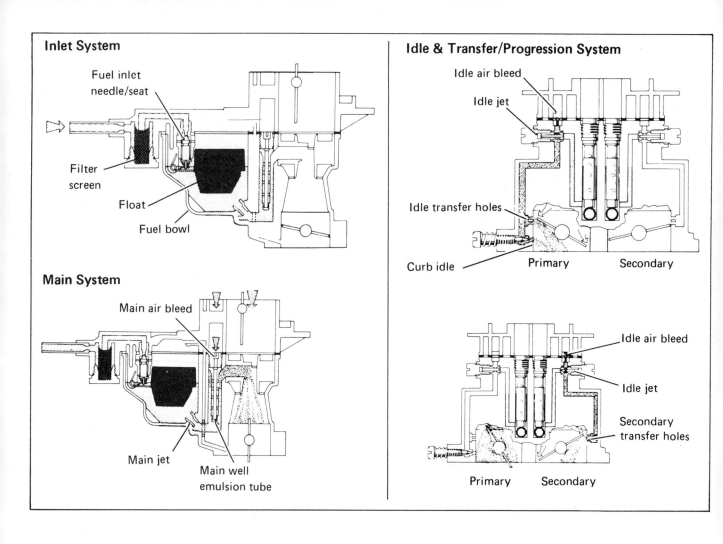

Inlet System

Fuel inlet needle/seat

Filter screen

Float

Fuel bowl

Main System

Main air bleed

Main jet

Main well emulsion tube

Idle & Transfer/Progression System

Idle air bleed

Idle jet

Idle transfer holes

Curb idle

Primary   Secondary

Idle air bleed

Idle jet

Secondary transfer holes

Primary   Secondary

Fuel Inlet—Fuel under pressure enters the fuel bowl through the fuel-inlet fitting in the air horn (carburetor cover) and through a filter screen. The 5210 has the usual GM-type sintered-bronze filter or a paper filter in the inlet.

The float is a closed-cell or hollow-plastic structure with two lungs. A small retaining clip hooked over the float-lever tang attaches to the fuel-inlet needle. This ensures the fuel-inlet needle with be pulled downward as the float drops. When the float is hanging down, a float-lever tang contacts a horizontal bumper spring to reduce float bouncing.

The fuel bowl vents to the air horn. Some models (usually for air-conditioned cars) have a fuel-return connection just above the fuel inlet. A portion of the fuel supplied by the pump is returned to the tank to ensure liquid fuel is supplied to the carburetor. Any vapors generated in the line between the fuel pump and the carburetor inlet during a hot soak are vented to the fuel tank.

Idle—In most cases there is an idle system for each barrel of the carburetor. The primary side is adjustable and the secondary side is used only as a transfer system. It supplies mixture as the secondary starts to open and before the time the secondary main system starts to operate.

Other than the adjustment on the primary side, the idle systems are essentially identical.

Power System—The primary power system valve is actuated by a diaphragm/rod combination operated by manifold vacuum.

The secondary power system is operated by air velocity through the secondary venturi, which creates a low pressure at the discharge opening in the air horn. Fuel flows from the bowl through a vertical passage containing a restriction. At the top of the passage, air from an air bleed is mixed with the fuel and the

fuel/air mixture flows through a cross passage into the air horn.

Accelerator Pump—The accelerator pump is a diaphragm type in the side of the body. It discharges into the primary side only. The pump shooter can be modified to give a pump shot into both sides if desired. Excess fuel vapor generated in the pump chamber during hot soaks is vented into the fuel bowl through a restriction.

Choke System—The automatic choke assembly on the carburetor body has a bimetal thermostatic coil that winds up when cold and unwinds when hot. The coil is attached to a shaft that has a fast-idle cam and a linkage to open/close the choke plates. On some models, engine coolant flowing through the water cover on the choke heats the bimetal coil to open the choke as engine temperature increases. Other models have an electric choke.

Power System (Primary)

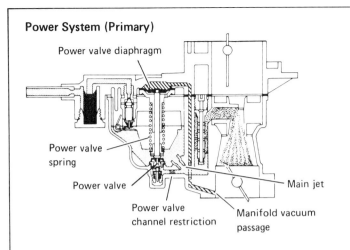

- Power valve diaphragm
- Power valve spring
- Power valve
- Power valve channel restriction
- Main jet
- Manifold vacuum passage

Power System (Secondary)

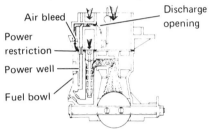

- Air bleed
- Power restriction
- Power well
- Fuel bowl
- Discharge opening

Deceleration System

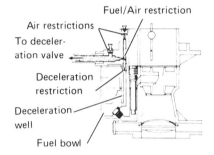

- Fuel/Air restriction
- Air restrictions
- To deceleration valve
- Deceleration restriction
- Deceleration well
- Fuel bowl

Accelerator Pump System

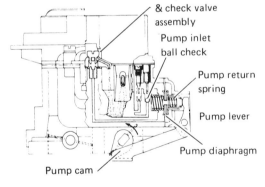

- Pump shooter & check valve assembly
- Pump inlet ball check
- Pump return spring
- Pump lever
- Pump diaphragm
- Pump cam

Choke System

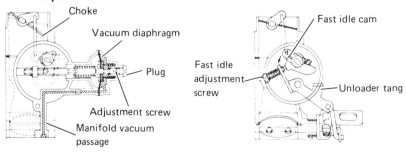

- Choke
- Vacuum diaphragm
- Plug
- Adjustment screw
- Manifold vacuum passage
- Fast idle cam
- Fast idle adjustment screw
- Unloader tang

Accelerator pump in middle position (2). Moving pivot pin to hole (1) decreases pump capacity; outside position (3) increases it. Early models had only two holes. Pump-lever housing should be removed when changing positions. Support pump casting while removing and inserting pivot pin to prevent casting breakage. Pivot pin (arrow) is removed by driving with a small punch from non-knurled side. Replace by driving from knurled side.

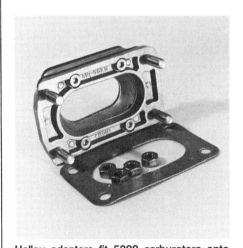

Holley adapters fit 5200 carburetors onto many imported automobiles. This 401-2 adapts 5200s to Datsun 1.4-liter engines. Other adapters are for Audi, Chevy LUV, Chrysler Mitsubishi, Ford Courier and other Datsun cars and trucks.

5200 features include booster venturis (1) and accelerator-pump shooters (2). Only primary side is drilled but secondary can be opened up. Main air bleeds (3) have emulsion tubes (4) underneath. Idle air bleeds (5), idle jets (6) are in individual holders (7). Secondary system power well is (8); deceleration system well is (9). Power valve (10) screws into bottom of bowl. Main jets are (11).

This 6510 was introduced in 1980 on Chevette. Model 6520 was used on Omni/Horizon cars. These are closed-loop 5200s. Duty-cycle solenoid is identified by electrical lead at left. Plastic connector at lower right is throttle-position sensor, which supplies input to ECU. See p. 38 for more information on closed-loop operation.

The choke system is activated by depressing the accelerator pedal before a cold start, which allows the coil to close the choke plates. A vacuum diaphragm and spring provide vacuum qualification of the choke opening once the engine is started.

Deceleration System—This supplies additional mixture to the engine to ensure against misfiring during deceleration, because that increases hydrocarbons. It operates only at manifold vacuums higher than normally expected at idle. When the carburetor is being used on an engine without deceleration valve, the 1/4-in. diameter brass tube on the air horn should be plugged. The 5210 and 5220 don't have the deceleration system.

During deceleration, high manifold vacuum is applied to a fitting on the carburetor air horn via a *deceleration valve* and vacuum line that are not part of the carburetor. This vacuum pulls fuel from a *deceleration well* in the fuel bowl and past a restriction. The fuel is mixed with air from an air bleed. Then, the mixture is metered through a restriction into the cross passage connected to manifold vacuum. Another air restriction in this cross passage adds a larger quantity of air to the mixture as it is drawn through the vacuum line and valve into the intake manifold.

Adjustment and repair of these carburetors is described in the section starting on page 175.

MODELS 2360 & 6360

In 1976, GM introduced the Dual-Jet or M2MC non-staged, two-barrel carburetor for V6 and small V8 engines (305-CID maximum). It is essentially the primary side of the Quadrajet. In fact, for the first couple of years the Rochester castings included the unmachined secondary half. In its closed-loop version, it was used through the late 1980 model years and the transition to fuel injection. It was used on both passenger cars and trucks. Along with the Q-Jet, it was one of the last original-equipment carburetors used.

Holley introduced the model 2360 in 1983 as a direct bolt-on replacement for the Rochester Dual-Jet. One basic criterion was to make every tube, fuel fitting, throttle linkage hook-up, vacuum signal, and so forth, virtually identical to the Dual-Jet.

Model 6360—This is exactly the same as the 2360 except that closed-loop control is added with a duty-cycle solenoid. Both are described in How Your Carburetor Works. The duty-cycle solenoid controls supplemental idle-air bleeds and main jets so complete mixture control is attained all the way from idle to WOT. The system is completely compatible with the on-board GM electronics. The wiring harness plugs in without modifications. GM began using closed-loop control carburetors in 1981.

Design Features—The venturi diameter is 1.200 in. with 1.375-in. throttle bores. Flow

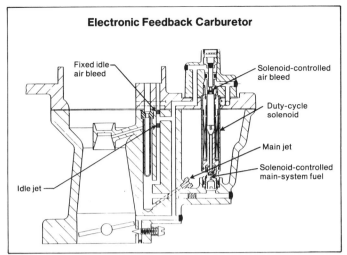

Electronic Feedback Carburetor

Fixed idle air bleed
Solenoid-controlled air bleed
Duty-cycle solenoid
Main jet
Solenoid-controlled main-system fuel
Idle jet
Idle jet

Duty-cycle solenoid is controlled by oxygen sensor in exhaust stream. Mixture is regulated by time solenoid is opened or closed; this is constantly adjusted by oxygen sensor.

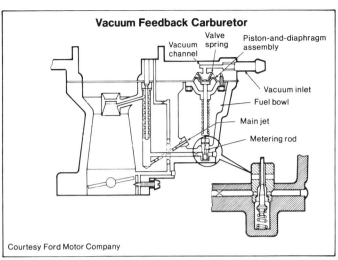

Vacuum Feedback Carburetor

Valve spring
Vacuum channel
Piston-and-diaphragm assembly
Vacuum inlet
Fuel bowl
Main jet
Metering rod

Courtesy Ford Motor Company

Vacuum feedback control of 5200 was introduced with Model 6500 on 1978 Ford 2.3-liter engines. Manifold vacuum is channeled to special diaphragm on carb. Diaphragm mechanically controls a bleed to revised power valve.

Model 2360 Holley replaces Rochester Dual-Jet or M2MC. All fittings are positioned to make this a simple bolt-on replacement for specific applications on 1976 and later GM cars and trucks.

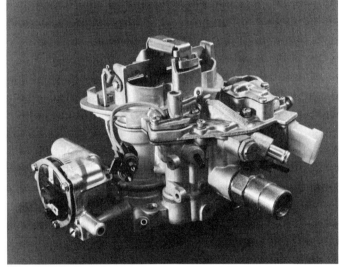

Model 6360 is closed-loop version of Model 2360. It features duty-cycle solenoid controled by vehicle ECU. Fittings are positioned to make this a simple bolt-on replacement for 1981 and later GM cars/trucks.

capacity is 260 cfm at 1.5 in. Hg. pressure drop. Construction is three-piece with aluminum air horn, zinc main body and an aluminum throttle body. The air horn is shaped to fit the stock air cleaner. The fuel bowl is integral with the main body. The throttle body fits the intake manifold without an adapter.

Cast-in double booster venturis ensure strong metering signals at low airflows to op-timize exhaust emissions, driveability and fuel economy. The automatic choke is either hot-air or electric to match the original-equipment in-stallation. A staged power valve provides a fuel delivery schedule closely tailored to engine re-quirements under all load conditions.

All bleeds and restrictions are pressed in. Main jets are the same metric type used in the 5200 family and Models 2280 and 4360. Ser-vice replacements are available with the 124-prefix number. See the chart on page 69.

A special feature allows setting the idle mix-ture of both bores simultaneously with a single adjustment screw. The idle mixture is divided equally between the two barrels. This first-of-a-kind approach was the idea of Bill Manning, Holley carburetor engineer *par excellence*, now retired.

Model 2280 two-barrel carburetor is standard on many 1978—'79 Chrysler 318-CID engines; replacement for 1962 and later Chrysler products with 273- and 318-CID engines. It replaces Rochester 2GC carburetors on 1964—'73 Chevrolets with 283-, 307- and 327-CID engines; and on 1968—'69 Buicks. Airflow capacity is 255 cfm. Three-piece aluminum design includes metric metering jets and gradient power valve. It has an SAE 1-1/4-in. throttle-body flange.

Model 6280 is closed-loop version of 2280 for Chrysler 318-CID engines, 1981—'87. Duty-cycle solenoid is hidden under air horn.

MODELS 2280 & 6280

The Model 2280 was designed in the mid-'70s. It has been used both as original equipment and for aftermarket applications. It was original equipment on Chrysler 318-CID V8s in passenger cars and trucks from 1978, until it was replaced by fuel injection in the late 1980s. Aftermarket usage on Chrysler products extends back to 1962., replacing the Carter model BBD on 225-, 273- and 318-CID engines. It also replaces the small Rochester 2GC on Chevrolet 283-, 307- and 327-CID engines. Buicks are covered for 1968—69 model years.

Design Features—Construction is three-piece: air horn, main body and throttle body. Because it is all-aluminum, it is a very light carburetor.

An air-horn diameter of 2-5/8 in. fits the original GM air cleaner. The original air cleaner bail snaps right on.

Most models are equipped with a divorced automatic choke. A few models have a manual choke. Choke qualifying is accomplished with a diaphragm unit.

The accelerator pump is of the piston type. Two holes on the pump lever allow pump-capacity adjustment.

Main jets are the smaller ones used in the model 5200 and others as described earlier. Booster venturis are part of a cluster assembly containing the idle and main air bleeds, as well as the pump shooters.

The vacuum-operated power valve is the piston-gradient type. Some 2280s have a

Model 6280 partially disassembled to show duty-cycle solenoid.

second power valve that is mechanically actuated by the accelerator-pump lever when the throttle nears wide open.

Fuel-inlet valve is integral with the fuel fitting. The float is a dual-lung type. Throttle bore

and stud spacings are SAE 1-1/4-in. standard. Throttle bores are 1-3/8in. Capacity is 255 cfm at 3 in.Hg pressure drop.

Model 6280—For automobiles with closed-loop control of fuel mixture, Model 6280 couples directly into the wiring of Chrysler cars with 318-CID engines. This carburetor was original equipment on these cars, beginning in 1981 and continuing through 1987.

This model is the same as the 2280 except that closed-loop control is achieved with a duty-cycle solenoid. Both are described in How Your Carburetor Works.

The duty-cycle solenoid controls supplemental idle-air bleeds and main jets so complete mixture control is attained all the way from idle to WOT.

MODELS 2210, 2211 & 2245

Model 2210 carburetors have been used as original equipment on Chrysler 360- and 383-CID engines. Aftermarket types are offered for both Chrysler and Chevrolet. Model 2245 was introduced on 1974 Chrysler Products. If differs from the model 2210 principally in its power-valve design. It is also used in the aftermarket to service other automobiles and trucks.
Model 2211—This is a replacement for the larger 1-1/2-in. SAE-flanged Rochester 2GC carburetor. Applications extend back into the late '60s. Airflow is 250 cfm. Although it is the same basic design as the 2210, the air horn diameter is changed to allow using the original air cleaner. An integral automatic choke mounts on the throttle body. A divorced-choke version is also available. Model 2211 was introduced in 1976 as an aftermarket-only, direct bolt-on replacement for the 2GC carburetor.

Side view of 2210 shows fast-idle linkage and cam, choke vacuum-qualifying diaphragm connected by hose to throttle body, and PCV and manifold-vacuum connections. Idle adjustment screw on this Chrysler unit grounds against an insulated stop used for changing distributor spark advance at idle. Tab on accelerator-pump lever (top left) opens evaporative control vent at idle so vapors are collected in storage canister or crankcase.

Model 2211, shown here with integral choke, is used on GM cars and trucks.

Systems Drawings for Model 2210

Inlet System

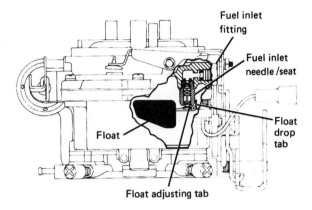

Fuel inlet fitting

Fuel inlet needle /seat

Float drop tab

Float

Float adjusting tab

Power System

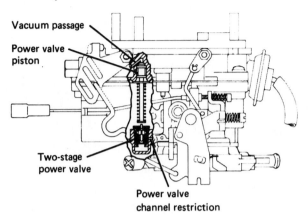

Vacuum passage

Power valve piston

Two-stage power valve

Power valve channel restriction

Idle System

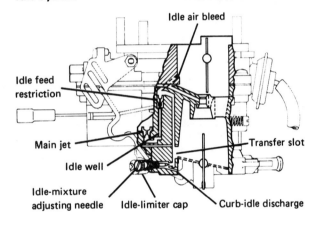

Idle air bleed

Idle feed restriction

Main jet

Idle well

Idle-mixture adjusting needle

Idle-limiter cap

Transfer slot

Curb-idle discharge

Accelerator Pump System

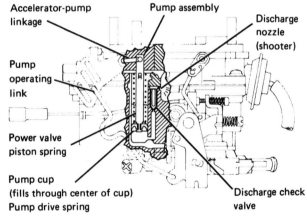

Accelerator-pump linkage

Pump assembly

Discharge nozzle (shooter)

Pump operating link

Power valve piston spring

Pump cup (fills through center of cup)
Pump drive spring

Discharge check valve

Main System

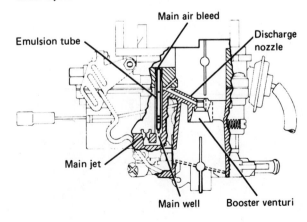

Main air bleed

Emulsion tube

Discharge nozzle

Main jet

Main well

Booster venturi

Choke System

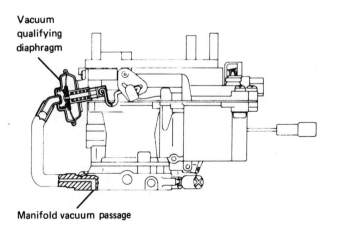

Vacuum qualifying diaphragm

Manifold vacuum passage

Model 1940 with integral choke.

Design Features—The 2210 and 2245 two-barrels flow 380 cfm at 3.0-in.Hg pressure drop. Throttle bores are 1-9/16-in. diameter in an SAE 1-1/2-in. two-barrel flange with a 2.00-in. x 3.68-in. stud pattern. The air-cleaner mounting flange is 4-3/16-in. diameter.

Three major castings are the zinc air horn and main body and an aluminum throttle body. A triple-venturi design is cast into the main body.

Two booster venturis plus the main venturi supply good atomization of the fuel as it leaves the discharge nozzle.

A closed-cellular float is side-hung in the fuel bowl. The piston-type accelerator pump is spring-driven.

The model 2210 power valve is either one- or two-stage, as required for specific vehicle-emission requirements. Model 2245 has a *gra-dient* or smoothly varying power valve.

An evaporation-control vent in the air horn vents the bowl to an external canister or storage device (crankcase on some Chrysler products). When the throttle is moved off-idle, the stored vapors are sucked into the carburetor base.

Idle screws are slanted for accessibility. Teflon-coated throttle and choke shafts reduce friction and provide long life. The divorced choke has a vacuum-qualifying diaphragm unit that is hose-connected to the throttle body. Hose connections include PCV, timed spark, manifold vacuum and evaporation control.

MODELS 1940, 1945, 1946 & 6145

The model 1940 has seen wide use on six-cylinder Ford car, truck and industrial engines, usually with an Autolite trademark on the carburetor body. It is also available as a Holley aftermarket replacement for Ford, Chevrolet and other makes.

Model 1945 is very similar to the 1940 except for the throttle, choke and power-valve. It was first used on Chrysler six-cylinder engines in 1974 and continued on passenger cars and trucks until the late 1980s.

The 1945 has a divorced choke in this description. The 1940 we've pictured has an integral choke, but some 1940s have divorced chokes.

Another version, the model 1946, was used as original equipment on Ford six-cylinder engines from 1978—83. Flow capacity is 200 cfm at 3.0 in.Hg.

Model 6145—For automobiles with closed-loop control of mixture, model 6145 connects directly into the wiring of Chrysler cars with 225-CID engines. This carburetor was original equipment on these cars, beginning in 1981 and continuing through 1987.

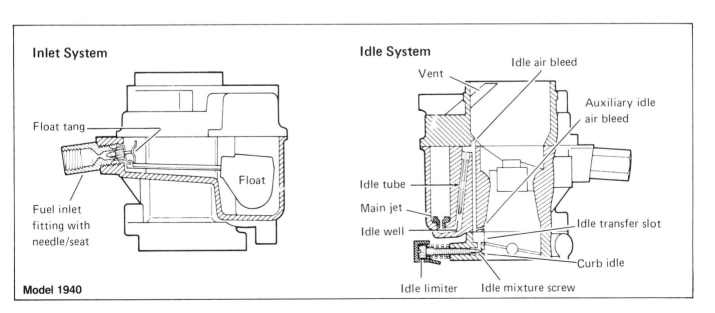

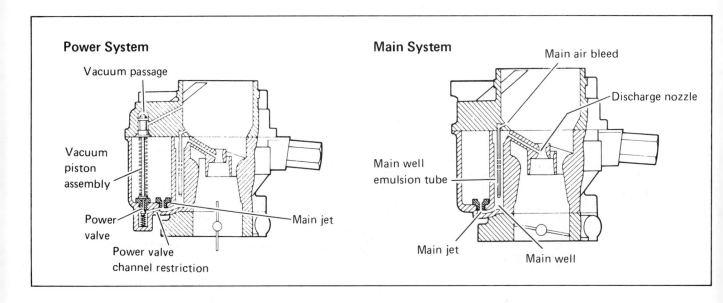

Power System

Vacuum passage

Vacuum piston assembly

Power valve

Power valve channel restriction

Main jet

Main System

Main air bleed

Discharge nozzle

Main well emulsion tube

Main jet

Main well

Model 1946 with integral choke used on 1979—'83 Ford and Mercury 200-CID engines.

This carburetor is the same as the 1945 except that closed-loop control is achieved via a duty-cycle solenoid. Both are described in How Your Carburetor Works. The duty-cycle solenoid controls supplemental idle-air bleeds and main jets so complete mixture control is attained all the way from idle to WOT.

Design Features—The single-barrel Model 1940 is available in three flow capacities: 170, 180 and 212 cfm (measured at 3.0-in.Hg pressure drop). Throttle bores are 1-7/16-, 1-9/16- and 1-11/16-in.

All share a 1-1/2-in. SAE flange, Ford models use a 2.68-in. stud spacing in this flange size; Chevrolet versions use a 2.92-in. stud spacing. Air-cleaner flange is 2-3/16-in. diameter. Model 1945 comes in one size with a 1-11/16-in. throttle bore. It flows 203 cfm at a 3.0-in.Hg pressure drop.

Three major castings are used. Air horn/bowl cover and bowl/body castings are zinc and the throttle body is aluminum.

A nearly concentric fuel bowl allows the carburetor to meet military-angularity specifications. Hose connections are provided for PCV valve and tapped openings for conventional timed spark or spark valve (early Ford vehicles) are included. A fresh-air pickup in the air horn supplies filtered air to an integral choke. Teflon coating on the throttle and choke shafts and on a choke lever minimizes friction and provides long-wearing capabilities.

Description of Operation—This description is applicable to all Model 1940, 1945 and 1946s. No attempt has been made to explain why certain actions occur in the functioning of the carburetor. Except as noted, operation is as described in How Your Carburetor Works.

Fuel Inlet—Fuel enters the fuel bowl through

a fuel fitting in the carburetor body. The Viton-tipped needle seats directly in the fuel-inlet fitting. It is retained by a cap. Fuel flows through holes in the side of the inlet fitting. The fuel bowl is designed so there is no need for a baffle. A dual-lung closed-cellular float mounts on a stainless-steel float lever hinged on a stainless-steel float pin.

Main Metering—At cruising speeds, fuel flows from the fuel bowl, through the main jet into the bottom of the main well. The main air bleed in the carburetor cover supplies filtered air to the emulsion tube in the main well. As fuel moves up the main well, it mixes with air as it passes the holes in the emulsion tube. This fuel/air mixture moves up the main well and across the discharge nozzle in the dual-booster venturi.

The main discharge nozzle passage is incorporated in the booster-venturi support that is a integral part of the carburetor body. Distribution tabs in the main venturi help to ensure equal distribution of the fuel/air mixture to all cylinders when the carburetor is used in conjunction with the original-equipment manifold.

Accelerator Pump—The accelerator pump is a spring-driven piston type in a cylinder in the bottom of the fuel bowl. The pump cylinder (cavity) fills through the center of the pump cup, loosely held onto the piston stem.

As the throttle lever is moved, the pump link operates through a series of levers. A pump drive spring pushes the pump piston down and seats the pump cup against the pump piston face so fuel can't escape into the bowl.

When the pump is not in operation, vapors or bubbles from fuel in the pump cavity escape around the piston stem through the floating piston cup inlet.

Power System—The power valve is either one- or two-stage, as required for specific vehicle-emission requirements. Some models have a gradient or smoothly varying power valve. Depending on application requirements, two power valves may be used: One actuated by manifold vacuum, the other mechanically actuated near WOT.

Choke System—The automatic choke system is controlled by a bimetal spring in a choke housing in the air horn.

When the engine starts, manifold vacuum applied to the choke diaphragm through a carburetor-body passage opens the choke valve to a preset vacuum qualifying position, called *choke kick*. A modulator spring gives correct initial choke opening after initial start in relation to outside temperature.

Manual-choke 1940s use a different air-horn casting. Some 1940s and all 1945s have divorced chokes. The 1946 has an electric choke.

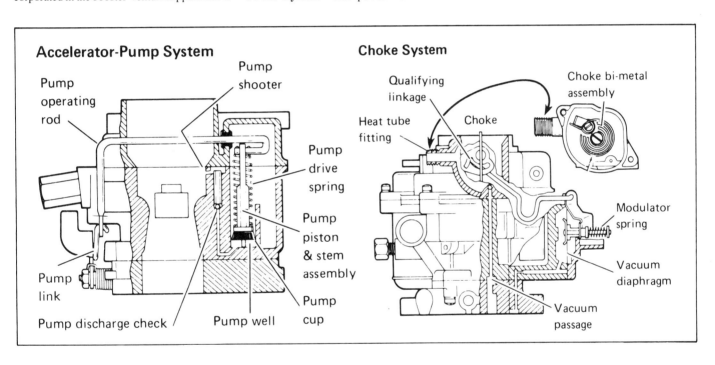

Accelerator-Pump System — Pump operating rod, Pump link, Pump discharge check, Pump shooter, Pump well, Pump drive spring, Pump piston & stem assembly, Pump cup

Choke System — Qualifying linkage, Heat tube fitting, Choke, Choke bi-metal assembly, Modulator spring, Vacuum diaphragm, Vacuum passage

4

SELECT & INSTALL YOUR CARBURETOR

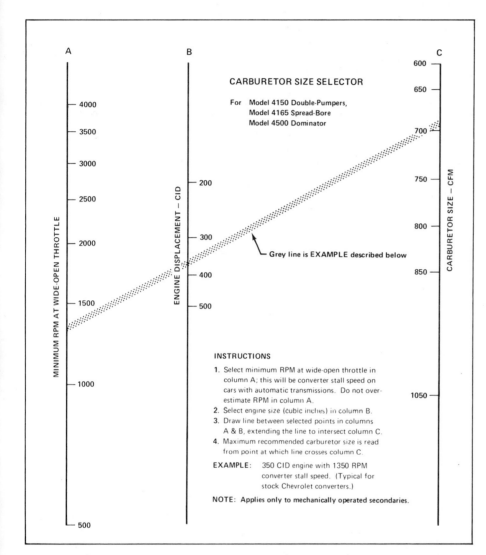

CARBURETOR SIZE SELECTOR

For Model 4150 Double-Pumpers,
Model 4165 Spread-Bore
Model 4500 Dominator

Grey line is EXAMPLE described below

INSTRUCTIONS

1. Select minimum RPM at wide-open throttle in column A; this will be converter stall speed on cars with automatic transmissions. Do not over-estimate RPM in column A.
2. Select engine size (cubic inches) in column B.
3. Draw line between selected points in columns A & B, extending the line to intersect column C.
4. Maximum recommended carburetor size is read from point at which line crosses column C.

EXAMPLE: 350 CID engine with 1350 RPM converter stall speed. (Typical for stock Chevrolet converters.)

NOTE: Applies only to mechanically operated secondaries.

When using this chart, keep a couple of points in mind. If your car has an automatic transmission, make sure you know the *converter stall speed* before using this chart. If in doubt, use the figure shown for a typical Chevrolet converter (1350 rpm). If using a modified converter for racing, make sure the stall speed is what you think it is.

If your car has a manual transmission, use the lowest rpm at which you use WOT. This must be a very conservative rpm (on the low side) and is found by observing your driving habits. Watch the tachometer! The heavier the vehicle and the lower the numerical axle ratio (higher gear ratio), then the lower this rpm must be.

With engines from 300—400 CID, the right choice usually works out to be a 650- to 700-cfm carburetor. A light car, such as a Camaro, Mustang or Duster may be able to use a 700- or 750-cfm unit, especially with a high numerical gear ratio (low gear ratio).

When in doubt, select a *smaller* carburetor size because it will typically give better acceleration times, even though power may fall off slightly at top rpm. You'll be satisfied with a smaller carburetor nearly every time!

Regardless of evidence to the contrary, a lot of carburetor buyers convince themselves that "bigger is better." Holley sells more large carburetors (800 and 850 cfm) because of the faulty logic that if a 650 is good, then an 850 must be that much better. Not true! Co-author Urich regularly gives this advice about airflow capacity: *"Don't buy it if you can't use it!"*

IMPROVED BREATHING INCREASES VE AND POWER

Stock passenger-car engines are fairly efficient air pumps up to 5000 rpm or slightly higher. And they provide a reasonably flat torque curve over this operating band. Pumping capabilities can be idealized (optimized) to provide better pumping within a narrower rpm band.

This is done by improving breathing. Reducing restrictions that cause pressure drop allows increased charge density to reach the cylinders. Typical improvements include:

- Carburetor changes (higher capacity).
- Intake-tract changes (manifold through the ports and valves).
- Exhaust system (headers or free-breathing mufflers).
- Valve timing (camshaft).

These design changes make a more efficient pump and optimize performance *at a particular rpm*.

But, there's a trade-off! Making the engine a better pump lifts the torque peak and the entire torque curve to a higher-rpm band. Then you can expect lower-rpm performance to be *reduced* accordingly.

Not all engines can be improved for higher performance (better breathing) without extensive modifications. In many cases the designers purposely optimized low-rpm performance. They used:

- Small-venturi carburetor.
- Tiny intake manifold and/or cylinder-head passages and ports.
- Small valves actuated by short-duration camshafts with lazy action.
- Low compression.
- Combustion-chamber design.
- Restricted exhaust systems.

Truck engines, low-performance passenger-car engines and industrial engines are good examples of these design characteristics.

As you may have heard, "You can't make a race horse out of a mule." Keep such factors in mind when selecting a carburetor. It is difficult—if not impossible—to upgrade engine performance with built-in restrictions.

If the engine is restricted so peak power occurs at 4000 rpm, don't select a carburetor to feed that engine at 6000—7000. *The engine will never run at those speeds.* A too-large carburetor will only worsen the previously available performance.

UNPACKING YOUR CARBURETOR

If you are buying your carburetor in a store,

unpack it before you pay for it. Look at the *inside* of the box. Note whether one side shows damage from carburetor movement. If so, check that side of the carb very carefully. Look it over slowly and thoroughly to make sure there is no shipping damage. Don't make a hurried examination.

Holley packaging engineers constantly improve packaging, but their best efforts are wasted when freight is mishandled. The *outside* of a carton may look perfectly intact while the contents are damaged.

Inspection—Visually inspect the carburetor. Hold the carburetor as you operate the throttle lever to make sure the throttles open fully and close without binding or sticking. A bent throttle lever can occur. When it does, the throttles may remain partly open (not return fully to idle or fast-idle position) when the lever is actuated. Is it all there? Are any parts missing? The instruction sheet may provide illustrations that will help in your inspection.

If the carburetor doesn't appear to be exactly right, don't buy that one. Ask to see another one and then check it out exactly the same way.

If your carburetor came through the mail, by United Parcel Service or some other delivery method, inspect it immediately when it arrives. Open the box and make sure it is the *correct* carburetor. That *is* important, as the wrong carburetor may have been shipped. Then check it thoroughly.

Manually operate the throttle lever and choke mechanism, checking for binding or other malfunction. Also, make a visual inspection of the carburetor, looking for missing parts, bent levers, or any shipping damage.

If there's a problem, proceed carefully if you try to fix it. If it is simple—such as a bent throttle lever—you may be able to remedy the problem easier than returning the unit. However-

er, if the casting has been damaged or if a shaft is bent, the carburetor must be replaced.

The firm you bought the carburetor from will replace it. Find out what the supplier requires *before sending it back for replacement*. In some instances, damage claims must be settled between yourself and the freight company (called *the carrier*). In other cases, the supplier takes care of this for you. Do not send the carburetor

to Holley. Warranty claims can only be handled by the dealer.

Timely Ordering—Order the carburetor *early*. It may not be obvious, but one of the first things to remember in building your engine is to get the correct parts together. Then assemble and test the car before setting impossible dates for completion and first competition attempts. Many cars don't show up at major events because the builder was over-optimistic about the amount of time required. The owner loses an expensive entry fee and misses the race.

It is possible the supplier may not have the unit you need in stock. He could have just sold the last one and be waiting for a new shipment to arrive. Or, the unit you require may be so popular that the factory temporarily cannot supply enough carburetors.

So, order your carburetor early—ahead of when you absolutely must have it. If you wait until the day before you have to race or use the car, you could end up buying the wrong carburetor. This means you will buy the right one later on, or use a carburetor not precisely right for your application.

Get the other pieces you need at the same time: fuel lines, fuel pump, spacer or adapter, studs and nuts, extra gaskets and jets, air cleaner, tubing wrench, new fittings and a fuel filter.

BEFORE INSTALLING YOUR CARBURETOR

Inspection—Really scrutinize the carburetor when you take it out of the box. Make sure the carburetor operates easily and opens to full throttle on both primary and secondary barrels. It should return easily to idle. Throttle shafts are equipped with adjustable stops. Throttle levers should return to rest against their adjustment screws when the choke is open, not against the throttle bores. Make sure there are no missing parts or bent levers.

Screw Check—Check for loose screws attaching the top of the carburetor or float bowls and

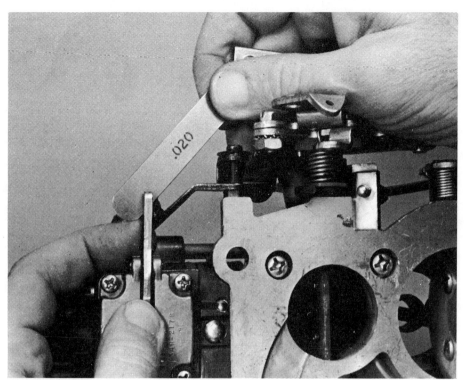

Essential pre-installation checks for each accelerator pump on carburetors with removable fuel bowls: (1) no clearance between the actuating-lever screw and the diaphragm lever at curb idle, (2) at WOT you should be able to move the diaphragm lever to allow inserting a 0.014—0.020-in. feeler gage as shown.

screws holding the accelerator-pump shooter/s. Also check the screws holding the castings together. Gaskets compress after they've been installed. It is important to check the screws so there will not be any fuel or air leakage when the carburetor is installed. Don't use too much force—anyone can strip threads by applying too much torque to the screws.

Hose Fittings—When you unpack the carburetor you will notice that some or all of the hose fittings are closed with rubber shipping plugs. These can be left installed when no hose will be attached to that fitting.

If the 3/8-in. PCV fitting extending from the rear of the base isn't used, replace it with a shipping plug or a piece of hose plugged at one end. Either must be clamped onto the fitting so a backfire won't blow it off. Or, close the tube with epoxy.

Don't use rubber componds like Silastic RTV to seal this fitting because gasoline turns them to jelly.

Disassembly For Checking—If you plan to take the carb apart to look at its insides, expect to replace bowl and metering block gaskets because these are usually destroyed by disassembly. Put the carb back together immediately upon finishing your inspection.

You will need new gaskets, spray-on gasket remover and a lot of patience. This is not a 5-minute job. Expect to spend at least an hour carefully removing the old gaskets from the metering block/s and fuel bowl/s.

Run Carb Before Changing It—In general, bolt on the carburetor and run it *before making any changes!* Chances are the carburetor will be very close to correct. Start with what Holley engineers have found to work successfully. They produce thousands of carburetors every year—for all kinds of applications.

Accelerator-Pump Check—Where pumps are in removable fuel bowls, check for correct accelerator-pump adjustment. Open the throttle wide, then move the diaphragm lever by hand. This 2-1/8-in. long lever pivots in the pump-cover casting. The lever must have an additional 0.015—0.020-in. travel at WOT throttle so the pump doesn't bottom in its housing. This ensures the throttle won't stick open because of excessive friction of the pump-operating lever against the plastic cam.

Also check that the pump-operating lever contacts the plastic cam at one end and the diaphragm lever at the other at idle. You should be able to wiggle the diaphragm lever back and forth slightly (horizontally) with your fingers. The slightest throttle movement should be transmitted through the pump lever, causing

the diaphragm lever to move.

The only exception: When a green cam is used, check for 0.010-in. clearance at WOT.

REPLACING YOUR CARBURETOR

Have a notebook and pencil handy for making sketches or notes of what you are taking apart. This is the mark of a professional. Keep track of what has happened so you won't have to guess on reassembly:

Air Cleaner—Remove the air cleaner, carefully detaching any vacuum lines to the cleaner and marking them with masking tape so they can be reassembled correctly. Cover the top of the carburetor with a rag or masking tape. You don't want spare nuts or other pieces falling into it.

Recommendation: Before proceeding, tag and number all vacuum hoses and other lines. This will help during installation. Remove the existing carburetor as follows but be aware that not all items apply to every application.

Fuel Line—Remove steel fuel-line fitting carefully because you'll probably reuse it. A fuel-line wrench that contacts four nut flats should be used. These are called *flare-nut* or *tubing* wrenches.

Fuel-line nuts are soft and tend to round off instead of turning. When this happens you will have to wreck the nut by using Vise-Grip pliers. To replace the nut requires cutting the fuel line very close to the end of the tubing. Cutting and reflaring requires a tubing cutter and a flaring tool. Rent them from an auto-parts house or hardware store.

Getting the line off the engine to allow this work requires disconnecting the fuel line at the fuel pump. If the nut at the carburetor rounded off, the same wrench is sure to round off the one on the fuel pump. So, buy a tubing wrench before taking off the fuel-pump fitting or you may have to create an entire new fuel line. The correct wrench is cheaper in the long run.

Seal the open end of the fuel line with masking tape or a clean, lint-free cloth so no foreign particles can enter.

Throttle Linkage—Disconnect throttle linkage, automatic-transmission controls and cruise controls from throttle lever. Save any retaining clips. Take off throttle-return spring/s and note anchor points for correct reassembly.

PCV Hose—Disconnect PCV hose, if it's attached to carburetor.

Vacuum Lines—Disconnect distributor spark hose/s, labeling these to keep vacuum and timed-spark hoses separate for correct reinstallation. Disconnect any other manifold vacuum hoses connected to the carburetor.

Other Hoses—Disconnect fresh-air hose and label it. Remove and label any other hoses such as gulp-valve hose (for air-injection-equipped cars) and connections to power brakes and so forth. Keep dirt out of all the hoses and lines you've removed.

Choke Linkage—Detach choke linkage at carburetor, noting whether it pulls or pushes to close the choke plate.

Remove Fasteners—Remove nuts and/or bolts and lockwashers attaching carburetor to manifold. Move any cable brackets out of the way. If you drop any nut, lockwasher, cotter key, piece of linkage or whatever, STOP! Find and recover it *before* proceeding.

Observe and note the position of any brackets held on the engine by the carburetor-attachment hardware. Lay these aside so they will not fall into the manifold when the carburetor is pulled off. Before you lift the carburetor, check carefully. Make sure nothing loose can fall into the manifold . . . such as a nut, bolt, fitting, cotter key or whatever.

Lift Carburetor—Carefully `pull carburetor off manifold. If it sticks, tap each side gently with a rubber or plastic mallet. Stuff a rag into the intake manifold opening/s. Clean the intake-manifold mounting pad thoroughly. Take care to keep gasket pieces out of the manifold.

INSTALL CARBURETOR

Install the new carburetor as follows, but be aware that not all steps apply to every application and installation.

New Studs—Install any new studs. Use the jammed double-nut technique to screw in the studs with a wrench. Use Loctite on studs.

Manifold Gasket—Install manifold-flange gasket. If a metal heat shield protects the carburetor base from exhaust gases in the heat-riser passage, place a thick (0.080-in.) manifold-flange gasket under the steel heat shield. No gasket is used between the shield and the carburetor. Pay attention to the gasket combination used by the automobile manufacturer. Duplicate it as nearly as possible.

Idle Solenoid—Sometimes the instructions ask you to transfer the idle solenoid and other items from the original carburetor to the new one. These may include linkage ball connections or lever extensions. If the original throttle lever has a non-removable ball, a corresponding ball will be in the loose parts supplied with the carburetor. These are in a plastic bag.

Adapting to the Installation—Some items on the new carburetor may have to be removed to adapt it to a particular application. Examples include a Chrysler-type throttle-lever extension on some two-barrel and four-barrel carburetors with universal throttle linkage. This must be removed to use the carburetor on Chevrolet or Ford installations.

Carburetor Base Gasket—One of the easiest ways to prevent manifold leaks is to check the carburetor base gasket. Hold it against the manifold flange. There should be adequate clamping area to hold the gasket. Make sure all openings match up. If the gasket is correct for the manifold, hold it against the carburetor base to

Throttle and transmission linkages, smog equipment connections and so forth are complex. Make a sketch BEFORE you take the manifold and/or carburetor off. Tag lines and connections with tape to identify each. Use any tactic necessary to help your memory: photos, drawings or sketches.

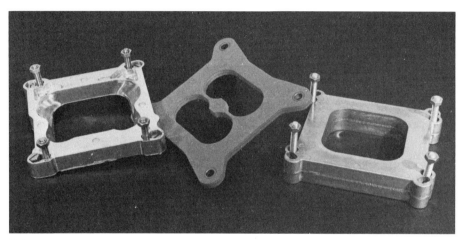

Holley adapters mate carburetor flanges to different manifold stud/bore patterns. Adapters must be used in some instances. Avoid flow losses by using a manifold with the matching stud/bore pattern for the carburetor. Holley Adapter 17-6 at left puts spread-bore onto square-flange manifold or vice versa. Center heat insulator gasket for Z manifolds, Holley 108-18, is 1/4-in. thick. Adapter at right, Holley 17-27, adapts square-flange carbs to spread-bore manifolds or serves as a 1-in. spacer for square-flange carbs.

STACKING GASKETS

Avoid gasket stacks or packs. These compress unevenly and the carburetor base can warp, binding the throttle shaft. They can cause a corner of the throttle base (mounting flange) to break off. Use the gasket supplied with the carburetor. Always use a thin gasket such as the 0.025-in. one supplied by Holley with a diaphragm-secondary carburetor. No gasket sealer is required if the carburetor base and manifold flange are clean and flat.

Don't stack gaskets to get clearance for lever operation, regardless of how badly you want to get your engine running. Do it right or you could end up buying an entire new car-

buretor body or throttle base.

These parts are not ordinarily stocked by even the largest dealers, and there is often a long wait for pieces to reassemble your carburetor. If the throttle body is not a separate part, you will have to buy a new carburetor because the main body is not sold as a replacement part.

If you need additional clearance to install a carburetor with a high-capacity accelerator pump, make a 1/4-in.-thick aluminum spacer and use a thin gasket on top of the spacer and one on the bottom. Spacers are available from Holley, too.

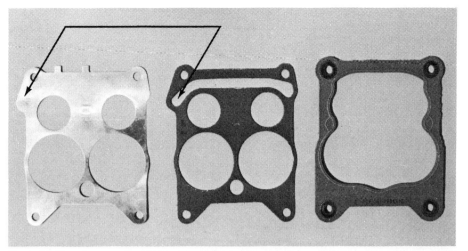

Heat shield surface marked TOP goes against carburetor base. This is Holley 108-20 or GM 3884576 (baffle). Center gasket, Holley 108-15 or GM 3884574, fits between heat shield and manifold flange. Arrowed sections must mate or there will be an exhaust leak. This arrangement was used on Chevrolets through 1969. In 1970 the heat shield was eliminated. Gasket/spacer at right, Holley 108-25 or GM 3998912 has bushings around stud holes.

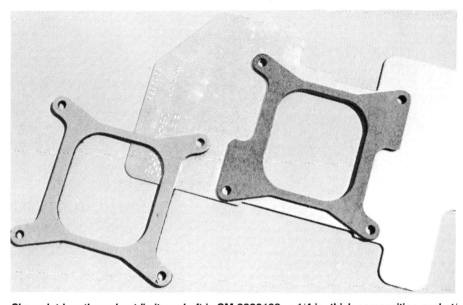

Chevrolet has these heat limiters: Left is GM 3999198, a 1/4-in.-thick composition gasket/spacer. Aluminum heat shield GM 3969835 for square-flange Holleys is at right. GM 3969837 (not shown) is an aluminum heat shield for a spread-bore. Both have attached gaskets to give 1/4-in. thickness. Cutouts clear 3310 and Chevrolet and Holley double-pumpers. Use a 1/4-in. spacer between carburetor base and shield for high-capacity accelerator pumps. Any gasket/spacer must have openings that *don't restrict* throttle bores or throttle operation.

expensive and time-consuming.

Vacuum-operated secondary throttles may never open if the base is warped by overtightening during installation. Hold the throttle wide open and operate the secondaries by hand. Make sure they open easily against the spring and close freely by spring action. If you fail to check this point, the secondaries may never work and you'll never get the performance you paid for.

Linkages—Connect throttle and transmission linkage. Attach throttle-return spring. Operate linkage to ensure nothing binds as the throttle is fully opened and then closed. With the choke held wide open, make sure the throttle returns to idle without sticking or binding

Make sure the levers don't hit anything when the throttle linkage is actuated from idle to WOT. Have a friend actuate the linkage with the foot pedal as you observe the linkage. See for yourself whether the throttle plates are 100% open in both the primary and secondary barrels.

Don't try to make this check by operating the throttle with your hand at the carburetor or by looking at what the levers *appear* to be doing. Slack or play in the linkage may allow full throttle when moved at the carburetor, but give less than full throttle when the foot pedal is depressed.

If foot-pedal movement doesn't give full throttle, examine the linkage to see what minor changes or adjustments may be needed in the linkage connecting to the carburetor. Don't change the linkage or levers on the carburetor itself. Simple adjustments are usually provided on the vehicle cable housing or linkage rods.

Don't think checking for full throttle is only for amateurs. Experts have been tripped up on this point . . . whether they admit it or not.

Check both the pump and the throttle levers to make sure nothing is in the way. Sometimes you'll have to install a spacer to clear high-capacity accelerator pump/s. Install the air cleaner and make sure it doesn't hit any portion

see if it fits the throttle bores, mounting holes and base shape. Place gasket on manifold.

Carb on Manifold—Place carburetor on manifold and add any brackets held in place by the attachment hardware. These may include throttle linkage, transmission kickdown, cruise control and solenoid brackets if such are used. Start the fuel line nut/s into the carburetor. Tighten them. Install nuts and/or bolts and tighten them gently against the carburetor flange. Then cross-tighten the bolts/nuts alternately to 5—7 ft-lb torque. This is not much force!

Overtightening can cause a warped throttle body. This will bind the throttle shafts so throttle action is stiff. In the worst case, overtightening may snap off a corner of the base. That *is*

of the linkage. Operate hand choke to check whether any clearance problem exists.

WARNING: Any binding or interference could cause the throttle to stick during operation and could result in a loss of throttle control (uncontrolled engine speed). This check should be made by operating the accelerator pedal from inside the vehicle.

Choke Linkage—Install choke linkage for divorced choke. Hold throttle lever partially open and activate the choke manually to make sure it operates freely. If the choke is electrical, make all the necessary connections. If the choke is integral, attach the necessary lines from the manifold.

Hoses—Reconnect appropriate hoses to carburetor. Transfer any additional fittings from the old carburetor if needed. Temporarily plug vacuum hose to air cleaner. Any vacuum connections on the carburetor which are not used should be closed with rubber plugs or caps.

Fuel Line—Flush fuel line to ensure no foreign particles enter the carburetor. Disconnect primary wire to coil (it's the small one connected to the + terminal) and insulate its end with a piece of tape so it won't spark. Hold a can under the open end of the fuel line and catch the fuel as you crank the engine several revolutions with the starter.

Connect fuel line to carburetor or fuel-line assembly. In some instances a minor bend in the fuel line may be needed. Or, you may have to shorten the fuel line and reflare the end.

If possible, install an in-line fuel filter to keep dirt out of your new carburetor.

Air-Cleaner Stud—Remove air-cleaner stud from old carburetor and install it in the new one, or use one provided with the carburetor.

HEAT INSULATION
Any time you can insulate the carburetor from engine heat, do it! Holley has several heat-insulator/spacers to consider. Holley 108-37 is an 11/16-in.-thick phenolic spacer for spread-bores, and 108-51 and -53 are for Model 4150/60. The 108-52 is for Model 2300. Others are shown on the following pages.

Check For Fuel Leaks—Set the parking brake and block the drive wheels to prevent any vehicle movement. Crank the engine or turn on the electric fuel pump to fill the carburetor with fuel. Check the fuel-inlet fitting/s for leaks. Tighten fittings to eliminate any leaks.

First Start—Reconnect the coil's primary wire, make sure the vehicle is in Neutral or Park, and ensure that it's safe to start the engine. Block the drive wheels and make sure the area in front and behind the vehicle is clear.

AIR LEAKAGE & IDLE SPEED
Any intake-system air leak affects idle speed and quality. Air leaks are caused by worn valve guides, worn throttle-shaft bores in the carburetor, holes in any hose connected to intake-manifold vacuum, and non-sealing gaskets where the manifold joins the cylinder head or carburetor. Leaks in any component attached to the manifold—vacuum motors, power-brake accumulators, and so forth can also cause problems.

Now, start the engine. Depress the accelerator pedal to floor and allow it to return. This charges the manifold with fuel and sets the choke and fast idle. With foot off accelerator pedal, crank engine until it fires. Repeat the previous two steps as required.

Flooded?—If carburetor floods over, there may be dirt in the needle-and-seat assembly.

If flooding continues, stop to correct cause. First try tapping the carburetor lightly with a screwdriver handle. If flooding doesn't stop, remove the fuel line and take off the carburetor top or float bowl.

Check float setting. If it's OK, chances are there is dirt under the needle. If the needle and seat are separate items pull the needle out of the seat and blow the seat with compressed air from both sides. If the needle and seat assembly is not a take-apart type, unscrew the entire needle and seat from the float bowl and agitate the assembly in solvent, then blow it dry with compressed air.

Setting Fast-Idle—Read the accompanying sidebar for precautions to take when setting fast-idle speed. This is usually adequate for most vehicles. If a particular application requires adjustment, use the following procedure. With a fully warmed engine running, advance throttle and place fast-idle cam so screw contacts top step of cam. On this step, set fast idle at approximately 1700—1900 rpm.

If your vehicle has T.C.S. (Transmission Controlled Spark advance) fast-idle speed adjustment is made with no vacuum advance and in Neutral. When the engine is cold, there will be vacuum advance and the speed may be too fast. Make changes to get it where it suits you.

Setting Idle Speed—Again, read the accompanying sidebar for precautions to take when setting idle speed. Set idle speed according to the decal in the engine compartment. On automatic-transmission-equipped cars the idle speed is usually set *with the parking brake on* and the transmission in Drive. On manual transmissions, put in Neutral and set the parking brake. Start the engine and check for vacuum and/or fuel leaks. Correct as necessary—temporarily plug vacuum hose to air cleaner.

Don't remove the idle-limiter caps. Idle-mixture screws are factory-preset for proper

emission values. Engine differences may necessitate slight adjustments to obtain a smooth idle.

NOTE: It's easier to make idle settings with the air cleaner removed, but to ensure final readings are correct, they should be taken with the air cleaner installed. If there is a throttle solenoid, set curb-idle speed by adjusting nut on the end of the solenoid (solenoid energized). Set the kill idle speed by adjusting the idle-speed screw on the carburetor with the solenoid de-energized. See under-hood decal for idle rpm and mixture setting.

Set Timing & Dwell—Before making final adjustments on the carburetor, check the ignition timing and dwell. Reset if required. Disconnect and plug the distributor vacuum line during this operation and reconnect the hose when completed. With the engine at normal operating temperature, place the transmission in Drive and adjust the hot-idle speed to the rpm indicated on the decal.

Air Cleaner—Install the air cleaner stud (provided). Install the air cleaner gasket (provided). Mark the stud 1/2 in. above the air cleaner and remove and cut any excess with a hacksaw. Reinstall the stud with Loctite. Connect the manifold vacuum to the air-cleaner connection. Connect any other air-cleaner hoses.

GET ACQUAINTED

Once you have installed your carburetor, live with the new combination for a few days before beginning any tuning efforts. Naturally you will want to set the idle correctly (to exact specifications if your car has emission-control devices), check the ignition timing with a timing light and make sure the spark plugs, points, cap and wires are all in tip-top shape.

By driving the car, you will learn what you have—a baseline condition. If you are drag racing, get your times consistent by working on your driving technique *before* you start tuning. There are enough variables without adding inconsistent driving. This is especially important if you have changed from an air-valve-secondary carburetor (such as a Q-Jet) or a vacuum-operated-secondary carburetor, to a double-pumper with a mechanical-secondary linkage.

More tuning details are provided in the Carburetor and Performance chapter.

CHECKING FUEL LEVELS OR FLOAT SETTINGS

Installing the carburetor and pumping fuel to it is the only easy way to check whether the needle/seat will seal correctly. Turning the carburetor upside down and blowing into the fuel inlet is not an adequate test. Your lungs cannot develop as much pressure as the fuel pump.

When the carburetor is installed and the engine is started, see if there is any flooding into the manifold. If there is no seepage or flooding into the throttle bores, chances are the fuel level is OK. If the carburetor doesn't have externally adjustable inlet valves and sight plugs, test drive the car. If it drives normally without dying at stops, the fuel level is probably fine. If the fuel level is too high, fuel spilling into the throttle bore/s will cause the engine to die at stops or after severe braking.

High-performance Holley carburetors have the advantage of externally adjustable inlet valves. Fuel-level sight plugs allow checking and setting fuel levels without taking the carburetor apart or taking it off of the engine.

Setting Fuel Level—If the engine has a mechanical fuel pump, lower the fuel level by loosening one bowl screw and allowing some fuel to leak out into a container (soda can cut in half) or a shop rag. Retighten the screw. Then run the engine to see whether the fuel level returns and stays where it is supposed to be.

Adjust the inlet valve so the level is just *below* the point where it would spill through the sight-plug hole. Check to see it stays there. Then raise the level until the fuel just spills through the plug hole. That way, you know the inlet valve is holding and the level is correct.

With an electrical pump, turn on the pump without running the engine. Make sure the inlet valves are holding and not "creeping." Then run the engine to make sure the level stays where it should. Be sure to reinstall the sight plugs after checking levels.

Warning: Don't drive the car without reinstalling the sight plugs!

The main problems with fuel-level changes are caused by the rough handling during shipping. Jarring forces can bend the tabs that establish the float/needle relationship. We've even seen float-bumper springs dislodged from the underside of floats.

Once a carburetor is installed on a car, the fuel level established by the float setting seldom changes. This means the simple task of level setting is usually a one-time operation with occasional checking to make sure it is still OK.

Don't raise or lower the fuel level except to get it to specification. It has been factory-calibrated for cornering, turns, spin outs, brake stops and accelerations. **Float levels are most critical with high G-loadings because those affect fuel handling.**

Slosh problems in the fuel bowls are severe. Just imagine trying to hold a cup of coffee in a car without sloshing during a burnout or a panic stop! That should give you some idea of what happens inside the carburetor fuel bowl/s. The only time the float level might be changed would be for drags or super-speedway use. The secondary level might be raised slightly, but expect brake-stop stalls as the result.

Avoid taking off the bowl cover or carburetor top on any carburetor with a built-in vacuum-piston for the power valve—unless you have a replacement gasket handy. If you take the top off and the gasket tears, the power valve may be constantly *held open*.

When a carburetor is being assembled and disassembled for calibration purposes, it is common practice to apply talcum powder to both sides of the gasket so sticking won't occur. Then use a new gasket when you are ready to reassemble the carburetor permanently. That will prevent dangerous fuel leaks.

BLUEPRINTING HOLLEY CARBURETORS

"Blueprinting" has become an important word in the enthusiast's vocabulary. As applied to an engine, it means correctly relating all parts of a production engine by matching and mating, balancing and rematching. The goal is to get the combination into a near-perfect state suitable for performance application. Blueprinting is often done on brand-new engines. This attention to detail can provide impressive performance improvement as an immediate payoff for the time and care invested in the project.

Blueprinting is now applied to the precise preparation and rebuilding of any engine or chassis component. But, it is a mistake to use the word or concept in relation to a Holley high-performance original-equipment or production-replacement carburetor. Tearing a new carburetor apart and attacking it with drills, trick linkages and so forth is like overhauling a new watch or micrometer when you first get it—something you probably wouldn't consider

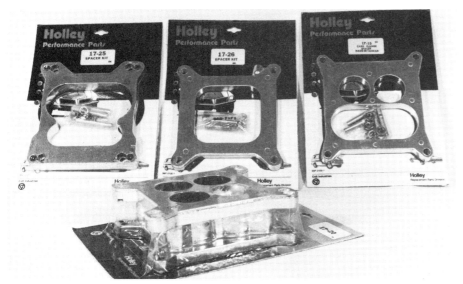

Popular adapters and spacers: 1/2-in. 17-25 (left) fits square-bore and spread-bore patterns, adapting between the two. 17-26 (middle) is an 1/2-in. spacer for square-bore pattern carburetors and manifold flanges. 17-15 (right) is required for 460-CID Fords when adaping Model 4150/60/80 to Ford Model 4300D manifolds. 17-20 (front) is 2-in. spacer to raise Model 4150/60/80 carbs above manifold flange.

doing. There is too much chance of ruining it and voiding the guarantee.

Carburetors are precisely made. They must accurately meter fuel and air into the engine. *They have to be correct before they are shipped.* Every carburetor to be used as original or replacement equipment on a production automobile must pass computer-controlled tests that check whether that individual carburetor performs. These tests ensure it will provide correct performance and low emissions when it is installed. If the carburetor is "out of spec," any "blueprinting" must be done by Holley before it is shipped. This requirement is law.

Production techniques have been developed over years of carburetor making. Each unit must work right when an automobile manufacturer, or an automotive enthusiast, bolts one onto an engine. Regardless of what you may have read to the contrary, very little needs to be done, or can be done, to one of these precise devices to "make it better" before you use it. Trick changes or special assembly techniques are not required to make the carburetor right for high performance. These would be incorporated and fully tested before the design was released to one of the Holley manufacturing plants.

Numerous magazine articles every year point out "fixes" to be made to new or used carburetors for more performance. Almost without exception, these have been tried at Holley's engineering labs and in field tests. And they are discarded as being unworkable or not generally applicable. Using care in selecting, installing and tuning your carburetor is the best

"trick" to get the utmost performance and satisfaction from it.

WHICH CARBURETOR IS RIGHT FOR YOUR ENGINE?

Enough different Holley carburetors are available as aftermarket models so almost any engine can be mated with a correct carburetor for the engine and application.

Some builders fall in love with a certain Holley size, such as the 850 cfm and disregard all other sizes. A larger or smaller carburetor might be correct for a particular application. Different types of carburetors are built because there are different kinds and sizes of engines. Their requirements are not the same. Holley would certainly prefer to build fewer types if this could be done and still match the needs of the engines that will use them.

It's obvious from outside appearance that many carburetors look quite similar. But, the mechanical secondary, vacuum secondary, double pumper, single pumper, non-pullover discharge nozzle with check valve just under it, rubber-type pump-inlet valve, ball pump-inlet valve, side-hung and center-hung float, and so on are all variations born of specific needs.

This may not be obvious if you are not a manufacturer, but every change costs money to design, to build and supply. So, these pieces exist for a reason. After you have read this book, the reasons will be easier to understand. You'll be right at home when you specify a particular carburetor for your own or a friend's engine.

Fuel Supply System—Read that chapter for

important details on fuel lines, fuel filters and fuel pumps.

Adapters—A carburetor should be installed directly onto its manifold without an adapter. Adapters don't usually provide optimum airflow characteristics. Many reduce the carburetor's flow capacity. It's best to buy a carburetor that fits the manifold to be used. It is sometimes possible to drill and tap the manifold to fit a slightly different stud pattern.

In the case of a four-barrel manifold with "standard" or "square" pattern, the double-pumper or a vacuum-secondary carburetor should be used. If the manifold is designed for a spread-bore pattern, the 4165, 4175 or 4360 can be used. An adapter may raise the carburetor so a special air cleaner or a hood "bump" will be required to gain hood clearance. And, an adapter can create problems with choke linkage, fuel-line attachment and fuel mixture distribution.

Heat Insulators/Spacers—Anytime you can insulate the carburetor from heat, do it! Holley has several insulator/spacers to consider. Holley 108-37 is an 11/16-in.-thick phenolic spacer for spread-bores. 108-51 and -53 are for Model 4150/60. 108-52 is for Model 2300. Others are shown on the following pages.

Spacers—These are often used to raise the carburetor on the manifold for better mixture distribution and improved power output. A spacer or heat insulator may raise the carburetor so a special air cleaner or a hood "bump" will be required to gain hood clearance. Throttle, choke linkage and fuel-line attachment must also be considered.

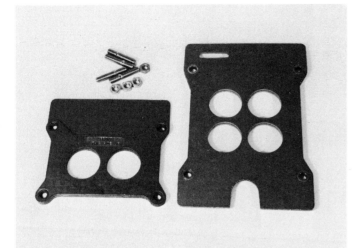
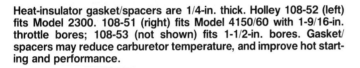

Heat-insulator gasket/spacers are 1/4-in. thick. Holley 108-52 (left) fits Model 2300. 108-51 (right) fits Model 4150/60 with 1-9/16-in. throttle bores; 108-53 (not shown) fits 1-1/2-in. bores. Gasket/spacers may reduce carburetor temperature, and improve hot starting and performance.

Have the correct gaskets before taking your Model 2300/05, 4150/60/80 carburetor apart! Holley's no-leak gaskets self-destruct on disassembly! Expect to spend 30 minutes or more cleaning off the old gasket with gasket remover.

GASKETS FOR MODELS 2300, 4150/4160, 4165/4175 & 4500

Several metering block, metering plate and fuel bowl gaskets are used for these carburetors. Few are interchangeable. Before disassembling your carburetor, get a complete set of new gaskets. Holley Performance Parts Catalog lists correct gasket numbers for most popular carburetors. Holley Illustrated Parts & Specs Manual lists gasket and Renew repair kit numbers for all Holley carburetors. Some Renew kits contain more than one type of gasket so one kit services several carburetor numbers.

Holley's current gaskets are adhesive-treated for improved sealing, so expect the gaskets to be destroyed when you disassemble the carburetor. Extra effort is required to disassemble carburetors with these gaskets. Cleaning off the remaining portions of adhesive-treated gaskets is not easy.

Use a spray cleaner such as CRC or Permatex Gasket Remover. These dissolving sprays strip old gaskets by dissolving the cements or binders that hold the material together. The sprays are powerful, so don't use them near any paint or plastics. Take care to mask off any surfaces you want to protect and read any precautions on the can about protecting your skin or lungs.

Directions for use are on the can. Most Holley bowl and metering-block gaskets require several spray applications, with a 5- to 10-minute wait after spraying before scraping off the gasket with a putty knife.

Be extremely careful to keep gasket residue out of the fuel and air-bleed holes in the metering blocks and fuel bowls. Wash the parts with water after using the gasket remover.

If you can save enough of the gasket to make a comparison with the new ones, that's a good idea. Be sure to replace the gaskets with the correct new ones.

To make gasket selection less confusing, the available gaskets are shown here with information on their general use. Locator pins on the metering blocks help line up the gasket and metering-block or fuel-bowl openings. If the gasket looks like it doesn't fit, flop it over and try it the other way.

SORTING OUT GASKETS

Throttle bores of square-flange Holley four-barrels range from 1-3/16—1-3/4 in. Spread-bore 4165/4175s have 1-3/8-in. primary and 2-in. secondary bores. The 4360 has 1-3/8-in. primary and 1-7/16-in. secondary bores.

Always check a new gasket against carburetor base. Make sure it doesn't hang into throttle bores to act as a restrictor or obstruct throttle operation. Some GM manifolds have heat tracks to warm the carburetor base with exhaust gas—others do not. The following info from the Chevrolet Parts Book and Holley's Performance Parts Catalog may help with your application.

Square-Flange Holleys—To mount on manifolds with heat tracks (through 1969). Use Holley 108-11 gasket with GM 3884575 0.010-inch stainless-steel heat shield.

For manifolds without a heat track, use Holley 108-10 or thin gasket (0.020-in.) for vacuum-secondary carburetors. A thin gasket won't compress much, so there is little chance of warping the base when tightening the flange nuts. Holley 108-14 can be used with mechanical-secondary carburetors if care is used in tightening so you don't warp the base.

Holley (Non-Spread-Bore)—For 1970 and later small-blocks use Holley 108-12, 5/16-in.-thick heat-insulator/spacer gasket. Or install Holley 108-51 or -53 1/4-in.-thick heat-insulator/spacer gasket. You could use GM 3999198 1/4-in.-thick hard-composition insulator/gasket.

Aluminum Heat Shields—For Holleys (any square-flange except 4500s). Use GM 3969835, 7 x 13 in., 1/4-in. thick at gasket area. Added 1/4-in. spacer (Holley 108-51, GM 3999198) required, or cutout if using high-capacity accelerator pump/s. A similar heat shield for spread-bores is GM 3969837.

Shield for 4165/4175 or 4360 with integral 1/4-in.-thick gasket area is GM 3969837. Requires cutout or 1/4-in. spacer GM 3998912 to clear high-capacity accelerator pump at rear of 4165.

Holley 4165/4175 or 4360—If replacing Quadrajet thru 1969 models, use Holley 108-20, 0.010-in. stainless-steel heat shield or GM 3884576 (baffle) against carburetor base. Holley 108-15 or GM 3884574 between heat shield and manifold flange.

If replacing Q-Jet on 1970 and later models, use Holley 108-25. It's a gasket with phenolic bushings around stud openings, or install GM 3998912.

GASKET ASSORTMENTS

These assortments cover popular Holley four-barrels. Each pack contains the number included (in parentheses) and gasket type.

Pack #	Contents
108-200	(2) 108-29
	(2) 108-33
108-201	(1) 108-29
	(1) 108-33
	(1) 108-30
	(1) 108-27
108-202	(1) 108-33
	(1) 108-31
	(1) 108-30
	(1) 108-27
108-203	(2) 108-32
	(2) 108-31
108-204	(1) 108-32
	(1) 108-31
	(1) 108-29
	(1) 108-27

(1) 108-13—Secondary metering-plate gasket for Model 4160 Chrysler and outboard Model 2300 on some 3 x 2 applications with diaphragm-operated throttles.

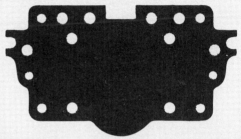

(2) 108-27—Secondary metering-plate gasket for some Model 4160s.

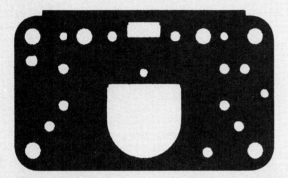

(3) 108-28—Primary metering-block gasket for Model 4160 Chrysler applications beginning in 1968

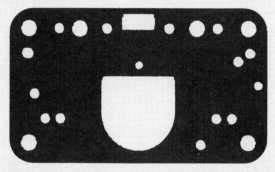

(4) 108-29—Primary metering-block gasket for most Model 4150s, some 4160s, early 4165 and most 2300 carburetors. Also used as secondary metering-block gasket on double-pumpers. Not used with accelerator-pump transfer tube. Also used for Model 4500s without an intermediate system. A similar gasket with idle-channel slots was discontinued because Holley's new gasket material eliminated swelling that was typical of old-style gaskets.

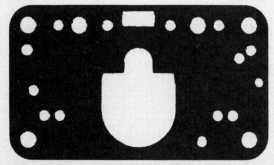

(5) 108-31—Used on same carburetors as 108-29 when equipped with accelerator-pump transfer tube. Used on all 4165/75s and a few 4150 carburetors. Used on primary side of some 4160s. Not interchangeable with 108-29, but a -31 can be made from a 108-29 by cutting half circle for the transfer tube.

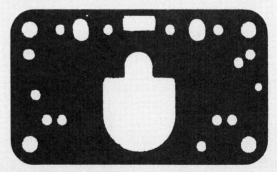

(6) 108-35—Metering-block gasket for Model 2300, List 6425 650-cfm two-barrel.

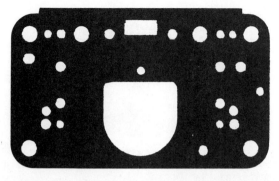

(7) 108-36—Primary and secondary metering-block gasket for Model 4500s with intermediate systems, such as List 6214 and 6464.

(8) 108-55—Primary metering-block gasket for Model 4180.

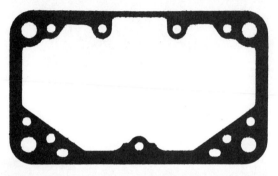

(9) 108-32—Fuel-bowl gasket for all Model 4165 and some 4150, 4160 (primary side) and 2300. Primary-bowl gasket for 4175, except computer-controlled. Accelerator-pump-discharge slot differs from 108-33 to work with pump discharge check in metering block.

(10) 108-33—Fuel-bowl gasket for Models 2300, 4150/60, and 4500 carburetors. *Note:* Both 108-32 and 108-33 have only one accelerator-pump hole. Early versions had two holes. Gaskets must be installed so holes line up or there will be no pump shot.

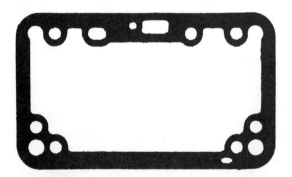

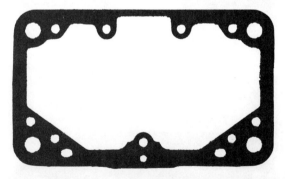

(11) 108-56—Primary-bowl gasket for Model 4180.

(12) 34-202—Primary-bowl gasket for computer-controlled Model 4175. Primary-bowl gasket for 4150/60 converted to Mile Dial configuration. Primary- and secondary-bowl gasket for 4150 converted to Quarter Mile Dial.

5

CARBURETOR / MANIFOLD RELATIONSHIP

DESCRIPTION

The intake manifold is the mount for the carburetor; it connects carburetor throats with cylinder-head ports. Ideally, a manifold divides fuel, air, exhaust residuals and recirculated exhaust (EGR) equally among the cylinders at all speeds and loads. Each cylinder should receive the same F/A ratio as all the others for minimum emissions, and maximum fuel economy and power production.

Manifold passages should have approximately equal length, cross-sectional area and geometric arrangement. For various reasons, this design goal is seldom met. Flow-equalizing features are often used to make unequal-length passages perform as if they were nearly equal.

The manifold designer must consider that some liquid fuel is usually moving around on the manifold's walls and floor. Both fuel vapor and liquid have to be distributed so the cylinders' F/A ratio stays the same. Liquid fuel is controlled by sumps, ribs and dams to ensure this condition.

The manifold floor and carburetor base are typically mounted parallel to the ground to avoid gravity's influence. It can cause uneven distribution of the liquid fuel. This usually means angling the carburetor pad/flange because the crankshaft centerline may be angled for drive-train alignment. It's not necessarily parallel to the ground.

Heating the manifold is essential in all but racing applications. Heat helps vaporize liquid fuel. Fuel may not vaporize as it leaves the carburetor. Or, it may drop out of the mixture due to an increase in absolute pressure or other reasons.

Small venturis aid mixture velocity through the carburetor and into the manifold. They generally aid vaporization and consequently distribution. High-speed airflow through the carburetor and manifold tends to maintain turbulence, but turbulence reduces flow. Velocity helps to keep fuel droplets in suspension, and thereby tends to equalize cylinder-to-cylinder F/A ratios.

If the mixture slows, as happens when passage size increases, fuel may separate from the air stream and deposit on manifold surfaces. Variations in the mixture supplied to the cylinders result.

Passage design should give sufficiently fast mixture flow to maintain good low- and mid-range throttle response without reducing volumetric efficiency at high rpm. Passages must be shaped to carry the mixture without

Holley's Pro-Contender plenum-type manifolds are available for small- and big-block Chevrolets and small-block Chryslers with W-2 heads. This is small-block Chevrolet unit. Small plenum volume and relatively short runners produce maximum horsepower in the 8000—9000 rpm range.

forcing the fuel to separate from the air on the way to the cylinder head.

When the mixture is forced to turn or bend, the air turns more quickly than the fuel and the two may separate. When this happens, a cylinder after the bend will receive a leaner F/A ratio than if the fuel had stayed in the mixture stream.

Pulsing within the manifold must also be accommodated. This action is called *back-flow* or *reversion*. It occurs twice during a four-cycle sequence. A pulse of residual exhaust gas enters the intake manifold during the valve-overlap period when both the intake and exhaust valves are off their seats. Another pulse reflects toward the carburetor when the intake valve closes.

Either of these pulses may hinder flow in the manifold. In severe cases, pulses pass through the carburetor into the atmosphere. A fuel cloud stands above the carburetor inlet. This is called *standoff*.

Standoff occurs as the fuel/air column starts and stops in the manifold in response to intake

valve opening and closing. Pulsing or bouncing movement of the column pushes fuel out of the air horns. Fuel is drawn back into the carburetor on the next intake stroke. But more bounces back out of the carburetor when the intake valve closes. The air column pulls fuel out of the discharge nozzle in both directions, on its way into the engine, and as it bounces back to the carburetor inlet.

Fuel is metered into the air stream *regardless of the stream's direction*—down through the carburetor or up through it from the manifold. This bi-directional flow occurs to some degree in most manifolds and in a marked degree in others.

F/A ratio differences between cylinders are often remedied by using unequal jet sizes. Richer (larger) jets are used in a section of the carburetor feeding lean cylinders. And leaner (smaller) jets are used for carburetor barrels feeding rich cylinders. Unequal jetting, commonly called *cross-* or *stagger-jetting*, is a partially effective remedy. Nevertheless, in such cases *the manifold is at fault*.

CROSS-H

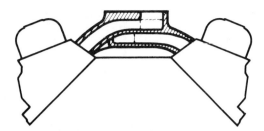

Cross-H or two-level manifold feeds half of cylinders from one side of carburetor—other half from other side of carburetor. Two sides of manifold are not connected.

SINGLE-PLANE

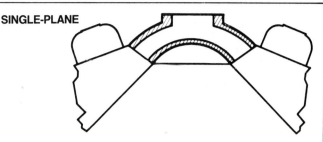

Single-plane manifold has all cylinder intake ports connected to a common chamber fed by the carburetor

PLENUM-RAM

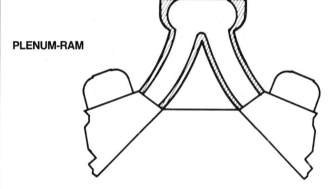

Plenum-ram manifold has a plenum chamber between passages to intake ports and carburetor/s.

ISOLATED-RUNNER

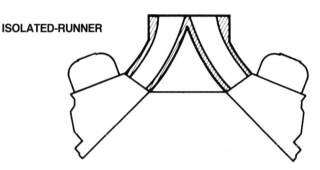

Isolated-runner (IR) manifold uses an individual throttle bore of a carburetor for each cylinder. There is no interconnection between the intake ports or throttle bores.

Big-block Chevy Strip Contender 300-4 or 300-5 is good example of a single-plane manifold. All cylinders share mixture from plenum cavity immediately under the carburetor. Typical of all Holley strip manifolds, there is no provision for EGR, choke or exhaust heat. Runners, plenum and carburetor mounting are separated from the tappet-chamber cover by an air gap. This tends to reduce inlet-charge temperature, thereby providing higher volumetric efficiency.

Stagger jetting is not very effective with plenum or single-plane manifolds because all cylinders share the output of all carburetor barrels.

Manifolds are also mounts for accessories. A manifold can be a tappet-chamber cover and have coolant passages or attachments. Provisions for choke operation can include a mount for a bimetal thermostat. Exhaust-heat passages to the carburetor flange and thermostat mount may be included too. Some have attachment points and holes for distributors. Old flat-head Fords mounted the generator on a manifold bracket.

MANIFOLD TYPES

There are a number of different manifold types:

- Single-plane.
- Two-plane.
- High-rise single- or two-plane.
- Individual- or isolated-runner (IR).
- IR with plenum chamber (Tunnel, Plenum or Channel-Ram).

Single-Plane—Roger Huntington, in a *Car Life* article, "Intake Manifolding" said, "The very simplest possible intake-manifold layout would be a single chamber that feeds to the valve ports on one side and draws from one or

Classic Cross-H (dual-plane) manifold design used by Ford engineers for their 427 CID single overhead cam drag racing engine. Vacuum-secondary Holley four barrels were mounted "backwards." Ford Motor Company photos.

more carburetor venturis on the other side. This is called a *common chamber* or *runner (single-plane)* manifold. Common-chamber manifolds have been designed for all types of engines—in-line sixes and eights, fours, V8s. It's the easiest and cheapest way to do the job. In fact, most current in-line four and six-cylinder engines use this type of manifold."

In the same article, Huntington also explained, "But we run into problems as we increase the number of cylinders. With eight cylinders there is a suction stroke starting every 90° of crankshaft rotation. They overlap. This means that one cylinder will tend to rob fuel/air mixture from the one immediately following it in the firing order, if they are located close to each other on the block. With a conventional V8 engine alternate-firing cylinders are actually adjacent—either 5-7 on the left in AMC, Chrysler, GM firing order, or 5-6 or 7-8 in the two Ford firing orders."

Two-plane (cross-H) manifolds, also called *dual-plane,* have been shown to be more throttle- and torque-responsive at low- and mid-range speeds than most single-plane designs. In 1970, single-plane performance manifolds began to appear in a new configuration. They keep mixture stream speed reasonably high at low- and mid-range engine speeds, yet offer low restriction to flow at high engine speeds.

Holley's Contender intake manifolds are good examples of this type of single-plane design. Careful selection of runner configuration, length and arrangement, coupled with optimum plenum volume, practically eliminate the low-speed disadvantage usually associated with single-plane manifolds. They keep the high-speed advantage over dual-plane manifolds.

Dual-runner *(dual-port)* manifolds appear to be two-plane designs, but they are actually two single-plane manifolds. A small- and a large-passage manifold are stacked one above the other in a single casting. The small-passage network is connected to the carburetor's primary side. This supplies high-speed mixture flow for good distribution and throttle response at low- and mid-range rpm. Larger passages are connected to the secondary portion of the carburetor. These supply extra capacity for high-rpm operation.

Experimental dual-runner *two-plane* manifolds have been developed by automobile manufacturers. Work on them was done by Ford, AMC, International Harvester, Holley Carburetor and the Ethyl Corporation. Its primary goal was emission reduction. Volvo's mid-'60s manifold used a similar idea. Mazda rotary (Wankel) engines also use the same manifolding concept.

Smaller carburetors can be used effectively with single-plane manifolds. The common

chamber damps out most pulsing, which reduces flow capability. A small carburetor quickens mixture flow and improves throttle response at low- and mid-range speeds.

Two-Plane—Two single-plane manifolds within a single casting are arranged so each is fed from one half (one side) of a two- or four-barrel carburetor. Each feeds one half of the engine. A cross-H manifold mounted on V8 is a familiar example.

Each carburetor half is isolated from the other, and from the other half of the manifold, by a plenum divider. Manifold passages are arranged so successive cylinders in the firing order draw first from one plane, then the other. In a 1-8-4-3-6-5-7-2 firing order, cylinders 1, 4, 6, 7 draw from one manifold plane and one half of the carburetor. Cylinders 8, 3, 5, 2 are supplied from the other plane and the other side of the carburetor.

Because there is less air mass to activate during each inlet pulse, throttle response is quicker and mid-range torque is improved—as compared with a conventional single-plane manifold.

Dividing the manifold into two sections causes flow restriction at high rpm. Only one half of carburetor flow capacity and manifold volume is available for any intake stroke. Thus, the divider is sometimes reduced in height, or removed completely. This makes more carburetor and manifold capacity available and increases high-rpm capability.

Bottom-end performance is limited when the divider is removed or reduced because the volume increase on each side or section decreases mixture speed at low rpm. This is not as severe as with a single-plane manifold, but it is a problem to consider when lowering divider height in a two-plane manifold.

Removable, interchangeable tops on Holley's Pro-Contender manifolds mount two 4500 or 4150 carburetors to discharge directly over the runners. The 300-201 at left is for Model 4500s; 300-202 at right fits Model 4150s. Manifolds for Chevrolet big-block and Chrysler small-block with W-2 heads have same capability.

Splendid high-rise example: Holley Strip Contender 300-25 manifold's carburetor is raised so runners have a straight downward shot to the cylinder-head ports. Air gap under plenum and runners helps keep fuel/air mixture cooler for more efficiency. Carburetor is Model 4150 0-8162 850-cfm double-pumper with secondary idle-mixture screws for improved idle air control. Increased throttle airflow compensates for modern racing camshaft profiles. Plumbed with Holley's universal chrome fuel line, Part 34-1.

On engines built for high-rpm operation, divider removal can be a tuning plus. Street and track applications combine careful selection of camshaft and other engine pieces to build torque into an engine. Leave the divider in place. The super-tuner can remove small amounts of it to reach the optimum height for a particular engine/parts combination and application. For street performance where 4000 rpm is rarely exceeded, a well-designed two-plane manifold is hard to beat.

Holley has three dual-plane manifolds: 300-36 and 300-38 for the small-block Chevy and the 300-39 for the small-block Ford.

High-Rise Or High-Riser?—Optional *high-rise* high-performance manifolds have been offered by some automobile manufacturers. Several aftermarket manifold makers have also made them. A high-rise manifold aligns the cylinder-head port angle with that of the manifold passage or runner. A nearly straight downward path connects the area under the carburetor to the intake port. In a V6 or V8 engine, the entire network of manifold runners is raised, along with the carburetor mounting.

High-rise should not be confused with *high-riser,* which refers to a spacer between the carburetor base and the manifold. It makes a longer riser and straightens flow disturbed by the throttle plate—before it enters the manifold. The spacer improves distribution by eliminating directional effects caused by partially-opened throttles.

High-rise and high-riser designs may be used with either single- or two-plane manifolds.

Independent-Runner (IR)—Independent- or isolated-runner manifolds are for racing applications. One carburetor throat and one manifold runner serve each cylinder-head inlet port. Each runner and throat combination is isolated from its neighboring cylinders.

Carburetors used with IR manifolds have fuel-metering for each barrel because cylinders cannot share functions (except accelerator pumps). There's a separate idle and main system for each barrel.

Sharp pulses occurring in two directions in an IR intake system start main metering operation very quickly. A large accelerator pump isn't required to cover up nozzle "lag." A power valve can't be used. It can't function correctly under the extreme pulsing conditions.

A benefit of an IR manifold is it allows tuning to take advantage of *ram effect.* This is a important point in manifold design. The shorter the tuned length, the higher the rpm at which peak torque occurs.

Carburetors used with IR manifolds must be *much larger* than for other manifold types. This is because each cylinder is fed by only one carburetor throat or barrel. A larger carburetor is required because the pulsing reduces carburetor flow capacity in the rpm range where standoff becomes severe.

IR manifold/carburetor combinations require standoff containment. Usually, a stack long enough to hold standoff is placed atop the carburetor inlet.

Some tuners say the IR carburetor venturi should be at least as large as the intake-valve diameter. Holley has made two Model 4500 carburetors specifically for IR use: List 6214 or 0-6214 (no longer made) and 0-9377. Even with their rating of 1150 cfm, two of these won't have enough capacity for a 302 CID V8. Holley calculated this engine would require *two* 1650 cfm four-barrels for IR.

Plenum-Ram—This manifold has a plenum chamber between the carburetor base and manifold runners. The chamber helps dissipate the strong pulsing, so less enters the carburetor to disrupt flow. Just as important, it allows the cylinders to share carburetor flow capacity. In the typical dual-quad plenum manifold, three or four cylinders simultaneously draw mixture from a plenum being fed by eight carburetor bores.

Sharing carburetor capacity makes the plenum-ram "forgiving" of carburetor capacity. This is true so long as the carburetors are not *too large* for the desired rpm range.

The typical Pro-Stock drag racer runs at 6800—8500 rpm. With a large-displacement engine, there is usually enough airflow at 6000 rpm to start the main systems, even with a pair of the largest 4500s.

The smaller the plenum cavity, the smaller the main-jet requirement. A smaller cavity sharpens pulsing to the carburetors. The main system starts sooner and more fuel is pulled out of the jets because of the pulsing.

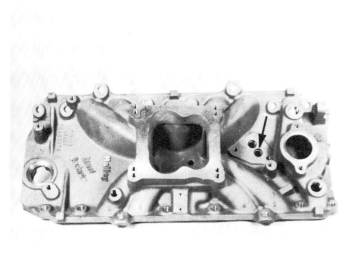

Holley 300-3 Street Contender manifold for big-block Chevrolet. Universal mounting pad accepts square-pattern or spread-bore carburetors without adapter. EGR provision (arrow) is in most Holley street manifolds. Plugs seal passages when no EGR valve is required. Plugs drive in easily and a little sealant helps prevent leaks. Overall height was kept low to clear modern hood lines. Photo at right shows clamp-on type EGR valve. Universal pad also accepts bolt-on valves.

Inside plenum of 300-7 Chrysler 318-CID Street Contender. Vanes help cylinder-to-cylinder distribution.

MULTIPLE CARBURETION

Until about 1967, two or more carburetors were considered essential for any modified or high-performance engine. No self-respecting auto enthusiast would consider building an engine with fewer than two carburetors—unless the rules required it. The current status is completely different. One four-barrel is usual and accepted for *all* street and many competition applications.

Now, sophisticated two- and four-barrel carburetors with small primaries and large progressively operated secondaries, are matched with single-carburetor manifolds for excellent performance and low emissions.

An application remains for multiple carburetion, at least as we once knew it: drag cars. It is also useful for the extended high-rpm operation at California dry-lakes events and the Bonneville Nationals Speed Trials.

Multiple carburetion is used to reduce the pressure drop across the carburetors to a minimum. This ensures the least possible HP loss from this restriction. Of course, low-rpm operation in these applications isn't a consideration. The extra venturi area and carburetor flow capacity don't create any problems.

A great many '60s and '70s engines were factory-equipped with two- and three-carburetor manifolds. By 1973 all U.S. manufacturers equipped their high-performance engines with single four-barrel carburetors. The majority of these single- and multi-carb factory manifolds used Holley two- or four-barrel carburetors with vacuum-operated secondary throttles—or secondary carburetors. Holley has reissued many of these original part numbers for Chevrolet, Chrysler and Ford muscle-car restorations. See your Holley dealer or performance catalog for specifics.

If you're the proud owner of a car with 2 x 4s or 3 x 2s, avoid buying mechanical linkages to open the throttles simultaneously. The need for adequate mixture velocity is stressed throughout this book. We explain how to obtain it by selecting the correct carburetor capacity for engine size and rpm.

Simultaneous opening of multiple throttles (except on IR manifolds) goes against these recommendations. The car is hard to drive because velocity through the carburetors is drastically reduced at low and medium speeds. Progressively operated secondaries are more desirable and improve driveability.

HOLLEY CONTENDER SERIES

Holley introduced a new and complete line of intake manifolds in 1976. These manifolds resulted from intensive engineering and development. Dynamometer, emissions, fuel economy, street driving and drag-strip testing were all used to create these manifolds.

Runners were designed for minimum flow loss using cross-section profile analysis. Infrared exhaust gas analyzing instrumentation accurately measured cylinder-to-cylinder fuel distribution. Good distribution was one of the paramount considerations in making manifolds that would not alter original-equipment emissions performance.

Holley is the only manifold manufacturer that also makes carburetors and fuel pumps. It considers the carburetor and manifold as a combination. Holley carburetors include design features to optimize performance of the total induction system.

Originally called *Dominator* manifolds, Holley changed them to *Contender* in 1987.

On the Street—Its engineers began with a "clean slate" to design a line of street manifolds. Some Holley street manifolds have universal carburetor flanges that mount either square-pattern or spread-bore carburetors without an adapter. Choke-operating features are also included.

Many of these Street Contender Manifolds

STRIP MANIFOLDS

Chevrolet Small-Block
2 manifolds 1-4V
1 manifold 2-4V

Chevrolet Big-Block:
oval or rectangular ports
2 manifolds 1-4V
1 manifold 2-4V
(rectangular ports)

Chrysler Small-Block:
273, 318, 340, 360 CID,
includes 340 & 360
with W-2 heads
2 manifolds 1-4V
1 manifold 2-4V
(W-2 heads only)

Ford 351C with 4V heads

STREET MANIFOLDS
(all 1-4V)

American Motors:
304, 343, 360, 390, 402
CID V8, 1970—'79

Buick V6:
196, 198, 225 CID: '79
231 CID: 1975—'79
Fits AMC Jeeps 1966—'71

Chevrolet V6:
200—229 CID to '80

Chevrolet Small-Block:
Five manifolds: 1957—'72;
1973—85

Chevrolet Big-Block:
396, 402 427, 454 CID
(oval-port only)

Chrysler Small-Block:
318—360 CID w/W-2 heads

Chrysler Small-Block:
318—360 CID,
2 manifolds

Chrysler Big-Block:
361—440-CID Low-Block
413—440-CID High-Block

Ford Small-Block:
221, 260, 289, 302 CID
(except Boss 302):
three manifolds

Ford:
351C, 351W, 351M,
400 CID: three manifolds

CARBURETOR

780 cfm with diaphragm secondaries
or 800-cfm double-pumper.
Two 4150s or two 4500s.

850-cfm double-pumper or Model
4500 with adapter.

Two 4150s or two 4500s.

780 cfm with diaphragm
secondaries or 800-cfm
double-pumper.

Two 4150s or two 4500s.

780 cfm with diaphragm secondaries
or 800-cfm double-pumper.

CARBURETOR

Model 4160 600 cfm for all-around performance, 800-cfm double-pumper for
competition.

Model 4360 for all-around performance,
4150 600-cfm double-pumper for competition. Jeeps use 390-cfm, R-8807. Spread-
bore or square-flange. Designed for engines, adapts to earlier models.

Model 4360 0-9694 specially calibrated for
this manifold.

Model 4360 for maximum economy, 4150/
60 600 cfm with diaphragm secondaries for
all-around performance. 650—750-cfm
double-pumper for best performance.
Spread-bore or square-flange carburetor.
Dual-plane manifolds use square-flange
only.

600 cfm with diaphragm secondaries for
good economy and mid-range performance. 650—850 cfm double-pumper for
best performance. Spread-bore or square-
flange carburetor.

600 cfm with diaphragm secondaries for
economy and good all-around performance.
780 cfm with diaphragm secondaries or 750
cfm double-pumper for best performance.
Square-flange only.

Model 4360 for maximum economy. 600
cfm with diaphragm secondaries for economy and good all-around performance.
600—700 cfm double-pumper for best performance. Spread-bore or square-flange.

600 cfm with diaphragm secondaries for
best economy and all-around performance.
780 cfm with diaphragm secondaries or
750-cfm double-pumper for best performance. Spread-bore or square-flange.

Model 4360 for maximum economy. 600
cfm with diaphragm secondaries for economy and overall performance, 600—700-
cfm double-pumper for best performance.
Kickdown linkage needed for automatic-
transmission applications. Spread-bore or
square-flange carburetor. Dual-plane has
square-flange.

600 cfm with diaphragm secondaries for
best all-around performance. 750-cfm
double-pumper for best performance. Kickdown linkage needed for automatic-
transmission applications. Square-flange.

Ford:
332, 352, 360, 390, 406,
428 CID. Also fits 427-CID
Low & medium-riser engines

Pontiac:
326, 350, 389, 400,421,
455 CID

Oldsmobile Small-Block:
330, 350 CID

Oldsmobile Big-Block:
400, 425, 455 CID

Toyota:
2.2-liter 20R engine
4-cylinder 1977—80

600—780 cfm with diaphragm secondaries
for best all-around performance. 750—800-
cfm double-pumper for maximum performance. Kickdown linkage needed for automatic-transmission applications. Square-
flange carburetor.

Model 4360 for maximum economy. Best
all-around performance with diaphragm
secondary 600—700 cfm, depending on
engine displacement. 650—800-cfm
double-pumper for best performance.
Spread-bore or square-flange.

Model 4360 for best economy. 600 cfm with
diaphragm secondaries for best all-around
performance. 650—750-cfm double-
pumper for maximum performance. Spread-
bore or square-flange.

Model 4175 with diaphragm secondaries
for best all-around performance. 750—800-
cfm double-pumper for best performance.
Spread-bore or square-flange.

Model 4360 0-9973 450 cfm for best all-
around performance. Model 4160 390 cfm
when "lugging" occurs.

Chart gives manifold applications as of 1987 with recommended carburetor
size and configuration. See current Holley Performance Catalog for manifold
and carburetor part numbers.

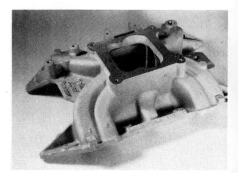

Chrysler low-block 361-, 383-, 400-CID engines get a performance boost with Holley
300-10 Street Contender manifold. Uses
spread-bore or square-flange carburetor.

Holley 300-8 Strip Contender manifold for
Chrysler small-block V8 engines: 318-, 340-
and 360 CID. Runners are raised above cam/
tappet cover with air gap so they will stay cool
for dense charge and best performance.

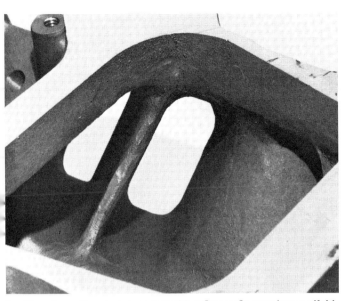

Looking down throat of deep-breathing Street Contender manifold. Note straight path for inlet charge from carburetor to cylinder-head port.

Holley 300-22 manifold for Buick V6 for 1975—'79 (and later for off-road use) and 1966—71 AMC Jeeps. Designed for street use, it includes exhaust crossover, EGR and all necessary mounting bosses. 30 HP was gained over stock manifold and 2-bbl. carburetor. Good performance results with 450-cfm Model 4360. Use 0-8516 for 1975—'76 odd-fire engines, and 0-8677 for 1977—'79 even-fire engines.

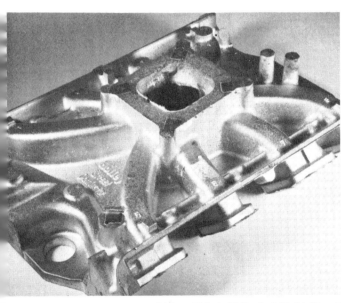

Aluminum casting prior to machining. This is Holley's 300-11 Street Contender manifold for the Ford big-block 352, 390, 428 engines with or without EGR. You'll need a crane to get original equipment manifold off engine because it weighs about 100 pounds.

Holley's manifold installation kits are complete for simple and trouble-free installation. You may find parts not needed for your particular engine. This one is for Chevrolet small-block V8.

have full emission-control provisions, including EGR. Tapped holes are provided for operating power brakes and other accessories. Exhaust-heat passages ensure fast warmup and good mixture distribution. Flange heights are kept as low as possible to fit under low hood lines.

The street manifold development effort emphasized making the manifold/carburetor supply good power with stock cast-iron exhaust systems. Further testing ensured the manifold/carburetor teams would also work well with headers. Incidentally, all Holley manifolds are 100% pressure-tested.

The installation kits are the most complete ever offered. Installation directions are written so inexperienced mechanics can install a manifold and make it work correctly.

On the Strip—Strip-type Contender intake manifolds are designed for maximum power on fully modified competition engines. They are not designed for street use. There is no provision for chokes, EGR or other emission-control equipment.

Holley 300-6 Street Contender for Ford 289/302-CID engines. EGR pad at rear can be plugged if not required.

Holley 300-7 Street Contender for Chrysler 318/340/360-CID engines. Flange accepts either spread- or square-bore carburetors.

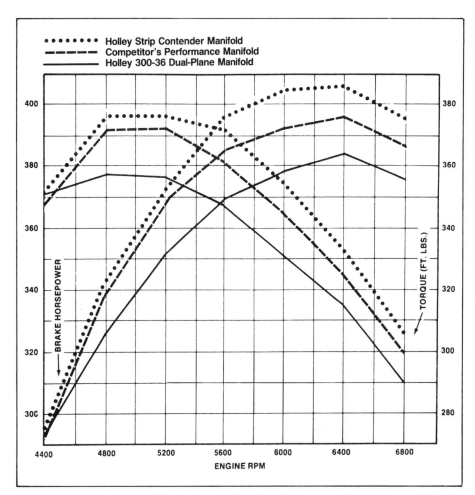

Dyno-power curve compares Holley Strip Contender manifold with high-rise dual-plane 300-36 Holley manifold and competitive performance manifold. Engine is 355 Chevrolet LT-1 with performance headers and 0-4781 (850-cfm double-pumper) carburetor used with "best-power" jetting for each manifold.

An air gap between the manifold valley cover and the intake runners reduces intake-charge heating from engine heat. Better power results from the cooler and denser intake charge to the cylinders.

These are true *racing* manifolds. Runner configurations and plenum volumes are optimized to favor all-out performance. Development and testing included dynamometer and drag strip work with actual competition engines. Development was conducted with headers to optimize power production above 4800 rpm.

See the nearby graph for performance comparisons between the Strip Contender and another competition manifold. Each used an 850-cfm Holley 0-4781 double-pumper carburetor. The Holley showed a 12-HP advantage on a 355-CID small-block Chevrolet engine.

Strip manifolds are designed for square-pattern Holley performance carburetors. Strip manifolds for Chrysler 318/340/360 CID engines work with both spread-bore and square-bore carburetors. Manifolds introduced during 1976 were Phase I of an ongoing testing and development program.

Pro-Stock 2 x 4 Contender—Phase II was the development of 2 x 4 maximum performance manifolds. Nearly a year of dynamometer and drag strip testing was used to evaluate virtually every combination of plenum volume, runner length and cross-sectional area. Manifolds are available for small- and big-block Chevrolet and small-block Chrysler with W-2 heads. Interchangeable tops allow using either two 4150s or two 4500s.

Construction is two-piece. The base contains the mating flanges to the cylinder head, the runners and part of the plenum. The top contains the upper portion of the plenum and the

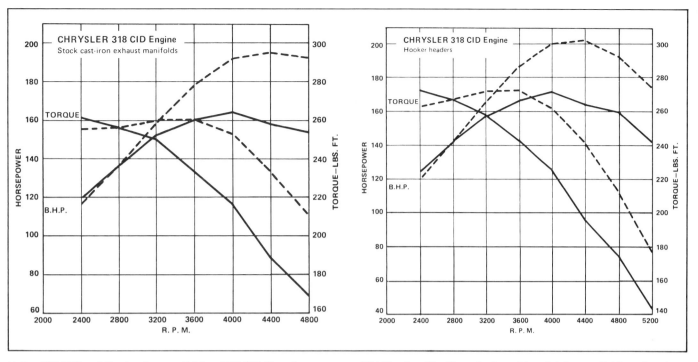

Holley 300-7 Street Contender manifold on 318-CID Chrysler gave over 30 HP gain with either stock cast-iron intake manifolds or headers. Headers kept power up at higher rpm. Solid line in both charts is original cast-iron intake manifold, 2-bbl. carb with no air cleaner. Dashed line in left chart represents 300-7 manifold with Model 4160, 0-7009 carb, 66—73 jets, and open-element air cleaner. Dashed line in right chart is same combination, but using 64—71 jets.

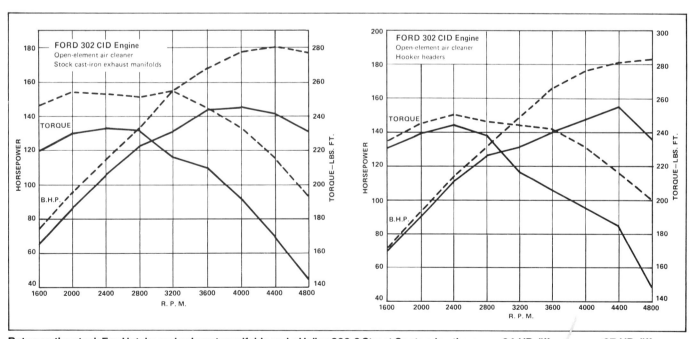

Between the stock Ford intake and exhaust manifolds and a Holley 300-6 Street Contender, there was 34-HP difference vs. 27-HP difference with headers. Headers gave slightly more power and carried power farther up the range. Solid line is stock cast-iron intake manifold and 2-bbl. carb. Dashed line is 300-6 manifold with Model 4160, 0-6919 carb, and 66—73 jets.

Ford small-block manifold is Holley 300-39.

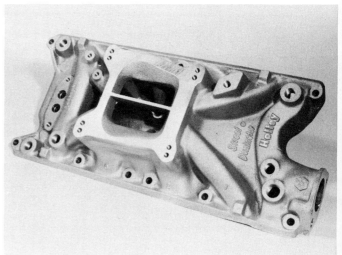

Holley "Z" manifold for small-block Fords (300-30Z) divides right and left sides of engine. Any gasket used on these manifolds should be Holley 108-18 to preserve separation between the two sides of engine. Balance passage between two rear cylinders provides excellent low-speed torque capabilities.

Chevrolet 90-degree V6, either 200- or 229-CID from 1978—'80 can be equipped with Holley's 300-34 manifold. Recommended carburetor is the 450-cfm Model 4360 0-9694, which is specifically calibrated for this engine/manifold combination. Air cleaner is Holley's Part 120-103 gold-finished 9-in. diameter air cleaner.

American Motors 304-, 343-, 360-, 390- and 401-CID V8 engines can use 300-31Z intake manifold. It applies to 1970—'79 engines with or without EGR. Shown here with Model 6150 0-8005 that has 600-cfm capacity, vacuum-operated secondaries and electric choke.

carburetor-mounting flanges.

Because plenum volume is relatively small, performance approaches that of an IR manifold. Plenum-chamber volume is adequate to damp pulsations and can be increased by placing spacers between the top and the base. Runners have a relatively straight path to the intake ports. Thus the intake charge has only minimal directional changes to make.

These manifolds are used on Modified and Pro-Stock cars with success. Quite a few also show up on street machines.

"Z" SERIES

The next development phase was the "Z" series. "Z" stands for Zora Arkus-Duntov of Corvette fame. Zora was a consultant to Holley after retiring from General Motors. After playing a very important role in the Contender 2 x 4 manifold program, Zora designed a new line of street-performance intake manifolds.

He made an important discovery: Connect-

ing the rear two cylinders with a balance tube minimized a classic problem of the single-plane manifold. The rear two cylinders on the left side (5 and 7 in a GM V8) rob each other of intake charge because they follow in the firing order. The balance tube provides another rear-cylinder charging source. The left and right side of the plenum chamber are also separated by a divider.

The result is an interesting performance compromise between single- and dual-plane

Toyota 1977—'80 2189cc engines can use this Street Contender 300-37 intake manifold. Model 4360 0-9973 is a 450-cfm carburetor calibrated for this manifold/engine combination. Manifold flange will also accept a square-flange Model 4150/60 carburetor for highly modified engines. Requires extensive throttle-linkage modifications.

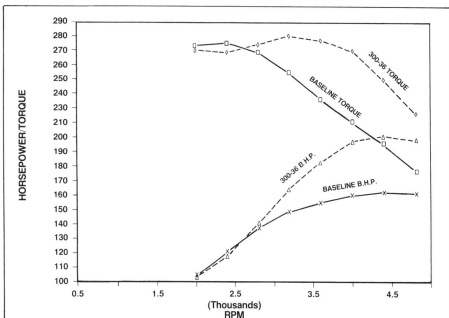

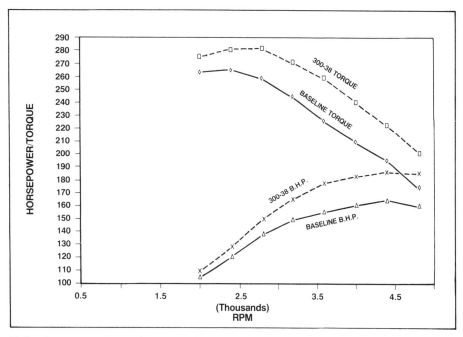

Holley dyno comparisons. At top are HP and torque outputs of 1983 305-CID Chevy V8 with no air cleaner, stock intake manifold, Rochester Q-jet, and Stahl 1.75-in. headers (solid line) vs. same engine with no air cleaner, Holley 300-36 dual-plane Contender intake manifold, 4160 0-1850 carb, and same Stahl headers (dashed line). At bottom is same stock engine configuration (solid line) compared with Holley 300-38 Contender manifold, 4160 0-1850-2 carb and same Stahl headers (dashed line).

manifolds. Low-rpm torque is improved over the single-plane and high-rpm power is improved over the dual-plane.

Four Holley Z manifolds are available for small-block AMC, Chevrolet, Chrysler and Ford engines. The "Z" suffix distinguishes this special series from other Holley manifolds.

HOLLEY DUAL-PLANE

Manifold experts and would-be experts have always argued the merits of single-plane versus dual-plane manifolds. Advocates on either side can make test data work in their favor. It is safe to say that single-plane manifolds tend to favor high rpm and horsepower. Dual-plane types serve best at low- and mid-range rpm and are basically *torque* manifolds.

To supply a complete line of manifolds, Holley added dual-plane manifolds in the early '80s. The only two active V8 engines at that time were the small-block Chevrolet and Ford, so the line is limited to these two engines. There are two Chevrolet manifolds and one for Ford.

The 300-36 Contender is a high-rise dual-plane manifold very similar to the Chevrolet LT-1 manifold. Match it with a 0-3310 750-cfm Holley carburetor and an open-element air cleaner and you've got a superior street package with good driveability, fuel economy and performance.

There is no EGR provision, so local emission regulations must be considered before installing it. Another word of caution, the manifold is about 1-1/4-in. higher than the stock cast-iron manifold, so measure hood clearance before

you buy.

The 300-38 Contender is a smaller dual-plane manifold for the small-block Chevrolet. Its low profile means there's no hood-clearance problem. This is the lowest-cost Holley V8

manifold. Because of the smaller, flatter-angle runner, both power and torque are reduced as compared with the 300-36. There is no EGR provision. The recommended carburetor is the 0-1850 600-cfm unit.

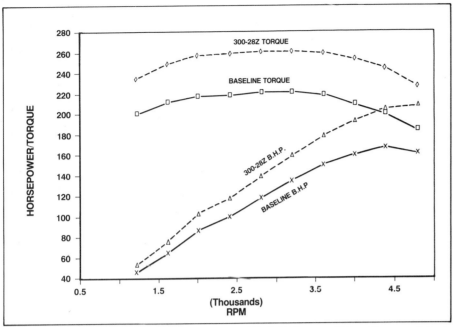

Holley dyno comparisons on 1979 305-CID Chevy V8. Solid lines are HP and torque of stock engine configuration with stock intake manifold, air cleaner, Rochester Q-jet and exhaust manifolds. Dashed lines represent HP and torque outputs of same engine with Holley 300-28Z intake manifold, Model 4160 0-9254 carb, stock exhaust manifolds and no air cleaner.

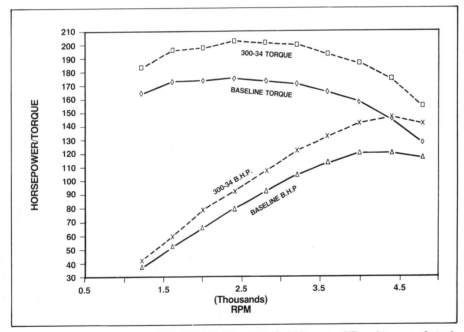

Holley dyno comparisons on 1980 229-CID Chevy V6. Solid lines are HP and torque of stock engine with stock intake manifold and Rochester 2-bbl. carb. Dashed lines are outputs of same engine with Holley 300-34 intake manifold with Model 4360 0-8516 carb. No air cleaner was used in both cases.

The 300-39 Contender follows the same design approach as the 300-38. It's for the Ford small-block engine. It is also a very good low-cost street manifold that has no hood-clearance problems.

DETECTING MANIFOLD LEAKS

An instant indicator of a manifold leak is a rougher-than-normal idle with the throttle at the factory-set curb-idle position. You may hear a hissing or whistling, but this can be masked by other engine noise. The roughness at idle is caused by the engine receiving more air than it needs. The mixture is being leaned.

Air leak symptoms appear more at idle than higher engine speeds because the engine is consuming so little fuel/air mixture. Additional air drastically alters the fuel/air mixture ratio. At higher engine speeds the air leak is small compared with the total fuel/air mixture. Consquently, the leak seems to disappear.

So how do you find the leak? First, inspect all hoses attached to the carburetor base or to the intake manifold. Make sure no hoses are cracked or broken. Take special care to check the underside or hidden portions of the hose where a leak might not be obvious. Make sure all manifold-vacuum ports have plugs installed.

Some mechanics spray a little solvent (carburetor cleaner or starting fluid) on hoses or the manifold to locate leaks when the engine is idling. The combustible solvent enters through a leak and the idle smooths and increases about 200 rpm.

Use this technique to check for worn throttle-shaft bores. Shafts and bores wear with use. An air leak and lumpy idle result. Spray the solvent directly at the throttle shaft where it enters the throttle body and note the idle response.

Use extreme care if applying this detection method because of the fire hazard of spraying combustible droplets on a running engine.

Other mechanics locate air leaks with propane. The gas can enter a small leak more easily than a liquid, and the fire hazard is reduced because the gas rises and leaves the work area.

Pinpoint any leaks by pointing the propane torch tip at the suspected area on an idling engine. Open the gas valve on the torch. An air leak will draw the gas into the manifold. Note the idle response as specified above.

Neither of these detection methods is a foolproof diagnostic procedure. Solvent or gas vapor can be sucked into the air cleaner or carburetor air horn and the idle will increase from this. You'll be mislead into thinking you've found an air leak.

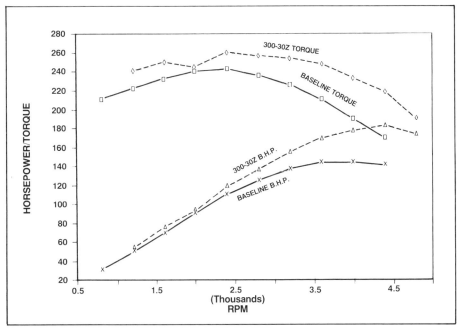

Holley dyno comparisons on 1975 302-CID Ford V8. Solid lines are HP and torque of stock engine with stock air cleaner, intake manifold, Motocraft 2-bbl. carb, and exhaust manifolds. Dashed lines are outputs of same engine with stock air cleaner, Holley 300-30Z intake manifold, Model 4150 0-6909 (62-71 jets) carb, and stock exhaust manifolds.

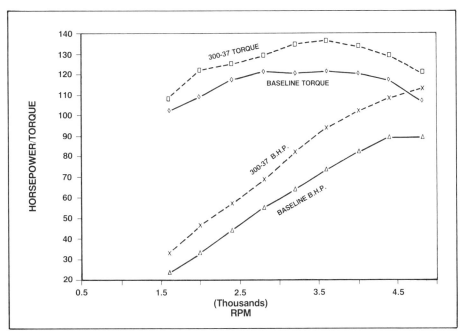

Holley dyno comparisons on 1979 2.2 liter 20R Toyota in-line 4 cyl. Solid lines are HP and torque of stock engine with stock air cleaner, intake manifold, and Aisan 2-bbl. carb. Dashed lines are outputs of same engine with stock air cleaner, Holley 300-37 intake manifold and Model 4360 0-9973 carb.

CARBURETOR & ENGINE VARIABLES

6

Testing programs require a dynamometer to measure effects of one engine variable at a time. This Chevrolet V8 engine is installed on SuperFlow SF-901 Computerized Engine Dynamometer System. Air inlet atop Holley carburetor measures airflow. Fuel flow is also measured so printout contains brake specific fuel consumption data, as well as horsepower and torque.

Many variables affect the operation of the carburetor and engine. Their relationships are examined here so you can see how each variable affects the others. Much of this information is important in understanding and tuning stock and racing engines.

SPARK TIMING

Late model cars have engine compartment labels specifying engine idle speed and spark advance settings. Carefully worked out by the factory engineers, these ensure that the engine in that vehicle will have emissions within specified limits.

Controlling Advance—In the early '70s, the trend was to detune the engine to meet emission requirements. Part of the detuning included retarding the spark at idle. Some emission control systems locked out vacuum advance in the intermediate gears. A temperature-sensitive valve allowed spark advance if the engine started to overheat and during cold operation. The advent of the catalytic converter in 1975 allowed more spark advance.

Three-way catalysts, discussed on page 136, limit HC and NOx in the exhaust stream, not by altering engine operation. This allows using more spark advance at idle and part throttle. Driveability and fuel economy are improved because engine efficiency is improved.

With the increased use of electronics to control engine operation, spark advance is even more closely controlled. The ECU receives inputs on engine speed, load, temperature and throttle angle and so on. It accurately changes spark advance to satisfy engine requirements based on the various sensor inputs.

Most carburetors have ports for timed spark and for straight manifold vacuum. Some Ford applications used a combination of venturi vacuum and manifold vacuum, called a *pressure-spark system*. Use of this ended in about 1972.

In general, a retarded spark reduces NO_X by keeping peak combustion pressures and temperatures at lower values than those generated by an advanced spark setting. It also reduces HC emissions. A retarded spark is good for reducing emissions, but bad for economy, driveability and coolant heating.

Fuel is being burned in the engine, but some heat energy is wasted as it flows into the cylinder walls. Because fuel is still burning as it passes the exhaust valve, the exhaust manifolds have to cope with more heat. This aggravates heating problems in the engine compartment. The cooling system has to work harder. Fuel is still burning as it passes the exhaust valve, so the engine's thermal efficiency is less because energy is wasted.

Using retarded spark requires richer jetting in the idle and main systems to get decent off-idle performance and driveability. A tightrope is being walked here. The mixture must not be allowed to go lean or higher combustion temperatures and NO_X will be produced. If mixtures are richened too far in the search for driveability, CO emissions increase.

Because retarding the spark hurts efficiency, the throttle plate must be opened farther at idle to get enough mixture in to keep the engine running. This must be considered by the carburetor designer in positioning the idle-transfer slot. High temperatures at idle and high idle-speed settings also promote dieseling.

Dieseling—Also called *run on,* is primarily caused by greater throttle opening. It is aggravated by higher average temperatures in the combustion chambers. Higher temperatures tend to cause any deposits to glow so self-ignition occurs.

Consider a car equipped with an *anti-dieseling solenoid.* Turning the ignition ON energizes the solenoid so the throttle is moved to its idle setting. Turning the ignition OFF de-energizes the solenoid to change the idle setting to about 50 rpm slower than a normal idle setting. This throttle idle position, which is more closed than normal idle, reduces any tendency to run on. If the engine can't ingest enough mixture to continue running, dieseling won't usually occur.

Timed Spark Advance—Carburetors equipped with timed spark advance (no advance at closed throttle) have a port in the throttle bore. This port is exposed to vacuum as the throttle plate moves past the port—usually slightly off-idle.

Spark-advance vacuum versus airflow calibration is closely established in manufacturing because this dramatically affects HC and NO_X emissions. Distributor advance, once considered so important for economy, is now an essential link in the emission-reduction chain.

VALVE TIMING

Valve timing has the greatest effect on an engine's idling and low-speed performance. A racing cam adds valve overlap and lift. While this allows the engine to breathe better at high rpm, it lowers manifold vacuum at idle and low speeds. Distribution and vaporization problems become obvious as the engine becomes hard to start, idles roughly (or not at all), and has a bad flat spot coming off idle. Very poor pulling power (torque) at low rpm is another characteristic. This is especially true when a racing cam is teamed with a lean, emission-type carburetor.

Because manifold vacuum is reduced, the signal available to pull mixture through the idle system is also reduced, and the mixture is leaned. Also, the throttle has to be opened farther than usual to get enough mixture into the engine for idling. This can place the off-idle slot/port in the wrong relationship to the throttle, so there is insufficient off-idle fuel to carry the engine until main-system flow begins.

And, the idle mixture has to be made richer to offset poor vaporization and distribution problems. Part of the uneven distribution and poor driveability problem stems from the overlap period.

When exhaust and intake valves open simultaneously, some exhaust gas is still in the cylinder at higher-than-atmospheric pressure. These gases rush into the intake manifold to dilute the incoming charge. Charge dilution effectively *lowers* the combustion pressure. This is especially true up to the rpm where the overlap time interval becomes short enough so the *reverse pulsing* becomes insignificant.

Reverse pulsing through the venturis at WOT adds to the fuel flow, making a richer mixture. Once the main system starts, the discharge nozzle delivers fuel in response to airflow in either direction. More information about valve timing and reverse pulsing is on page 108.

When manifold vacuum is reduced (pressure increases toward atmospheric), the power valve may start to operate. Or it may flutter open and close as manifold vacuum varies wildly. These aren't valid reasons to remove the power valve, but do select a power valve that will be closed at the lowest vacuum (highest pressure) during idling. Use a power valve with a lower vacuum rating, i.e., a smaller number stamped on the valve.

In extreme cases, a wild racing cam magnifies these problems so the car becomes undriveable for anything except competition. This is especially true if carburetion capacity is increased to match the cam's deep-breathing characteristics.

When a racing cam is installed at the same time the carburetor is changed, the carburetor gets blamed for poor idling. The real culprit is the racing camshaft. Information on engine tuning with a racing cam is in on page 121.

TEMPERATURE

Temperature affects carburetion. It affects mixture ratio because air becomes less dense as temperature increases (approximately 1% for every 11F). The density change reduces VE and power, even though main-jet corrections of approximately one main-jet size smaller (old-style jets) for every 40F ambient temperature increase will keep mixture ratio correct.

Maximum power production requires keeping the inlet charge as cool as possible. For this reason, racing engines are designed or assembled so the intake manifold is not heated by exhaust gas. Some stock passenger car and truck engines use an exhaust-heated intake manifold because the warmer mixture, although not ideal for maximum power, helps driveability.

Supplying a warm-air inlet to the carburetor, or an exhaust hot spot in the intake manifold aids vaporization. Good vaporization ensures more even mixture distribution to the cylinders because fuel vapors move more easily than liquid fuel.

Icing—This occurs most frequently at 40F (5C) and relative humidity of 90% or higher. It is typically a problem at idle: ice forms between the throttle plate and bore. It usually occurs when the car has been driven a short distance and stopped with the engine idling. Ice builds around the throttle plate and shuts off mixture flow so the engine stops. Once the engine stalls, vaporization stops and the ice promptly melts. The engine can be restarted. This may occur several times until engine temperature warms the carburetor body so vaporization doesn't cause icing.

ICE CAN CAUSE DAMAGE

The accelerator pump is the lowest point in the fuel inlet system of a Holley with removable fuel bowls. Water can collect there, particularly in a carburetor that isn't used regularly. If this water freezes, using the carburetor could rupture the pump diaphragm.

To avoid this problem, purge water from the carburetor's fuel system . Add a can of "dry gas" compound to the gas tank to absorb water in the fuel supply system so it will be carried into the engine with the fuel. This should be done at the start of the cold-weather season and anytime humidity is high.

Turnpike icing occurs in the venturi system when running at a relatively constant speed for a long period under ideal icing conditions. Ice buildup gradually chokes down the venturi size so the engine runs slower and slower.

Fuel vaporization removes plenty of heat from the surrounding parts of the carburetor.

So, there is a greater tendency for this phenomenon to occur in small venturis where vaporization is best. Icing is no longer a major problem because cars are factory-equipped with exhaust-manifold stoves to warm the air supplied to the air cleaner inlet. In some applications thermostatic flapper valves shut off hot airflow when underhood temperatures reach a certain level.

On some high-performance engines, a vacuum diaphragm opens the air cleaner to a hood scoop or other cold-air source at low vacuums/heavy loads.

Percolation—At the other end of the thermometer there's a phenomenon called *percolation*. It usually occurs when the engine is stopped during hot weather or after it has been run long enough to be fully warm. Engineers call this a *hot soak*.

In this case, no cooling air is being blown over the engine by the fan or vehicle motion. Heat stored in the engine block and exhaust manifolds is radiated and conducted directly into the carburetor, fuel lines and fuel pump.

Fuel in the main system between the fuel bowl and main discharge nozzle can boil or percolate. Vapor bubbles push or lift liquid fuel out of the main system into the venturi. The action is similar to that in a percolator coffee pot.

Fuel falls onto the throttle plate and trickles into the manifold. Excess vapors from the fuel bowl, and from the bubbles escaping from the main well, are heavier than air and drift down into the manifold. This makes the engine difficult to start and a long cranking period is required. In severe cases, enough fuel collects in the manifold so it runs into cylinders with open intake valves. Fuel washes oil off the cylinder walls and rings, causing excessive engine wear.

Percolation is aggravated by fuel boiling in the fuel pump and in the fuel line to the carburetor. Because this creates fuel pressure as high as 15—18 psi, the inlet valve needle may be forced off its seat. Fuel vapor and liquid fuel are forced into the bowl, raising the fuel level. This makes it that much easier for the vapor bubbles to lift fuel to the spillover point.

Solving percolation problems requires a systematic approach. The main system is designed so vapor bubbles lifting fuel toward the discharge nozzle tend to break before they can push fuel out of the nozzle. Fuel levels are carefully established to provide as much lift as can be tolerated. In some instances, the fuel must pass through an enlarged section at the top of the main well or standpipe to discourage vapor-induced spillover.

Gaskets and insulating spacers are used between the manifold and carburetor, and between the carburetor base (throttle body) and fuel bowl. An aluminum heat deflector or shield keeps some engine heat away from the carburetor.

Hot-starting problems are reduced by internal bleeds in the fuel pump. A vapor-return line may also be used on the carburetor ahead of the inlet valve. When the bleed and return line are used, any pressure buildup in the fuel line escapes harmlessly into the fuel tank or fuel-supply line.

Another bad high-temperature effect is boiling fuel in the fuel line between the pump and the fuel tank. Fuel can even boil in the fuel pump. When the fuel pump and line are filled with hot fuel, the pump supplies a mixture of vapor and liquid fuel to the carburetor.

Very little liquid fuel is delivered during an acceleration after a hot soak, so the fuel level drops, causing leaning. The bowl may be nearly emptied, partially exposing the jets. When the jets are partially exposed, the carburetor can't meter a correct fuel/air mixture because the jets are designed to work with liquid fuel—not a combination of liquid and vapor.

This condition is called *vapor lock*. Holley carburetors are especially resistant to the problem. Their large bowl capacity holds enough liquid fuel, even though some has escaped as vapor, until the fuel pump can supply more liquid fuel.

In difficult cases, fuel lines may have to be rerouted to keep them away from extreme heat, such as the exhaust system. If the lines cannot be relocated, it is usually possible to insulate them. This is especially important for racing vehicles. Cool cans help, as do high-performance electric fuel pumps located at the tank to *push* fuel to the carburetor.

AIR DENSITY

In the air requirements section of Engine Requirements, page 9, we related VE of the engine to the density of the fuel/air mixture received by its cylinders. We showed that the higher the density, the higher the VE.

The mixture density depends on atmospheric pressure, which varies with altitude, temperature and weather conditions. And, mixture density is also affected by intake-system layout. Density increases when the carburetor is supplied with cool air and when the intake manifold is not heated.

Density is reduced if the inlet air is heated or if the fuel/air mixture delivered by the carburetor is heated as it enters the manifold. Further density reductions occur as the mixture picks up heat from the manifold and cylinder head passages, hot valves, cylinder walls and piston heads.

As with almost all other engine variables, there are tradeoffs. Warming the mixture reduces its density, but also improves distribution, especially at part-throttle.

Density has an effect on carburetor capacity and mixture. The *major* density changes that occur are due to altitude changes. Let's consider the effects of driving from sea level at Los Angeles to the 5000 ft. at Denver. The flow and pressure-difference expressions look like this:

$$Q \sim A \sqrt{\frac{\Delta_p}{\gamma}} \quad \text{or} \quad \Delta_p \sim \left(\frac{Q}{A}\right)^2 \times \gamma$$

where

Q	=	volume flow
γ	=	density
Δ_p	=	pressure difference
A	=	carburetor-venturi area

Regardless of density, the volume taken in remains the same at a given rpm, but going from sea level to 5000 ft. drops density to 83% of its sea-level value. Pressure difference or Δ_p is also 83% of the original value, so the carburetor acts as if it were larger.

Because Δp increases inversely as the square of the area, area must be reduced only by a ratio of $\sqrt{0.83}$ or 0.91 to restore the same pressure difference with the original carburetor at sea level. In other words, the carburetor acts as if it were 9% larger. This is only a problem if carburetor size was marginally too big to begin with.

Consider a carburetor on the verge of stumbling and having flat spots in acceleration at sea level due to late turn-on of the main system. These problems will worsen at high altitudes because the carb size *effectively* increases due to reduced air density.

WOT fuel/air ratio is determined mainly by venturi size and main jet size, assuming fuel and air density never change.

A rule of thumb is to reduce Holley jet size by one number for each 2000-ft. altitude increase. Holley engineers usually figure approximately 4% fuel flow change between jet sizes. Thus, two jet sizes smaller will keep nearly equivalent fuel/air ratios at 5000 ft. altitude.

COMPRESSION RATIO (CR)

High compression improves engine performance by increasing the burning rate of the fuel/air mixture. Peak pressures and peak torque can approach the maximum of which the engine is capable. High compression also increases HC and NO_x emissions.

Lowering the compression reduces HC emissions by reducing the combustion chamber's surface-to-volume ratio. The greater the surface-to-volume ratio, the more surface cooling occurs, thereby increasing HC.

Until about 1970, high-compression engines with up to 11:1 CR were available in high-performance cars. By 1971, manufacturers were reducing compression ratios and by 1972 most cars had no more than 8.0—8.5:1.

Reducing compression slows the burning rate of the fuel/air mixture so peak pressures that encourage NO_x formation aren't reached. Reduced compression also increases heat transfer into the cylinder walls. Burning continues as the piston is descending, thereby raising the exhaust temperature.

Low compression increases the fuel/air requirement at idle. More residual exhaust gas remains in the clearance volume and combustion chamber when the intake valve opens, causing excessive mixture dilution. This can cause off-idle driveability problems. In effect, low compression promotes some EGR without emissions plumbing or hardware.

With the advent of the three-way catalytic converters, microprocessor control of engines and higher octane unleaded fuels, engineers were able to tune up engines. Compression ratios were again increased so that by 1986, 9.0—10.0:1 CRs were fairly common in production cars.

Raising or lowering the compression ratio of an engine doesn't normally affect the main system fuel requirements, so jet changes aren't usually required. Raising compression may require slightly less ignition advance in some cases.

CR and Fuel Octane—Compression ratio and octane requirements are closely related. As compression is increased, octane must also be increased. A higher octane fuel is required to avoid detonation and preignition—often called *knock*.

After World War II, high-compression engines were designed and produced to obtain higher efficiencies. By 1969, some had 11:1 compression!

Then the requirement for reduced emissions began to be tackled in earnest. First, the auto makers asked the fuel companies to start "getting the lead out" for emission equipment that wouldn't be able to tolerate lead in the exhaust.

Engineers created engines to operate on lead-free gasoline. Tetraethyl lead (Ethyl compound) was one of the most commonly used anti-knock additives used as an octane-increaser in gasolines. Lead compounds affect plant life, the atmosphere and humans. Consequently, there are serious health and ecological concerns about lead content in car fuels.

But, these weren't the only reasons engineers wanted to eliminate lead from fuel. The expensive catalyst used in converters (standard parts from 1975 on) is destroyed when contaminated with lead and lead byproducts.

The engineers, along with the oil companies, designed a small filler orifice for the gas tank. The unleaded gas pumps were equipped with nozzles to fit. This was an attempt to ensure that drivers couldn't use gasoline that could wreck the catalytic converters.

At the start of the measures, unleaded regular was 87 octane (pump reading). Premium unleaded was 91 octane (pump reading), but it was difficult to find. Premium unleaded of 92 octane (pump reading) is readily available in the '80s. Gasoline refineries have steadily reduced octane ratings and the trend is to still lower ones. Although 100+ octane gasolines were commonplace in the late '60s, 87 octane unleaded regular was a primary fuel by 1986.

EXHAUST BACK PRESSURE

Exhaust back pressure has little effect on carburetion at low speeds. For high performance, low back pressure is desired to obtain the best volumetric efficiency through optimum breathing. The effects of exhaust restriction increase approximately as the square of rpm.

Using headers may change the main jet requirement. Either richer or leaner main jets may be needed, depending on the interrelation of the engine components.

Dieseling Or "Run On"—This is the tendency of an engine to continue running irregularly and roughly after the ignition has been switched off. This problem is aggravated by:

- Anything that remains hot enough to ignite fuel/air mixtures—such as any sharp edges in the combustion chamber.
- High idle-speed settings used to meet emission requirements.
- Combustion chamber deposits.
- Low-octane fuel.

7

CARBURETOR & PERFORMANCE

Butch Leal's Pontiac has a momentary lead on Wally Balchunas' Mercury. All Pro Stocks use Holley 4500 carburetors.

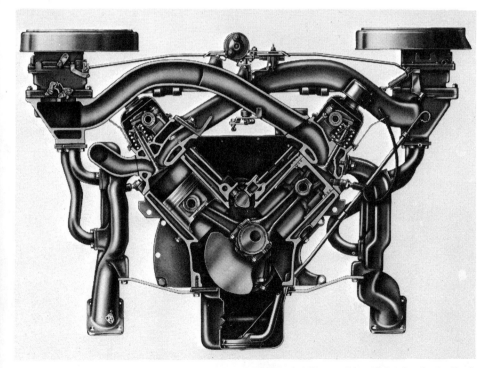

1963 Chrysler 413-CID 300J Ram Induction engine had eight equal-length intake ducts. Each four cylinder set was fed by one carburetor. An equalizing tube connected the two sets. Duct lengths were selected to give 10% torque improvement at 2800 rpm. The strong torque increase provided a noticeable acceleration improvement over a 1500-rpm range: from 50—80 mph. This engine is a classic example of ram tuning in a production car.

When we made this chapter different from Carburetor & Engine Variables, it was difficult to decide which chapter should include what subjects. Because the variables covered in the previous chapter do affect performance, be sure to read both chapters if you want maximum performance.

RAM TUNING

Ram tuning can give better cylinder filling and improved VE in a narrow speed range. A combination of engine-design features are involved:

- Intake and/or exhaust-system passage or pipe lengths.
- Valve timing.
- Velocity of intake and exhaust gases.

Although ram tuning improves torque at one point or narrow rpm band, the improvement tends to be "peaky." Power falls off sharply on either side of the peak. It is generally understood that ram tuning is a resonance phenomenon. Resonance is sought at a tuned peak with the knowledge that *the power gained at that point may be offset by corresponding losses at other speeds.*

Ram tuning can add mid-range torque. Chrysler's six-cylinder and V8 engines in the early '60s are good examples. These gains are obtained at the expense of top-end power. Or, more usual for high-performance engines, low-

and mid-range torque may be sacrificed to take advantage of top-end improvements.

Individual intake-manifold passages for each cylinder (ram or tuned length) can be measured from the intake valve to a carburetor inlet, if there is one venturi per cylinder. Or, the length may be measured from the intake valve to the entry of a plenum chamber fed by one or more carburetors. This measurement is a function of manifold design.

The tuned length at WOT can be considered to be the distance from the venturi throat (or from the carburetor inlet) to the intake valve. Either of these situations may be true. If venturi size is significantly smaller than the passage *between* the venturi and the valve, the venturi forms a reflection point and defines tuned pipe length.

If the venturi is about the same size as the passage between the venturi and the valve, then it does not form a reflection point. The tuned pipe length is determined by the next large change in section outward—probably the air horn or carburetor inlet.

For a well-shaped air horn, the reflection point will be about halfway along the bellmouth entry. There may be multiple reflections and *two* tuned lengths. One is measured from the valve to the venturi and the other to the bell-mouth entry of the carburetor air horn or velocity stack.

Engine speed at which ram effect is most pronounced varies inversely with tuned length. Therefore, the shorter the tuned length, the higher the rpm at which peak torque will occur. Conversely, the longer the passage length, the lower the rpm at which peak torque occurs.

Equations have been written to describe where ram-tuning effects will occur, but most are over-simplifications. They leave out the effects of manifold-passage size and the sizes of intake ports and valves. Making any of these larger raises the rpm at which best filling occurs. This explains why best driveability and street performance is obtained with small-port manifolds.

The torque peak can be modified by valve lift, overlap and by adding a plenum chamber between the runners and the carburetors. Using a plenum under the carburetors tends to lower the torque peak which can be achieved, but it also broadens the torque peak over a wider rpm range. Thus, the engine becomes less *peaky* and easier to tune.

Installing a plenum also reduces fuel stand-off and allows each cylinder to draw additional mixture from the other carburetor barrels at the top end of the rpm range. This greatly reduces the carburetor airflow-capacity requirement for the engine.

Valve timing greatly affects rpm capabili-

Chrysler's production plenum-ram for Hemi engine was constructed to provide peak power around 6800 rpm. Branch length and plenum volume were varied to fit specific racing applications. Large-block wedge engines had a similar manifold. Holley offers 0-4235 and 0-4236 770-cfm Model 4160s as replacements for the original List 3116 vacuum-secondary carbs with 1-11/16-in. throttle bores.

> **RAM TUNING**
> Complete details on ram-tuned intake systems are in Philip H. Smith's book, *The Scientific Design of Exhaust & Intake Systems*. This book is available from Classic Motorbooks, P.O. Box 1, Osceola, WI 54020. One of the best single articles written on the subject was by Roger Huntington in the July 1960 Hotrod magazine, "That Crazy Manifold." July and August 1964 Hotrod magazines had two articles by Dr. Gordon H. Blair, Ph.D. All are worth reading. Using a dynamometer to measure the real performance of a specially constructed "tuned" system (either intake or exhaust) is absolutely essential.

ties. Cylinder filling is aided at high rpm by holding the intake valve open past BC (Bottom Center). At low speeds, holding the valve open past BC allows part of the intake charge to be blown back onto the intake manifold as the piston rises on its compression stroke. This reversed charge reduces manifold vacuum and drastically affects idle and off-idle F/A mixture requirements.

As rpm increases, faster piston movement creates a greater pressure drop across the car-buretor. Air enters the carburetor with higher velocity, giving greater acceleration (and momentum) to the mixture traveling toward the valve. Thus, as the piston approaches BC on the intake stroke, cylinder pressure is rising toward that at the intake port. And, pressure at the intake port is being increased by air-column momentum in the intake-manifold passage supplying it. Thus, filling improves with rpm until friction losses in the manifold exceed the gain obtained from delayed valve closing.

The past two paragraphs are true, regardless of whether ram tuning is used or not. Now let's consider what happens in the manifold passage as the valve is opened and closed. When the piston starts down on its intake stroke, a *rarefaction* or negative-pressure pulse is reflected to the carburetor inlet.

As this pulse leaves the carburetor, atmospheric pressure rushes in as a positive-pressure pulse. When the passage length is optimum for the rpm at which peak torque is sought, the positive-pressure pulse arrives near the time when the valve is closing. The pulse assists in the last part of cylinder filling. Note the interrelationships of passage length, mixture velocity, valve timing and rpm. It's a complex process, to say the least!

The mixture attains a velocity of up to 300 ft

per second or more (depending on rpm) as it travels through the port during the intake stroke. Because the mixture has mass (weight), it also has momentum. This is useful for aiding cylinder filling when the intake valve is held open after BC (sometimes to 100° past BC) while the piston is rising on the compression stroke.

Manifold design must be considered because an isolated-runner (IR) type allows much longer delay in closing the intake valve than the usual single- or two-plane manifolds. This is because the IR system supplies only one cylinder per carburetor venturi. There is no other cylinder that affects mixture dilution, sharing (robbing) or adverse pulsing.

When the intake valve shuts, incoming mixture piles up or *stagnates* at the valve backside, reflecting a compression (positive-pressure) pulse or wave toward the carburetor inlet. As this wave leaves the carburetor inlet, it is followed by a negative-pressure pulse back to the valve. This bouncing or reflective phenomenon repeats several times until the inlet valve again opens. Pressure at the carburetor inlet varies from positive to negative as the wave bounces back and forth in the inlet passage.

At certain engine speeds, the reflection or resonance phenomenon will tend to be in phase (synchronized) with intake valve opening and closing. The positive pulses will tend to "ram" the mixture into the cylinder. Improved filling is the result.

Although the pulsations are in phase only at certain speeds (yes, there can be multiple peaks!), the mixture column in the intake passage provides some ram effect at all speeds because of its own inertia. Best filling is obtained with intake-system and exhaust-system resonances in phase at the same rpm.

On the exhaust side, exhaust gas enters the pipe at 80 psi or higher because the exhaust valve opens before BC (before the power stroke ends) while there is still pressure in the cylinder. Thus, the exhaust gets a "head start" so the piston does not have to work so hard pushing out the exhaust. The exhaust "pulse" starts a pressure wave traveling at the speed of sound (in hot gas) to the end of the system. From the end of the system, a rarefaction or low/negative-pressure pulse reflects back to the exhaust valve at the same speed.

Tuned systems are constructed with lengths to allow this pulse to arrive during the overlap period. The idea is to reduce exhaust residuals in the clearance volume and ensure complete emptying of the cylinder. This reduces charge dilution and provides more volume for F/A mixture—hence greater volumetric efficiency.

Main-Jet Requirements—With an IR manifold, ram tuning has a dramatic effect on main-jet requirements because strong pulsing at WOT pulls fuel out of the discharge nozzle in *both* directions. This is not of any consequence

if you're not concerned about part-throttle performance. Main-jet size can be established for WOT operation. Otherwise, the F/A mixture must be richened for part-throttle operation. An inverted power valve can accomplish this. Or, add a plenum chamber to the manifold or carburetor base to soften high-rpm WOT pulsing and use a compromise jetting. This usually handles both part-throttle and WOT operation.

The bigger the carburetor in relation to the engine size, the greater the need for an inverse power valve. The smaller the carburetor in relation to the engine size the less difference between part-throttle and WOT F/A mixture.

Tuned-exhaust effects on the main-jet requirement vary. If the exhaust causes stronger intake system pulsing, a smaller main jet could be used. Or, if the effect lessens pulsing, a larger jet may be required. Predicting these effects is extremely difficult, so tuners tackle each situation by trial and error.

Summary of Ram Tuning—Peaky results obtained with ram tuning can seriously reduce engine flexibility. Don't overlook this point. It is all too easy to get over-excited about spectacular results obtained from racing motorcycle engines, so let's look at them briefly.

Motorcycle engines are built as single-cylinder units, each with its own carburetor and exhaust pipe. This allows the designer to take advantage of two very important features: (1) no mixture-distribution problems, and (2) pressure phenomena in the intake and exhaust systems can be relied on for ramming or "supercharging" the cylinder at a very high rpm.

Thus, high-output bike engines obtain outputs of up to 2.9 HP per cubic inch! However, racing motorcycles with such engines have 8- to 11-speed gearboxes to use the extremely narrow rpm band in which power is produced. Some of these engines won't produce noticeable power below 6000 rpm.

RAM AIR

The forward motion of your car can induce some air pressure into the intake system, provided a forward-facing inlet is connected to the carburetor. This duct should have air straighteners in it. These allow air to enter the carburetor smoothly, preferably through an air cleaner or other diffusing device to break up turbulence. The scoop should mate with a tray under the carburetor/s so any ram-air pressure is not lost into the engine compartment.

While very minor pressure increases are obtained, even a minor pressure aids induction at high rpm and gives more HP where the engine is starting to "run out of breath." According to Gary Knutsen of McLaren Engines, pressures of 6 in. of water (about 0.22 psi) were obtained at racing speeds on the Chaparral race cars. On very long straights this pressure provided measurable performance benefits as op-

posed to cars running without a ram-air inlet.

Other writers claim the improvement can amount to as much as +1.2% at 100 mph, +2.7% at 150 mph and +4.8% at 300 mph. No matter what the capability of an engine, such increases can make the difference between winning and losing.

You may have noted some race cars equipped with a forward-facing air scoop over the induction system. These typically have the scoop opening ahead of the hood. It should be far enough above the hood or roll bar, so the scoop picks up relatively unturbulent air.

BLOCKED HEAT RISERS

Blocked heat risers may prove acceptable for street driving in the summer. When it starts to get chilly, change to the exhaust-heated manifold. Otherwise, the long time required for the engine to warm the manifold for acceptable vaporization and smooth running will make the car miserable to drive. Having exhaust heat during cold weather plays an important part in making the engine last longer. If you insist on feeding a poorly vaporized mixture to the cylinders during cold weather, excess gasoline will wash oil from the cylinders and wear out the engine in a hurry.

COLD AIR & DENSITY

Mixture density has been thoroughly discussed in Engine Requirements. There we show that higher density inlet air improves the engine's VE proportionate to the density increase. So, let's examine the practical aspects. What can you do to keep density "up" to get best HP from your engine?

First, underhood temperature is not ideal for HP production. Even on a reasonably cool day, air reaching the carburetor inlet has been warmed by passing through the radiator and over the hot engine components. Underhood temperatures soar to 175F (80C) and higher when the engine is turned off and the car stands in the sun. An engine ingesting warm air loses more power than you might imagine. Assume that the outside (ambient) air temperature is 70F (21C) and the underhood temperature is 150F (66C). Use the following equation:

$$\gamma oa = \sqrt{\frac{460 + t_{uh}}{460 + t_{oa}}} \times \gamma uha$$

$$\gamma oa = \sqrt{\frac{460 + 150}{460 + 70}} \times \gamma uha$$

$$\gamma oa = \sqrt{1.15} \ (\gamma uha) \text{ or } 1.072 \ \gamma uha$$

where

γoa	= outside air density
γuha	= underhood air density
t_{oa}	= outside air temperature
t_{uh}	= underhood air temperature

You can calculate relative air density from barometer and temperature readings, but most tuners prefer an *air density meter.* It can be used to help select correct main-jet area according to square root of air-density changes (in percent). Air density changes from hour-to-hour and day-to-day, and most certainly from one week to the next and one altitude to another.

Pro Stock car with hood-mounted air scoop has base that seals carburetor inlets into scoop so ram air can be fully used.

In this example, outside-air density is 107.2% of underhood-air density, or 7.2% greater. Because mass airflow increases in direct proportion with density, HP with outside air will increase at the square root of 1.15, which is 1.072 or 7.2%. If the engine produces 300 HP with 150F (66C) air-inlet temperature, it can be expected to produce 322 HP with 70F (21C) air-inlet temperature. The density increase caused by using outside air is considerable.

Cold air gives more improvement than ram air because approximately 1% HP increase is gained for every 11F drop in temperature. This assumes the mixture is adjusted to compensate for the density change and there is no detonation or other problems. Using outside air instead of underhood air is climate-limited because too-cold temperatures may cause carburetor icing.

Air Scoops—If air scoops are used to duct air to the carburetor, do not connect the hose or scoop directly to the carburetor. Instead, connect the scoop to a cold-air box or to the air-cleaner housing to avoid creating turbulence as the incoming air enters the carburetor air horn.

If you use a cold-air kit that picks up cold air at the front bumper, be prepared to change the air-cleaner filter element at regular intervals. You may have to change as often as once a week in dustier areas. If you leave the filter out of the system, plan on new rings or a rebore job because your engine will quickly wear out.

You are better off ducting cold air from the cowl just ahead of the windshield. This high-pressure area ensures a supply of cool outside air to the carburetor. That area still gets airborne dust, but it is several feet off of the ground and away from some of the heavier grimy grit encountered at road level. Using fresh air from the cowl is another way to get performance while keeping your car looking stock.

Cars with stock hoods and stock or near-stock-height manifolds may be equipped with fresh-air ducting to the air cleaner by using parts from some high-performance cars.

Or, you may prefer to use one of the fresh-air hoods offered on some models. These typically mate a scoop structure on the hood with the air-cleaner tray on the carburetor/s. Thus, underhood air is kept out of the carburetor.

If a tall manifold such as an IR or plenum-ram type is used, the hood must be cut for clearance and a scoop added to cover the carburetor/s. Whether the scoop opens at the front or back depends on airflow over the car. The optimum air entry into the scoop may have to be determined by testing. An optimum entry provides an above-atmospheric-pressure air supply that is non-turbulent.

In general, scoop-opening area should be approximately 12% larger than carburetor-venturi area. The scoop roof should be positioned 1-1/2-in. above the carburetor inlet. Any more clearance may create detrimental turbulence and any less restricts airflow into the carburetor.

Econo Dragster has velocity stack sealed to base of scoop. Carburetor is on a 2-in. spacer to increase plenum volume, straighten mixture flow and improve distribution.

Fresh-air hood components on Camaro. Former Chevrolet engineer Gerry Thompson holds air cleaner base that fits on two four-barrel Holleys. Hood is open at back by cowl. Hood duct mates with foam rubber gasket.

Chevy high-rise manifold for Z-28/LT-1 has oil shield under heat-riser area. Shield and blocked heat riser help keep intake charge cool.

INCREASED DENSITY EQUALS LARGER JETS

No matter how a density increase is obtained, by increased atmospheric pressure, a cold manifold or a cooler inlet-air temperature, it must be accompanied with larger main jets. Area size increase is directly proportional to square root of density increase in percent.

Fuel-cooling can (*cool can*) is often used by drag racers. Fuel passing through coiled line is cooled by ice or dry ice and alcohol in can. Cooler fuel temperature ensures carburetors receive liquid fuel. Cold fuel under pressure isn't likely to flash into vapor when it drops to atmospheric pressure as it enters carburetor.

Like fresh-air hoods, scoop-equipped hoods should mate with a tray under the carburetor/s to keep warm underhood air out of them.

Drag racers always keep the hood open and avoid running the engine between events so the compartment stays as cool as possible. It is helpful to spray water onto the radiator to help cool it. This ensures the engine water temperature will be lower and the radiator will not heat incoming air any more than is necessary.

Although "seat-of-the-pants" feel may indicate stronger performance from a cold engine, the fact of the matter is that the engine coolant temperature should be around 180F (82C) or so to allow minimum friction inside the engine. Keep the engine oil and water temperature at operating levels while taking care to keep down the inlet-air temperature.

While we are talking about improving density by using cold inlet air, let's remember that a heated manifold reduces density. Exhaust heat to the manifold should be blocked off to create a "cold" manifold for performance.

There are various ways to do this. In some instances intake-manifold gaskets are available to close off the heat openings. Or, a piece of stainless steel or tin-can metal can be slipped between the gasket and manifold to block off the opening. Many competition manifolds have no heat riser and therefore the manifolds are "cold" to start with. Some car makers offer shields that fit under the manifold to prevent hot oil from heating a cold manifold, or at least to reduce that tendency. This can be a cheap way to gain a few HP on a small-block V8.

AIR CLEANERS

Because every engine needs an air cleaner to reduce expensive cylinder wear caused by dust, it makes sense to use one that will not restrict the carburetor's airflow capabilities. Avoiding restrictions allows your engine to develop full power.

The only time an engine might possibly be run without an air cleaner is on engines being operated where there is no dust in the air or pits, which is an unlikely condition. Even then, when an air cleaner is removed from the carburetor, the air cleaner base or something similar should be retained because its shape may provide a efficient entry path for the incoming air. It also will help to keep incoming air from being heated by the engine.

K & N Filters makes an air entry device to smooth airflow entering the carburetor. They call it a *Stubstack,* and suggest it be used in conjunction with one of their air cleaners. A device such as this can be worth several HP.

The table on this page shows the results of tests which dispel some common fallacies about air cleaners and their capabilities. In general, a tall, open-element air cleaner provides the least restriction. It also increases air-inlet noise.

Note that some air cleaners allow full airflow capability. These air cleaners should be used by racers, even if their use requires adding a hood "bump." An air cleaner that gives full-flow capability to the carburetor provides impressive top-end power improvements, as compared with one that restricts flow. For instance, the use of two high-performance Chevrolet air cleaners stacked together (instead of one open-element cleaner) improved a 1969 Trans Am Camaro's lap times at Donnybrook, Minnesota by one full second.

It is very important to check clearance between the upper lid of the air cleaner and the top of the carburetor's *pitot* or *vent* tubes. Air-cleaner elements vary as much as 1/8 in. in height due to production tolerances. Shorter elements can place the lid too close to the pitot tubes so correct bowl reference pressures are not developed. Whether the pitot tubes are angled or flat on top, there should always be at least 3/8-in. clearance between the tube tip and the underside of the air-cleaner lid.

You have noticed the long *snorkle* intakes on modern air cleaners. These are intake-noise reducers, not performance improvers. High-HP engines nearly always have two snorkles for more air and perhaps for image, too. For competition, the snorkle can be removed where it joins the cleaner housing. Additional holes can be cut into the cleaner housing to approximate an open-element configuration to improve breathing. Or, it may be possible to expose more of the element surface by inverting the cleaner top. An open-element design is least restrictive.

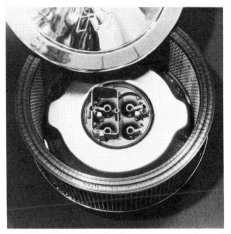

K & N 14-in.-dia. air cleaner uses 5-in. tall reusable oiled element. Shown here on Holley 4150 alcohol carburetor. It can be cleaned and reused. This type of filter is popular for off-road and dirt-track competition.

K & N Stub-Stack is another air-entry device for Holley two- or four-barrel carburetors. Flow improvements of several percent are claimed. Device can be used with or without an air cleaner.

AIR CLEANER COMPARISON Model 4165, List 6210	
Cleaner Type	**WOT Airflow (cfm)**
None	713
Chevrolet 396 closed-element with single snorkle	480
Chevrolet 396 closed-element with single snorkle cut off at housing	515
Same as above, but with two elements	690
Chevrolet high-performance open-element unit	675
Same as above, but with two elements	713
14-in. diameter open-element accessory-type air cleaner	675
Chevrolet truck-type element (tall) used with accessory-type base and lid	713
Foam-type cleaner (domed flat-funnel type)	675

NOTE: All data obtained with same carburetor. New clean paper elements used in all cases.

Holley Tests
October 1971

When it's time to race, use a clean filter element. Keep the air cleaner base on the carburetor if you possibly can, even if you have removed the air cleaner cover and element. Be sure to secure the cleaner and/or base so it cannot vibrate off to strike the fan, radiator or distributor.

Because the carburetor is internally balanced, that is, the vents are located in the air-horn area, no jet change should be required when the air cleaner is removed.

Dual snorkles or inlets are usually a trademark of factory high-performance vehicle. One at left is a 1972 Pontiac GTO. Right photo shows Chevrolet Z-28 air cleaner. This high-performance air cleaner is one of least restrictive single-element cleaners available.

Holley tests showed a 2.4% flow improvement when 3-1/2-in. velocity stacks were added to a 1050-cfm Model 4500. Velocity stacks clean up air entry so there is less flow-robbing turbulence.

TABLE OF VELOCITY STACK EFFECTS				
For Four-Barrel Carburetors				
Carburetor	No Stack	3-1/2" Stack	5" Stack	Improvement
Model 4500, 0-4575	1005 cfm	1030 cfm		baseline +2.4%
Model 4150, 0-4781	825 cfm	830 cfm	833 cfm	baseline +0.6% +0.9%
Model 4165, 0-6262	812	845	845	baseline +4%
Holley Tests July 1971				

VELOCITY STACKS

Velocity stacks are often seen on racing engines. These can improve cylinder filling (charging) to a certain extent, depending on many other factors. For instance, when velocity stacks are used on an isolated-runner manifold, the stacks may form part of a tuned length for the air column.

Velocity stacks also provide a straightening effect to the entering air. And, they can contain fuel standoff, which is typical with isolated-runner-design manifolds. Remember that velocity stacks need space above them to allow air to enter smoothly. Mounting a hood or air-box structure too close to the top of the stacks reduces airflow into the carburetor. Two inches should be considered a bare minimum clearance between the top of a velocity stack and any structure over it.

When an air cleaner is used on a carburetor equipped with stacks, keep the 2 in. recommended clearance between the top of the stacks and the underside of the air-cleaner lid. This may require using two open-element air cleaners fastened together with RTV or another sealant—and a longer stud between the carburetor top and the cleaner lid.

Holley carburetors designed for use with velocity stacks, such as the Model 4500, can sometimes obtain as much as 7—9% airflow improvement. On the usual four-barrel with the 5-in. air cleaner base, wide-mouthed entry devices provided improvements ranging from insignificant (less than 1%) to as much as 4%.

DISTRIBUTION CHECKING

Distribution checking determines whether all cylinders are receiving an equal mixture. This is extremely important when a manifold or carburetor change is made. A previous carburetor/manifold combination may have provided nearly perfect distribution, but you cannot take the chance that one or more cylinders will be running lean. Several ways of checking distribution are detailed in the distribution section of the Engine Requirements chapter.

Exhaust Temperature—If you have a Superflow or other computer-controlled dynamometer, an exhaust temperature printout for all cylinders will help you check distributuion. Strive for differences of not more than 100F (38C), and preferably less. Chevrolet Performance Products Engineer Bill Howell suggests a temperature range of 1450—1550F (788—844C) for the Chevrolet V6 or V8 small block. Other engines may require slightly different exhaust temperatures for peak power output.

Reading Sparkplugs—At the race track there's only one way to do it. You have to rely on the appearance and color of the plug electrodes and porcelains. These can provide a lot of valuable information about what is happening in the engine.

An accompanying plug color chart explains some things to look for. The part of most interest is the base of the porcelain. Because it is "buried" in the plug shell, an illuminated magnifier should be in your tool box.

Checking plug color gives only a rough idea of what is occurring in the way of mixture ratio and distribution. It is difficult to see a change in plug color without changing the main jet at least four sizes.

In How Your Carburetor Works, we describe Holley's Quarter Mile Dial System. It allows changing fuel/air ratio up to 20% or 5 main jet sizes *without removing the fuel bowl*. Changes

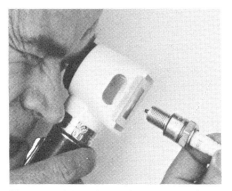

Plug porcelain color and appearance being checked with sparkplug illuminator. These include a magnifier to aid in plug reading. One should be in every tuner's tool kit. Engine must be "cut clean" by turning off ignition and declutching or getting into Neutral at the conclusion of WOT full-power run in top gear. If this method isn't used, plug readings are meaningless.

can be made as the car is driven. This tuner's tool is especially helpful once you've established basic jetting. It can be used to fine tune for atmospheric or altitude changes.

Many items cause plug-appearance variations. Using plug color to check distribution is only helpful when the engine is in good condition. Engine condition can be checked quickly with a compression gage to make sure all cylinders provide equal compression at cranking speed. For a more accurate check, a leakdown test can compare cylinder condition.

New plugs take time to "color"—even three or four drag-strip runs may fail to "color" new plugs. Plug color is only meaningful when the engine is declutched and "cut clean" at the end of a high-speed full-throttle, high-gear run. If you allow the engine to slow with the engine still running, plug appearance will be meaningless. Plug readings can be made after full-throttle runs on a chassis dyno with the transmission in an intermediate gear so the dyno is not overspeeded. But road tests require high gear to load the engine correctly.

Plug checks can be useful where the engine has been running at full throttle against full load applied by an engine dyno. It is easier to get good plug readings on the dyno because full power can be applied and the engine cut clean without difficulty. Plugs can be read quickly because you can get to them easier than in the usual installation. However, don't think that plug heat range and carburetor jetting established on an engine dyno will be absolutely right for the same engine installed in your racing chassis. Airflow conditions past the carburetors can easily change the requirements—perhaps so unevenly that different cylinders will need different changes.

It would be nice if every plug removed from an engine looked like the others from the same engine—in color and condition. But this is seldom ever achieved! Color and other differences indicate combustion-chamber temperatures and/or fuel/air ratios are not the same in every cylinder—or that related engine components need attention. The problem is greatly complicated in engines where there is a great difference between the cylinders in turbulence and efficiency. The big-block Chevrolet is a notable example.

If differences exist in the firing end of the plugs when you examine them, the cause may be due to one or more factors:

● Unequal distribution of the mixture.

● Unequal valve timing (due to incorrect lash or a worn cam).

● Poor oil control (rings, excess clearance or valve-stem seals).

Ignition Checking—Problems within the ignition system can also lead to plugs not reading the same or misfiring:

● Loose point plate.

● Arcing in the distributor cap.

● Defective rotor, cap or plug wires/connectors.

● Cross-fire between plug wires.

● Defective primary wire or even a resistor that opens intermittently.

Pay special attention to the cleanliness of the entire ignition system including the inside and outside of the distributor cap and the outside of the coil tower. Also, clean the inside of the coil and cap cable receptacles. Any dirt or grease here can allow some or all of the spark energy to leak away.

If the cylinders have equal compression and the valves are lashed correctly, a difference in plug appearance may indicate a mixture-distribution problem. It is sometimes possible to remedy this with main-jet changes.

For instance, if one or more plugs show a lean condition, install larger main jets in the throttle bore/s feeding those cylinders. Should one or more plugs show a rich condition, install smaller main jets in the throttle bore/s feeding those cylinders.

The real problem occurs when several cylinders fed from the *same* throttle bore show different mixture conditions: some lean with some correct, or some rich with some correct, or perhaps a combination of all three conditions! This reveals a manifold fault that can't be corrected with jet changes. Correcting such conditions requires manifold rework beyond the scope of this book.

HEADER EFFECTS VS. JETTING

Headers usually reduce exhaust back pressure so the engine's VE is increased—it breathes easier! The main effects of headers are seen at WOT and high rpm.

Using headers may change the main-jet requirement. Either richer or leaner jets may be needed, depending on the interrelation of the engine components.

The preceding ram-tuning section details how a tuned exhaust system that alters the pulsing seen by the carburetor may make main-jet changes necessary to compensate for any increase/reduction in intake-system pulsing.

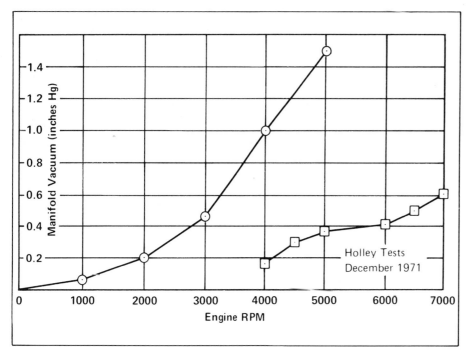

Chart shows minimum restriction by using two four-barrel carburetors for drag-race or competition engine. Such installations provide horsepower equivalent to racing fuel-injection systems. Linked circles represent Holley Model 4165, 0-6210 650-cfm carb on Chevy L-46 350-CID engine. Linked boxes are two Holley 4160, 0-6224 carbs on 350-CID Chevy racing engine with plenum-type manifold.

CARBURETOR RESTRICTION

Carburetors are tested at a given pressure drop at WOT to obtain a cfm rating indicative of flow capacity. One- and two-barrel carburetors are tested at 3.0-in.Hg pressure drop. Three- and four-barrel carburetors are tested at 1.5-in.Hg pressure drop.

When you want to make comparisons, use these formulas:

$$\text{Equivalent flow at 1.5 in.Hg} = \frac{\text{cfm at 3.0 in.Hg}}{1.414}$$

$$\text{Equivalent flow at 3.0 in.Hg} = \text{cfm at 3.0 in.Hg} \times 1.414$$

The one- and two-barrel rating was adopted because low-performance engines typically showed WOT manifold-vacuum readings of 3.0 in.Hg. When four-barrel carburetors and high-performance engines became commonplace they were rated at 1.5-in.Hg pressure drop because of *two* reasons.

First, this rating was close to the WOT manifold vacuum being seen in these engines. Second, most carburetor testing equipment had been designed for smaller carburetors. Pump capacity on this expensive test equipment would only provide 1.5-in.Hg pressure drop through larger carburetors. Hence the 1.5-in. rating came about as a "happy accident."

For maximum output, it is essential to have the carburetor as large as possible—*consistent with the required operating (driving) range.* Driving range (maximum rpm) must be considered as discussed in the chapter, Select & Install Your Carburetor.

Using a lot of flow capacity, more than calculations indicate necessary for the engine, can reduce inlet-system restriction and increase VE at WOT and very high rpm. Such carburetion arrangements compete with fuel injection in terms of performance because the restrictions are minor. But note that the dual-quad installations typically used by professional drag racers are not capable of providing usable low- or mid-range performance. These engines typically operate in a very narrow range of 6000—8500 rpm or so.

TOOLS REQUIRED

Start with patience! You need more than the feel in the seat of your pants and the speedometer for serious tuning. Specific tools are required, but you'll especially need a patient and methodical approach to the project. This means you cannot be in a hurry. If you have no intention of really getting serious about tuning, run your Holley as it comes out of the box and leave your tool box locked up.

A vacuum gage, fuel-pressure gage and a stop watch are essential. So is a tachometer. Vacuum and fuel-pressure gages are an extra set of "eyes" to let you see what's happening inside of the engine. For serious competition on a regular basis, an air-density gage is especially helpful. You'll also want a 1-in. open-end wrench, preferably the MAC-141. It's specifically designed for fuel-inlet nuts on two- and four-barrel carburetors with center-hung floats. A broad-blade screwdriver can be used for jet changes.

TIMING DEVICES

Although a stop watch can be used for some very fine tuning, you may want to consider getting your own timing device with associated photocells, or rent a portable unit so you can set up the lights at varying distances. Pro-Stock racers often test acceleration over a initial 60 ft to work out starting techniques, tire combinations and carburetion. Most races are won in the critical starting period and by initial acceleration over the first few feet.

A FEW PARTS WILL BE HELPFUL

When you are working on a two- or four-barrel with detachable fuel bowls, have a few parts available. Foremost among these are extra bowl and metering-block gaskets and bowl-screw gaskets. Be especially careful to buy the correct bowl gaskets for carburetors with the non-pullover pump discharge nozzles (such as the 4165s or the 6425). Although similar to those used on 4150/60 and 2300, they are NOT the same. O-rings for the transfer tube, if used, should also be on your shopping list.

Before you buy any main jets, find out what size is already in the carburetor. If the carburetor is new, check Holley's Illustrated Parts & Specs catalog to see which jets are *supposed* to be in the carburetor. Or, check the Holley High-Performance Catalog.

Neither is foolproof because Holley changes jet sizes to fit specific application requirements and catalogs must be printed before some of the carburetors are finalized. Take the top off of the carburetor or pull off the fuel bowls and look for yourself to be absolutely sure. Mark the jetting on the bowls.

Once you know what jets you have, buy four sizes lean and four sizes rich for each main jet in your carburetor. This will handle most engine variations and most atmospheric-condition changes (density).

Or, you can install Holley's Quarter Mile Dial System to change fuel/air ratio up to 20%

Jet extensions and modified float for secondary bowl on Econo-Dragster. These cars leave starting line so fast that fuel moves away from main jets, leaning the mixture. Notched float clears tubes. Holley Tech Rep made this mod at Indianapolis Drags; an example of Holley's racing support.

Holley released these main-jet *slosh tubes* for Ford NASCAR application with backwards-mounted carburetor. When they are soldered or Loctited into place to hold them in the jets, jet changing can become a real chore.

or 5 main jet sizes *without removing the fuel bowl*. This tuner's tool is especially helpful once you've established basic jetting. It can be used to fine tune for atmospheric or altitude changes. Each switch position is one-half jet number size, or 2%.

Main jets are not necessarily the same size in a four-barrel. Secondaries may contain different jets than the primary side. And, if you are running a big-block Chevrolet with an open-plenum manifold, the carburetor should use three different jet sizes because it is "stagger-jetted."

For plenum-type all-out drag-race manifolds, install at least two sizes larger main jets. These are the only two cases where jets should be changed *before* running the engine. Otherwise, make your first tests with the carburetor jetted *exactly as supplied by Holley*. There are no other exceptions.

For any four barrel with a 650—850-cfm main body, main jets are usually between 76—81, assuming power valves are installed in the carburetor, if they were there originally. If the carburetor you are working with is a four barrel in this size range and the jets are more than four sizes away from the 76—81 spread, chances are that whoever jetted the carburetor lost his bearings and got off course with the jetting. Put back the original jetting before you start tuning. Mark the jetting on the bowls.

Drag racing often requires richer jets. For instance, if 80s worked fine on the dynamometer, you may need 82s or 84s at the strip. Jets have to be rich to get a mixture equivalent to that obtained on the dynamometer with rock-steady conditions. Double-pumpers or carburetors with a high-capacity pump may not

need extra-rich jetting for the strip because the pumps usually inject enough fuel to cover up the airflow lag.

ONE CHANGE AT A TIME

It never occurs to some would-be tuners, and even some old-timers, that changes must be made ONE at a time. It's too easy to be tempted, especially when you are sure you need a heavier flywheel, different gear ratio, other tires, a different main jet, two degrees more spark advance and a different plug heat-range. Changing one of these at a time would be just TOO SLOW.

You, or your buddies convince yourself of that. And, first thing you know, you've lost the baseline tune and you don't know where you're at or how you got there. When you are trying to tune your carburetor (a complex piece of equipment in itself) there's all the more reason to make one change at a time. Then check it against known performance by the clocks, or by your stopwatch and tachometer as described elsewhere in this chapter.

Anytime you change more than one thing, you no longer have any idea of which change helped (or hindered) performance. It's even possible that one change provided a positive improvement that was cancelled by the negative effects of the other change. The net result *seemed to be* no change.

When tuning, follow a procedure and stick to it. The less help (and therefore, advice) you have, the better. Concentrate. Be deliberate. And don't be surprised when the process eats up more time than you ever though it could. If planning other changes soon, such as a different manifold, camshaft, air cleaner, distributor-advance curve, cylinder heads or exhaust system, then put off tuning until the car and engine are set up as you expect to run it. Otherwise, your tuning effects will be wasted and you can look forward to a repeat performance of the entire tuning process.

Whatever you do, don't fall into the common trap of rejetting the carburetor to some specialized calibration that you read about in a magazine article or heard about at the drag strip last week. Holley spent thousands of dollars getting the calibration correct. There is good reason to believe they used more engineers, technicians, test vehicles, dynamometers, flow benches, emission instrumentation and other equipment and expertise than you may have available. Remembering these hard facts will save your time, effort, money and temper.

When you make jet changes from standard, use a grease pencil or a marking pen to mark the bowls with the main-jet sizes you've installed. Some tuners use pressure-sensitive labels on fuel bowls for noting which jets are installed. Others write the information on a light-colored portion of the firewall or fenderwell where it won't be wiped off during normal tuning activities such as plug changes.

Noting what jets have been used saves a lot of time when tuning because no time is wasted in disassembly and reassembly to see what jets are in the carburetor/s. Even the best memories are guaranteed to fail the jet-size memory test.

BEFORE YOU START TUNING

Now that you've gathered the tools, spare jets and other paraphernalia, here are a few more details. First and foremost, check the accelerator pumps to make sure they operate with the slightest movement. And, check that there is at least 0.015—0.020-in. added travel in the diaphragm-operating lever at WOT.

The Select & Install Your Carburetor chapter also discusses checking and setting fuel levels for bowls with sight plugs. Do it! If your car-

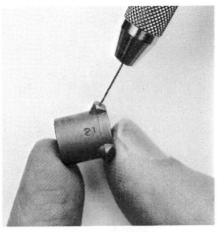

Use a pin vise to hold drill for accelerator-pump shooter. "21" stamped on shooter is original hole size in thousandths of an inch.

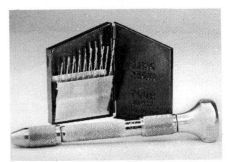

Wire drill index with drills from 0.0135—0.039 in. (Numbers 80—61) is useful item for serious tuners. Pin vise holds drill bit. Use only your fingers to twist these tiny drills.

buretor does not have removable bowls, be sure the fuel level is correct before proceeding.

Remove the air cleaner (temporarily!) so that you can look into the air horn. Have someone else mash the pedal to the floor as you check with a flashlight to make sure the throttles fully open (not slightly angled). If they're not opening fully, figure out why and fix the problem. Any time you remove and replace the carburetor, check again to ensure that you have a fully opening throttle. It is the easiest item to overlook and the cause of a lot of lost races or poor times. Any honest racing mechanic will admit that he's been tripped up by a part-opening throttle *at least once.*

For drag racing, air cleaners are generally not used. For any other competition where dust is involved, be sure to use a low-restriction paper-element cleaner, such as a tall open-element AC type and replace it often. Combination paper-element and oiled-foam cleaners should be used for very dusty conditions. If the cleaner is removed, the engine can suck in a lot of abrasive dirt by merely running back down the return road. If the engine has to last, then stop at the turn off and put the air cleaner on, or push the car back to the pits.

The air cleaner directs air into the carburetor so the vents work correctly and air gets into the air bleeds correctly. You have probably read a lot of articles that said to be sure to leave the air-cleaner base in place, even if you had to remove the air cleaner for some obscure reason. Lest you think the writers were kidding you, one dyno test series showed a 3 HP loss by removing the air-cleaner base. It causes air to flow into the carburetor with less turbulence. It is essential! As previously mentioned, use a shaped air-cleaner base or K & N Stubstack to promote smooth air entry into the carburetor.

Air cleaners also protect against fires caused by starting "belch-backs," reduce intake noise, and reduce engine wear. Intake noise can be horrendous, even worse than exhaust noise, on

an engine turning a lot of rpm. Air cleaners greatly reduce that noise.

Before leaving the subject of air cleaners, look at how the stock cleaner is designed before you invest in some flat-top, flat-bottom, short cleaner because it looks good. Note that the high-performance cleaner stands high above the carburetor air inlet. Adequate space allows the incoming air to enter correctly and with minimum turbulence. With a flat filter sitting right on top of the air inlet you may lose HP.

For racing, take the sintered-bronze filters out of the inlets to the fuel bowls. Make sure a filter is in the line between the pump and the carburetor/s. Also make sure the choke is locked open (for racing only!). If you remove the choke, plug all holes left when you take out the shaft, operating mechanism and fast-idle linkage. It's not really necessary to remove the choke.

ACCELERATOR-PUMP TUNING

The engine's ability to come off the line "clean" indicates a pump "shot" adequate for the application. A common complaint, heard again and again, is "It won't take the gas." Actually it's the other way around because the engine is not getting *enough* gas and a "bog" is occurring.

Two symptoms often appear. The first of these is the car bogs—then goes. This can be caused by pump-discharge nozzles that are too small so not enough fuel is supplied fast enough. The second symptom is one of the car starting off in seemingly good fashion, then bogging, then going once more. We are talking

about drag-race starting here. In this second case, the pump-discharge nozzles may be correctly sized. But, the pump is not big enough to supply sufficient capacity to carry the engine through.

Solving the first problem may mean using larger pump-discharge nozzles, which may require a larger pump, too. More details on tuning discharge-nozzle size appear a few paragraphs later.

In the second case smaller nozzles may be tried in the hope that the existing pump size will then handle the capacity requirement. If that fails, then try a larger pump with the original nozzles.

As a general rule, the more load the engine sees, the more pump shot needed in rate and volume. If the engine sees less load as the vehicle leaves the line, shooter (discharge-nozzle) size can be reduced. Less load occurs when an 1800 rpm stall speed converter is replaced with a 3000 rpm converter in an automatic transmission. The same is true when replacing a light flywheel with a heavier one.

Valve timing affects pump-shot requirement. Long valve timing (duration) and wide overlap create a need for more pump shot than a stock camshaft requires.

Carburetor size and position also affect pump-shot requirements. More pump shot is needed when the carburetor is mounted a long way from the intake ports, as on a plenum-ram manifold or a center-mounted carburetor on a Corvair or VW.

The larger the carburetor flow capacity in relation to engine displacement and rpm—the more need for a sizeable pump shot. This covers up the "hole" caused by slamming the throttles wide open. This is especially true with mechanically operated secondaries.

Think about this for a moment and you'll see clearly why Holley warns against converting vacuum-operated secondary throttles to mechanical operation. There's no pump to cover up the "hole" caused by secondary opening. That's the reason for "double-pumpers." They give an adequate pump shot to cover up mechanically opening the secondaries.

Sometimes a carburetor is changed from one engine to another or the engine is changed into a different vehicle. Or, drastic changes may be made in the vehicle itself. The main problem will always be tip-in performance. Work may be needed to get the accelerator-pump system to perform as you'd like.

Shooter-size tuning is best done by increasing the nozzle diameter (or decreasing it) until crisp response is obtained when the throttle is "winged" (snapped open) on a free engine (no load). When crisp response is obtained, increase the nozzle size another 0.002 in. The combination will probably be drivable for a drag application.

Pump-Shot Duration—Pump-shot duration can be timed by shooter size, pump-cam lift and pump capacity. Shooter size also determines the rate fuel is fed from the accelerator-pump system during WOT "slams." The override spring is a safety valve that "gives" (compresses) when the throttle is slammed open. Compressed spring force against the lever operating the diaphragm establishes delivery pressure in the pump system. Delivery rate then depends on system pressure and shooter size.

The override spring must never be adjusted so it is *coil-bound* or has no capability of being compressed. Never replace the spring with a solid bushing to improve pump action. Either course of action will cause a ruptured pump diaphragm and/or a badly bent pump linkage because gasoline won't compress. Something has to give or break if the throttle is slammed open and there's no shock absorber.

If the pump cam provides full lift and therefore full travel for the pump diaphragm, cam *shape* is not important for drag-race applications. The cam merely provides a way to compress the override spring so the spring causes the pump to deliver its shot. *Position* of the cam on the throttle shaft is very important for the drag racer. The relation of throttle opening to cam lift is shown in a graph on page 31 of How Your Carburetor Works. This clearly shows that if the throttle is opened very far to provide staging rpm, so much of the cam lift is used up that the pump cannot deliver a full shot.

Determine what throttle opening is required to obtain the desired staging rpm. Then rotate the cam backward on the shaft until the pump lever again rests on the heel of the cam (no-lift

position). You may find one of the existing holes will line up with a hole in the throttle lever, or you may have to drill another hole in the plastic cam.

Check that there is NO clearance between the pump actuating lever and the cam. Resetting the throttle to a lower idle speed can move the cam away from the lever and delay the pump shot. A mere 2° throttle movement should move the pump lever. When readjusting the pump-operating-lever adjusting screw to reestablish contact with the cam, check that there is 0.015—0.020 in. additional travel for the diaphragm lever at WOT between the lever and the adjusting screw.

Various cams are offered for the 2300, 4150/60/80, 4165 and 4500 carburetors. These are primarily for use in tuning the actuating of the accelerator pump/s on carburetors used for engines being driven with varying throttle openings. This includes street and highway use, road courses and circle-track racing.

Carburetors that don't use cam actuation of the accelerator pump can sometimes be modified for added capacity by lever/linkage changes to get maximum pump stroke. The pump piston should nearly bottom in its well. Stroke increases may be gained by lifting the piston to a higher starting position but not past the fill slot or pump-well entry. Each carburetor must be examined to see whether the diaphragm bottoms in its housing. If not, minor linkage/cam modifications may allow added travel so the diaphragm is just short of bottoming at full lift.

In a carburetor that doesn't have removable shooters (passages drilled into body), drilling the discharge nozzle/s may require disassembling the carburetor. A lead ball or other plug may have to be removed to allow access to the discharge passage.

POWER-VALVE TUNING

You may immediately think, "I know just what to do—take it out!" No, regardless of all the material written to the contrary, *there is seldom any real reason to take out the power valve* and replace it with a plug, even though Holley sells plugs for that purpose.

The power valve in the secondary is especially important because it allows using smaller main jets. Braking forces don't cause the engine to run excessively rich and there is no tendency for the engine to load up or run rich at part-throttle. Holley's engineering staff has found many advantages by leaving power valves in place.

The valves have an important purpose or they would not be installed in the first place. If they could be left out, Holley could reduce their manufacturing costs. The power valve is the "switch" between the mixture ratio for cruising and that required for full power.

Power-valve tuning requires using a vacuum

gage. Let's use as an example a car equipped with a camshaft that provides such low manifold vacuum at idle or part-throttle that the power valve opens, giving richer mixtures or perhaps flutters on and off due to vacuum fluctuations. In this instance, a power valve that opens at a still lower vacuum should be installed. If a 65 power valve is in the carburetor and the vacuum occasionally drops to 5 in.Hg at idle or part-throttle, install a 40 power valve (opens at 4 in.Hg). This ensures that the power valve will not open until its added fuel is needed.

It is essential to know what the manifold vacuum is at idle. It is also one situation where it is necessary to have a gage that is not highly damped, that is, the needle has to "jump" to follow vacuum fluctuations or you won't know how low the vacuum is getting.

Another application that demands a vacuum gage is racing in a class where carburetion is limited to a certain carburetor type or size that is too small for the engine. A class demanding the use of a single two-barrel is typical. Here, manifold vacuum may remain fairly high as the car is driven through the traps at the end of the quarter. That's just one example, of course.

The power valve should always have a higher opening point than the highest manifold vacuum attained during the run, especially at the end. If this is not the case, the power valve will close and the engine will run lean. Disaster will result—usually in the form of a holed piston. Sometimes it will get lean enough to cause "popping" sounds from the exhaust.

For example, a carburetor is equipped with a 30 (3.0 in.Hg) power valve. Testing shows that manifold vacuum is 4.0 in.Hg through the high-speed portion of the course. Change the power valve to a 65 or 85. Keep in mind the previous example so the power valve does not open at idle because of manifold-vacuum fluctuations created by camshaft characteristics.

> **POWER VALVE CHANNEL RESTRICTION (PCVR)**
> A large-area PVCR is sometimes used on secondaries to allow using smaller main jets for best fuel control under severe braking. If *reducing* PVCR diameter, close original hole with lead shot or Devcon F aluminum-base epoxy compound. Then redrill to the desired size. Or, drill the PVCR in a metering block to allow pressing in idle-feed restrictions obtained from an old metering block. Press in the brass restriction and redrill to needed size.

LOCK SCREW

ADJUSTING NUT

SIGHT PLUG

Adjustable needle/seat assemblies used on some Holleys with removable fuel bowls are adjusted by loosening lock screw. Turn nut to raise or lower fuel level. Locking the adjustment is only function of lock screw.

Flat-track racing (especially with super-modified cars) and slaloms, are the only applications that generate G loads high enough to move fuel away from the power-valve inlet so air can enter to lean the mixture. If the secondary power valve is removed, the main-jet size must be increased to compensate for the lost area of the power-valve channel restriction/s. Then flooding through the main jets and out the discharge nozzles will occur during braking or hard stops. The extra-rich mixture during part-throttle operation may cause plug fouling or loading up during "light-throttle" use such as warming up or running slowly during caution laps.

TUNING IN THE VEHICLE

A lot of engine-development work related to getting carburetion correct can be done on an engine dynamometer. However, some tuning has to be done with the engine installed. In general, it is safe to jet up (richer) one or two jet sizes when moving the engine from the dyno to the chassis.

For tuning you need a place that is always available whenever you want to use it for tuning purposes. You also need a vacuum gage and a stopwatch. The reason for using the same place is that subtle changes in roads can really throw off your best tuning efforts. Always use the same strip. A road can look perfectly level and

Whistle vent in top metering block ensures bowl venting and reduces possibility of fuel spewing out of bowl vents under cornering acceleration and braking forces. It provides foam control under hot conditions, too. First whistle vents were supplied in carburetors used by Ford at Le Mans. Vents are available as Holley Part 26-40. Bent-brass baffle with triangular opening (middle block) is used in current production, usually only on primary bowls of four-barrels. It keeps foam out of bowl vents under hot conditions. Perforated baffle in lower metering block was first baffle type used. No longer used in production, it is available as Holley Part 26-39.

yet include a substantial grade of several percent. You won't be able to tell this with your naked eye. Surveyor's apparatus is needed to make this kind of judgment.

If you are tuning for top-end performance, and you know the engine rpm at the end of the quarter mile, a lot of tuning can be accomplished with a stopwatch. Start the watch as you accelerate past an rpm point which is 2000 or 3000 below where you want to be at the top end. Stop the watch when you reach the rpm

marking the end of the range in which you are interested. Use the highest gear to eliminate gear changes. Eliminating these gets rid of one more variable in the tuning procedure.

Stop-watching runs from 3500 rpm to the peak rpm that will be used gives a very accurate indication: Is a change helping or hurting performance? High gear stretches the time required to pass through the rpm range of interest and eliminates wheelspin that often occurs at gear changes. You can see the effects of changes in main-jet size or pump calibration.

The race course is a poor place to tune during actual competition. There is never enough time to get the combination running exactly right and there is always a lot of confusion in the busy, exciting and emotion-charged atmosphere of racing day. The competitor who has to do any more than fine tuning or adjustments is literally not ready to race. Further, at a drag race, conditions constantly change so the times change. As more rubber is laid down at the starting line, traction "out of the hole" improves and times get faster—without changing the car.

If you can use the drag strip where you ordinarily race, this is an excellent place to tune. If the timing devices can be installed and operating, you'll get instant feedback on your tuning efforts. Use timing devices and the convenience of an unchanging stretch of road or drag strip to get things exactly right without any time pressures from competitive action.

Really serious racers are using on-board computers to take data during tuning or actual race events. A printout can be evaluated to see the effects of changes.

Standardize your starting procedure, preferably eliminating any standing starts because wheelspin at the line makes a lot of difference in your times. Wheelspin will confuse your best tuning efforts. If you want to work on your starting techniques, do that separately when you have the car tuned to your complete satisfaction.

Times or speeds that a car is turning—assuming good, consistent starting techniques—are a good indication. Is the mixture ratio being supplied by the carburetor/s correct? If a jet change makes the vehicle go faster, the change was probably made in the right direction, regardless of what sparkplug color tells you. As long as a change produces improvement, keep making changes in that direction until the speed falls off. Then go back to the combination that gave the best time.

Unless plugs indicate the mixture is rich, keep richening until times start to fall off. Plug color can indicate perfect mixture, even though the engine is getting into detonation at the upper end. That's why some tuners prefer to look at the piston crowns to get an idea of what's happening in the engine.

Because the drag-race engine spends such a

Underside of 0-4412 version of Holley 2300 500-cfm two-barrel shows factory holes in throttle plates (arrows). These allow throttles to be more closed at idle so they relate correctly to idle-transfer slots. Holes are on same side of throttle as transfer slots. Light behind carburetor shows all around throttles. Throttle plates are not seated against throttle bores. This correct clearance is established by Holley. Don't make plates fit tightly against throttle bores.

small portion of the run at a peak-power condition, sparkplugs—especially in a quench-type (wedge) combustion chamber—may need to be bone white for the best times. Don't be concerned about plugs not coloring in drag events so long as the times keep improving. Just keep making one change at a time—and *only one!*

When reading sparkplugs, remember plugs have tolerances, too. One set of plugs may read one way. Another set with the same heat range may read differently. If you can't get plugs to read correctly, try one step colder plugs—then one range hotter. Plugs often give you a clue as to how the mixture is being distributed to the various cylinders. This is true if the engine is in good tune and the compression is the same in all cylinders—and all valves are seating.

STAGGER JETTING

If you are working with an engine that has stagger jetting, make jet changes up or down in equal increments. If one jet is normally 78 and another an 80 and you are richening by two steps, move up to an 80 in the 78 hole and an 82 in the 80 hole. Move everything equally.

If the engine has "square" jetting (same size in all four holes or same size in primary barrels with a different "same size" in the secondaries), make the changes equally for each jet position.

SPECIAL PROCEDURES FOR "WILD" CAMSHAFTS

The next few paragraphs are very specialized and apply only to the pro racer. Normally such modifications are not required, even with a wild camshaft. So be sure you try the carburetor in its "box-stock" condition before proceeding with such changes.

Holley performance carburetors, such as the Model 4150 double-pumpers, may be rich enough through the idle and mid-ranges to handle a wild cam without changing the idle feeds. Modifying with a hole in each primary throttle plate is common, especially on very large engines with wild cams, such as the big-block Chevrolet with a long-duration camshaft.

A wild racing camshaft with lots of valve-timing overlap can cause seemingly insurmountable tuning problems. Fortunately, solutions are available, although they are not widely known. If your racing requires a wild "bumpstick," you should not mind the extra effort required. You want to ensure that the engine will idle at a reasonable speed and not load the plugs when the car is run slowly—as on warm-up laps, caution laps or running back to the pits after a drag run. This work makes the engine more controllable in approaching the staging lights at the drags. This effort is worth the time it takes.

Pre-Installation Checks—The first thing to do is to follow the normal pre-installation procedures of checking the accelerator-pump setting and making sure the bowl screws are tight. Look at the underside of the carburetor with the throttle lever held against the curb-idle stop (not against a fast-idle cam). Note the position of the primary throttle plates in relation to the transfer slots or holes. This relationship was established by the factory engineers to give the best off-idle performance. Reasons for these slots/holes are described in the idle system explanation, page 28.

Check the throttle-plate-to-throttle-bore clearance with a feeler gage or pieces of paper as you hold the throttle lever against the curb-idle stop. Note this clearance in your tuning notebook. Record everything as you proceed, regardless of your wonderful memory.

Install Carburetor—Install the carburetor on the engine and start the engine. If you have to increase the idle-speed setting to keep the en-

Throttle/transfer-slot relationship

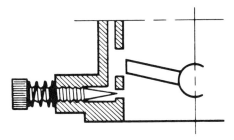

A — Transfer slot in correct relation to the throttle plate. Only a small portion of the slot opens below the plate.

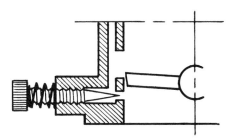

B — Throttle plate closing off slot gives smooth idle with an off-idle flat spot. Manifold vacuum starts transfer fuel flow too late. Cure requires chamfering throttle plate underside to expose slot as in **A**.

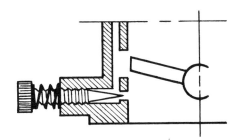

C — If slot opens 0.040 inch or more below throttle, rough idle occurs due to excessive richness and little transfer flow occurs when throttle is opened. A long flat spot results.

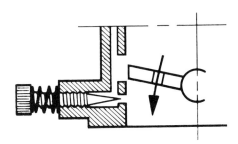

D — Correcting condion in **C** requires resetting throttle to correct position **A** and adding hole in throttle as described in text.

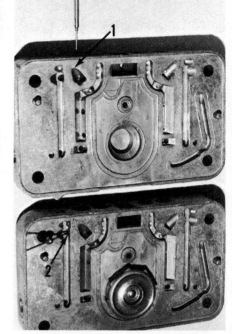

Two more idle-fuel-restriction locations. Left is restriction at lower end of idle fuel well. One of these press-in brass restrictions has been placed on a drill inserted in actual restriction. "Chrysler" type metering block at right is also used on Model 4500 0-6214 and 0-6464. It has idle-fuel restriction in bottom of tube inserted into main well. One of these idle-feed-restriction tubes on block shows relative location. This tube is the idle well. Metering block with tube idle well is identified by two aluminum spots and four lead balls on top.

gine running, note how many turns or fractions of a turn open the throttle to this point. Adjust the idle-mixture screws for the best idle. If the mixture screws don't seem to have any effect on the idle quality, note that fact.

Use a responsive (not highly damped) vacuum gage to measure manifold vacuum at idle. If manifold vacuum occasionally drops to a value lower than required to open the power valve, a power valve that will remain closed at idle must be installed before proceeding with the next changes.

Drilling Throttle Plates—Take off the carburetor. Turn it over and note where the throttle plates are in relation to the transfer slot. If you can see more than 0.040-in. of the transfer slot between the throttle plate and the base of the carburetor, drill a hole in each primary throttle plate on the same side as the transfer slot.

If holes already exist in the throttle plates, enlarge these holes. Some Holleys are equipped with such holes. In the case of a 400- to 450-CID engine, the hole size required often works out to be 0.125—0.140 in. Smaller engines require smaller holes. Start with a 1/16-in. drill on your first attempt and then work up in 1/32-in. steps. Before reinstalling the carburetor, reset the idle to provide the same throttle-plate-to-bore clearance you measured at the beginning of this procedure.

Start the engine. If the engine idles at the desired speed, the holes are the correct size. Too slow an idle means the holes need to be larger; too fast means smaller holes. If holes have to be plugged and redrilled, solder the holes closed or close them with Devcon "F" Aluminum.

Idle restrictions may be pressed into the top of the idle well. Brass restriction has been placed on a drill inserted in the actual restriction (arrow).

When you have the holes at the correct size (which may require the use of number or letter drills to get the idle where you want it), note the size. Where there are two throttle plates on the primary side, both plates should have the same size hole.

Drilling Idle Feeds—Do the idle-mixture screws provide some control of the idle quality? That is, do they cause the engine to run rough as the idle needles are opened? If not, open up the idle-feed restriction approximately 0.002 in. at a time until some control is achieved. Correct control is indicated when the engine runs as smoothly as possible and turning the idle-mixture screw either way causes the engine rpm to drop and roughens the idle as the mixture is leaned or richened.

Idle feeds are very small holes. You'll need a wire-drill set. Proceed in very small in-

Idle-feed restriction may be a brass tube in top of idle well (1), or brass restriction in cross channel between idle well and idle down leg (2).

crements. Even a 0.002-in. increase in idle-feed restriction of 0.028 in. is an area (and hence, flow) increase of 13%. Wire drills, incidentally, are not used in a power drill. Hold a wire drill in a pin vise and turn it with your fingers. Pin vises are available where you buy wire drills, namely at precision tool supply houses, model shops, or through the Sears Precision Tool catalog.

Transfer Fuel Mixture—An adequate accelerator pump setup usually eliminates any need to work on the transfer fuel mixture. This is controlled by the idle-fuel-feed restriction (IFR). The mixture can be checked by opening the throttle with the idle screw until the main system just begins to start. Then back off the screw until it just stops. If richening or leaning with the idle-mixture screw causes rpm drop-off, the mixture is correct. On the other hand, if leaning it causes the rpm to increase, the mixture is too rich and vice versa.

Even if the carburetor is really too big for the engine, try it before making *any* changes to the idle system. If idle and off-idle performance turn out to be unacceptable, increase the idle-feed restriction slightly.

Make changes in very small increments. It is all too easy to drill out certain items of the metering block so there is no easy way to get back to the starting point. Sometimes this requires a new metering block. And, it's easier to take the carburetor off to increase a hole size in the throttle plate/s than it is to solder or epoxy the hole closed and drill another one.

If you are in a time bind and have to go racing before you can make the recommended sequence of tests and adjustments, then a quick fix may help. However, it is only part of the cure for this situation in which the throttle is too far open at idle.

We have discussed pump delivery vs. cam type. Pump cam lift is all in by about 20° throttle opening on most of the cams. Thus, a wide throttle opening can use up 40—50% of the available pump shot. Cams on Holley two- and four-barrel carburetors can be rotated to a second position to regain part of the pump-shot capacity. Only the primary pump cam is moved. Even if you use the cam-relocation "quick-fix" you'll still have to take the time to replace the power valve/s with one/s with an opening point occurring at a lower manifold vacuum than you measured with the engine idling.

ROAD-RACE TUNING

Drag racers usually limit carburetion tuning to straightforward and reasonably minor changes: Main-jet size, idle-mixture-screw setting and selection of a power valve that will not open at idle.

Road-race tuning is something else. These racers go further in their search for the "ultimate tune." We will tell you what these tuners do to get their carburetion "spot on." At the same time we must warn that this is not for the Average Mechanic. This tuning takes experience. Understand it is easy to go "too far" in modifying parts that are not easily replaced— or put back in their original condition.

Tuning involving idle-fuel restriction (IFR) and power-valve-channel restriction (PVCR) is modification close to carburetor engineering. It requires infinite care and patience, more than most mechanics could ever imagine.

Tuning Procedure—Once the correct carburetor size has been selected, tuning proceeds like this.

1. First, set the idle by turning the mixture screw in until the engine falters. Then back it out 1/8—1/4 turn.

2. Free-engine (no-load) rpm is increased *slowly* to 3000 rpm to see if there is any point where the engine stumbles or misses. Do this so fuel from the accelerator pump will not confuse the lean condition being checked for. Missing or stumbling indicates a lean condition.

3. Back out the mixture screw slightly to see if this helps the condition.

4. If the screw has to be backed out more than 1/2 turn from the best idle setting previously established, open the IFR 0.002 in. at a time until there is no stumble or miss to the 3000 rpm point.

NOTE: Read the earlier material on curb-idle throttle-plate positioning related to the transfer slot or holes as detailed for racing camshafts.

5. Once the IFR is correctly established for the free-engine tests, road test the car for surging at low constant speeds and about 14—16 in. of manifold vacuum. Mixture is controlled by the IFR from curb idle through 30 mph steady speed or light-load conditions If the car "feels good" leave it alone.

6. If it surges, try opening the IFR another 0.002 in. to cure the condition.

7. Starting at 30 mph, a series of "crowds" are made with the driver "crowding" a certain manifold vacuum as observed on a gage. Crowds are light accelerations made while keeping the manifold vacuum constant. First crowd 12 in., then 10 in., then 8 in. and so on—to the point of power-valve opening.

8. If there is a lean surge during these crowds, increase primary-jet size until acceptable driveability is obtained.

NOTE: A rich condition is seldom found— except in some high-performance carburetors. Richness causes the engine to "lay-down" or seem "lazy."

9. Keep track of the main-jet size that provides the desired driveability because you have to know that size at the conclusion of the next test.

10. Test at WOT from 20—80 mph in high gear. Increase or decrease main-jet size to get the best time determined by stopwatch.

11. If jet size turns out larger than established for driveability in the previous test, increase the PVCR area to compensate for the difference in area between the two main-jet sizes.

A drill size that provides the desired area increase is used to open the PVCR. Reassemble and install the carburetor. If a smaller PVCR is required, this is more difficult to accomplish because many PVCRs are merely holes drilled through the metering block from the power-valve area to the main channel. In general, reducing the PVCR area is more difficult than increasing it because the hole will have to be plugged and drilled to a smaller size.

12. Retest to ensure the changes have been made correctly.

Accelerator Pump Tuning—This tuning has been described for street and drags, but a road racer may have to modify pump-cam phasing on the secondary (assuming a double pumper is used). This may be needed to get correct throttle response coming off of a turn that requires slowing down to the point where the secondaries are just starting to open or are slightly open. This kind of tuning can only be done for the individual track/course situation and is only mentioned as one of the items to be considered.

Remember that conditions vary from hour to hour and day to day. Your tuning results will only relate to all changes accomplished on the same day. Always take the time to rerun your baseline or best times to make sure this has not changed because of variables such as engine condition, plug condition, tires, atmospheric pressure and so forth.

TUNING VACUUM SECONDARIES

Vacuum-operated secondary throttles are initially opened by a signal (vacuum applied to the diaphragm) from the primary venturi. Airflow through the venturi increases with engine rpm. This signal is bled off by a second, smaller hole into the secondary venturi (called a *kill bleed*) so the signal being applied to the diaphragm increases smoothly. When primary air flow gets high enough to create a signal that overcomes the diaphragm spring, the secondary throttles begin to open.

As airflow starts to increase through the secondary venturi, the secondary bleed hole adds signal to that from the primary. This signal helps to open the secondaries, and eliminates "hunting," "flutter" or unstable operation of the secondaries near the opening point.

The reason for vacuum-operated secondaries is to ensure that the secondaries won't open ahead of the time when the airflow is needed. The engine is never over-carbureted, even if the driver punches the throttle wide open at low speed. The engine goes right on operating on two primary barrels for good low-end response until the engine builds up rpm. When there is sufficient primary airflow so the diaphragm opens the secondaries, the engine is ready to use the extra capacity.

Vacuum-operated secondaries will open at different full-throttle rpm, depending on the spring installed behind the operating diaphragm. A larger engine opens the secondaries sooner than a smaller displacement engine because the larger engine generates higher airflow.

Opening point and rate of opening for secondary throttles can be tailored to the engine and application by diaphragm spring choice. This is the only item to consider changing when working with vacuum-actuated secondaries. This spring counterbalances the vacuum signal from the venturis.

It holds the secondary throttles closed against the curb-idle stop until the diaphragm receives sufficient vacuum force to compress the spring and open the throttles. Atmospheric pressure against the offset secondary throttles assists in keeping them closed. Inconsistent idling can be caused by using a clipped spring or a non-standard spring behind the diaphragm.

Always start your tuning efforts with the standard spring and then use springs from Kit 20-13 to accomplish any changes. Page 37 of How Your Carburetor Works provides a graph of spring height versus load. The yellow spring allows secondaries to open quickest. This spring has the lowest load at a given height. Carburetors are usually supplied with a green,

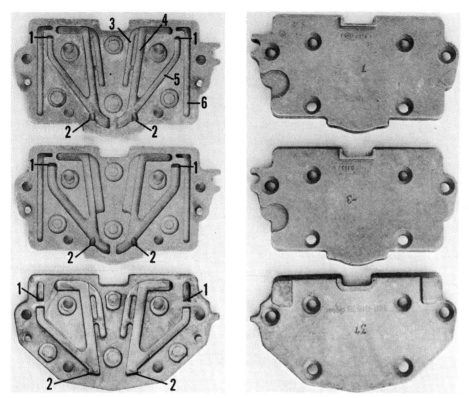

Secondary metering plates. At top is first design used on 3160 and 4160. Center version supplied on some 4160s for Chevrolet had larger well capacity. Aluminum plate (instead of zinc) at bottom is for Chrysler 4160s. Numbers identify features: (1) idle-feed restriction, (2) main restriction, (3) main air well, (4) main well, (5) idle well, and (6) idle down leg.

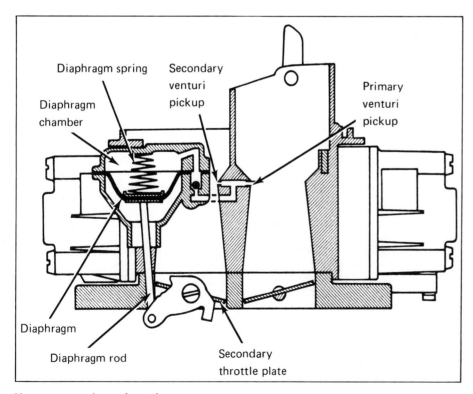

Vacuum secondary schematic.

purple or red spring.

If you have the triple two-barrel setup with vacuum-operated end carburetors, you'll have yellow springs in a Chrysler setup; brown springs in a Chevrolet. Play with different springs if you like.

A number of "tricks" have been touted as important modifications for vacuum-secondary Holleys. Most are almost, if not completely, useless!

AIR CLEANER AFFECTS DIAPHRAGM SECONDARIES

A weaker diaphragm spring is required to get the same secondary opening point when the air cleaner is removed—unless engine had a very low-restriction air cleaner. The air cleaner restricts airflow, providing a higher vacuum signal to operate the diaphragm at a lower rpm. This is typical of diaphragm-equipped carburetors from early Fords and Chevrolets with single-snorkle air cleaners. A yellow spring is a good choice when starting tuning. If secondaries open too quickly, then try other springs for slower action until you find the desired opening point.

Why Remove the Check Ball?—The first action many mechanics do is take out the check ball. It's easy to do, even if they don't understand what happens. A bleed groove in the ball seat allows the signal from the venturis to build at a controlled rate so the secondaries don't open suddenly. When the throttles are closed, the ball unseats to bleed the vacuum signal from the diaphragm immediately, thereby allowing the secondaries to close quickly. Closing the throttles quickly is more important than allowing them to open suddenly in nearly every instance.

Taking the ball out of the circuit allows you to "feel" the secondaries open. Many mistakenly interpret what they feel as an increase in acceleration. Surprise! What they are really feeling is a bog or sag in the acceleration curve.

Why Change to Mechanical Opening?—The recommendation most often heard, and one that has destroyed the driveability of more carburetor/engine combinations than any other, is that of changing diaphragm carburetors to mechanical secondary operation.

A screw is placed in the secondary lever and the diaphragm or its spring is removed. Secondary operation is then mechanically controlled by the primary throttle shaft. Those advocating this conversion overlook the fact that the carburetor now requires more care in driving.

No pump is available to cover up the hole or bog created when throttles are opened suddenly without regard to engine rpm. This is especially true when the secondaries are operated simultaneously with the primaries (1:1 throttle action). If you want mechanical secondaries for a racing application, then get a carburetor with two

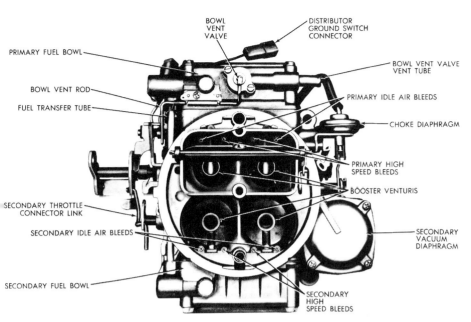

Holley sometimes refers to main air bleeds as *high-speed bleeds*. Here is typical Model 4160 with secondary metering plate and primary metering block. Float bowls are side-hung types with non-adjustable needle/seat assemblies. Secondary throttles are vacuum-actuated.

Labels on figure:
- PRIMARY FUEL BOWL
- BOWL VENT ROD
- FUEL TRANSFER TUBE
- SECONDARY THROTTLE CONNECTOR LINK
- SECONDARY IDLE AIR BLEEDS
- SECONDARY FUEL BOWL
- BOWL VENT VALVE
- DISTRIBUTOR GROUND SWITCH CONNECTOR
- BOWL VENT VALVE VENT TUBE
- PRIMARY IDLE AIR BLEEDS
- CHOKE DIAPHRAGM
- PRIMARY HIGH SPEED BLEEDS
- BOOSTER VENTURIS
- SECONDARY VACUUM DIAPHRAGM
- SECONDARY HIGH SPEED BLEEDS

accelerator pumps or a center-shooter type.

The best recommendation we can make is to let the engine open the secondaries. Change the opening point by swapping springs if you like. But keep the original spring so you can reinstall it if you don't find improvement through using different ones. Watch the acceleration times closely so you are not misled by the feel in the "seat of your pants."

So you won't spend a lot of time fighting a problem that has been overlooked by many—check secondary-throttle operation by hand as you hold the primary throttle wide open. The throttle shaft should move easily against the resistance of the diaphragm spring and close easily against the stop. Binding can be caused by deposits on the shaft if the secondaries have not been used. And, it is quite common for the shaft to bind due to incorrect and uneven tightening of the carburetor attachment nuts/capscrews. This problem arises most often when a soft gasket or a gasket pack has been used.

OFF-ROAD TIPS

With the increasing popularity of off-road and recreational vehicles, many have asked about optimizing carburetor performance for these applications. Two basic problems are involved: (1) angularity and (2) vibration.

Angularity—Visualize the problem as you tip the carburetor. Consider how changing fuel level changes its relationship to the main jets, discharge nozzle and fuel-bowl vents. Note that the angle can affect the height of the discharge nozzle in relation to the fuel level.

In some attitudes, a 40° tilt may cause fuel to drip or spillover from the discharge nozzle. Other than using a military-vehicle carburetor, a Model 1940 or older Holley center-float carburetors (1901, 2140 and 4000), there is one fix. Drop the fuel level approximately 1/16 in.

Problems caused by lowering the fuel level are: power valve and main jets are uncovered sooner and nozzle "lag" may create a noticeable off-idle bog. Part of this lag can be offset with increased pump. Either open the discharge nozzle/s or "shooters," or use a larger accelerator pump—or both.

Some lag or "bog" is almost inevitable, especially if the carburetor is too large for the engine and rpm being used. Minimize the problem by using a carburetor no larger than absolutely required for peak rpm expected in actual driving. You seldom need large carburetors for off-road use.

Vibration—The float takes a real pounding in off-road applications. The bumper spring under the float must be selected so it will assist in damping the float's wild gyrations as it vibrates. In general, the spring should be strong enough so it will just allow the float to drop of its own weight.

In some instances this could require using two bumper springs wound together, or a spring from another carburetor. Two springs are offered for side-inlet fuel bowls (4150/60, 4165, 2300). 38R-757 is the standard one with a plain-steel finish. 38R-803 is stronger and has a blue finish.

Vent or Pitot Tubes—Extend these upward as high as possible. You don't want fuel sloshing out of the vent tubes under severe braking and bouncing. Off-road cars with remotely-mounted air cleaners may be equipped with small hoses to carry the vents all the way up into the air cleaner.

Throttle Linkage—Using a cable drive is recommended for off-road installations. It transmits less vibration to the driver's foot. Many stock automobiles are now equipped with such arrangements. It is usually easy to obtain a cable throttle linkage with everything made to fit the job at hand.

Hydraulic linkages are also popular, but it is quite easy to overstress the throttle levers with such hook-ups. The hydraulic linkage should be installed so full travel of the actuating cylinder provides WOT. In some instances, cylinder mounting has to be carefully thought out so there is not an overcenter condition during throttle operation.

Air Cleaner—The best possible air cleaner completely encloses the carburetor, with the throttle operated by a cable. The cable housing can be sealed where it enters the baseplate for the air cleaner.

If the air cleaner assembly is very heavy, support it with special brackets. Avoid overloading the single tie-down stud in the center of the carburetor.

COMMON RACING PROBLEMS

Holley has been a major sponsor with representation at races across the country for many years. This includes circle track and drag racing. Tech reps talk with thousands of racers at Holley Clinics and at their trailers where they work on carburetors. From these contacts they've compiled the most common problems. While slanted toward the drag racer, some are common to road and track, too.

Dirt or Rust—Remove the fuel bowl and there it is. Good old ferrous oxide (rust). Looks just like Georgia mud. The cause is a corroded fuel tank. The tank might be one that sat for a while in a high-humidity environment or one purchased secondhand from someone who may not have known it was rusty or dirty.

Rust is the most common foreign material to invade the fuel system. But sometimes plain old dirt finds its way in through poor fuel handling practices. Whatever the contaminant, flooding usually results because something gets between the inlet needle and seat. Electric fuel pumps are also susceptible. Contaminants can interfere with operation of the internal regulator valve.

A temporary fix is a new unrestrictive in-line filter. Eventually a dirty tank must be flushed and a rusty one replaced. By the way, always use an in-line filter as a safeguard even with a new clean tank.

Fuel Pressure—Most common is running out of fuel at the top end or near maximum WOT rpm, where fuel demand is the highest. The problem is either an inadequate pump, restrictive system or perhaps the pressure was set too low in the first place. You need a pressure gage to confirm this. Remember, pressure below 3 psi at the top end is marginal.

You also need the pressure gage to set pressure at idle for systems with an adjustable regulator. If pressure is too high the flooding tendency is greater. We've seen racers try to run the Holley high-pressure pump without a regulator. The result is 15 psi to the inlet and guaranteed flooding.

Incorrect Float Level—Correct procedure for setting the externally adjustable floats is covered in detail in the Model 4150 Repair & Adjustment section, page 158. Most racers use carburetors with these bowls. Remember fuel level should be reset after changing the fuel-inlet valve or fuel pressure. Fuel level must be checked on a new carburetor because shipping shocks can alter the float setting.

Accelerator Pump—This is usually adjusted incorrectly. The proper method is shown in the Model 4150 Repair & Adjustment section, page 160. Remember the pump-operating lever should contact the pump lever at idle (or at staging rpm throttle opening). And the pump lever should have a little travel left at WOT. When you've done this you've got a full stroke. We've seen bent pump-operating levers. Don't do it unless you can't get a proper adjustment with the screw, which is rare.

Using Non-Holley Parts—Most common are gaskets, jets and inlet valves. Some are good, but most are not up to Holley standards. Some gaskets are made of less-expensive material and probably not tested with racing fuels. Not all non-Holley jets are flow-checked. Many so-called "high-flow" inlet valves actually flow less fuel than Holley items. Stick with Holley parts in Holley Carburetors.

Removing Power Valves—We see an alarming amount of this. The only reason for removing the power valve is where the induction system is so restrictive that manifold vacuum at WOT gets above the rating of the power valve. In this case the valve will close and lean the mixture. The correct solution is to use a higher rated valve. If you remove the power valve you must jet up 6—8 jet sizes to compensate. Then the part-throttle mixture will be 6—8 jet sizes too rich.

Incorrect Jetting—Sometimes this occurs because the power valve has been removed and the basic calibration gets twisted around. Reading the plugs as described in the performance section helps guide you in your jet changing. It can show if stagger jetting is necessary to correct a fuel/air distribution problem. Once you've become confused with jet changes for whatever reason, the best action is go back to the original jetting with the correct power valve/s and make changes in small increments from that reference point.

Altering Secondary Actuation—Some tuners screw in the secondary-throttle lever on diaphragm-operated carburetors. This converts a diaphragm-operated secondary to a mechanical one. The problem is, there is never enough accelerator pump shot to get you through without a bog on a WOT "punch." Worse yet, in some cases the throttle can jam open. This can lead to an exciting and expensive drive.

Don't do this little trick. Buy a double-pumper if you want mechanical secondaries. Or change the secondary diaphragm spring to get the opening characteristics you want. Use a stop watch or timer to evaluate changes.

Dirt Clogged Air Bleeds—When this happens the metering of the idle and/or main systems is altered. Sometimes these can be freed with a little spray-on solvent. If they are clogged badly, remove the bowls and metering blocks, spray with a solvent, and then blow out the passages.

Carburetor Worn Out—It's amazing how long some carburetors stay around going from car-to-car and hand-to-hand. After a few years they can get into pretty sad shape. You have to make up your mind whether to replace or repair. If the carburetor is the size and type that is just right for your car and the castings and shafts are sound, you might want to repair it. Read the Repair & Adjustment section for your particular carburetor. Remember to get a Holley Renew kit before you start.

8

CARBURETOR & FUEL ECONOMY

TEST METHODS

Fuel economy and data about it are interesting to read about. So many different numbers are quoted and so many disclaimers made, you can get downright confused. We'll explain the more commonly quoted numbers and clear up some of the confusion.

EPA ECONOMY NUMBERS

The Environmental Protection Agency (EPA) issues two different economy numbers: city and highway. Among other things, this Federal agency sets automotive emission standards and test procedures. And it conducts vehicle certification tests to make sure the manufacturers are in compliance.

EPA economy numbers are derived from data taken from the *Constant Volume Sampling* (CVS) test. The engine starts from cold after standing for at least 10 hours. Exhaust gases are measured in grams per mile during test runs over a simulated 7.5 mile route. All compounds containing carbon, namely CO, CO_2 and HC, are recorded.

Because the relationship between carbon and hydrogen atoms in fuel is known, the weight of carbon in the fuel can be calculated in grams per gallon. Tests results give each of the carbon compounds in grams per mile. Using the molecular weights of carbon, hydrogen and oxygen, total weight of emitted carbon can be calculated in grams per mile. Dividing grams per gallon by grams per mile results in miles per gallon. How about that!

The EPA released this data for the first time with the 1974 car model certification data. Why didn't they simply measure the fuel consumed during the test and divide it into 7.5 miles? Holley engineering tried it on one test and got numbers 9% higher than those calculated by the EPA method.

A lot of criticism was directed at the EPA during 1974 because of their low numbers. This could have been predicted because this cycle represented only city driving. For 1975 and later, the cycle just described was designated as *city economy*. The EPA designed a *highway* fuel economy procedure and began releasing these numbers, too. The highway economy test and calculations are conducted similarly with major exceptions. Tests are with a completely warmed-up engine. The driving cycle has a higher average speed with fewer accelerations and decelerations. Trip distance is 10.24 miles.

Some of Holley's Economaster Carburetors. From lower left and going clockwise are Models 1920, 2300, 4360, 5210, 2210, 1940. Center carburetor is a 5200.

SAE ECONOMY NUMBERS

The automotive industry traditionally measured fuel economy by driving the vehicle through a prescribed course and measuring actual fuel consumption. Manufacturers have a slightly different procedure, but all give city, highway and constant-speed fuel economy.

In 1974, the SAE (Society of Automotive Engineers) designed a standard fuel economy test consisting of a driving-event schedule for three distinct cycles. The city portion has a 15.6 mile per hour (mph) average with seven stops. A suburban cycle runs at a 41.1 mph average with two stops. The non-stop interstate cycle averages 55 mph.

In November 1974 Union Oil Company and the National Association Stock Car Auto Racing (NASCAR) ran SAE economy tests at Daytona using 58 vehicles from all the 1975 models. Results were reported in the November 18 and 25, 1974 issues of "Automotive News."

Union Oil and NASCAR used the same kinds of vehicles the EPA used in their certification and fuel economy reporting for direct comparison. All vehicles were emission-tested and only those that passed were used. City-economy results averaged 18% lower than EPA city numbers; interstate numbers averaged 8% lower than EPA highway results.

OTHER TEST METHODS

Another traditional way of deriving fuel economy is the *constant-speed* or *road-load-hook* method. The vehicle is driven at constant speeds, usually from 20—60 mph while fuel consumption is measured by one of many metering devices. Distance is measured with a fifth wheel trailing behind the vehicle. Economy is calculated in miles per gallon. Main jets are changed in the carburetor and the tests re-run. This allows plotting fuel economy versus main-jet size at each speed for that particular vehicle package. This same procedure can also be used to evaluate the effects of other engine variables such as spark advance.

Steady-state economy can be run on the dynamometer. Such tests vary among manufacturers. One method is to determine engine load for various vehicle speeds by actual test or empirically. Engine test speeds are determined by multiplying vehicle speeds by a ratio: engine rpm divided by vehicle speed in mph. This is called the *N/V ratio* for the vehicle.

The engine is maintained at a given load and speed on the dynamometer. F/A ratio is changed by varying fuel-bowl pressure or by changing main jets. Throttles are opened or closed to maintain power. The test is repeated at other speeds and loads. Data are plotted as brake specific fuel consumption pound per HP hour versus manifold vacuum. These plots not only allow selecting the most economic fuel flow at each speed, but also permit engine-to-engine comparisons.

Hope we haven't confuse you some more. The EPA method is probably the best simply because so many factors like temperature and vehicle load are closely controlled. Therefore, results, while not having great significance on an absolute basis, are very repeatable, yielding a good benchmark for year-to-year and vehicle-to-vehicle comparisons.

CARBURETOR EFFECTS

Liquid fuel doesn't burn very well, so the object is to get it vaporized or at least atomized into the smallest possible droplets. The carburetor can help by supplying strong metering signals with small venturis and efficient booster designs. Proper preparation of the fuel/air emulsion in the main well also affects atomization. Heat supplied to the inlet air or to a hot spot in the intake manifold aids vaporization and hence improves economy. But heat reduces power by lowering charge density. Once you've got the fuel in suspension, good manifold design helps keep it that way.

If leaning out at any load and speed can be prevented, the overall mixture can be kept less rich and economy improves. For example, the idle system is controlled by manifold vacuum. So, a low-speed, low-manifold-vacuum condition reduces the idle-metering signal and there is a leaning effect. Idle system fuel feeding almost completely stops. The best way to overcome this problem is with an efficient, early-operating main system. An ideal carburetor allows programming the correct F/A ratio at any load, speed and transient condition.

We are frequently asked: Which gives better fuel economy, a two-barrel or a four-barrel carburetor? The question is not always easy to answer. Staged carburetors expand the effective metering range. It all depends on how we choose to use that expanded metering range.

When the primary size of a staged carburetor is the same as a non-staged carburetor it replaces, you can expect about the same fuel economy. If you split this metering range by using an even-smaller primary size, you can expect to run leaner mixtures and get better fuel economy. The greater total flow still gives some power advantage. Earlier staged carburetors tended to follow the former route, while in recent years the trend has been toward the latter. Examples are Models 4165, 4175 and 4360 four-barrels and Models 2305, 5200 and 5210 staged two-barrels.

If you drive these carburetors the same way you drive a non-staged one, economy is usually improved. If extra performance is there, you may be overpowered by a strong temptation to use it. That consumes more fuel!

Good cylinder-to-cylinder fuel/air distribution is essential for improved fuel economy. Running all cylinders at nearly the same F/A ratio allows keeping the overall mixture leaner. Vaporization, atomization and good intake manifold design are critical in getting good cylinder-to-cylinder distribution. To optimize distribution, the carburetor and manifold must be treated as a integrated system.

Another item used to aid fuel economy is staged or gradient power valves. These valves allow moderately increasing the F/A ratio in the higher end of the part-throttle range, while bringing in full-power enrichment as late as possible. Most new Holley carburetors and some of the old ones have this capability. Operation of these valves is explained in detail on page 26.

OTHER ENGINE FACTORS

Timing—Spark timing greatly affects fuel economy. Engine-modification emission packages in the '70s included spark retard to control unburned HC and NO_X. Engines were made less efficient so higher *exhaust temperatures* would reduce hydrocarbons and peak temperatures in the cylinder. This lowered NO_X, but caused higher engine-compartment temperatures that deteriorated hoses and other rubber and plastic parts. Reduced efficiency also reduced fuel economy.

Compression Ratio—A higher compression ratio increases engine efficiency. There has been a trend toward lowered ratios in recent years for the reasons stated above, as well as for lowering the octane requirement so unleaded fuels can be used. Unfortunately, this also hurts fuel economy.

Catalytic Converter—These were introduced in 1975, allowing some improvements in spark advance. In the '80s, three-way catalytic converters and feedback carburetion or fuel injection allowed for inceased engine performance. Spark advance and compression ratios returned to pre-emission levels.

Exhaust Gas Recirculation (EGR)—EGR systems route part of the exhaust gas back into the intake manifold. This helps control NO_X. Burning speed is reduced, so efficiency and fuel economy drop. Diluting the intake charge requires a richer mixture and the throttle has to be opened farther to get the desired power. These also adversely affect fuel economy.

Camshaft—Another changed part on emission-controlled engines is the camshaft. By adding overlap (the time when both intake and exhaust valves are open) the cam provides added EGR through the manifold. Then a low numerical gear ratio is chosen for the rear end. Thus the engine can never operate in an rpm range where it can effectively use the added overlap for speed or power. The result further reduces fuel economy.

There *is* some good news. Most manufactur-

ers are using high-intensity electronic ignition systems to ensure burning leaner mixtures, thereby aiding economy. Adding a catalytic converter aids fuel economy because it treats emissions in the exhaust system after the burning process is over, allowing the car makers to put some performance and efficiency back into the basic engine.

Other items affect fuel economy:
- Drive train and rear-axle ratio.
- Vehicle weight.
- Wind resistance and aerodynamics.
- Accessory loads.
- Engine size.

ECONOMY CARBURETORS

With all of the concern and emphasis on fuel economy, Holley began redesigning a line of Economaster replacement carburetors in 1975. Development programs indicated areas of potential improvement. Existing designs were studied to figure out how to incorporate newly found economy improvements in older replacement carburetors.

A goal of 5%—10% improvement was set, using EPA test procedures as a baseline. Three other objectives included reduced cost, easier installation and wider application. The same carburetors had to meet emission standards for recommended applications on several vehicles.

HOLLEY TEST PROCEDURES

EPA highway tests were run according to federal procedures. The EPA city cycle was slightly altered. Instead of starting with a cold vehicle, testing was done with a warmed-up one. Very small gains were being sought and sometimes day-to-day and test-site variations were greater than the improvement itself.

To achieve repeatable comparative results, the vehicle was placed on the emission rolls and warmed up. Then city and highway economy were run with a given carburetor combination. Leaving the vehicle on the rolls, the carburetor was changed and the tests rerun immediately. As a result, Holley's absolute city-economy numbers are a little higher than would be obtained on the EPA cycle. This method also allowed getting a lot of data in a short period.

Actual exhaust-emission tests to verify compliance were run according to EPA procedures from a cold start. The carburetors were also evaluated on a road test: A 200 mile city and highway trip through southeastern Michigan.

There are several different models with a total of about 250 part numbers. Models include the 1940, 2210, 2300, 2280, 5200, 5210 and 4360. All are described in detail elsewhere in this book, so we'll discuss applications, new features and test results. All test data are presented as a percentage compared to the baseline or original carburetor. The model 4360's economy features are discussed in its own section.

You can see economy booster nozzle when looking in throat of 1920. Vanes help move fuel around for better mixing.

Two-stage power valve for 1920. Plastic tangs are different lengths so the two valves open at different points, performing a stepped function.

Two 1920s demonstrate opened-up idle systems. Economy unit at left has much wider transfer slot (arrows).

Model 2300 economy carburetor's fuel bowl attaches directly to original fuel line.

MODEL 1940

This single-barrel model is for six-cylinder Fords 1962—73, AMC 1970—74, Chevrolet, Buick and Oldsmobile 1968—74 and Pontiac 1970—71. The booster venturi in these carburetors is undercut slightly to aid in fuel dispersion. A high-velocity idle system is used with staged power valves on some applications. Economaster gains 11.6% city, 8.2% highway and 6.2% road test.

MODEL 2210 & 2245

Applications for this two-barrel are Chrysler V8s 1963—74 and Pontiac, Chevrolet and Buick 1968—74. Special features include the high-velocity idle system and a two-stage power valve. Economaster gains: 2.9% city and 5.4% highway.

MODEL 2300

This two-barrel carburetor serves V8 Fords 1961—74 and AMC 1968—74. Because this carburetor is the oldest of the group, it required the greatest number of changes.

Some were to make the carburetor an easier bolt-on replacement. A new fuel bowl was added with a fuel inlet matching the vehicle fuel line. The choke housing was redesigned to connect directly to the vehicle choke tube. The throttle body now incorporates a universal PCV tube and eliminates the need for a spacer in some applications.

Changes for economy include new discharge

Model 2300 staged power valve installed in metering block.

Traditional booster venturis on left; Economaster improved vaned types on right. Larger, more complex economy booster slightly reduces airflow capacity.

nozzles, high-velocity idle systems and a two-stage power valve. Economaster gains: 5.8% city and 6.5% highway.

MODELS 5200 AND 5210

The Model 5200 is used on Pinto and Capri vehicles from 1971—74. The 5210 is for the 1973—74 Vega. Because these staged two-barrel carburetors are relatively new, little could be done to improve them. Double booster venturis on the primary side give stronger signals and better atomization. Economaster gains: 4.9% city and 3% highway for the Ford 2300cc engine; 5.4% city and 6.3% highway for the 140-CID Vega engine.

LIMITED APPLICATIONS

As we moved into the late '70s and early '80s the original equipment manufacturers (OEM) placed greater and greater emphasis on fuel economy. Federal legislation required that corporate average fuel economy (CAFE) increase incrementally through the years. On top of this, the world went through several fuel crises, making fuel economy a high priority for the whole industry.

As Holley began calibrating replacement carburetors for these model years, it became more and more difficult to meet the 5%—10% improvement design goal. If a carburetor didn't meet the test requirements, it wasn't included.

In addition, feedback carburetion became commonplace in the early '80s. Because feedback systems run at chemically correct or *stoichiometric* mixtures, there is no F/A ratio difference between carburetors, and little chance for fuel economy improvement.

Consequently, many Holley Economaster carburetors are available for 1960 through mid-

Economaster throttle body on left is thicker, allowing use of a universal PCV tube and eliminating parts.

'70 vehicles. This availability decreases for late 1970 vehicles and only a few are made for '80s cars, ending with 1983 models.

SUMMARY

While these economy gains seem relatively small, they are significant when you consider most of the carburetors were already good to begin with. As we state again and again in this book, the carburetor is only one of many factors affecting fuel economy.

Conservation of energy and gasoline shortages have brought fuel economy into sharper focus than ever before. Carburetor and engine engineers have long been concerned with the factors affecting fuel consumption.

Cylinder-to-cylinder mixture distribution and good vaporization are a couple of these factors. Overall F/A ratio is another one. There are definite limits of F/A ratio that will support combustion. Most current carburetors are calibrated very near the lean limit in the part-throttle or economy range.

Minor improvements can sometimes be made by recalibration, but the old fairy tale about a carburetor that gives 50 mph on a 450-

CID engine in a 5000 pound vehicle is just that—a tale. There are inspections and actions *you* can do to get the maximum fuel economy out of your vehicle.

Tuneups—Keep your engine tuned. A fouled spark plug really affects fuel economy and power. A completely misfiring plug means that cylinder is pumping all of its fuel/air charge out the exhaust pipe.

Timing—Make sure basic distributor timing is correctly set and all vacuum lines are secure and intact. Engine efficiency drops off with spark retard and that is more money out of *your* pocket.

Air Cleaner—Inspect the air-cleaner element. A dirty filter causes greater resistance to airflow, thereby creating stronger metering signals and richer mixtures in some carburetors. This added restriction also reduces horsepower capability.

Choke—The choke plate should be in a vertical position when the engine reaches normal operating temperature. Just remove the air cleaner and take a look. Consult the troubleshooting section if a problem exists.

Tire Pressure—Increase tire pressure. This

Old choke housing on right, new at left. New one connects directly to vehicle plumbing.

causes a slightly harsher ride, but rolling resistance is lower, which increases economy. Your tires will last longer, too.

Driving Habits—Avoid unnecessary hard accelerations. By sensing manifold vacuum, the carburetor automatically increases F/A ratio as load is increased. Keep manifold vacuum as high as possible as you drive. Mixtures in the power range are 10%—15% richer than the economy range. If you have a vacuum gage in your vehicle, keep vacuum above 6 in.Hg.

Plan your trips. One trip with several short stops is much better than a lot of short trips several hours apart. The object is to keep the automatic choke (with its richer mixtures) from coming back on. Also, frictional horsepower or the power required just to move all the engine parts is greater with a cold engine.

Watch your speed. More horsepower is required to move a vehicle at 70 mph than at 50 mph because wind resistance increases with speed. Keep your speed constant. Don't let it drift up and down. Acceleration requires energy. The accelerator pump also gives a little squirt every time you move the throttle. Use a cruise control for highway driving.

9

CARBURETOR & EMISSIONS

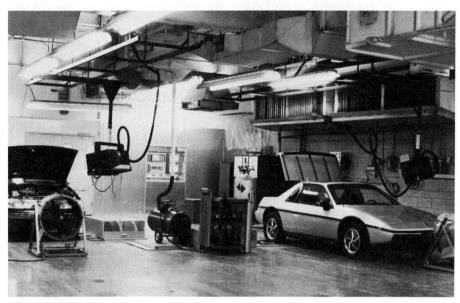

Holley Emission Test Laboratory. Vehicles are rolled onto chassis dynamometers and load is controlled as dictated by federal test procedures. Analyzers and computer are in temperature-controlled room seen in background. Plastic sample bags above and behind Fiero hold exhaust-gas sample to be analyzed later. Analysis determines mass value of each constituent.

Air pollution is a worldwide problem. This atmospheric condition is not limited to urban or industrial areas—it is now almost impossible to get away from pollution. Growth in population and fuel use has been a major contributing factor. The magnitude of the problem, and the concern of the public, is manifested in legislation to regulate contaminants that can be put into the atmosphere by automobiles. Standards for industrial emissions have also been set, but the major focus and enforcement has been in the area of new-automobile manufacturers. Makers of aftermarket (replacement) parts that directly influence emissions, including Holley, also are affected.

California, specifically Los Angeles and San Francisco, has one of the worst smog problems. Hence this state has led in exhaust-emission-control regulations.

So what is *smog,* anyhow? It is a simple term for a complex happening. When unburned hydrocarbons (HC) and oxides of nitrogen (NO$_X$) combine in the atmosphere and are acted upon by sunlight a complicated chemical reaction occurs to produce *photochemical smog.*

Both cities mentioned have all of the necessary ingredients: HC + NO$_X$ + sunlight. These are helped to combine by inversion lay-

ers over these areas. This is a dense layer of the atmosphere which prevents escape of the ingredients into the upper atmosphere where they might be dispersed by winds. The inversion layer is like a lid on a pot. It holds the ingredients right there so the reaction has plenty of time to take place—often for several days.

Smog causes nose, throat and eye irritations. And, like carbon monoxide (CO), is extremely harmful to animal and plant life (including trees). Smog also causes deterioration of some plastics, paint, and the rubber in tires, seals, weatherstripping and windshield-wiper blades.

There are three major types of vehicle emissions:

- Crankcase
- Exhaust
- Evaporative

CRANKCASE EMISSIONS

The first emission-control device, required by California in 1961, was subsequently required nationwide. It was a metering valve plumbed between the crankcase and intake manifold. Before 1961, all engines vented the crankcase into the atmosphere through a road-draft ventilation tube. The vent spewed unburned hydrocarbons and carbon monoxide

into the atmosphere.

The first Positive Crankcase Ventilation (PCV) systems used in 1963—67 were of the *open* variety. Air was pulled into the crankcase through the wire mesh of the oil-filler cap. A PCV valve connected the base of the carburetor to one of the rocker covers.

The PCV valve has a spring-loaded poppet and a fixed restriction. At periods of high manifold vacuum, as at idle or on the overrun, flow is only through the restriction, so very little flow occurs. As manifold vacuum drops, the spring in the valve overcomes manifold pressure so PCV flow increases with engine speed.

But, by 1968 all engines used a *closed* PCV system. Air from the air cleaner or a filter enters the crankcase, usually through a tube connected to an oil-filler cap in one of the rocker-arm covers. Air flows through the engine and enters the base of the carburetor through a tube containing a PCV valve. This closed system also allows the crankcase to vent through the air cleaner under low manifold vacuum conditions. Keeping this valve and restriction clean is essential to the correct operation of the engine. This is the only crankcase venting.

Crankcase emissions were attacked first. These are approximately one-third of all engine emissions. And, it was obvious from looking at the old road-draft vents that tons of pollutants were being spewed into the atmosphere. If an early car (pre-'65) is running, you'll smell the escaping crankcase fumes.

EXHAUST EMISSIONS

This area is more complex by far than the crankcase or evaporative ends of the problem. Exhaust emissions include unburned hydrocarbons, carbon monoxide and oxides of nitrogen.

In the 1966 model year, California applied standards for tailpipe emissions of CO and HC, together with test procedures and sampling methods. The California emission test was conducted by operating a vehicle on a chassis dynamometer. It simulated a 20-minute drive through downtown Los Angeles.

Actual exhaust emissions from the tailpipe were measured for concentrations in analyzers and recorded. These recordings were reduced to an average reading. More weight was given certain operational modes.

The federal government adopted the California test procedures and standards in 1968 and required, as California had earlier, all manufacturers to certify and prove that their vehicles met the prescribed standards.

In 1973 the federal government introduced a new test procedure called *Constant Volume*

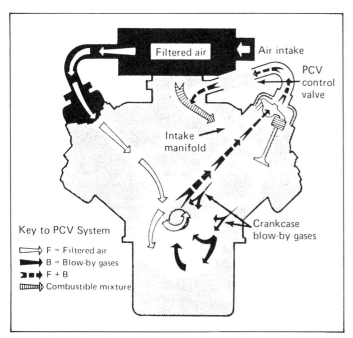

Schematic of PCV system with valve open.

Close-up of analyzers used to obtain final mass values of each gas, plus a continuous reading throughout test. Analyzers feed computer that prints out final test results. These include a volume and mass concentration of each gas for each driving mode, i.e., idle, acceleration and so forth. This mode readout is a valuable analytical tool for the development engineer.

Sampling or CVS system. The vehicle is *soaked* (left standing) with the engine off for 10 hours. The test is run on a chassis dynamometer loaded proportional to engine displacement and vehicle weight. The cold start is included in the test. A specific driving schedule consists of idle, acceleration, cruise and deceleration modes in a non-repetitive sequence. No two modes are alike. The test simulates 7.5 miles over 23 minutes. The test fuel type is specified for uniformity.

All exhaust gas is mixed with outside air and routed through a constant-volume pump that mixes and measures the flow. A specified proportional part of the mixture is collected in a plastic bag. After the test is run, bag contents are analyzed for concentrations of HC, CO and NO$_X$.

Because volume and concentrations are known, the actual mass of each gas can be calculated. The standards are written on a mass basis. Air in the test room is constantly monitored in a background bag. The mass of each constituent in the background bag is calculated and subtracted from values obtained in the sample bag.

This exhaust-emission procedure was modified beginning with the 1975 car model year.

The first 8.5 minutes or 3.6 miles of the test is rerun after a 10-minute engine-off period. Kept in a separate bag, this sample is called the *hot-transient portion.* An equal part of the first test is called the *cold-transient portion.* Its exhaust sample is also collected in a separate bag. These two sample bag values are averaged to allow for the fact that not all starts are cold starts.

The sample from the remainder of the first test is collected in a third bag called the *hot-stabilized portion.* The average of the hot and cold transient portions are combined with this portion to yield final exhaust-emission results.

CO forms whenever there is insufficient oxygen to complete the combustion process. Generally speaking, the richer the mixture, the higher the CO concentration. Even if the fuel/air mixture is chemically correct, CO cannot be reduced to zero. Perfect mixing and cylinder-to-cylinder distribution is nearly impossible to achieve.

Gasoline is composed of numerous and varied hydrogen and carbon compounds, hence the name *hydrocarbons.* Unburned hydrocarbons are just that: gasoline that did not burn on its trip through the engine. There are several reasons why this happens. Rich mixture is one. Fuel

that does not burn because of lean misfiring is another. So, either a lean *or* a rich F/A mixture increases HC emissions.

Other factors affect HC concentration. Higher compression increases combustion-chamber surface-to-volume ratio and thereby increases HC emission. Spark advance and high vacuum under deceleration also affect HC.

Standards for oxides of nitrogen emissions were established by California for 1971. These became nationwide law in 1973. Oxides of nitrogen (NO$_X$) form in the combustion chamber under high temperature and pressure conditions. Combustion pressures increase as the engine is loaded. The tendency to form NO$_X$ is increased as the mixture is leaned because of the increased availability of free oxygen. Maximum NO$_X$ production occurs at 0.062 F/A (16:1 A/F).

EMISSION CONTROL APPROACHES

There are various approaches to the problem of making engines and vehicles meet the emission standards. The first approaches were engine modification and air injection.

As of 1972, another engine modification was being used: Exhaust Gas Recirculation or *EGR.* By 1975, most exhaust systems used either a

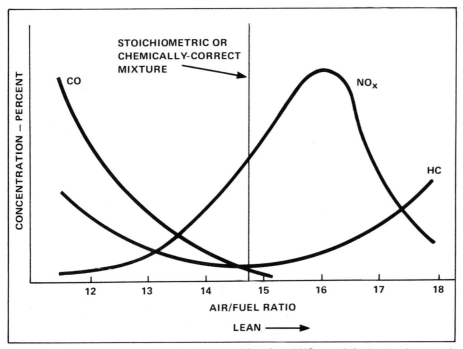

Plot shows approximate relationship between CO, HC and NOₓ as air/fuel ratio changes. It shows the problem faced by carburetor calibrator. Leaning mixture to lower HC and CO emissions increases NOₓ emissions. Best calibration is a compromise holding all three at acceptable levels.

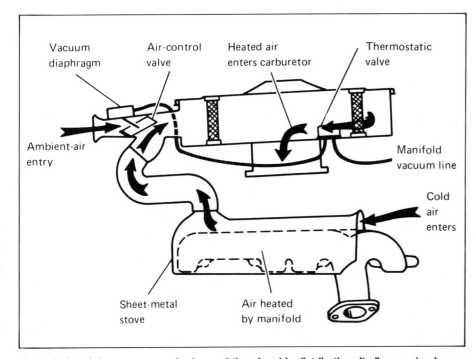

Heated inlet air improves vaporization and thereby aids distribution. It allows using leaner fuel/air mixtures to reduce emissions. Thermostatic valve modulates temperature of air entering carburetor by opening flapper to admit ambient air when underhood temperature exceeds 85F (29C). Heated air supply is shut off by flapper when underhood temperature exceeds 125F (52C). Chrysler illustration.

thermal reactor or a catalytic converter.

The thermal reactor appears in various forms. It is a restriction in the exhaust system ahead of the muffler. It retains heat in the front part of the system, encouraging burning excess HC. It also reduces flow rate to give more time to complete combustion of HC. Thermal reactors are used in combination with the already complex assortment of controls and gadgets to reduce emissions.

The catalytic converter, an addition to the exhaust system, assumes a major role in emission reduction as described in a later section. When a catalytic converter is used, some of the stringent controls applied to the engine can be eliminated, resulting in better driveability and fuel economy.

Engine Modifications—These include carburetor calibration and operational changes, along with distributor spark-advance settings, curves and operational changes.

Carburetors are set up with leaner mixtures in the part-throttle range. Mechanical limiters are placed on idle-mixture adjustment screws to prevent excessively rich idle mixtures. Dashpots and throttle retarders, plus special idle setting solenoids are used. And, the choke is designed to "come off" very quickly after the engine starts. Inlet air is heated to ensure good fuel vaporization and distribution.

Decelerations create very high manifold vacuum unless special controls are used. With a closed throttle, so much exhaust is sucked back into the intake manifold that the F/A mixture is diluted (leaned). Borderline firing occurs, causing missing and consequent high emission concentrations of unburned hydrocarbons.

Several controls can be used singly or in combinations:

● Shut off the fuel flow so there will be no unburned hydrocarbons—because no fuel will be entering the manifold. This creates a "bump" when the fuel is turned back on near normal idling manifold vacuum.

● Supply a richer mixture to ensure burning. This was done by a deceleration valve and special deceleration fuel/air feed circuit on some Pintos, for example.

● Retard throttle closing to avoid high vacuum build up. Although commonly used, it reduces the braking effect that would have been obtained from the engine during deceleration with a closed throttle.

Distributors are set up with more retard at idle and part-throttle. Various switches, valves and other controls are used to provide advance or retard as required to meet emission requirements. Spark retard is an effective means of reducing HC. This is because exhaust temperatures are increased so the hydrocarbons are burned completely.

Additionally, basic engine modifications are being made, including reducing compression ratio to reduce combustion pressures and temperatures, valve-timing variations and combustion-chamber redesign.

Sorting out which modification accomplishes what is difficult. Let's over-simplify and say retarded spark helps reduce HC emissions by raising exhaust temperatures, hence ensuring complete burning. Retarded spark does not let the engine develop peak pressures it is capable of, so NO_x is also reduced.

Combustion-chamber alterations include eliminating flat quench surfaces to slow burning and keep NO_x down. By eliminating the cooler surfaces of quench areas, HC emissions are dropped. Piston design is important. If the rings are higher or the piston top is tapered toward the top ring—there's less volume in which unburned HC can "hide," and this further reduces HC.

Keeping the chamber hot reduces deposits, which provide still more places for unburned HC to "hide." All these are minimal changes, but the game of reducing emissions is made up of these. Keeping compression ratio down reduces peak pressures—reducing NO_x.

Reducing emissions is a super balancing act—just like tightrope walking. The major complexity facing engine designers is the engine's tendency to produce more NO_x whenever HC and CO are being reduced—and vice versa.

Air Injection—This system causes additional burning in the exhaust ports and manifolds. The exhaust manifold becomes an oxidizing reactor. A slightly richer mixture is used and extra air is added to oxidize (burn) unburned hydrocarbons and carbon monoxide. An engine-driven air pump and an air manifold deliver air to each exhaust port. This is a costly approach, but it allows using a slightly richer mixture to make the car more driveable with less tendency toward midrange surging.

The first major use of air injection was on 1966—67 California cars. GM called the system *AIR* for *Air Injection Reactor*, Ford termed theirs the *Thermactor* system. The air pump is supplied with filtered air from a built-in air cleaner/filter or from the carburetor air cleaner. The pump is protected from exhaust gases by a one-way check valve. It only allows air to flow *toward* the exhaust system. A vacuum-controlled diverter valve shuts off air flow to the exhaust system during deceleration (overrun) so backfiring will not occur. This diverter valve dumps all of the pump output through an air muffler.

Some engines have been equipped with AIR or Thermactors ever since the method was first introduced. These systems were usually used on high-performance engines. As of 1972, air-injection systems were used more widely to help meet increasingly stiff HC and CO emissions requirements.

More efficient oxidation is provided by redesigning the exhaust manifold into a better

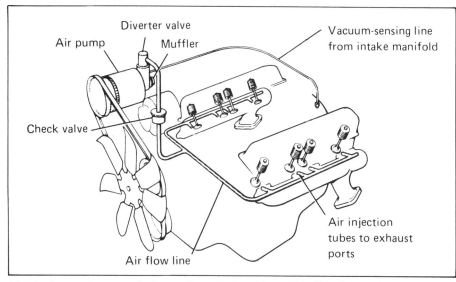

Air-injection systems are similar on all cars that use them. This Chrysler version appeared on 1972 California cars. Pump adds controlled amount of air to ensure complete burning of the exhaust gases in the exhaust manifolds. Chrysler drawing.

reactor by restricting flow and providing insulation to keep the heat in. These two items provide more time and higher temperatures so HC and CO are further oxidized. Added restriction cause excessive loss of power and higher temperatures require more expensive materials. The Mazda rotary and some BMWs have used the reactor approach, but to date, U.S. manufacturers have avoided it.

Exhaust Gas Recirculation (EGR)—This method began to be used later than the other modifications. The first two production uses of EGR with built-in plumbing to accomplish it were on 1972 California versions of some Buick and Chrysler automobiles.

Beginning with 1973s, virtually all vehicles had an EGR valve of one type or another. The ERG valve controls exhaust gas routed either from the exhaust crossover in the intake manifold or directly from the exhaust manifold. Exhaust gas is introduced into the intake manifold either directly or through a spacer beneath the carburetor. In all cases, care is taken to distribute exhaust gas equally to all cylinders. This becomes more important as EGR rates are increased.

There are many types and configurations, but these valves are easily recognized by a large operating diaphragm. Some are simple on-off types. Most use a tapered stem to increase exhaust gas flow with engine through-put. Some sense exhaust back pressure to make the recirculation rate more proportional to actual mass flow rate through the engine.

The carburetor usually supplies the signal for the EGR valve from a probe in the venturi or from a port in the throttle body. This port is not

Holley replacement EGR valve has three calibration washers with different openings to vary EGR into intake manifold. One closest to original valve size inserts in counterbore on base.

EGR valve with tapered pintle has an opening size controlled by vacuum signal applied to diaphragm.

Three vacuum-controlled EGR valves. Chrysler valve on left, GM at top, Ford on right.

exposed to manifold vacuum at idle, much the same as a spark port, to prevent EGR at this point.

The venturi pickup gives a signal proportional to airflow through the carburetor. In some cases the carburetor signal is multiplied by routing it through a mechanical vacuum amplifier. EGR at heavy loads is unnecessary because NO_X does not form readily at richer power mixtures. This is handled automatically in some cases because vacuum signal to the valve drops off with load.

The carburetor must also be considered because driveability is adversely influenced as EGR rate is increased. Simply richening the mixture is not the answer because this increases HC and CO emissions. Efforts must be extended to improve vaporization, mixture preparation and cylinder-to-cylinder distribution.

Don't disconnect your EGR because it's illegal to do so. And, your engine will have excessive part-throttle knock just before the power valve opens. This is because the exhaust gases mixed with the fuel/air mixture slowed burning, giving the same effect as an antiknock additive.

Catalytic Converter—Catalytic converters were used for the first time on 1975 vehicles. Some also used an air pump. The catalyst is more effective when used with an air pump, but this adds cost. A catalyst and air-injection combination can have an efficiency as high as 90%

under optimum conditions.

A catalyst is an element or compound that helps promote a chemical reaction but doesn't actively take part in it. The catalyst is not changed chemically by the reaction. The first automotive catalysts were of the oxidizing variety: They helped oxidize the HC and CO into water (H_2O) and carbon dioxide (CO_2).

Most auto catalysts are the Platinum Group Metal (PGM) type that includes platinum, palladium and ruthenium. These metals are mounted on beads or monolith honeycomb supports made of less-expensive material such as alumina. The catalyst is installed in a can somewhere in the exhaust system, usually under the floor.

The carburetor supplies slightly richer part-throttle mixtures to assure a reaction and this improves driveability somewhat. The distributor is advanced more than non-catalytic packages, aiding both driveability and fuel economy. In other words, engine modifications are lessened because HC and CO are handled by aftertreatment in the exhaust stream.

The catalyst is guaranteed for at least 50,000 miles. Most are lasting far longer than the warranty period. Replacement catalysts are available from the car manufacturers and from major muffler manufacturers.

The catalyst must be used with unleaded fuel. Lead in the fuel "poisons" the catalyst in just a few miles, rendering it ineffective.

Typical EGR installation on 1973 Chrysler. Valve transfers gas from exhaust-gas crossover to intake manifold.

The catalysts described above are the *oxidizing* type. In 1981 catalysts that control NO_X as well as CO and HC were introduced. Known as *three-way* catalysts, these require holding the fuel/air ratio to very close limits. A controlled or *feedback* system (also called "closed-loop" control) is used in the carburetor. A explanation of the basics of three-way catalysts and feedback systems is in the How Your Carburetor Works chapter.

Evaporative Emissions—Here is the third

EGR amplifier used on 1973 and later Chryslers. Carburetor venturi vacuum is input signal. By a complex system of valves and diaphragms, amplifier modifies manifold vacuum to supply stronger signal to EGR valve. Four hoses are for venturi vacuum in, manifold vacuum in, EGR signal out, and temperature override signal to switch off output at lower engine temperatures. Latter function isn't always used.

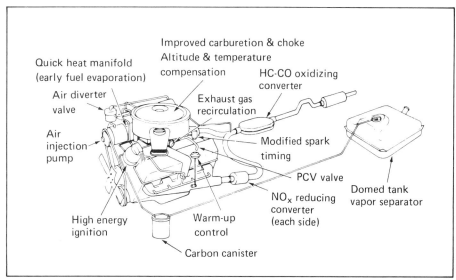

Emissions control technology progressed from simple PCV to complete system. Cost and complexity increased, too.

major area for discussion. Evaporative emission includes hydrocarbon materials contained in fuel spilled or evaporated from fuel tanks and carburetors. You might consider this an insignificant part of the emission picture, but it is estimated that evaporative emissions equal the emissions that would occur if crankcase ventilation were uncontrolled.

The gas tank and carburetor were traditionally vented to the atmosphere—until 1970 in California, and 1971 nationwide. Venting got rid of vapors, aiding the hot-starting capabilities of the cars. There was no real concern about the emissions caused by spilled fuel during over-filling or by gasoline sloshing out of vents during sudden maneuvers.

The most obvious part of this solution is the charcoal canister in the engine compartment. But, sophisticated measures are used in the fuel-tank-filling and tank-construction areas.

Thermal expansion is provided for by trapping as much as three gallons of air during tank filling. Ford cars use a limited-fill method, whereas GM and Chrysler have another tank area or bell inside the tank. These tanks trap air during filling, then allow it to escape to the top of the main tank where it vents to a charcoal canister.

Vent lines are very special. They incorporate vapor-separation devices, which are small tanks located near and slightly above the main gas tank. Any liquid trapped therein drains back to the tank, but the vapor passes on to the

canister. In the case of some Chrysler products, it is stored in the crankcase.

In some instances, vapor-collection lines connect the carburetor to the charcoal canister. The canister is about the size of a small cookie jar and located wherever room can be found in the engine compartment. Fuel vapors are adsorbed onto the surfaces of the charcoal granules. When the car is restarted, vapors are sucked into the carburetor or intake manifold to be burned in the engine.

Canister purging varies widely with make and model. In some instances a fixed restriction allows constant purging whenever there is manifold vacuum. In others, a staged valve provides purging only at speeds above idle. In 1972, GM incorporated a thermal-delay valve so the canister is not purged until the engine reaches operating temperature. Purging at idle or with a cold engine creates other problems, such as rough running and increased emissions because of the additional vapor added to the intake manifold.

In 1970—'71, total evaporative emissions allowed from any car were six grams per hot soak. In 1972, the allowance was reduced to two grams per hot soak.

Altitude—Beginning with the 1977 car model year, all vehicles sold at altitudes above 2,500 ft had to meet emission standards at the altitude at which the vehicle is sold. In most cases, the carburetor has a different calibration; others use automatic altitude adjustments.

EMISSION SETTINGS

All manufacturers are required to install a specification label in the engine compartment. It details the correct carburetor and distributor adjustments needed to maintain legal emission levels for that vehicle. No matter how effective or sophisticated the control system, a weak spark, fouled plug, bad plug wire, cracked distributor cap, or any of many other things, can wreck the system's efficiency. It only takes one thing going wrong to cause the car to become a pollutant emitter of a worse nature than a car without any controls.

A single bad spark plug is a good example. In SAE Paper 710069, "Exhaust-Emission Control for Used Cars," the authors pointed out that a single fouled plug increased HC emission level six times: from 605 ppm to 3,609 ppm.

WHAT'S IT COSTING?

The whole point of emission controls is to clean up the environment—namely the air we breathe and live in. But, as is always the case when you get down to the facts—there is "no free lunch." Anything costs *something*. That something includes reduced driveability, increased gasoline consumption, increased tune-up costs, and a car that weighs more.

To these obvious costs we must add increased complexity of the entire vehicle with associated cost increases in both engineering and manufacturing.

Racer checking throttle-return spring action on Pro Stock car. Two Holley 4500s and Holley electric max-pressure pump are standard on these cars.

it without having to take your eyes off the driving course. Drag racers mount their fuel pressure gages on the cowl outside of the windshield because common sense and rules prohibit fuel lines or containers in the driver's compartment.

In case it's not immediately obvious why the fuel system should be routed outside the driver's compartment, just think about what happens when a clutch, flywheel or transmission (standard or automatic) explodes and cuts any part of the fuel system plumbing. Sparks are sure to occur at some point during such an incident.

Similarly, if a car crashes, fire danger is always present. You want to have as much safety margin as possible for yourself or your driver. We lost a very good friend in 1960. Wayne Ericksen perished in a fire caused by fuel in the driver's compartment.

The sensible way to install a fuel pressure gage in the cockpit is to use an electrical gage with a remote pressure sender. Install it where you would take off pressure for a mechanical pressure gage. This is at the intersection of the Y that feeds both float bowls (on carburetors with two inlets) or at the connection to the carburetor. Several aftermarket manufacturers make Y and in-line fittings that have a tapped hole for a fuel-pressure sender.

FUEL SYSTEM PROBLEMS

Racers often get into leaning-out problems that are no fault of the carburetor or its jet combination. The problem is insufficient fuel pressure. These problems can be easy to identify because increasing main-jet size doesn't help the problem and probably worsens it at low- and mid-range rpm.

Inadequate fuel supply at the carburetor can be caused by:

• Pump with insufficient capacity.

• Restrictive fittings or fuel lines too small; inlet seats too small.

• Too many bends in a fuel line, or a crimped fuel line.

• Tank outlet or filter screen restricted.

• Plugged fuel filter/s.

• Use of a high-restriction filter between tank and pump instead of between pump and carburetor.

• Dirt anywhere in the fuel-supply system.

• Fuel line too near a heat source, causing boiling in the line.

FUEL PRESSURE

Fuel pressure should be measured with a 0—10 psi fuel-pressure gage. Monitor the fuel

pressure to avoid wasting a lot of time and money applying corrective measures to areas that aren't contributing to fuel-supply problems. Measuring pressure just ahead of the carburetor ensures you will know what fuel pressure is available at that point.

The most important fuel-pressure measurement is made just as the engine is at its rpm peak for the course. This is where it is using the most fuel. Pressure at this point should be at least 3.5 psi, but any pressure between 3.5—8 psi is OK. Six (6) psi is considered a normal fuel pressure by Holley engineers.

Any pressure lower than 3.5 psi is not acceptable. It indicates the pump or fuel-supply system is not keeping up with engine fuel requirements. Using fuel pressure above 8 psi should be approached with caution and accompanied with appropriate fuel-level changes in the fuel bowl.

Pressures over 6 psi overcome the closing force applied to the inlet needle valve, creating unnecessarily high fuel level in the fuel bowl. Each added psi raises fuel level approximately 0.020—0.030 in. over the nominal level established at 6 psi.

Mount the fuel pressure gage so you can see

FUEL LINES

Fuel lines must be routed away from heat and firmly secured so that they will not vibrate and fatigue. Fittings must be non-restrictive. Some fittings have built-in restrictions. Check every fitting you use in your fuel supply system. Make sure the passage is the same size all the way through the fitting. You may be able to open up the passage with a drill.

Avoid 90° (right-angle) fittings wherever possible. These cause the most fluid friction and therefore are more restrictive than straight-through or 45° fittings. A right-angle fitting has the same restrictive qualities as a piece of tubing several feet long.

If a mechanical fuel pump is used, install a 1/2-in. ID line (not fuel hose!) from the tank to the pump. Fuel hose can collapse from the vacuum applied by the pump, effectively shutting off or reducing fuel flow to it. Make sure the fitting connecting to fuel tank is as close to fuel line ID as is consistent with safety.

Where the fuel line attaches to the fuel tank is one junction commonly overlooked by mechanics who are just getting started in competition. They will install a large line, but try to feed fuel through a tiny 1/4 in. or smaller dia-

Pro Stock racers understand the wisdom of keeping fuel lines cool. Refrigeration-line insulation is used to reduce effects of heat rising from exhaust headers. Flat piece atop carburetors seals against underside of air scoop, preventing heated engine compartment air from mixing with air supplied to carburetors.

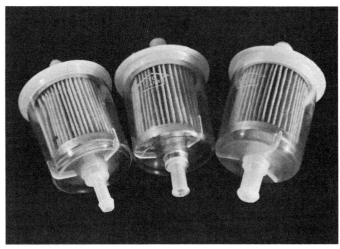

See-through in-line filters are available for 5/16-, 1/4- and 3/8-in. fuel line. It's easy to see when one of these is dirty.

meter opening. This is another place where steel, copper or aluminum tubing is a better choice than fuel hose.

Tube fittings usually allow a larger passage than you can get with hoses. This is because a hose fitting's wall thickness must withstand the clamping pressure applied by a hose clamp. Tubing fittings can have openings very close to the actual ID of the tubing itself, thus giving less restriction.

The important point is to keep fuel supply to the pump unrestricted. The pump outlet (for a engine-mounted mechanical pump) or regulator outlet connection to the carburetor/s can be through 5/16- or 3/8-in. tubing or hose.

FUEL FILTERS

A fuel filter should be used between the fuel pump and the carburetor. Never use any kind of filter, other than a simple screen, on the suction side of a fuel pump. This is true regardless of the fuel pump that is used. The usual screen at the tank outlet will usually be OK if it is clean.

The filter in the line to the carburetor should be non-restrictive. *Paper element* filters such as those supplied by Holley are excellent for the purpose. If you are concerned about pressure drop through the filter, Y the fuel line to run through two filters so each one supplies a carburetor. Or, use two filters in parallel in the line. Mount the filter canister to allow easy replacement of the element.

Sintered-bronze (Morraine) filters are in the inlets of many two- and four-barrel carburetors. These are OK for street use if there is little dirt

Holley canister-type fuel filters with tube and hose connections are neat and functional additions to any fuel system. Replacement element is in center.

in the gasoline and if the tank itself is clean. How often can you be sure of these? If the fuel supplied to the pump is dirty (which can happen in a dusty area) remove the sintered-bronze filters from the inlets and install an inline filter between the pump and the carburetor.

Pay attention to the fuel filter and replace paper elements in throwaway inline filters when fuel pressure drops. This indicates the filter has done its work and it is time for a new one.

For competition, remove the sintered-bronze filters from the inlets and install an inline filter.

FUEL PUMPS

There are two common types of fuel pumps: *mechanical* and *electric*. Although the carburetor never "knows" which one supplies its fuel, let's briefly examine each.

Mechanical Fuel Pumps—Engine-mounted mechanical pumps are diaphragm types driven by camshaft/crankshaft eccentrics operating a

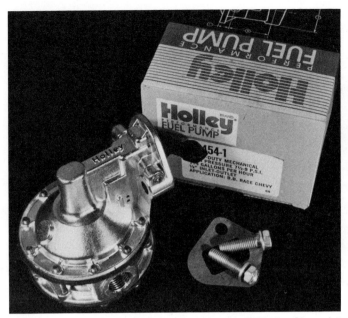

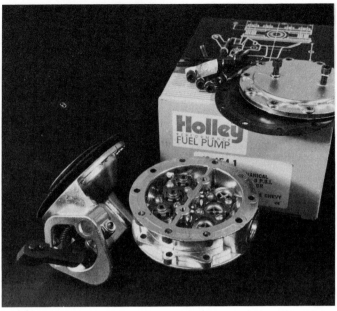

Holley's high-output mechanical pumps are available for Chevrolet 90° V6, small- and big-block V8, and Ford 289, 302 and 351W engines. This pump is competition model for big-block Chevy.

Disassembled high-output mechanical pump shows 6 valves: 3 inlet, 3 outlet. Inlet/outlet ports are 1/2-in. NPT.

Holley 12-833 mechanical pump for small-block Fords disassembled to reveal construction details. Also available for Chrysler and GM, these pumps feature 60-gph capacity. Large inlet/outlet ports (allows hose to 3/8-in. ID) in rotatable housings can be turned to allow easiest plumbing routing.

rod or lever. Advantages include low first cost, simple plumbing and mounting, low noise level and familiarity of the general public with the type. Millions have been used over the years.

A major disadvantage is transferral of engine heat into the fuel, especially when the engine is stopped. The mechanical pump sucks fuel through a long line from the tank, promoting the fuel's tendency to flash into vapor, especially on warm days.

Electric Fuel Pumps—These pumps have become widely used as original equipment since the mid-'70s. Most are submerged in the fuel tank and operate quietly and efficiently. The electrical pump has a higher first cost, is noisier than a mechanical pump and requires connection to the car's electrical system. It must be plumbed to the tank outlet and to the fuel line.

An electrical pump is typically installed mounted at the rear, near the tank, as a "pusher." Fuel pushed forward to the carburetor has less tendency to flash into vapor as it moves through the line. For competition or hot-weather, the rear-mounted electrical pump provides insurance against vapor lock.

When installing an electric pump, eliminate the mechanical pump if at all possible. It heats the fuel and limits pressure by acting as a restrictor in the line from the tank. Block-off plates are available to close the fuel pump opening in the engine block.

There are several types of electrical fuel pumps: fixed-vane, sliding-vane and solenoid-operated.

HIGH-OUTPUT MECHANICAL FUEL PUMPS

Holley's line of high-output mechanical fuel pumps is designed for maximum flow, reliability and flexibility of application. Both street and competition versions are available.

Street pumps flow 110 gallons per hour (gph, free-flow) at 8000 rpm. Shut-off pressure is 6.5—8 psi. Inlet and outlet ports are 3/8-in, National Pipe Thread (NPT).

Competition pumps flow 114 gph at 8000

rpm. Shut-off pressure is 7.5—9 psi. Ports are 1/2-in. NPT. These pumps use the same part number as street versions, except that "-1" is added.

Common features include three high-capacity inlet valves and three high-capacity outlet valves, for a total of six. Multiple valves ensure adequate and continuous fuel flow. Repair kits are available to service these pumps.

HOLLEY GPH 110 PUMP

This electric fuel pump is a positive-displacement type. Pumping action is accomplished by four sliding vanes spaced in a rotor at 90° intervals. Vanes are thrown out against the rotor chamber walls by centrifugal force. The rotor is offset in its pumping chamber so the inlet side is larger than the outlet side.

A pumping segment created by two vanes picks up fuel as the segment passes the inlet port. Vanes move the fuel from the "larger" side of the chamber to the "smaller" side. *Dead-head pressure* (pumping against pressure built up in a closed-end pipe) is regulated by an internal spring-loaded bypass valve that routes fuel from the outlet to the inlet side.

Power for the pump is supplied by a 12-volt permanent-magnet DC motor that runs dry, that is, no fuel is in the motor portion of the pump. A seal on the motor shaft keeps fuel out of the motor. Bronze bearings are used at each end of the motor shaft.

Both low-pressure and high-pressure (high-performance) versions of the pump are offered.

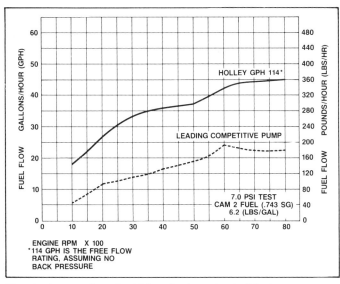

Flow-test comparison for high-output mechanical fuel pumps.

Holley electrical pump (left) pushes fuel from tank at about 9 psi to regulator near carburetor. Standard pressure regulator 12-803 (middle) covers fuel-pressure range of 3—10 psi. Pressure switch 12-810 (canister with contacts) is essential component. It senses engine oil-pressure to shutoff fuel pump when engine is stopped, whether ignition is turned off or not. Pump is mounted on 12-809 insulator mounting bracket. Standard rubber-lined clamp supplied with pump is at right.

Although most of the other components are the same, the low-pressure pump has a different bypass valve and a motor with a lower rating and a different winding. This pump's dead-head pressure rating is 7 psi. It is designed for street and highway use without a fuel pressure regulator. It is not designed for competition.

The high-pressure pump (dead-head pressure is 14 psi) is supplied with a remote fuel pressure regulator that should always be mounted near the carburetor/s. A spring operates against the regulator diaphragm to open the internal valve. Line pressure against the same diaphragm closes the regulator valve to maintain a preset pressure.

Regulated output (downstream) pressure can be externally adjusted from 3—10 psi, and dead-head pressure is altered by changing the spring-preload adjustment screw. A locknut maintains the setting. All pump and regulator inlets and outlets are tapped for 3/8-in. NPT.

INSTALLING A HOLLEY GPH 110

Wiring—Include a safety switch in the wiring circuit so the pump won't work unless there is oil pressure. Holley's 12-810 switch can be mounted on a 1/8-in. pipe tee. Put the stock pressure switch for the idiot light on the other side. The fuel pump will shut off if the engine stalls with the ignition ON.

Using the switch to turn the engine with the starter energizes the pump from the starter solenoid. Once the engine is running, the switch supplies voltage to the pump so long as there is oil pressure to keep the switch turned on. A

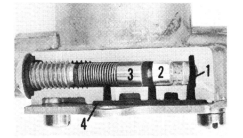

Pump passages provide output-pressure regulation. Cutaway of pressure-relief valving shows how this works. Fuel at higher-than-desired pressure from outlet side (1) enters hollow seat (2) to act against spring-loaded piston (3). Pressure pushes piston off seat so high-pressure fuel is routed back to inlet side of pump (4), thereby regulating pressure. Rotor (5) is offset in pumping chamber (6) formed by vanes (7) in wear sleeve (8).

Cutaway side view shows rotor (5) with sliding vanes (7), wear sleeve (8), wear plates (9) on top and bottom of pumping chamber, seal (10) and bronze bushing (11) for armature shaft.

schematic showing sample wiring for the switch is included here.

Mounting—Place the pump in as cool an area as possible; keep it away from any exhaust system components. Any fuel pump mounted to the chassis will transmit some noise into the car's body structure. This is no problem on a race car with open exhaust, but it can be a source of annoyance on a dual-purpose car that is driven on the street.

The optimum way to reduce this noise is to mount the pump on Holley's 12-809 insulator mounting bracket. And to reduce the noise further, mount this bracket on four rubber-insulated studs attached to a chassis member or onto a stiffened body section.

Never mount the pump directly onto a large flat sheet-metal surface. The result will be amplification of the noise, just the opposite of what you are trying to achieve. Always mount the pump near the fuel tank (usually at the rear of the car) and as low as possible so suction height is kept to a minimum.

Creating a vacuum (low absolute pressure) on the end of a fuel line, especially a long one, tends to allow the fuel to flash into vapor, which is very hard to pump. This is why professional racers replace the engine-mounted mechanical pump with an electric pump near the fuel tank; it's positive insurance against vapor lock.

When fuel is pumped forward at high pressure, there is another advantage: this offsets pressure losses caused by line loss (friction) and by acceleration (g forces). Pumping the fuel forward at high pressure and reducing pressure before feeding it to the carburetor/s ensures there will always be adequate pressure available at the carburetor/s.

Holley pump installation in Wally Booth's old Pro Stock Camaro shows bypass line installed in location normally occupied by screw for pressure-relief valve. Hose contained a 0.060-in. restrictor. Arrow points to bypass line. Wally hasn't raced in many years, but this is still a good idea.

Fuel Lines—Keep the pump-inlet line short and large. If a filter is used between the fuel tank and the pump inlet, it must be a screen-type. There must not be any pressure drop at this point. That could cause fuel vaporization and consequent pump cavitation. It is preferable to position the pump so its inlet is slightly below and behind the tank so the fuel level creates a *head* or positive pressure at the inlet. Acceleration forces will tend to keep fuel at the inlet.

Stock-size (5/16 or 3/8 in.) fuel lines can be used on a street machine, but the pump per-

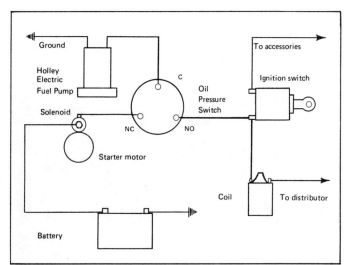

Typical wiring diagram for electric fuel pump. Holley's pressure switch 12-810 ensures pump won't operate unless engine is running or ignition switch is energizing starter solenoid. Starter circuit from ignition switch not shown in drawing.

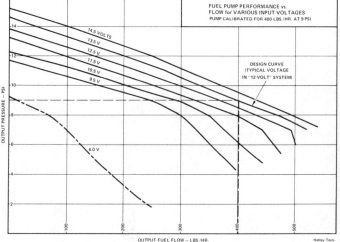

Note how pump performance drops off as voltage drops. This emphasizes importance of keeping battery charged. Pumps are designed to operate at 13.5 volts—nominal regulated voltage of 12-volt systems. At 13.5 volts, pump draws approximately 4 amperes.

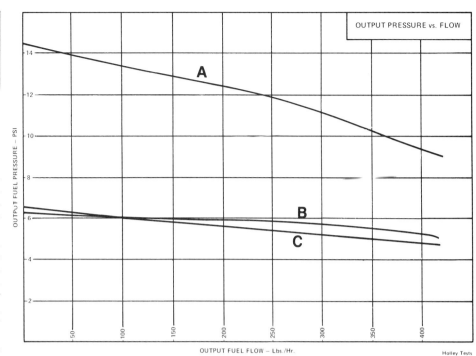

OUTPUT PRESSURE vs. FLOW

OUTPUT FUEL PRESSURE – PSI

OUTPUT FUEL FLOW – Lbs./Hr.

Holley Tests
June, 1971

Curve (A) shows dead-head pressure of Holley Max-pressure pump #12-802 (non-regulated) is 14.5 psi; pump can supply 420 lb/hr (75 gph) at 9 psi non-regulated output pressure. Curve (C) notes with regulator set for 6.5-psi output, 420 lbs/hr is maintained while pressure drops to 4.75 psi. (B) shows pressure and flow characteristics of standard pressure pump #12-801 (non-regulated).

formance will be compromised by such an installation. Small lines, sharp bends and kinks, or right-angle fittings will cause a pressure drop.

Because only one GPH 110 pump is needed for adequate fuel delivery (even on a Pro-Stock race car) part of the money that would have been spent for a second electric pump can be applied to the purchase of large fuel lines.

Keep the lines away from exhaust system components to avoid excessive heat. Make sure no part of the body will deflect the exhaust from open headers back onto the line. If a line passes near the exhaust system and there is no other place to route it, thoroughly insulate the fuel line. Clamp the line against the chassis or body structure with rubber-lined aircraft clamps.

Pressure Regulator—Mount the pressure regulator as close to the carburetor/s as possible. Lines between the regulator and carburetor/s can be 3/8-in. ID. There are two outlets on the Holley regulator. If the carburetor has fuel bowls with individual inlets, connect each bowl to an outlet. Where two carburetors are used, connect each carburetor to an outlet. Some racers prefer using two regulators, one at each carburetor, for insurance.

Pressure at the carburetor must be set with the engine idling so there will be some flow to allow the regulator to function. Use a fuel pressure gage at the carburetor and adjust the reg-

ulator to supply 6—7 psi output (factory-setting).

Cool Can—When running the car at high ambient temperatures, a cool can should be used just ahead of the regulator (upstream) on the high-pressure side so fuel won't tend to

flash into vapor when it is changed to a lower pressure by the regulator.

Fuel Bypass—Some racers install a separate bypass from the pump outlet to the tank. Then the pump doesn't continually pump the same fuel in a loop from the outlet back to the inlet.

Two fuel-pressure gages and two regulators on Pro Stock car. Fuel pressure can be observed during warmups in pits. Second regulator is hidden behind water hose; it is mount for electrical sender for fuel-pressure gage inside cockpit.

Dual fuel-pressure regulators supply these Model 4500s on Pro Stock car.

The external bypass allows fresh fuel to appear at the inlet, even at low-demand conditions such as idling.

The bypass should be through a 1/16 in. (or 0.060) restriction. Even with this bypass, capacity of the high-performance pump is 360 lb per hr of fuel at 9 psi.

BYPASS SPRING REPLACEMENT
Warning: Avoid heavy bypass springs. A 19-psi bypass spring is being sold by another company for Holley's 12-802 max-pressure pump. Holley tests show that using this spring reduces pump life by 75%.

ELECTRIC FUEL PUMP SERVICE KITS

A service kit for the 12-802 high-pressure pump allows repairing a functional pump that leaks because of a worn armature bushing or seal. The kit (12-808, Lower Housing Service Kit) includes a new pump housing with the seal assembly located to ride on a previously unused portion of the shaft.

The rotor, pump vanes, motor and bottom cover are removed from your old pump and installed in the new housing. The new housing includes a Permalube bearing with a lubrication wick and also includes heavier bosses for the fuel line fittings. These two features were added to all Holley fuel pumps in 1978.

Other simple repair kits are 12-805 for low-pressure and 12-806 for high-pressure pumps. These include a pump check-valve assembly and an inlet screen. A rotor service kit (12-811) has a new rotor and vanes. An armature cap and brush kit, 12-855, is used to fix pumps with worn brushes.

WATER IS THE ENEMY!

Holley's electric pumps are reliable. Yet Holley Technical Representatives fix several at every drag race where Holley is represented. There is always a rash of failures at the first races of the season.

Inevitably, failures are caused by water in the fuel. Where does the water come from? Humid conditions are common in most of the

---

FIRE—A HAZARD YOU CAN MINIMIZE
by Howard Fisher

Carburetors and fuel-supply system components carry or contain gasoline—a very flammable liquid. Careful installation and observation of what is happening when fuel pressure is applied to the carburetor (watching for flooding, for example) greatly reduces the possibility of fire.

Workplace—When a car or a carburetor is being worked on in a closed area containing a flame—such as the pilot light or burner of a water heater or furnace—**fire danger is extreme!** One spill can generate sufficient vapor to be carried across the floor to the flame. Then the trouble begins in the form of an explosion or a fire or both. Remember—any carburetor removed from a car contains gasoline. Drain it before carrying the carburetor inside to work on it. This is especially true when you work in an area with any kind of open flame.

Air Cleaner—Seventy-five percent (75%) of all auto fires directly result from leaving off the air cleaner. Fuel spews out of the carburetor onto the manifold—or standoff collects on the underside of the hood—then a backfire ignites the fuel.

Fire experts point out that the air cleaner prevents a backfire from igniting any stray fuel. The air cleaner itself doesn't support combustion very well. It's interesting to note that flame arresters are required on the carburetors of all marine inboard gasoline engines. If a fire starts in the air cleaner, a lot of smoke can be expected, but not much burns if the element is the usual paper type. Other auto fires not caused by leaving the air cleaner off are due to a bad fuel line or connection between the fuel pump and carburetor.

What To Do—Immediately call the fire department when a fire breaks out. Don't wait until you've used up your extinguisher and the fire is still raging. Get the fire department on the way just in case.

If you have a fire under the hood, don't throw the hood open because hot gases and flames will rush out. Open the hood just a

crack and shoot the extinguishing agent in. Better yet, shoot it in from under the engine.

Check everything before restarting the engine or you could start a worse fire—just when your extinguisher is all used up. Check all ignition wires, battery cables and the fuel lines to see whether they have burned or melted. Check fuel-line connections to make sure they have not loosened.

Fire Extinquishers—If a fire extinguisher is carried in the car, the fire can usually be put out quickly and with little damage. A 2-pound *ABC* dry-chemical extinguisher covers all three classes of fire found in cars. *A* is for upholstery and the interior, *B* refers to gasoline/oil fires, *C* is an electrical fire.

Dry Chemical—Volume-for-volume, powder has much better extinguishing capabilities than carbon dioxide (CO_2)or Halon FE-1301 (Bromotrifluoromethane). Also, powder retards reignition of the fire at hot spots and wiring.

Drawbacks of the dry-chemical extinguisher are that the powder goes *everywhere,* leaving a mess to be cleaned up afterward. And, the powder can get in the engine, especially if there is no air cleaner. If a lot of powder has to be directed into the carburetor air inlet, some may get into one or more cylinders through an open intake valve.

When you attempt to restart, a piston will compress this into a cake that may prevent the engine from turning. Even if you can crank the engine, the powder is abrasive. So, if very much gets in the engine, pull the cylinder heads and clean out the powder before running the engine.

Carbon Dioxide—CO_2 extinguishers are preferred by many because they cannot damage the engine and there is no after-mess. This is their greatest *plus*. But, because CO_2 fights fire by displacing oxygen, a much larger extinguisher (than dry chemical) is required to match the power of a dry-chemical unit. Fire experts we talked with recommended a 50-pound CO_2 unit! In open areas, especially when the wind is blowing, CO_2 dissipates

very quickly and sometimes will not put out a burning fuel line or wire.

Halon—An alternative to CO_2 is Halon FE-1301. This is the only approved extinguishing agent. Chemical products formed when Halon FE-1301 is exposed to flame interrupt the reactive process essential to fire. A concentration of only 4% (by volume) of Halon FE-1301 extinguishes the flames of most common fuels.

While the makers of systems using this extinguishing agent claim that a concentration of 20% can be breathed safely with no ill effects, material from the National Fire Protection Association (NFPA) disagrees. The NFPA says, "Halon 1301 vapor has low toxicity. However, decomposition products (as in a fire) can be hazardous. When using these extinguishers in unventilated places such as small rooms, closets, motor vehicles or other confined spaces, avoid breathing gases produced by thermal decomposition of Halon 1301."

Halon dissipates afterward with no mess or harm to the engine or other components. Pound-for-pound, Halon has three times the extinguishing power of CO_2. Even so, it dissipates rapidly in open areas or where the wind is blowing.

A 5-pound Halon extinguisher is an excellent item to carry in your car or have handy in your garage. If you have a CO_2 or Halon and a dry-chemical extinguisher on hand, always use the CO_2 or Halon first.

Many racecars are equipped with on-board Halon FE-1301 extinguisher systems. The added safety margin for a the driver who may have to exit from a flaming vehicle offsets the seemingly high first cost.

They pipe pressurized Halon into the driver's cockpit as low and far forward as possible. To avoid frostbite, keep the cockpit nozzle 18-in. away from any part of the driver. This location reduces the possibility of airflow sucking the Halon out of a low-pressure area. Additionally, nozzles direct Halon over, under and around the engine.

U.S. and Canada, especially during the summer months. Water condenses on the tank surfaces and falls into the fuel, settling in the bottom of the tank and in the pump. Sometimes, water is pumped into your tank with the gasoline.

Because the pump is usually the lowest point in the fuel system, water settles in the pump and sits there, causing corrosive damage. We see pumps corroded so badly that the rotor won't spin. Vanes are stuck in the rotor and the pressure-relief valve is stuck tight. Although these problems are easily fixed with Holley's service parts kits, it takes time. And it's aggravating to miss out on the racing.

If the vehicle is used every day, occasionally add a can of methanol-based fuel treatment to the fuel. This mixes with the fuel and the water so the water is harmlessly carried through the system and into the engine.

On a race car, drain the fuel system any time the car will be left sitting for several days. Use the fuel pump to drain the tank, then remove the pump-inlet hose connections and make sure the tank is empty. Squirt oil into the pump and turn it on and off to coat its internals. Squirt in more oil, then reattach the inlet hose. The next time you head for the races you'll know your pump is in good condition and ready to do its job.

Rust accumulation in bottom of electric pump isn't unusual. Drain gas tank and complete fuel system before storage. Disconnect pick-up line to pump and squirt some motor oil in so vanes won't freeze in rotor. Take bottom off pump and occasionally clean out any accumulated dirt and rust to prolong its life.

CARBURETOR TROUBLESHOOTING POSSIBLE CAUSE	PROBLEM	Stalling	Rough Idle	Flooding	Hot Start	Economy	Hesitation	Acceleration	Surge	Back Fire (cold)	Power	Stalling (cold)
Idle Adjustment		X	X		X	X	X		X	X		X
Idle Needles (Damaged)		X	X									X
Idle Vent Adjustment		X	X		X							X
Fast Idle Adjustment		X										X
Idle Passages (Dirty, Plugged)		X	X				X		X	X		X
Auto. Choke Adjustment										X		X
Choke Diaphragm Adjustment										X		X
Choke Rod Adjustment										X		X
Choke Unloader Adjustment										X		
Metering Jets (Loose, Plugged)						X	X	X	X	X	X	
Power Valve (Loose, Sticking)						X		X		X	X	
Fuel Inlet Needle & Seat (Loose, Leaking)		X	X	X	X	X	X				X	
Float (Leaking, Rubbing, Wrong Setting)		X	X	X	X	X	X		X		X	
Gaskets (Brittle, Improper Seal)		X	X			X	X		X			
Pump Discharge Holes (Dirty, Plugged)							X	X		X		
Pump Diaphragm (Worn, Cut)							X	X		X		
Pump Ball Checks (Dirty, Sticking)							X	X		X		
Choke Diaphragm Adjustment (Vacuum Leak)										X		X
Choke Valve & Linkage (Dirty, Sticking, Damaged)										X		X
Secondary Carb. Linkage Adj.							X	X		X	X	
Secondary Lockout Adjustment							X			X		X
Throttle Valves (Loose, Damaged, Sticking)		X	X				X		X			X
Venturi Cluster (Dirty, Loose)		X			X	X	X	X	X	X	X	X

Chart specifies carburetor problems only. It's assumed engine is in good mechanical condition and in tune. Many ignition and carburetor problems have same symptoms. Don't assume fault is with carburetor.

ANALYZING CARBURETOR PROBLEMS

There are three reasons to take wrench and screwdriver in hand and lay your carburetor open from choke plate to idle screw.

1. You're curious.
2. You're a racer or performance enthusiast.
3. You've got a driving problem with your vehicle and want to fix it.

If you are a number 1 or 2, skip to the appropriate section on disassembly and repair. If you belong to group 3, this section was written *just* for you.

How can you be sure the problem is with the carburetor, or involves it at all? An experienced carburetor tuner we know claims he's fixed a lot of "carburetor problems" by changing sparkplugs and distributor points. There's lot of truth in that statement. Replacing plug wires is another instant "magical" fix.

When analyzing engine malfunctions you have to look at the *total* system. That's what the next few pages are all about. Common problems associated with carburetors are presented with some probable solutions. Look under the Problem List for the malady that is occurring. The numbers refer to possible answers in the Solution List.

We also list non-carburetor causes for a simple reason. Disassembly and repair of a carburetor is truly time-consuming. It sure is disappointing to go through the whole exercise only to discover *later* that the problem is in some other component or system. Our objective is to get you to the solution quickly and simply.

PROBLEM LIST

A. Hard starting—cold engine:
   1, 2, 3, 4, 5, 6, 7, 8, 9, 10, 11.
B. Hard starting—warm engine:
   1, 10, 12, 13, 14, 15.
C. Rough idle and stalls:
   4, 7, 8, 16, 17, 18, 19, 20, 21, 22, 33, 53.
D. Deterioration of fuel economy:
   1, 4, 7, 18, 20, 23, 24, 25, 26, 30, 49, 52, 53.
E. Sag or hesitation on light accelerations:
   8, 10, 14, 18, 24, 25, 27, 28, 30, 32.
F. Sag or hesitation on hard accelerations:
   23, 27, 29, 30.
G. Surge under cruising and light loads:
   8, 10, 14, 18, 24, 25, 26, 30, 31, 32.
H. Surge at high speeds and heavy loads:
   23, 25, 26, 31, 34, 35.

Mass confusion! Excellent example of why you must identify all hoses and connections. Make a sketch for reassembly. Your memory is guaranteed to fail when reconnecting all these hoses!

I. Misfire or backfire:
   1, 4, 21, 27, 31.
J. Loss of power and top speed:
   1, 14, 18, 20, 23, 31, 34, 35, 36.
K. Fast idling or inconsistent idle return:
   8, 19, 37, 38, 39, 40, 41, 42, 43, 44.
L. Vapor lock—loss of power, stall or surge on acceleration after short engine-off period in high temperatures:
   10, 34, 35.
M. Inoperative secondary system (diaphragm-operated):
   45, 46, 47, 48.
N. Engine bucking or emitting black exhaust smoke:
   1, 23, 49, 50, 51, 52.
O. Poor cold driveaway:
   1, 2, 3, 29, 30, 51.

SOLUTION LIST

1. Binding or sticky choke plate or linkage. This can sometimes be repaired without removing the carburetor. If you have a remote or divorced choke, disconnect the choke rod from the carburetor to isolate the problem. *Never use lubricating or household oil to free the choke.* Oil gathers dust and grime and stiffens at low temperatures, creating an even worse problem. Commercial solvents for carburetors work well. Penetrating oil works just great.

Sometimes vibration or a few backfires will cause the choke plate to shift on the choke shaft. Repair requires loosening the choke plate screws and realigning the plate in the air horn. If the choke is held on by screws with lock washers this is easy. Most have staked screws to prevent loosening. Loosening any staked screw requires considerable care to avoid twisting off the screwhead.

Use a small file to remove the upset or staked material from the screw and proceed with caution. You must restake the screws when you reinstall them. The opposite side of the shaft must be firmly supported so you won't bend the shaft in the process. Disassemble the carburetor to allow staking the screws. With a divorced or remote choke, the linkage or bimetal in the choke pocket in the intake manifold can rub against the side, causing binding. Move the choke rod up and down to detect this condition.

2. Incorrect choke adjustment. There are two basic adjustments—the bimetal index and qualifying or pull. See next section.

3. Overstressed bimetal. If the choke unit doesn't exert enough force to close the choke plate when the engine is cold and ambient temperature is below 60F (15.5C), this could be your problem. A new bimetal is required. Because replacement bimetals are not always readily available, try resetting the choke in the

RICH direction. Most automatic-choke housings have an arrow indicating RICH and LEAN directions.

4. Fouled or old sparkplugs. You can easily spot this with an engine analyzer but not many of us have this tool. Pull a plug or two and take a look. If you see a deposit build-up or burned electrodes on one or two, then change the *whole* set. Sparkplugs are inexpensive and the benefits of good firing are numerous, especially for economy. If plugs and wires are over a year old, replace the whole set regardless of how good they look.

5. Wrong distributor point gap or dwell. Detect with a dwell meter or by physical measurement. With the point rubbing block set on one of the cam lobes, the points of most non-electronic distributors should be open about 0.017 in. Check with a feeler gage or a No. 77 drill. Check the points for pitting or build-up.

Point changes can be accomplished on the engine but it is easier and less risky if the distributor is removed. If you remove the distributor, note the position of rotor and housing and have a timing light handy to re-time the distributor correctly when you reinstall it. You must make sure the distributor drive mechanism fully engages with the oil pump if it drives the pump.

6. Water condensed in the distributor cap. This can happen with warm humid days and cool nights. Remove distributor cap and wipe with a clean dry cloth. Check inside the cap for cracks or carbon tracking while you have it off. Either means a new cap.

7. Poor compression. This condition could result from worn piston rings or leaky intake or exhaust valves. A compression or leak-down test will give a quick answer. Consult a service manual for desired compression values. If one or more cylinders has more than 20% less compression than the others, you've got problems. A leak-down tester is better than an ordinary compression tester because it helps you find the leak.

8. Intake leaks. Look very closely at all rubber vacuum hoses. Make sure they are not split, leaking or disconnected. These hoses become hardened with age. Cracks are often hidden in bends or on the underside, so look carefully. Be sure to check the hoses to the automatic transmission. Manifold-to-head-gasket leaks can be detected by spraying a little carburetor cleaner all around the intersection while the engine is idling. If the engine speeds up or smooths out, you've found the culprit.

WARNING: Be careful when spraying flammable carburetor cleaner on an idling engine— don't let it ignite! Use it sparingly and in a well-ventilated area.

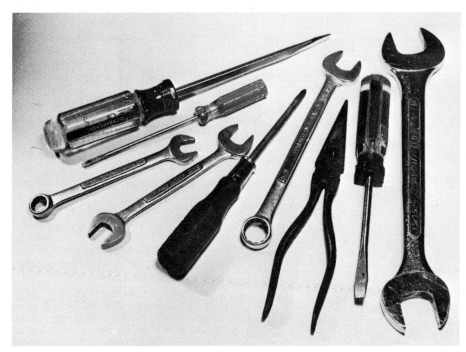

These are ordinary tools for working on carburetors. A clutch-head screwdriver is also needed for 4160/80 carburetors. Other essential tools include tubing wrenches, Corbin-clamp pliers and fuel-inlet open-end wrench.

9. Low battery voltage. Slow cranking speed is the giveaway here.

10. Fuel volatility. Oil companies change the *volatility* or *vapor pressure* of their fuels so they are highest in mid-winter and lowest in mid-summer. This allows quick cold starts with little cranking in January and minimizes long cranking to get a hot engine started in July. Volatility is also varied geographically, with higher values in the North and lower ones in the South. An unusually warm winter day always brings a rash of hot-starting problems. Avoid filling up at low-volume gas stations—especially in the spring and fall.

11. Water in the gasoline. Modern gasoline additives make this less of a problem than it once was. Nevertheless, always fill your tank completely to minimize the opportunity for water vapor to condense in the unused volume. It also reduces the likelihood of rust formation in your fuel tank. For the same reasons avoid purchasing fuel at low-volume stations. It is a good idea to add a can of water-absorbing fuel-tank cleaner like Dry Gas or STP Gas Treatment once in a while.

12. Incorrect carburetor fuel level. An excessively high fuel level causes rich die-outs on sudden stops due to fuel spillage. There is also a greater tendency toward *fuel percolation*. It boils over from the bowl into the manifold.

A low fuel level can cause sags when accelerating because it delays the main system

start-up. Fuel starvation (leanness) on turns and maneuvers can also result from a low fuel level.

Some Holley carburetors have externally adjustable fuel levels and removable sight plugs. With the engine idling the lock screw should be loosened and the adjustment nut turned until the fuel level is just at the bottom of the sight-plug hole.

Other carburetors require disassembly for float adjustment. This is treated in more detail for specific carburetors in later sections. The Holley Illustrated Parts & Specs Manual gives fuel-level adjustments for most popular Holley carburetors.

13. Leaky fuel-inlet valve. Is the valve worn or is foreign material lodged between the inlet and seat? New inlet valves and seats are included in most repair kits. Fuel levels are noted in the Renew Kit instructions. Always check fuel level when changing fuel-inlet valves or floats.

14. Sticking exhaust-manifold heat-control valve. Most vehicles built before 1969 had heat-control valves. This valve diverts some exhaust gas through an intake-manifold passage to create a "hot spot." A valve stuck in the closed position makes the hot spot run excessively hot. This causes vapor formation and boiling in the carburetor fuel bowl. Hard starting and rough idling result. A valve stuck open will not allow the hot spot to reach high enough temperature. Low and mid-range driveability

problems are the symptom.

Free the valve with commercial solvents designed for this purpose. Penetrating oil or WD-40 is especially good. If the valve has been stuck for some time, it may take several applications, a little time and friendly persuasion with light hammer taps.

15. Mechanical bowl-vent adjustment. Bowl vents are often found on pre-'68 carburetors. The vent should be slightly open (approximately 1/16 in.) at idle and engine off and closed at all other conditions.

16. Carburetor icing. Icing can occur when there is high relative humidity and temperatures in the 30—50F (-lC—10C) range. While the engine is warming up, ice forms between the throttle plate and bore. Check the carburetor-air preheat system on 1969 and later vehicles. On earlier models check the exhaust-manifold heat-control valve (see 14, above). A slightly higher idle speed helps minimize icing.

17. Idle-mixture adjustment. Turn the idle-mixture screw in until engine speed drops slightly, then back out the screw about 1/8 turn. This is the *lean-best-idle setting.* For 2- and 4-barrel carburetors, set idle mixture on one side and repeat on the opposite side. Then go back to the original side and repeat the process one more time just to be safe. On 1968 and later vehicles, idle-adjustment range is limited for exhaust-emission purposes.

18. Clogged air bleeds or passages. This usually requires a carburetor teardown just to determine if it really is the problem. Try swabbing and squirting the exposed bleeds with a little Gum-Out, STP Carb Cleaner, other carburetor solvent, or isopropyl alcohol. This may open up the blockage and save you a lot of work.

19. Idle-speed adjustment. Specific carburetor sections show the location of the idle-speed adjustment screw. Vehicles from 1970 and later have recommended idle speed on a tag in the engine compartment. For earlier vehicles, use 600 rpm for manual transmissions and 550 rpm in Drive for automatics.

Be careful when setting the idle on cars with automatic transmissions. Don't stand in front of the car or drape yourself on the fender. Make sure the parking brake is ON and the wheels are blocked. Don't "flick" or "blip" (snap the throttle on quickly and then release) the throttle or you could have an out-of-control vehicle.

20. Restricted or dirty air cleaner. Place a 100-watt bulb inside the cleaner element and look at the outside. You can see the dirt pattern. Most times the element can be cleaned with pressurized air. If it looks hopeless, buy a new element, they're inexpensive.

21. Old and/or cracked sparkplug wires. With the engine idling on a dark night, open the hood and observe the sparkplug wires. If sparks jump from the wires, it's time for a new set. Sometimes the center of carbon-core (TVR)

Holley Illustrated Parts & Specs

Manual For Current Carburetor Models

Covers Model Numbers:
2300, 4150, 3160, 4160, 1920, 1940, 2210, 2245, 2211, 5200,
4165, 4175, 4500, 5210, 1945, 6145, 4360, 2280, 1946
6146C, 6500, 6510, 5220, 4180, 4190EG, 5740, 6740, 6520

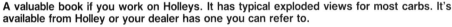

A valuable book if you work on Holleys. It has typical exploded views for most carbs. It's available from Holley or your dealer has one you can refer to.

Top: Staked choke-plate-retaining screw (arrow). Bottom: Staked throttle-plate screws. Screws are staked to prevent loosening and falling into engine. Staking must be removed before taking screws out. Restake with a small punch and hammer on reassembly. Support shaft while staking to prevent bending shaft. Avoid removing staked screws whenever you can. It's seldom necessary for carburetor rebuild.

wires can separate. This even happens with new TVR wires. Ignition wires must be removed from the plugs by tugging on the connectors—never by pulling on the cables.

22. Leaky intake or exhaust valves. A compression or leak-down test will usually detect this problem; the exception is a hanging or sticking valve that acts up sporadically.

23. Power valve stuck. A piston-type valve can stick open or closed. Diaphragm-type valves seldom stick, but leaking is possible. A leaky diaphragm causes an abnormally rich condition, evidenced by a black, smoky exhaust and extreme difficulty in restarting.

24. Distributor vacuum-advance line disconnected or leaky. Hoses become dry and crack with age. Connections should be snug because small leaks have great effects.

25. Incorrect basic distributor setting. Cars from 1970 and later have the recommended setting listed on a tag under the hood. For earlier models, see the service manual.

26. Wrong size main jets. This commonly occurs with racers or enthusiasts, and with used carburetors. Main-jet sizes for most popular Holley carburetors are listed in the Holley Illustrated Parts & Specs Manual.

27. Accelerator-pump failure. Remove the

air cleaner and observe the pump nozzles while opening the throttle. A steady stream of fuel should shoot out as you open the throttle. Make sure you install the fuel-bowl gasket so the pump passages are not blocked.

28. Clogged idle-transfer slots or holes. This condition requires a carburetor teardown to find and remedy.

29. Wrong accelerator-pump adjustment. Specific carburetor sections explain some of the adjustments for your particular carburetor. Renew Kit instructions and the Holley Illustrated Parts & Spec Manual give correct settings and describe how to check the settings.

30. Carburetor too large for the application. Usually an enthusiast-caused problem. The How To Select & Install Your Carburetor chapter deals with this subject.

31. Clogged main jets. Requires internal carburetor inspection. It seldom happens.

32. Hot inlet air system inoperative. This system preheats inlet air by routing it past the exhaust manifold. It is common on 1969 and later vehicles.

33. Clogged PCV valve. This valve is usually installed in a grommet or cap in the valve cover. Inspection is quick and easy. Most can be cleaned with a little kerosene or solvent. You'll know it's clean when you can blow through it in one direction (toward the carburetor) but not the other. Be sure to install it correctly.

34. Clogged fuel-inlet filter or screen. In some cases this can be inspected without removing the carburetor. Some vehicles have an in-line filter between the fuel pump and carburetor. Don't hesitate to change it if you suspect it.

35. Low fuel-pump pressure. A pressure gage can be installed between the fuel pump and carburetor. Typical idle pressures are 3.5—6 psi. Less than 2.5 psi at top speed is a sure danger signal. *Don't plumb fuel lines to a pressure gage inside your car!* Mount a fuel-pressure gage on the cowl outside of the windshield.

36. Throttle plates not reaching wide-open position. All carburetors have a wide-open stop on the throttle lever. Have someone depress the throttle pedal to the floor while you check to see if the throttle lever reaches the wide-open stop. If it doesn't, readjust the throttle linkage or cable. Hold the throttle lever against the stop while looking down to see whether the throttle plates are actually vertical (wide-open position).

37. Throttle plates not seated in the bores. They're not supposed to seat in the bores! They're factory-adjusted to be slightly open at idle. If the throttle plates have shifted or have become loose, then you *may* want to consider recentering them. This is not a job we recommend for the amateur.

It requires removing the throttle body and reseating the plates. And it is a ticklish operation on most carburetors because throttle-plate screws are staked to prevent loosening. Care is needed to prevent twisting off the screw heads. Remove the upset or staked material with a small file and remove the screws with great care. Back off the idle-speed screw, reset the plates in the bores and retighten the screws. Support the opposite side of the shaft and restake with a small prick punch.

Important: These screws *must* be restaked to avoid screws and/or plates entering the engine to cause serious damage.

38. Dashpot binding or misadjusted. The dashpot slows the throttle return. If the idle-

Contents of Holley Renew Kit for Model 4150. Read the instruction sheet! It contains tips and adjustment specifications. All necessary parts are here to rebuild carburetor to original specifications. Included are gaskets, pump diaphragm/s, inlet valves, power valves, and float gage.

speed screw never returns to the stop, the dashpot is binding or misadjusted. Normally, the dashpot should have approximately 3/32-in. additional travel beyond closed throttle. Readjustment can be made by turning the dashpot after the locknut has been loosened. Be sure to tighten the locknut after the readjustment.

39. Vehicle linkage binding. Separate the vehicle throttle linkage from the carburetor to isolate the problem. Look for sticking or binding along the linkage. Lubrication may solve the problem. Cable-operated linkages sometimes require minor cable rerouting to avoid binding.

40. Anti-dieseling solenoid incorrectly adjusted. This solenoid acts as the idle stop while the engine is running. It is withdrawn when the ignition is turned off so the plates can close further in the bore to prevent after-run or dieseling. Make sure the solenoid plunger moves as the ignition is turned on and off. Idle speeds should be set with the solenoid *activated* (holding throttle slightly away from closed position).

41. Fast-idle cam bound or stuck. Squirting a little solvent on and around the cam and its associated linkage may correct this.

42. Overstressed throttle-linkage return spring. Check the spring from the carburetor

throttle lever to some mounting point on the engine. If coil separation indicates an overstressed condition, replace the spring.

43. Bound or bent throttle shaft. Separate the throttle-actuating linkage from the carburetor throttle lever and check for binding or sticking. If deposits and dirt are the problem, squirting a little solvent on the shaft may help. A bent shaft will probably have to be replaced. Binding is sometimes caused by over-torquing carburetor-attachment nuts, warping the throttle body. This can prevent diaphragm-operated secondary throttles from opening.

44. Worn throttle-shaft bearings. Separate the vehicle throttle linkage from the carburetor and wiggle throttle shaft up and down. If movement is noticeable, shaft bearings are worn. Replace the throttle body.

45. Failed secondary operating diaphragm. Remove the cover and inspect the diaphragm. Replace the diaphragm if it is torn or broken. Diaphragms are available as a service item. Part numbers are in the Holley Performance Parts Catalog or the Holley Illustrated Parts & Specs Manual.

46. Plugged secondary vacuum-signal port. This can be repaired by cleaning, but requires disassembly of the carburetor.

Spray-on gasket remover is almost essential to remove stuck on Holley gaskets. Follow manufacturer's application instructions and precautions. Spray on, then let soak in for a few minutes. Rub or scrape off gasket. Use your fingernail or plastic scraper to avoid damaging cast-in raised bead that ensures sealing. Wash part in solvent or water after using gasket remover. Be careful where you spray because these are *powerful* paint removers!

Carb Spray Cleaner by STP is helpful for cleaning up carbureter and fuel system parts. It's also useful for removing residue and cleaning parts after using spray-on gasket remover.

A lug or protrusion on metering block is good prying point when gasket is stuck. Avoid penetrating gasket more than 1/4 in. because you can chisel off hidden locating tabs or dowels.

47. Binding secondary-throttle shaft. This shaft must be free to rotate to function properly. Over-torqued carburetor hold-down nuts or capscrews or using a thick soft gasket may result in throttle-body warping and hence throttle binding. Another, less-common cause may be loose or shifted throttle plates.

48. Secondary operating vacuum hose leaky or disconnected. This applies only to 3 x 2 (three-carburetor) applications.

49. Flooding. This is the condition when fuel continues to enter the carburetor uncontrolled by the float and inlet valve. Fuel spills out of the carburetor into the intake manifold. Look for leaky or worn fuel-inlet valves or foreign material holding the valve off the seat.

Foreign material is often rust or dirt from the vehicle or gasoline station fuel tank. Flooding can also be caused by a faulty float. Brass floats may develop a leak and lose buoyancy. This seldom happens with closed-cellular or hollow-plastic floats. Although they too can absorb fuel over time and lose their buoyancy.

50. Broken power valve diaphragm. Remove the power valve and inspect. Excessive backfiring can be the cause.

51. Slow choke come-off. Can be caused by a choke misadjustment. A more common cause with hot-air chokes is clogging or rupturing of the tube bringing hot air from the stove in the

exhaust manifold or crossover to the choke unit. If hot air doesn't get to the choke bimetal, the choke will open late or remain in a partially closed position. On a completely warmed engine, the integral-choke unit should be quite hot to the touch.

52. Wrong metering-block gasket. Check to make sure you have the correct one. Note if it should be used with a carburetor not having an accelerator-pump transfer tube.

53. Model 1920 carburetors. Engines using the crankcase for fuel-vapor storage must have a PCV valve in good condition. Because the fuel bowl is vented to the crankcase, high-mileage engines can produce sufficient blowby to pressurize the bowl. This can cause a rich mixture with consequent reduced economy and stalling during idle.

PREPARING FOR CARBURETOR REPAIR

Once you've analyzed the problem and decided it lies with the carburetor, you've set yourself up for *another* decision. Here are your options:

1. Take the carburetor apart, make the critical repair and put it back together.
2. Make an economy carburetor repair.
3. Perform a complete carburetor disassembly and repair.

Which Option?—If you've done a little carburetor work and you're fairly sure where the problem is and time is important, option 1 is probably the best approach. You might be able to perform this operation without removing the

carburetor, but it isn't really a good idea. Bending over the fender is difficult and parts are easily lost.

If time allows, remove the carburetor from the engine. For this option you need, at the bare minimum, new gaskets. Gasket numbers for the Model 4150/60/80 and 4165/75 are in the Performance Parts Catalog or in the Holley Illustrated Parts & Specs Manual (Holley Part 36-51-6). Your dealer probably has both. For other carburetors you may have to purchase a complete Renew Kit to obtain the gaskets you need.

The catalog and manual contain a wealth of information about specific Holley carburetors and can be obtained by writing:

Technical Service Department
Holley Replacement Parts Division
601 Space Park North
Goodlettsville, TN 37072
(615) 859-4924

These are both inexpensive. There is also another Holley Illustrated Parts & Specs Manual for Older Carburetor Models, 36-51-5. It too is inexpensive. The Technical Service Department is also a good place to get quick service on hard-to-find parts that may not be immediately available at your dealer.

It is seldom necessary to do option 3, disassembling the carburetor and soaking it in a special cleaner as most manuals and printed instructions direct you to do. First of all, it is very time-consuming. Most sub-assemblies must be taken apart. Non-metal components

Holley Renew Kits have original parts. Many other kits don't and their parts may not perform to specifications.

Place carb on stand while disassembling to protect throttle plates. Many good ones are available, but four 5/16-in. bolts and eight nuts are inexpensive and work just great.

Open throttles extend below throttle body. Handle carburetor with care when it's off manifold. Damage inevitably occurs when throttles are held open, then carburetor is set down hard. You can't use carburetor until you've purchased new throttle plates.

Don't even think about reusing this gasket! Holley's fuel bowl and metering block gaskets seal well, but they self-destruct on disassembly. Remove residue with spray-on gasket remover, time and patience. Be sure to blow out all passages where gasket pieces could create problems. Be extremely careful not to scrape off cast-in raised-bead sealing surfaces!

can't be exposed to the cleaner. Commercial carburetor cleaners are expensive and the Environmental Protection Agency may require special and expensive paperwork and disposal procedures. So, unless you plan to rebuild several carburetors or are in the carburetor-rebuilding business, this procedure is usually expensive.

We think option 2—the economy carburetor repair method—represents the best compromise of cost, time requirement, and satisfactory results. Cleaners such as kerosene, Stoddard solvent and mild paint thinners allow you to clean up delicate plastic and synthetic parts together with metal parts, making complete disassembly unnecessary.

Cleaning—A small open can, a brush, a small scraping tool and some elbow grease let you do a fine job of washing. For dissolving deposits, use lacquer thinner, toluol, MEK, Gum-Out, Chem-Tool, STP Carb Cleaner or any of the many brands of cleaners available. These must be used in a well-ventilated area away from fire or pilot lights—such as on a gas range, water heater or furnace. Use with a brush on large surfaces to dissolve deposits. Use a common ear syringe to shoot the solution through passages. Wear safety glasses and keep your hands out of any dissolving-type chemicals. One way or another you can do a good job without exotic equipment.

Passages and orifices should be blown out with compressed air. If compressed air isn't available, you can always use a bicycle or tire pump to do the job. Never use a wire or drill to clean orifices and restrictions because the slightest mark can change flow characteristics.

Renew Kits—For options 2 and 3 get the correct Renew Kit listed in the Holley Performance Catalog or the Illustrated Parts & Specs Manual. Holley Renew Kits contain the same components as originally installed in the carburetor. Not many other repair-kit manufacturers can make this claim.

The Renew Kit contains all gaskets including the one that goes between the carburetor and intake manifold. Also included are fuel-inlet valves, power valves, accelerator-pump diaphragms or cups and a service instruction sheet giving adjustment specifications and procedures. When similar gaskets or parts are included, compare with the original parts and choose the parts most similar to the original.

Parts will probably be left over from your kit when you've finished. Don't panic! The kits were designed to service more than one application in most cases. Consolidating parts reduces the number of kits the dealer has to stock. It is actually more economical to include a few extra parts so each kit will service several different carburetors.

Tools—Common tools are usually good enough for carburetor disassembly and repair. You will need standard and Phillips screwdrivers, regular and needle-nose pliers and the usual set of open-end wrenches. A sharp scraping tool is good for removing deposits as well as old gaskets from the intake manifold.

Be extremely careful with gasket surfaces on carburetor parts. Zinc and aluminum are easily scratched. Small "beads" or raised surfaces may be cast in to provide positive sealing. Because they are hidden under stuck-on gasket material, they're easily damaged.

Spray-on gasket remover is essential for removing gaskets stuck onto carburetor surfaces. Take your time and use several applications if that's what it takes to loosen the old gasket material so you can get it off with a soft plastic scraper—or your fingernail.

A special 1-in. open-end wrench (MAC S-141) may be required to remove the fuel-inlet fitting on Models 4150/60/80 and 4165/75 carburetors. You can sometimes do this with a standard open-end wrench. Corbin-clamp pliers and tubing wrenches are good to have for carburetor removal and installation. Tubing wrenches are a *necessity* if you are working with soft fuel-line nuts.

Follow the instructions in Select & Install Your Carburetor for removing and installing the carburetor. There's no way to overstress the

importance of tagging and identifying each vacuum hose with a piece of tape or other tag. Take a few minutes to make a schematic diagram showing all of the hookups. This saves a lot of grief, especially on vehicles with complicated emission-control systems.

A holding fixture should be used to prevent damage to the throttle plates while working on the carburetor. Many stands are available, but 5/16 bolts and nuts work just fine. Use a second nut on each bolt to lock the throttle body onto the bolts, preventing wobble.

Now you're ready for the job. Specific carburetor sections include disassembly, repair and assembly procedure for most popular Holley carburetors. In some cases, we discussed the complete disassembly even though you may be using the economy method.

We couldn't include every variation of every model carburetor Holley ever made. We limited our discussion to typical carburetors, but yours may be slightly different. Expect to do a little thinking and analysis of your own application from the basics presented here.

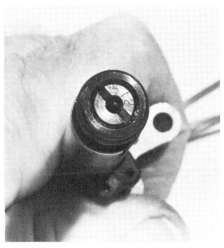

Closed-loop carbs have removable duty-cycle solenoid. Don't put it in strong carburetor cleaners! Don't remove the screw-in jet in end. To test if it's working, put your hand on it when engine is running. If you can feel it vibrating, it's probably OK.

Models 4150/4160/4180, 4165/4175, 2300 Repair & Adjustment

NOTE: The 4150 family of carburetors includes Models 4160, 4180, 4165, 4175, and 2300. Because of their similar construction they are discussed in one set of disassembly, repair and adjustment procedures. For demonstration purposes we used a popular Model 4150 which incorporates more sub-assemblies than most carburetors. If you can make it through this one, you won't have any problem with any other carburetor in this family.

(2) Remove four secondary fuel-bowl screws. Remove fuel bowl and gasket and metering block and its gasket. Separating these assemblies may require a rap from screwdriver handle or plastic mallet. Separating fuel bowl, metering block and carburetor main body may be difficult on carburetors with Holley's black gaskets. If inserting putty knife or anything else to loosen gasket, don't push in more than 1/4 in. or you may shear off one of the locating dowels.

Model 4160 carburetors have metering plate instead of metering block. These also tend to stick after removing clutch-head screws. A rap should loosen it. The carburetor used here is a Model 4150 with dual inlets and no fuel-transfer tube between bowls.

(1) Before disassembly, mount carburetor on holding fixture or set of 5/16-in. bolts. Loosen fuel-inlet fitting and also fuel-bowl sight plugs, and needle and seat lock screws. These are easier to do when carburetor is completely assembled. We prefer to loosen these parts while carburetor is still securely bolted to manifold.

(3) Here is single-inlet carburetor with balance tube between bowls. Note O-ring (arrow). Don't worry about preserving it when rebuilding, new ones are in Renew Kit. Just slide fuel bowls off tube. On reassembly, use petroleum jelly or oil on O-rings. Twist tube slightly to ease O-ring entry into each bowl. Make sure no part of O-ring gets pinched over bead of tube. Fuel under pressure is contained in tube, so don't make mistakes or you could cause leaks.

(4) Now repeat procedure on primary side. On Model 2300 two-barrel, this is where you begin. Use plenty of torque when replacing bowl screws: 50 in-lb.

(5) Remove choke unit. With integral chokes, first remove hairpin retainer from bottom of rod connecting choke-control (unit through main body casting) up to choke lever. Use needle-nose pliers.

(6) Note position of mark on black bimetal housing relative to marks on choke casting. Strut in middle of these marks on casting is called *index mark*. Choke adjustments are made relative to this mark. Draw a picture so you can reassemble choke in the same position. Choke settings are called out in marks RICH or LEAN from the index.

(7) Remove three screws holding bimetal housing retainer and remove retainer, gasket and bimetal housing. Don't remove bimetal from housing.

(8) Remove metal choke housing from main body by extracting three attachment screws.

(9) For carburetors with divorced or remote choke: remove two screws holding vacuum break, the retainer holding fast-idle cam and lever, and choke rod retainer (if there is one). Disconnect vacuum hose at throttle body and remove all choke parts. Here is choke lever and vacuum break from typical divorced or remote-choke application.

(10) Remove clip from shaft (arrow), take out three screws mounting vacuum break housing to main body and remove housing.

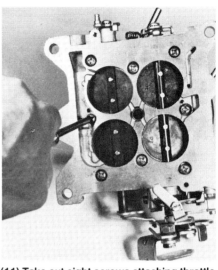

(11) Take out eight screws attaching throttle body to main body. These are often tough to turn. Impact driver is helpful. You now have carburetor broken down to major subassemblies and can begin their disassembly, if needed.

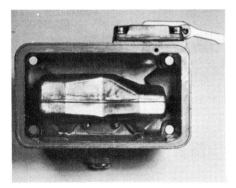

(12) Center-pivot-float fuel bowls hinge primary floats at front and secondary floats at back. This bowl can have either single or dual inlets. With dual inlets, one side is closed with plug and other side has inlet fitting.

(13) On bowls with front-mounted floats, first remove inlet needle-and-seat assembly. Loosen lock screw and turn hex nut counterclockwise. It slips over needle-and-seat assembly. Now remove two screws holding float-mounting bracket and remove bracket and float from fuel bowl.

(14) Fuel bowl with side-mounted float. Remove baffle (arrow) surrounding inlet valve and then retainer from float hinge pin. Float assembly can then be removed. Nonadjustable inlet valves must be removed from inside with open-end wrench. Take out fuel-inlet fitting you previously loosened. Remove it with integral filter and spring, see (15). Remove sight plugs if used. Fuel bowls are completely disassembled. This fuel bowl has externally adjustable needle/seat.

(15) Disassembled side-mounted-float fuel bowl with non-adjustable inlet valve.

(15a) Plastic float in side-mount fuel bowl with externally adjustable inlet valve.

(16 & 17) Primary bowls (and secondary bowls on double-pumpers) contain accelerator-pump assemblies. Remove four attachment screws and lift pump diaphragm and housing from bowl. Some have hanging-ball inlet. Clearance between ball and retainer (arrow) should be 0.011—0.013 in. with bowl inverted. Others have a rubber-umbrella inlet valve (top photo). Remove rubber valve before putting fuel bowl in cleaner.

(18) Remove main metering jets with wide-blade screwdriver. The screwdriver must cover both sides of slot or you will damage jets. Primary and secondary jets are often different sizes. Small jets go in primary side if carburetor has smaller primary venturis. On rare occasions jets will differ from side to side in same metering block. Always check jet sizes and locations and write this down *before* you take out jets.

Remove bowl-vent splash shield and any vacuum fittings if used. DON'T REMOVE ANY PRESSED-IN VACUUM TUBES. Turn each mixture screw in gently until it seats. Record how many turns it took. Take out idle-mixture screws and seals.

EXCEPTION: Model 4180 mixture screws are sealed in throttle body. It is such a chore to unseal and remove them that this isn't recommended for cleaning/rebuilding.

Remove power valves with a 1-in. wrench. A socket is preferred, but open end is OK if you use it carefully. The 1-in. wrench for large fuel-inlet fittings works fine.

It usually isn't necessary to disassemble metering blocks any further. Although there are tubes inside main and idle wells, these can usually be cleaned with compressed air. Small metering plate from secondary side of Model 4160 requires no further disassembly.

Metering blocks with O-ringed tube connecting them to main body should have this tube removed before proceeding further. Use new gaskets on reassembly. When you reassemble carburetor, install mixture screws 1-1/2 turns off their seats as starting point.

(19 & 20) Take good look at choke assembly before taking it apart. Note fast-idle cam and choke lever relationship. Remove choke shaft nut, lock washer and spacer, and then slide shaft and fast-idle cam from housing. Next remove choke qualifying piston. Make sure it operates freely in its bore. Remove cork gasket that surrounds restriction on back side of choke housing. Use new gasket on reassembly.

(21) Disassemble secondary diaphragm. Remove four attachment screws; a rap will separate upper and lower housings. Remove spring and diaphragm. Pencil points to cork gasket that should be removed. Use a new gasket on reassembly.

CLEANING & ASSEMBLY

The carburetor is completely disassembled and ready for cleaning. Remember if you doing a complete carburetor repair, only metal parts should be put in carb cleaner. Don't immerse electrical parts in strong cleaners. All non-metal parts, including choke bimetal and housing, Teflon bushings and plastic accelerator-pump cams should be cleaned with milder cleaner such as kerosene or paint thinner. Once all cleaning is done, inspect parts for undue wear and replace as required. If using a Renew Kit, all gaskets, pump diaphragms, secondary diaphragms (in some cases), fuel-inlet valves and power valves are included.

(20a) Details of electric choke caps. Top one is heated by resistance wire (arrow). Lower one uses solid-state heater that raises resistance and lowers current flow as temperature rises.

(22) If putting the main body in carburetor cleaner, remove choke plate and shaft to remove little plastic guide. If using the economy repair method, choke-shaft removal is seldom necessary and we don't recommend it. If removing choke plate and shaft, first file staked portion of choke screws. Then take out screws and lift choke plate out of shaft. The choke shaft can now be removed from main body, allowing removal of choke rod and guide. Remember, restake choke-plate screws at reassembly. That requires supporting shaft so it won't be bent.

Remove pump-discharge-nozzle screw, nozzle and gasket. Turn body over to remove pump-discharge valve. Double pumpers have two pump-discharge assemblies. Models 4165/4175 don't have pump-discharge valve at this location.

(23) It's seldom necessary to disassemble throttle body and immerse all of its parts. Only a few metering restrictions and small passages are in it and throttle-plate screws must be removed and restaked upon assembly. That's a job and if not necessary, why do it? Cleaning with brush and milder solvent is usually more than adequate. If determined to do complete disassembly, then remove: idle-speed screw and spring, diaphragm-operating lever from secondary throttle shaft and fast-idle lever from primary shaft, and cotter key and connecting link between primary and secondary throttle levers. File off staked ends of throttle-plate attachment screws, remove screws and throttle plates. Slide shafts out of flange. Take out Teflon bushings (typical on secondary side of carburetors with diaphragm-operated secondaries).

(24) When reassembling carburetor, simply follow disassembly instructions in reverse order. Pictures and exploded views will help. When assembling fuel-supply tube, use petroleum jelly (Vaseline) on O-rings so they'll slip in easier. When assembled properly, you can rotate tube with fingers.

Thoroughly restake choke and throttle-attachment screws. If one loosens and goes into engine, it could be very expensive. Other than very small choke and throttle screws, don't be shy about torquing assembly screws, especially throttle-body and fuel-bowl screws. Once you've gotten all in, go around again and give them a little extra tweak.

Be sure secondary diaphragm is sealed all the way around when attaching its cover to the lower housing. Unload diaphragm spring by pushing up on rod. This will cause diaphragm to lay flatter and make it easier to get screws and cover installed. On Models 4165/4175, short bowl screws go on top. Don't forget to replace all gaskets. Some small ones are easy to overlook.

(25) Some bimetals have hooked end while others have loop as shown. Make sure you capture choke-lever tang with end of bimetal when installing bimetal housing. Rotate housing back and forth before tightening retainer and choke plate should move.

(26) Externally adjustable fuel-bowl float levels can be set on car. Remove sight plug. Loosen lock screw at top of assembly and turn adjusting nut until fuel level is at bottom of sight-plug hole. To confirm setting, flush fuel bowl a few times by accelerating engine with transmission in NEUTRAL. Tighten lock screw while holding adjustment nut and replace sight plug. This operation is difficult to do accurately on rough-idling car.

ADJUSTMENTS
A number of adjustments should be made as you reassemble carburetor. Adjustment procedures are shown in accompanying photographs. Specific dimensions are in instruction sheet supplied with Renew Kit and in Holley Illustrated Parts & Specs book.

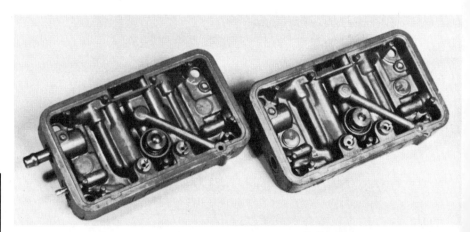

(27) Primary metering block can be distinguished from secondary because it contains idle-mixture screws and may also have one or more tubes. Metering-block gaskets are properly installed when they line up with dowels on metering block.

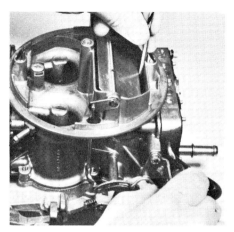

(28) Dry float setting is usually measured between bowl casting and float end with bowl inverted. Holley Renew Kits give correct spec and may include a gage. Adjust float level by bending tang as shown, being careful not to mar contact surface.

(29) Choke-qualify adjustment. Specification is clearance between choke plate and casting on either top or bottom edge as noted. Renew Kit or Holley Illustrated Parts & Specs gives dimension. Hold choke plate closed and measure clearance while operating vacuum break by hand or with vacuum source. Vacuum source is best; engine is excellent one. Adjust by bending vacuum break link on divorced-choke carburetors.

(30) Dechoke spec is measured between choke plate and housing with throttle wide-open. Adjust by bending end of choke rod as indicated by screwdriver.

(31) Emission-type vent valve connects to charcoal canister. Clearance should be 0.015 in. as shown with throttle at normal or curb idle. Adjust by bending lever.

(32) Old-style external vent clearance is usually around 3/32-in. Adjust by bending lever.

(34) Normal or curb idle is set as shown. Set it to correct engine rpm later.

(33) Pump lever should have at least 0.015—0.020-in. additional travel beyond screw when throttle is wide-open. Screw and lever should also be in contact at idle. Adjust screw to accomplish both. With a green cam, added pump-lever travel should be 0.010 in. Pump cam is shown in position (2) at arrow. To reduce capacity and change delivery, remove screw, move cam and insert in hole (1) and screw into alternate hole in cam.

(35) Secondary idle-speed adjustment. About 1/2 to 1 turn away from having plates seated in bore is good initial setting.

(36) Fast-idle adjustment is made with fast-idle screw on highest step of fast-idle cam. Clearance between primary throttle plate and throttle bore should be 0.025 in., measured as shown.

(37) Dashpot setting refers to additional travel of dashpot when throttle is at curb idle. Consult Holley Illustrated Parts & Specs or Renew Kit instruction sheet for exact setting. 0.090—0.120 in. is common. Adjust by loosening locknut and turning dashpot assembly.

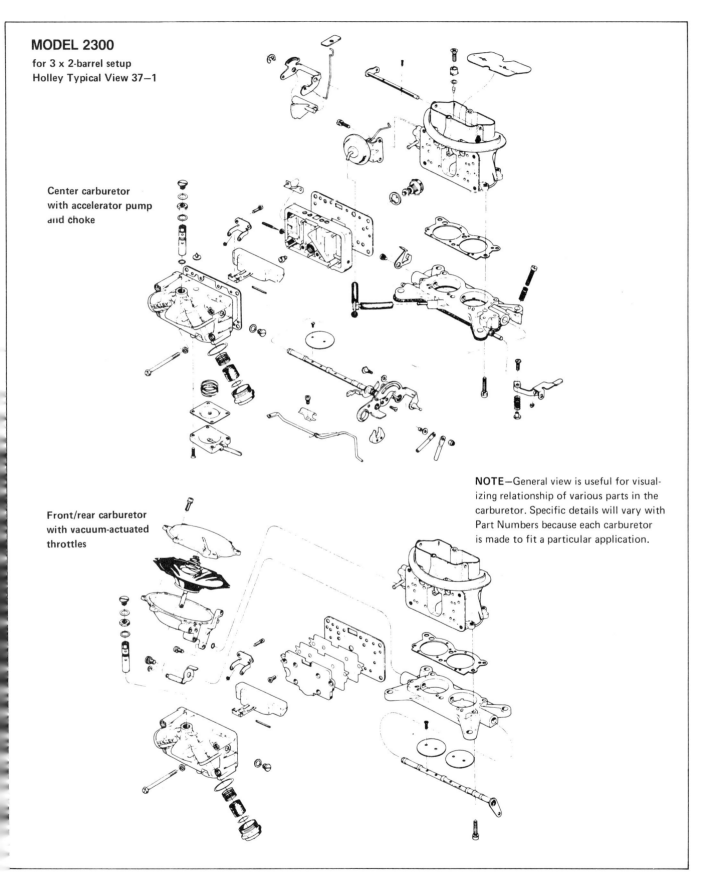

MODEL 2300

for 3 x 2-barrel setup
Holley Typical View 37—1

Center carburetor
with accelerator pump
and choke

Front/rear carburetor
with vacuum-actuated
throttles

NOTE—General view is useful for visualizing relationship of various parts in the
carburetor. Specific details will vary with
Part Numbers because each carburetor
is made to fit a particular application.

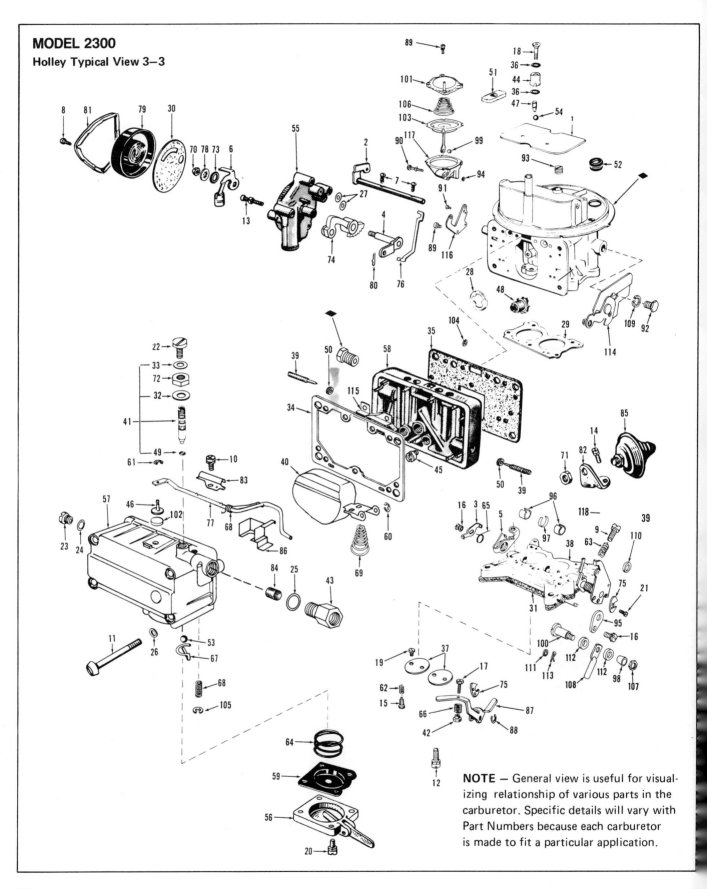

MODEL 2300

Holley Typical View 3–3

NOTE — General view is useful for visualizing relationship of various parts in the carburetor. Specific details will vary with Part Numbers because each carburetor is made to fit a particular application.

1	Choke plate	58	Main metering body & plugs assy.
2	Choke shaft assembly	59	Pump diaphragm assembly
3	Fast idle pick-up lever	60	Float spring retainer
4	Choke hsg. shaft & lev. assy.	61	Air vent retainer
5	Fast idle cam lever	62	Fast idle cam lev. scr. spring
6	Choke therm. lev., link & piston	63	Throttle stop screw spring
7	Choke plate screw	64	Pump diaphragm return spring
8	Therm. hsg. clamp screw	65	Fast idle cam lev. spring
9	Throttle stop screw	66	Pump oper. lev. adj. spring
10	Air vent rod clamp scr. & LW	67	Pump inlet check ball retainer
11	Fuel bowl to main body screw	68	Air vent rod spring
12	Throt. body scr. & LW	69	Float spring
13	Choke hsg. scr. & LW	70	Choke thermostat shaft nut
14	Dashpot brkt scr. & LW	71	Dashpot screw nut
15	Fast idle cam lever screw	72	Fuel valve seat adj. nut
16	Fast idle cam lev. & throt. lev. screw & LW	73	Choke therm. lever spacer
		74	Fast idle cam assembly
17	Pump oper. lev. adj. screw	75	Pump cam
18	Pump discharge nozzle screw	76	Choke rod
19	Throttle plate screw	77	Air vent rod
20	Fuel pump cov. assy. scr. & LW	78	Choke therm. shaft nut LW
21	Pump cam lock scr. & LW	79	Thermostat housing assembly
22	Fuel valve seat lock screw	80	Choke rod retainer
23	Fuel level check plug	81	Thermostat housing clamp
24	Fuel level check plug gasket	82	Dashpot bracket
25	Fuel inlet fitting gasket	83	Air vent rod clamp
26	Fuel bowl screw gasket	84	Filter screen assembly
27	Choke housing gasket	85	Dashpot assembly
28	Power valve body gasket	86	Baffle plate
29	Throttle body gasket	87	Pump operating lever
30	Choke therm. housing gasket	88	Pump operating lev. retainer
31	Flange gasket	89	Adapter mounting & diaphragm cover assy. screw
32	Fuel valve seat adj. nut gskt.		
33	Fuel valve seat lock scr. gaskt.	90	Throt. diaphragm hsg. scr.
34	Fuel bowl gasket	91	Adapter passage screw
35	Metering body gasket	92	Choke bracket screw
36	Pump discharge nozzle gasket	93	Air adapter hole plug
37	Throttle plate	94	Throt. diaphragm hsg. gasket
38	Throt. body & shaft assy.	95	Throttle lever
39	Idle adjusting needle	96	Throttle shaft bearing
40	Float & hinge assy.	97	Throttle shaft brg. (center)
41	Fuel inlet valve & seat assy.	98	Throttle connector pin bushing
42	Pump oper. lev. adj. scr. fitting	99	Diaphragm check ball
43	Fuel inlet fitting	100	Throttle connector pin
44	Pump discharge nozzle	101	Diaphragm housing cover
45	Main jet	102	Air vent cap
46	Air vent valve	103	Diaphragm housing assembly
47	Pump discharge needle valve or check ball weight	104	Diaphragm link retainer
		105	Air vent rod spg. retainer
48	Power valve assembly	106	Diaphragm spring
49	Fuel valve seat "O" ring seal or gasket	107	Throttle link connector pin nut
		108	Throttle connector bar
50	Idle needle seal	109	Choke brkt. scr. lock washer
51	Choke rod seal	110	Throt. link connector pin washer
52	Choke cold air tube grommet	111	Throt. connector pin washer
53	Pump inlet check ball	112	Throttle connector pin spacer
54	Pump discharge check ball	113	Throt. connector pin retainer
55	Choke hsg. & plugs assy.	114	Choke control lever bracket
56	Fuel pump cover assy.	115	Metering body vent baffle
57	Fuel bowl & plugs assy.	116	Throt. diaphragm adapter
		117	Diaphragm housing
		118	Idle adj. needle spring

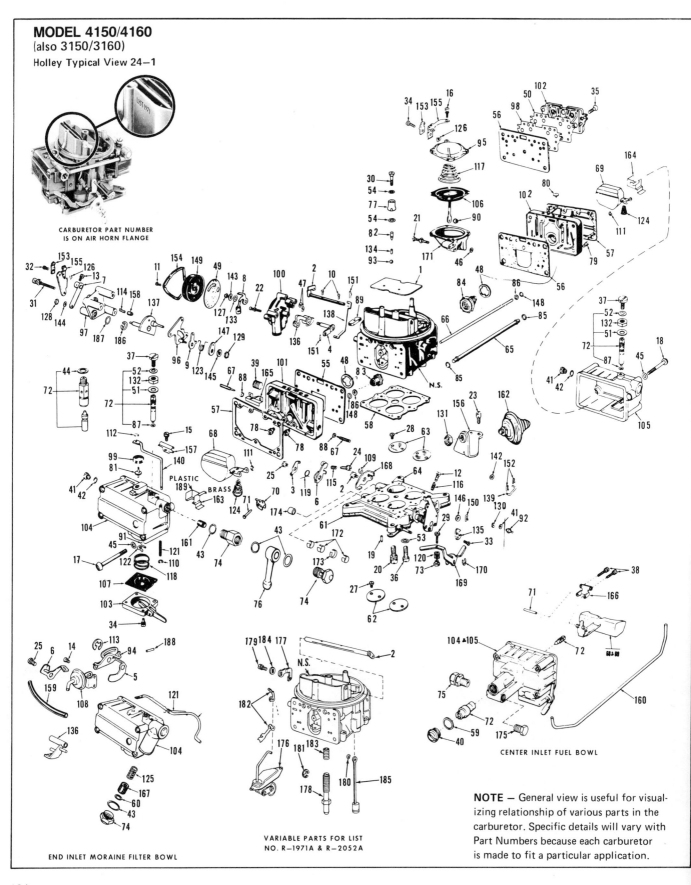

MODEL 4150/4160
(also 3150/3160)
Holley Typical View 24—1

CARBURETOR PART NUMBER
IS ON AIR HORN FLANGE

PLASTIC
BRASS

N.S.

END INLET MORAINE FILTER BOWL

VARIABLE PARTS FOR LIST
NO. R–1971A & R–2052A

N.S.

CENTER INLET FUEL BOWL

NOTE — General view is useful for visualizing relationship of various parts in the carburetor. Specific details will vary with Part Numbers because each carburetor is made to fit a particular application.

1 Choke plate	61 Flange gasket	128 Choke control lever nut
2 Choke shaft assembly	62 Throttle plate — primary	129 Back-up plate stud nut
3 Fast idle pick-up lever	63 Throttle plate — secondary	130 Throttle lever ball nut
4 Choke housing shaft & lever assy.	64 Throt. body & shaft assembly	131 Dashpot nut
5 Choke control lever	65 Fuel line tube	132 Fuel valve seat adj. nut
6 Fast idle cam lever	66 Balance tube	133 Choke thermostat lever spacer
7 Choke lever & swivel assy.	67 Idle adjusting needle	134 Pump check ball weight
8 Choke therm. lev., link & piston assembly	68 Float & hinge assy. — primary	135 Pump cam
9 Choke rod lev. & bush. assy.	69 Float & hinge assy. — secondary	136 Fast idle cam assembly
10 Choke plate screw	71 Float lever shaft	137 Fast idle cam & shaft assembly
11 Therm. housing clamp screw	72 Fuel inlet valve & seat assy.	138 Choke rod
12 Throttle stop screw	73 Pump lever adjusting screw fitting	139 Throttle connecting rod
13 Choke lever assembly swivel screw	74 Fuel inlet fitting	140 Air vent push rod
14 Choke diaph. assy., brkt. scr. & lock washer	75 Fuel transfer tube fitting assy.	141 Throttle lev. ball nut washer
15 Air vent clamp screw & LW	76 Fuel inlet tube & fitting assy.	143 Choke shaft nut lock washer
16 Sec. diaph. assy. cov. scr. & LW	77 Pump discharge nozzle	144 Choke control lev. nut lock washer
17 Fuel bowl to main body screw — primary	78 Main jet — primary	145 Back-up plate stud nut lock washer
18 Fuel bowl to main body screw — secondary	81 Air vent valve	146 Throt. connector pin washer
19 Diaph. lever adjusting screw	82 Pump discharge needle valve	147 Choke spring washer
20 Throt. body screw & lock washer	83 Power valve assy. — primary	148 Balance tube washer
21 Diaph. hsg. assy. scr. & LW	85 Fuel line tube "O" ring seal	149 Therm. hsg. assy. — complete
22 Choke housing screw & LW	86 Balance tube "O" ring seal	150 Throt. connector pin retainer
23 Dashpot brkt. screw & LW	87 Fuel valve seat "O" ring seal	151 Choke rod retainer
24 Fast idle cam lever adj. screw	88 Idle needle seal	152 Throt. connecting rod cotter pin
25 Fast idle cam lev. scr. & LW	89 Choke rod seal	153 Choke cont. wire brkt. clamp
26 Diaph. lev. assy. scr. & LW	90 Diaphragm housing check ball — sec.	154 Thermostat housing clamp
27 Throt. plate screw — primary	91 Pump inlet check ball	155 Choke control wire bracket
28 Throt. plate screw — secondary	92 Throttle lever ball	156 Dashpot bracket
29 Pump lever adjusting screw	93 Pump discharge check ball	157 Air vent rod clamp
30 Pump discharge nozzle screw	94 Choke diaphragm assembly link	158 Fast idle cam plunger
31 Fast idle cam plate scr. & LW	95 Sec. diaphragm housing cover	159 Choke vacuum tube
32 Choke cont. wire brkt. clamp scr.	96 Back-up plate & stud assembly	160 Fuel transfer tube
33 Pump cam lock screw	97 Fast idle cam plate	161 Filter screen
34 Fuel pump cov. assy. scr. & LW	98 Secondary metering body plate	162 Dashpot assembly
35 Secondary metering body screw	99 Air vent cap	163 Baffle plate — primary (brass)
36 Throt. body screw — special	100 Choke hsg. & plugs assembly	164 Baffle plate — secondary
37 Fuel valve seat lock screw	101 Main metering body & plugs assy. — primary	165 Metering body vent baffle
38 Float shaft brkt. scr. & LW	102 Main metering body & plugs assy — secondary	166 Float shaft retainer bracket
39 Spark hole plug	103 Fuel pump cover assembly	167 Fuel inlet filter
40 Fuel bowl plug	104 Fuel bowl & plugs assy. — primary	168 Diaphragm lever assembly
41 Fuel level check plug	105 Fuel bowl & plugs assy. — secondary	169 Pump operating lever
42 Fuel level check plug gasket	106 Secondary diaph. & rod assy.	170 Pump operating lever retainer
43 Fuel inlet fitting gasket	107 Pump diaphragm assembly	171 Secondary diaphragm housing
44 Fuel valve seat gasket	108 Choke diaphragm assembly — complete	172 Throt. shaft bearing — sec (ribbon)
45 Fuel bowl screw gasket	109 Secondary diaph. link retainer	173 Throt. shaft bearing — sec. (ribbon)
46 Sec. diaphragm housing gasket	110 Air vent rod spring retainer	174 Throt. shaft bearing — pri. (solid)
47 Choke housing gasket	111 Float retainer	175 Fuel bowl drain plug
48 Power valve body gasket	112 Air vent valve retainer	176 Choke assy. — complete (divorced)
49 Choke thermostat housing gasket	113 Choke control lever retainer	177 Choke shaft lever
50 Sec. metering body plate gasket	114 Fast idle cam plunger spring	178 Idle by-pass adj. screw
51 Fuel valve seat adj. nut gasket	115 Fast idle cam lever screw spring	179 Choke lever screw & LW
52 Fuel valve seat lock screw gasket	116 Throttle stop screw spring	180 Choke piston link retainer
53 Throt. body screw gasket	117 Secondary diaphragm spring	181 Fast idle cam retainer
54 Pump discharge nozzle gasket	118 Diaphragm return spring	182 Choke rod clevis clip
55 Metering body gasket — primary	119 Fast idle cam lever spring	183 Idle by-pass adj. screw spring
56 Metering body gasket — secondary	120 Pump lev. adj. screw spring	184 Choke piston lever spacer
57 Fuel bowl gasket	121 Air vent rod spring	185 Choke piston & link assembly
58 Throttle body gasket	122 Pump inlet check ball ret. spring	186 Choke oper. lev. spring washer
59 Fuel bowl plug gasket	123 Choke spring	187 Choke oper. lever washer
60 Fuel inlet filter gasket	124 Float spring — pri. & sec.	188 Choke clevis pin
	125 Fuel inlet filter spring	189 Baffle plate — primary (plastic)
	126 Choke cont. wire brkt. clamp scr. nut	
	127 Choke thermostat shaft nut	

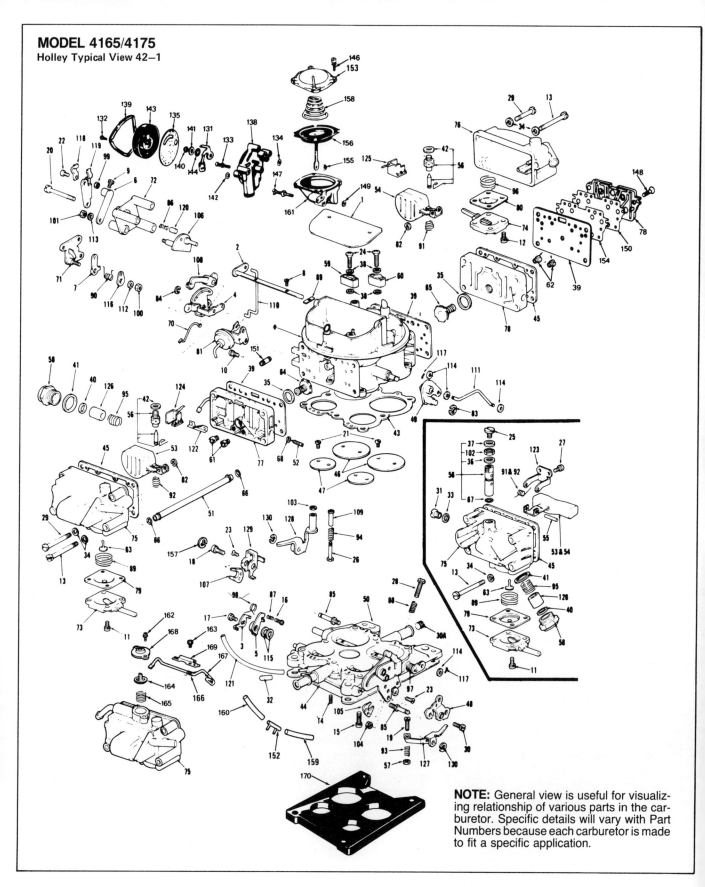

NOTE: General view is useful for visualizing relationship of various parts in the carburetor. Specific details will vary with Part Numbers because each carburetor is made to fit a specific application.

1	Choke plate	57	Pump lever adj. screw fitting	114	Secondary connecting rod washer
2	Choke shaft assembly	58	Fuel inlet fitting	115	Throttle seal washer
3	Fast idle pick-up lever	59	Pump discharge nozzle - primary	116	Choke spring washer
4	Choke control lever	60	Pump discharge nozzle - secondary	117	Secondary connecting rod cotter pin
5	Fast idle cam lever	61	Main jet — primary	118	Choke wire bracket clamp
6	Choke lever & swivel assembly	62	Main jet — secondary	119	Choke wire bracket
7	Choke rod lever & bushing assembly	63	Pump check valve	120	Fast idle cam plunger
8	Choke plate screw	64	Power valve assy - primary	121	Choke vacuum hose
9	Choke lever swivel screw	65	Power valve assy — secondary	122	Metering body vent baffle — pri. & sec.
10	Choke diaphragm bracket screw & LW	66	Fuel line tube "O" ring seal	123	Float shaft retaining bracket
11	Fuel pump cover screw & LW — primary	67	Fuel valve seat "O" ring seal	124	Baffle plate — primary
12	Fuel pump cover screw & LW — secondary	68	Idle needle seal	125	Baffle plate — secondary
13	Fuel bowl screw (long) pri. & sec.	69	Choke rod seal	126	Fuel inlet filter
14	Pump lever adjusting screw — secondary	70	Choke diaphragm link	127	Pump operating lever — primary
15	Throttle body screw & LW	71	Back-up plate & stud assy.	128	Pump operating lever & guide assy. — sec.
16	Fast idle cam lever adj. screw	72	Fast idle cam plate	129	Pump cam lever — secondary
17	Fast idle cam lever screw & LW	73	Fuel pump cover assy. - primary	130	Pump operating lever retainer — pri. & sec.
18	Pump cam lever screw & LW	74	Fuel pump cover assy — secondary	131	Choke therm. lever
19	Pump lever adj. screw — primary	75	Fuel bowl & plugs assy — primary	132	Choke therm. cover screw
20	Fast idle cam plate screw & LW	76	Fuel bowl & plugs assy — secondary	133	Choke housing screw
21	Throttle plate screw — pri. & sec.	77	Metering body & plugs assy — primary	134	Choke housing gasket
22	Choke wire bracket clamp screw	78	Metering body & plugs assy — secondary	135	Choke therm. cover gasket
23	Pump cam screw	79	Pump diaphragm assy. — primary	136	Tube & "O" ring seal
24	Pump discharge nozzle screw	80	Pump diaphragm assy. — secondary	137	Idle adj. needle limiter cap
25	Fuel valve seat lock screw	81	Choke diaphragm assy.	138	Choke housing & plugs assy.
26	Pump operating lever adj. screw	82	Float hinge retainer	139	Choke therm. cover retainer
27	Float shaft bracket screw & LW	83	Cam follower lever assy. retainer	140	Choke therm. shaft nut
28	Throttle stop screw	84	Choke control lever retainer	141	Choke shaft nut lock washer
29	Fuel bowl screw (short) pri. & sec.	85	Pump lever stud	142	Choke housing screw & L.W.
30	Throttle lever extension screw	86	Fast idle cam plunger spring	143	Choke therm. cover assy.
30A	Throttle body channel plug	87	Fast idle cam lever screw spring	144	Choke shaft spacer
31	Fuel level check plug	88	Throttle stop screw spring	145	Cam follower stud
32	Vacuum tube plug	89	Diaphragm return spring — primary	146	Secondary diaphragm cover screws
33	Fuel level check plug gasket	90	Choke spring	147	Secondary diaphragm housing screws
34	Fuel bowl screw gasket	91	Float spring — secondary	148	Secondary metering body screws
35	Power valve gasket	92	Float spring — primary	149	Secondary diaphragm housing gasket
36	Fuel valve seat adj. nut gasket	93	Pump lever adj. screw spring — primary	150	Secondary metering body plate gasket
37	Fuel valve seat lock screw gasket	94	Pump lever adj. screw spring — secondary	151	Tube & "O" ring assy.
38	Pump discharge nozzle gasket	95	Fuel inlet filter spring	152	Four-way connector
39	Metering body gasket — pri. & sec.	96	Diaphragm return spring — secondary	153	Diaphragm cover machine
40	Fuel inlet filter gasket	97	Throttle return spring — secondary	154	Secondary metering body plate
41	Fuel inlet fitting gasket	98	Fast idle cam lever spring	155	Secondary check valve
42	Fuel valve gasket — pri. & sec.	99	Choke wire bracket clamp screw nut	156	Secondary diaphragm
43	Throttle body gasket	100	Back-up plate stud nut	157	Secondary diaphragm link retainer
44	Flange gasket	101	Choke lever nut	158	Secondary diaphragm spring
45	Fuel bowl gasket - pri & sec.	102	Fuel valve seat adj. nut	159	Choke vacuum hose
46	Throttle plate — secondary	103	Pump operating lever adj. nut	160	Choke vacuum hose
47	Throttle plate — primary	104	Throttle lever ext. screw nut	161	Secondary housing & seat assy.
48	Throttle lever extension	105	Pump cam — primary	162	Vent valve screws
49	Cam follower lever assy.	106	Fast idle cam & shaft assy.	163	Air vent rod clamp screw & L.W.
50	Throttle body & shaft assy.	107	Pump cam — secondary	164	Vent valve body assy.
51	Fuel line tubing	108	Fast idle cam assy.	165	Vent valve spring
52	Idle adjusting needle	109	Pump operating lever screw sleeve	166	Vent rod spring
53	Float & hinge assy. — primary	110	Choke rod	167	Vent valve rod
54	Float & hinge assy. — secondary	111	Secondary connecting rod	168	Vent valve clamp assy.
55	Float shaft	112	Back-up plate stud nut LW	169	Air vent rod clamp
56	Fuel inlet valve & seat assy.	113	Choke control lever nut LW	170	Throttle body spacer

MODEL 4180C .

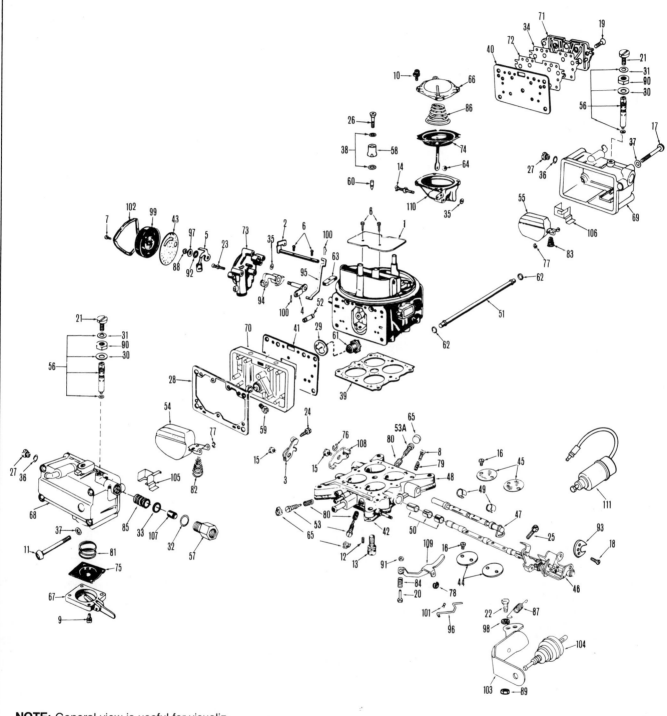

NOTE: General view is useful for visualizing relationship of various parts in the carburetor. Specific details will vary with Part Numbers because each carburetor is made to fit a specific application.

1 Choke plate
2 Choke shaft & lever assy.
3 Fast idle cam lever
4 Choke housing shaft & lever assy.
5 Choke thermostat lever & piston assy.
6 Choke plate screw
7 Choke thermostat clamp screw
8 Throttle stop screw
9 Pump cover screw and 1.w.
10 Secondary diaphragm cover screw & 1.w.
11 Fuel bowl screw (primary)
12 Secondary idle adjust screw
13 Throttle body screw & 1.w.
14 Secondary diaphragm housing screw & 1.w.
15 Fast idle cam lever & secondary diaphragm
   lever screw
16 Throttle plate screw
17 Fuel bowl screw (secondary)
18 Pump cam lock screw
19 Secondary metering body screw
20 Pump lever adjusting screw
21 Needle & seat lock screw
22 Modulator bracket screw
23 Choke housing screw & 1.w.
24 Fast idle adjusting screw
25 Transmission kickdown adjusting screw
26 Pump discharge nozzle screw
27 Fuel level check plug
28 Fuel bowl gasket
29 Power valve gasket
30 Needle & seat adjust nut gasket
31 Needle & seat lock screw gasket
32 Fuel inlet fitting gasket
33 Fuel inlet filter gasket
34 Secondary metering plate gasket
35 Secondary diaphragm & choke housing gasket
36 Fuel level check plug gasket
37 Fuel bowl screw gasket
38 Pump discharge nozzle gasket
39 Throttle body gasket
40 Secondary metering body gasket
41 Primary metering body gasket
42 Flange gasket
43 Choke thermostat gasket
44 Primary throttle plate
45 Secondary throttle plate
46 Primary throttle shaft assy.
47 Secondary throttle shaft assy.
48 Throttle body & shaft assy.
49 Throttle shaft bushing
50 Throttle shaft bushing
51 Fuel transfer tube
52 Pump transfer tube assy.
53 Idle adjusting screw
54 Primary float & hinge assy.
55 Secondary float & hinge assy.

56 Fuel inlet needle & seat assy.
57 Fuel inlet fitting
58 Pump discharge nozzle
59 Primary main metering jet
60 Pump discharge nozzle check needle
61 Primary power valve assy.
62 Fuel transfer tube 0-ring seal
63 Choke rod seal
64 Secondary diaphragm check ball
65 Idle limiter cap
66 Secondary diaphragm housing cover
67 Pump cover assy.
68 Primary fuel bowl & plugs assy.
69 Secondary fuel bowl & plugs assy.
70 Primary metering body & plugs assy.
71 Secondary metering body
72 Secondary metering body plate
73 Choke housing & plugs assy.
74 Secondary diaphragm & link assy.
75 Pump diaphragm assy.
76 Secondary diaphragm link retainer
77 Float & hinge assy retainer
78 Pump lever retainer
79 Throttle stop screw spring
80 Idle adjusting needle spring
81 Pump diaphragm return spring
82 Primary float spring
83 Secondary float spring
84 Pump lever adjusting screw spring
85 Fuel inlet filter spring
86 Secondary diaphragm spring
87 Transmission kickdown lever spring
88 Choke shaft nut
89 Throttle modulator lock nut
90 Needle & seat adjusting nut
91 Pump lever adjusting screw nut
92 Choke thermostat lever spacer
93 Pump cam
94 Fast idle cam assy.
95 Choke rod
96 Throttle connecting rod
97 Choke housing shaft lock washer
98 Bracket screw lockwasher
99 Choke thermostat & cap assy.
100 Choke rod retainer
101 Throttle connecting rod retainer
102 Choke thermostat clamp
103 Throttle modulator bracket
104 Throttle modulator assy.
105 Primary fuel inlet baffle
106 Secondary fuel inlet baffle
107 Fuel inlet filter
108 Secondary diaphragm lever assy.
109 Pump operating lever
110 Secondary diaphragm housing
111 Idle solenoid assy.

(1) Place carburetor on stand or 5/16-in. bolts and nuts to prevent throttle-plate damage.

(2) Remove hairpin clips from bottom of choke link and top of accelerator-pump operating link (arrows). Watch the rascals, they get away and are hard to find. Note accelerator-pump-link position; put it back in same hole. Note how lower end of accelerator-pump link fits into throttle-lever slot.

(3) On divorced-choke 4360 remove two screws (1 & 2) holding choke vacuum-break assembly onto main body. Disconnect vacuum-break link from choke-operating lever and vacuum hose from tube in throttle body. Don't immerse vacuum break in strong cleaner. Check for leaks. Push stem in, then hold finger over tube in back. If stem moves replace vacuum-break assembly. Next, remove clip (3), holding choke-operating lever and fast-idle cam onto their common shaft. Be careful, clip is easy to lose.

(4) On divorced-choke 4360 it isn't necessary to remove choke lever and cam. If you do, disconnect small assist spring by lifting tang out of hole in shaft (arrow). Note spring position. Choke lever and link are separated by rotating lever as you remove it. Now remove accelerator-pump-link from its lever. Note relationship between choke lever and fast-idle cam. Torsion spring adds extra closing force for cold starts. Note its relationship to lever and shaft.

(5) On integral-choke 4360, remove hairpin from choke link behind bimetal housing. Don't disassemble automatic-choke mechanism unless there is a problem or if immersing entire carburetor in strong cleaner. Don't put choke or vacuum break in strong cleaner.

(6) If removing choke link, rotate it when pulling it through hole in air horn. On most rebuilds this link can remain attached to choke lever in air horn.

(7) Note position of choke-link plastic guide. Choke won't work correctly if you reverse guide on reassembly.

(8) Remove 10 screws holding air horn to main body: four long ones across center of air horn, six shorter ones around edge. Remove air horn. It may require prying with screwdriver as shown, and/or light rap will help loosen gasket.

(9) Lift air horn straight up to prevent damaging power-valve-piston stem. On reassembly, be extremely careful not to bend power-valve stem. Get pump piston started correctly in its bore. Be sure power-valve stem inserts between float legs.

(9a) Top view of air horn with vent cover swung aside. Accelerator-pump lever remains installed.

(10) Remove accelerator-pump lever by taking out screw-fulcrum. Unhook lever from pump link, freeing all pump components. Replace pump cup on reassembly. Remove rubber boot from air horn; replace it on reassembly. Be sure to replace spring perch (item 67 in exploded view) on reassembly. On assembly, check for 7/16-in. accelerator-pump travel. Adjust by bending accelerator-pump link.

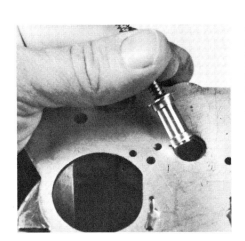

(11) If power-valve-piston doesn't move up and down freely, first squirt carburetor cleaner around stem and try to move piston up and down. If this fails, remove piston assembly. Because this requires removing staked material from around retainer and restaking upon reassembly, don't do it if you don't have to. A screwdriver and a few raps with hammer can accomplish restaking.

(12) Check choke plate and shaft for binding or damage. If either exist, remove choke assembly. Don't do so unless absolutely necessary because staking must be removed from attachment screws. Screws must be restaked during reassembly; support choke shaft to prevent bending. Here is disassembled air horn showing vent baffle, power valve and accelerator pump removed. It's ready for cleaning.

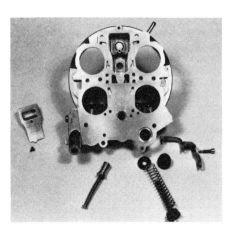

(13) Before separating main and throttle bodies, remove fuel-inlet plug and fitting with 7/8- and 1-in. socket wrenches, respectively. Remove filter, spring and gasket from inlet cavity. Sintered-metal filter can be cleaned and reused. Remove fuel-inlet valve with wide-blade screwdriver. Remove float by lifting combination hinge and retainer. Turn remaining portion upside down, being careful not to damage primary booster venturis. Remove six screws holding main and throttle bodies together; separate the castings. Photo shows main-body components. Remove main jets, noting numbers on jets so you can put them back in same position. Primary main jets are smaller than those for secondaries. Remove power-valve. Use wide-blade screwdriver, taking care not to bend valve stem. Note: Early 4360 power valves were three pieces: seat, spring and valve.

(14) Main body and integral fuel bowl. Components are power valve (1), primary main jets (2), and secondary main jets (3).

(15) Main jets and power valve. Larger diameter main jets are for secondary side. This carburetor had 187 primary and 550 secondary jets. Power valve (#39 in exploded view) was originally three pieces. It is now one part.

(16) Remove limiter caps from idle-mixture screws with screwdriver or pliers. Turn mixture screws in gently, counting turns to seat. Record for reassembly. Remove mixture screws and springs. It isn't necessary to remove throttle plates unless there is damage or wear. Don't do it unless it's necessary—and it's usually not!

(17, 18 & 19) If putting throttle body in strong cleaner, remove primary throttle lever and shaft assembly because there is a plastic sleeve under return spring. If you remove plates, staking material must be removed from attachment screws. These screws *must be* restaked upon reassembly to prevent them from loosening and causing engine damage. If total disassembly of throttle body is needed, these photos show correct relationship of all levers and springs.

4360 ASSEMBLY TIPS

Carburetor is ready for cleaning. Remember, don't immerse any plastic, rubber or electrical parts into strong cleaners—only metal parts! Clean all surfaces thoroughly and blow out all passages with compressed air.

Before reassembly, inspect all parts to be reused for undue wear or damage. Pay particular attention to choke and throttle shafts and float. In most cases parts in Renew Kit, such as inlet and power valves, pump cup and all gaskets, are *only* ones that need to be replaced.

CAUTION: Float can be installed upside down. Make sure float tang contacts inlet-valve needle when float is raised.

In reassembling carburetor simply reverse disassembly process. Screws attaching air horn and throttle body to main body require about 30 in-lb of torque for good retention. If you don't have a torque wrench, turn them down snugly.

Note two dowels in throttle body which mate with corresponding holes in main-body casting. A dowel in main body mates with hole in the airhorn.

(20) Remember to check float setting before installing air horn. Float can be set dry by holding float tang against inlet valve, being careful not to raise float hinge pin. Dimension at forward edge of float should be 1/8-in. below gasket surface. Adjust by bending float tang.

(21) Idle-speed adjustment screw. Back off screw until throttle plates seat in bores. Then rotate screw 1-1/2 turns clockwise for beginning idle set. Reset idle speed to specs after carburetor is installed.

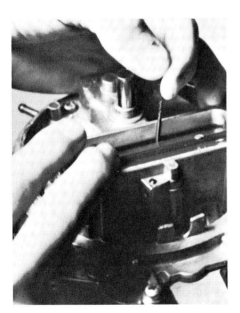

(22 & 23) Choke-qualify set. Apply vacuum source to vacuum break. Apply slight closing force to choke lever while measuring for 9/62-in. clearance at low side of plate. Adjust by bending link (arrow). Even though there is a dechoke provision, adjustment is unnecessary because mechanical secondaries provide more than adequate unloading.

(24) Rough fast-idle adjustment. With fast-idle-adjustment screw (arrow) set on top step of cam, adjust so 0.024-in. drill (No. 72) fits between throttle plate and bore as shown. If you don't have a drill, estimate and reset to specification on vehicle. You'll probably want to do this anyway. If you don't have spec, about 1700 rpm with engine warm and vehicle in NEUTRAL is good baseline.

Manually operate throttle and choke mechanisms, checking for binding or other malfunctions. Any binding or interference could result in uncontrolled engine speed. Once carburetor is on car, check to be sure there are no leaks or flooding that might cause a fire.

MODEL 4360

NOTE: General view is useful for visualizing relationship of various parts in carburetor. Details vary with carb P/Ns because each carburetor is made to fit a specific application. Parts deginated with a diamond are not available for service. Power valve #39 was originally three pieces. It is now one part.

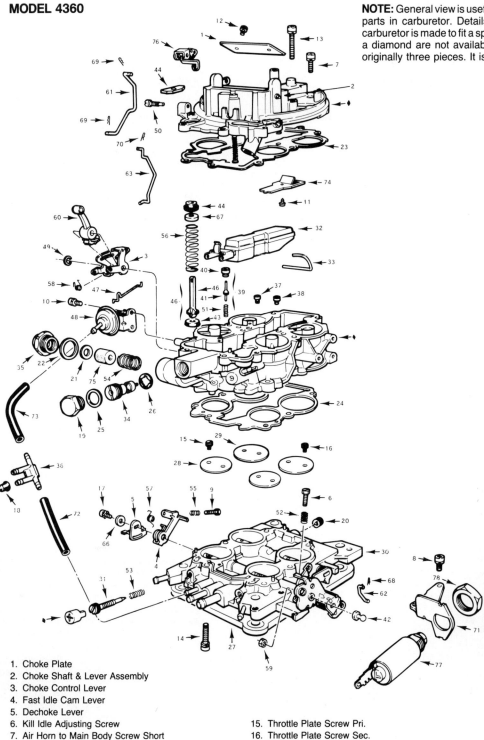

24. Throttle Body Gasket
25. Fuel Inlet Plug Gasket
26. Fuel Valve Seat Gasket
27. Flange Gasket
28. Throttle Plate Pri.
29. Throttle Plate Sec.
30. Throttle Body & Shaft Assy.
31. Idle Adjusting Needle
32. Float & Hinge Assy.
33. Float Hinge Shaft & Retainer
34. Fuel Inlet Valve Assy.
35. Fuel Inlet Fitting
36. TEE Connector
37. Main Jet Primary
38. Main Jet Secondary
39. Power Valve Assy. (now one piece)
40, 41. No longer apply
42. Throttle Lever Ball
43. Pump Cup
44. Choke Rod Seal
45. Pump Stem Seal
46. Accelerating Pump Assy.
47. Choke Diaphragm Link
48. Choke Diaphragm Assy.
49. Choke Control Lever Ret.
50. Pump Lever Stud
51. No longer applies
52. Kill Idle Screw Spring
53. Idle Needle Spring
54. Fuel Inlet Filter Spring
55. Fast Idle Screw Spring
56. Drive Spring
57. Fast Idle Cam Lever Return Spring
58. Choke Control Lever Spring
59. Throttle Lever Ball Nut
60. Fast Idle Cam Assy.
61. Choke Rod
62. Secondary Connecting Rod
63. Accelerating Pump Rod
64. Throttle Lever Ball L.W.
65. Connecting Rod Washer
66. Dechoke Lever Retaining W.
67. Spring Perch Washer
68. Connecting Rod Retainer
69. Choke Rod Retainer
70. Pump Rod Retainer
71. Solenoid Bracket
72. Choke Vacuum Hose
73. Choke Vacuum Hose
74. Fuel Bowl Baffle
75. Fuel Inlet Filter
76. Accelerating Pump Lever
77. Solenoid Idle Stop
78. Solenoid Nut
Parts not shown on illustration
P.C.V. Tube Plug
Throttle Lever Ball
Throttle Lever Ball L.W.
Throttle Lever Ball Nut
Trans Kick-Down Stud
Trans Kick-Down Nut

1. Choke Plate
2. Choke Shaft & Lever Assembly
3. Choke Control Lever
4. Fast Idle Cam Lever
5. Dechoke Lever
6. Kill Idle Adjusting Screw
7. Air Horn to Main Body Screw Short
8. Solenoid Bracket Screw & L.W.
9. Fast Idle Adjusting Screw
10. Choke Diaphragm Bracket Screw
11. Fuel Bowl Baffle Screw
12. Choke Plate Screw
13. Air Horn to Main Body Screw Long
14. Throttle Body to Main Body Screw & L.W.

15. Throttle Plate Screw Pri.
16. Throttle Plate Screw Sec.
17. Dechoke Lever Screw & L.W.
18. TEE Plug
19. Fuel Inlet Plug
20. Power Brake Plug
21. Fuel Inlet Filter Gasket
22. Fuel Inlet Fitting Gasket
23. Main Body Gasket

Model 5200/10/20, 6500/10, 5220/6520 Repair & Adjustment

(1) Model 5210 on left is for GM; 5200 on right is used on Ford. Both carburetors are very similar. Most are used on 4-cylinder engines. Mount carburetor on stand to protect throttle plates. Loosen fuel-inlet fitting while carburetor is still intact. Remove fitting, gasket, filter and spring. New gasket and filter are in Renew Kit. The 5200 has non-replaceable plastic filter.

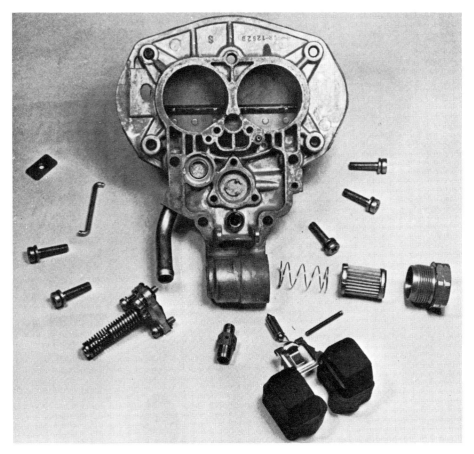

(2) Remove retainers from both ends of choke-operating link and free link from both levers. Remove five screws holding air horn to main body and lift air horn straight up. A slight rap from plastic hammer or the handle of screwdriver may be required to separate the castings. Slide choke-operating link through slot in air horn and turn casting to side, letting little plastic guide slide out. Remove float hinge pin with small drift punch. Lift out float and inlet valve. Remove three screws holding power valve and remove this assembly. Now it will be easier to remove fuel-inlet seat and gasket. Photo shows how far you usually have to go with air horn. If choke plates or shaft are damaged or binding, remove them also. First, file staking from threaded end of screws and remove these screws with great care. Now slide plates from slotted shaft and shaft from air horn. When you reassembly choke plates, hold air horn up to a light to make sure plates are properly seated before tightening attachment screws. Screws will have to be re-staked with a prick punch or small chisel. Support shaft while you do this.

(3) Choke assembly. Before removing it, note relationship between mark on bimetal housing and marks on choke casting. Restore this bimetal setting on reassembly. As you face choke housing, clockwise rotation causes richer setting.

(4) Next, remove hot-water-housing retaining screw, washer, housing and gasket. This may require rap from screwdriver handle. Remove three screws and retainer holding bimetal housing and gasket. Don't remove bimetal from housing. Don't place plastic gasket in harsh cleaner. Remove three screws holding choke casting to main body, then remove choke casting and assembly. Photo shows hot-water stove and bimetal assembly removed from choke casting. Disconnect fast-idle link when you do this.

(5) Choke and vacuum break assembly. Replace O-ring (1) with new one. This passage provides manifold vacuum to vacuum break. Note relationship between fast-idle cam, choke lever and spring. Tang (2) is bent for dechoke adjustment. Fast-idle screw is (3). Remove O-ring from vacuum passage. Remove three screws holding vacuum break cover. This allows you to remove cover, spring and diaphragm and stem assembly. Normally, this is as far as you have to go.

(6) If you choose to go further, note relationship of spring between fast-idle cam and choke lever. Refer to photographs for help. Remove choke shaft nut and lock washer. Choke lever, fast-idle cam, spring, cup, spacer, and Teflon lever and shaft can all be removed. Remove screw retaining fast-idle-cam lever spacer and washer. Photo shows choke lever and fast-idle parts disassembled in correct relation to one another.

(7) Choke vacuum-break assembly. Check diaphragm for holes or cracks.

(8) Go next to main body. Where this applies, remove two screws holding anti-dieseling solenoid bracket to main body. Remove main air-bleed restrictions and well tubes from primary and secondary wells. Sometimes they can be difficult, so use paper clip with hook on end. It slips into tube so you can pull it. Ordinarily you shouldn't put wires into orifices, but this one isn't critical. Remove primary and secondary idle-retainer plugs and jets on each side of carburetor.

(9) If used, jet holder (retainer) contains idle-feed restriction. Idle jets have number stamped on one surface. Remove main metering jets from bowl bottom.

(10) Record the numbers as you remove each jet and note where each one was placed so you can reinstall it correctly. Jets in this carburetor are different in every location. Some carburetors have idle-feed restrictions (1) for primary and secondary. Bleed restrictions (2) are stamped on top. Well tubes (not shown) are stamped on bottom. Main jets (3) are stamped on side.

(11) Remove power-valve seat, valve and spring. Don't bend valve stem. Photo shows main jets (1) and power valve (2) adjacent to their respective tapped holes.

(12) Turn limiter cap (if there is one) as far clockwise as it will go. Remove limiter cap with pliers, taking care not to bend mixture screw (bottom arrow). Turn mixture screw in with fingers until it reaches its seat, counting turns. Use this as rough idle setting on reassembly. Remove mixture screw and spring. Remove four screws holding accelerator-pump housing to main body, allowing removal of housing, diaphragm and spring. Remove pump-nozzle screw, nozzle, gaskets, and check balls. This is as far as you should go with disassembly, especially with the economy method. For complete job, be prepared to spend more time and follow instructions closely. Photo shows accelerator pump and discharge nozzle disassembled. Discharge check and nozzle are installed in hole (top arrow). Some list numbers have two discharge-check balls.

(13) Next, remove locking retainer (arrow) from primary throttle shaft nut by bending away metal tabs.

(14) Remove retaining nut (1), and all mechanism attached to primary throttle shaft can be removed, which includes primary throttle lever (2), secondary operating lever (3), idle lever (4), return spring (5), and several spacers. Photo shows relation of all primary and secondary throttle levers and their return springs. If you remove these, use this for guidance. Unlike Model 5200, 5210 secondary-throttle plates must be removed before secondary throttle lever and spring can be taken off because lever is riveted to shaft. Unless throttle bore area is quite dirty, plates are nicked, or shaft is loose or sticky, don't do it. The staking must be removed from throttle-plate screws with a file and they must be restaked with a punch at reassembly. Before torquing screws, hold carb up to light and make sure plates seat in their bores when both primary and secondary stop screws are backed off.

(15) Note return-spring positions for primary and secondary throttle shafts.

(16) Choke-qualify dimension. With a light closing force on choke plate, push diaphragm stem toward diaphragm as far as it will go. With a third hand measure clearance between lower edge of plate and casting, using drill (arrow). Correct dimension is listed in Renew Kit or Holley Illustrated Parts & Specs Manual.

(17) Choke qualify is adjusted as shown. Turning in screw gives a smaller or richer qualifying dimension. Turning out has the opposite effect. Some Model 5200s have slotted adjustment screw inside removable cap.

5200 CLEANING & ADJUSTING

Now the carburetor is completely disassembled and ready for cleaning. Do the cleaning by either method, but remember: Only metal parts can be immersed into commercial-type carburetor cleaners. Non-metal parts (plastic, rubber and electrical) must be cleaned with a mild solvent such as kerosene. When you've thoroughly cleaned all of components, blow out passages with compressed air. If you don't have an air compressor, a hand tire pump will do nicely. Most metering restrictions are removable and easily cleaned. Never stick wires or drills into these restrictions.

Now go through all of the components not included in the repair kit, and hence must be reused. Look for excessive wear. Pay particular attention to the two throttle shafts and the choke shaft. If the bearings are very loose, replace the complete carburetor. This is very seldom the case. Check the booster venturi for tightness. A loose fit could also require carburetor replacement. For reassembly, work your way back through photos for disassembly.

Several adjustments must be made during assembly. These are dry float setting, bumper-spring adjustment, choke bimetal setting, choke pull-down or qualify, fast-idle-cam phasing, dechoke setting, and rough settings for curb and fast idle. Procedures are demonstrated in the photographs, but consult the Renew Kit or Holley Illustrated Parts & Specs Manual or vehicle shop manual for specific dimensions.

(18) Dry float setting is measured between float lung and casting as shown—without gasket and with air horn inverted. Adjust by bending float tang contacting inlet valve. Be careful not to mar contact surface. Dimension is in Renew Kit or Holley Illustrated Parts & Specs Manual.

(19) Make sure bimetal loop fits over tang upon reassembly. Rotate bimetal housing to make sure choke plate moves.

(20) Fast-idle-cam phasing. With a 5/32-in. drill between choke plate and casting as shown, there should be 0.010—0.030-in. clearance between choke-lever tang (pen points to it) and fast-idle cam with fast-idle screw against second-highest cam step. Bend tang to adjust. Adjustment assures correct choke and fast-idle-cam relationship.

(21) Measure dechoke dimension between choke plate and casting with throttle wide open. Adjustment tang is shown in previous photograph.

(22) Rough normal or curb-idle adjustment (1) is 1-1/2 turns from where plate seats in bore. Set to correct rpm on engine. When an anti-dieseling solenoid is used, idle speed is set with screw (2) with solenoid activated.

(23) With fast-idle adjustment screw against top step of cam, a rough fast-idle adjustment is 0.035-in. clearance between throttle plate and casting as shown. Fast-idle screw is shown in choke casting and assembly photograph.

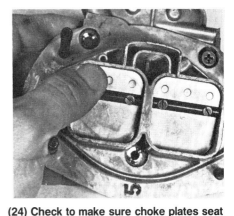

(24) Check to make sure choke plates seat well in housing and open and close without sticking or binding. With air horn off, hold choke plate and housing up to light and check for uniform clearance. Manually operate throttle and choke mechanisms, checking for binding or other malfunctions. Any binding or interference could result in uncontrolled engine speed. Once carburetor is on car, check to be sure there are no leaks or flooding that might cause a fire.

(25) Secondary idle-speed adjustment (1) should be 1/4—1/2 turn from where throttle plate is seated in bore.

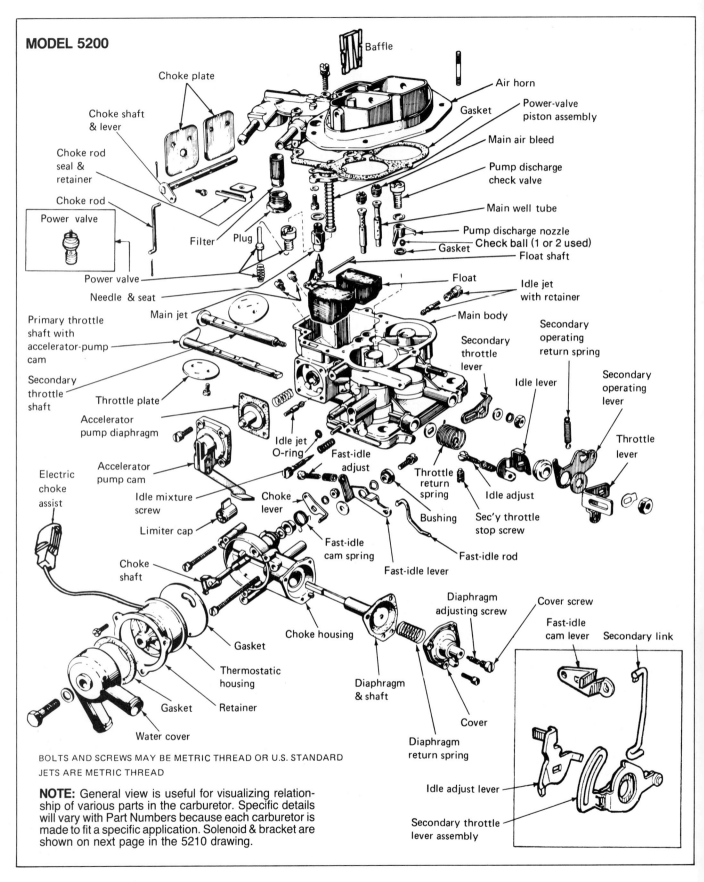

MODEL 5200

Baffle

Choke plate

Choke shaft & lever

Choke rod seal & retainer

Choke rod

Power valve

Filter

Plug

Power valve

Needle & seat

Main jet

Primary throttle shaft with accelerator-pump cam

Secondary throttle shaft

Throttle plate

Accelerator pump diaphragm

Accelerator pump cam

Idle mixture screw

Limiter cap

Electric choke assist

Choke shaft

Gasket

Thermostatic housing

Gasket   Retainer

Water cover

Air horn

Gasket

Power-valve piston assembly

Main air bleed

Pump discharge check valve

Main well tube

Pump discharge nozzle

Check ball (1 or 2 used)

Gasket

Float shaft

Float

Idle jet with retainer

Main body

Secondary throttle lever

Secondary operating return spring

Idle lever

Secondary operating lever

Throttle lever

Idle jet O-ring

Fast-idle adjust

Throttle return spring

Idle adjust

Sec'y throttle stop screw

Bushing

Fast-idle rod

Choke lever

Fast-idle cam spring

Fast-idle lever

Diaphragm adjusting screw

Cover screw

Fast-idle cam lever

Secondary link

Choke housing

Diaphragm & shaft

Cover

Diaphragm return spring

Idle adjust lever

Secondary throttle lever assembly

BOLTS AND SCREWS MAY BE METRIC THREAD OR U.S. STANDARD

JETS ARE METRIC THREAD

NOTE: General view is useful for visualizing relationship of various parts in the carburetor. Specific details will vary with Part Numbers because each carburetor is made to fit a specific application. Solenoid & bracket are shown on next page in the 5210 drawing.

MODEL 5210

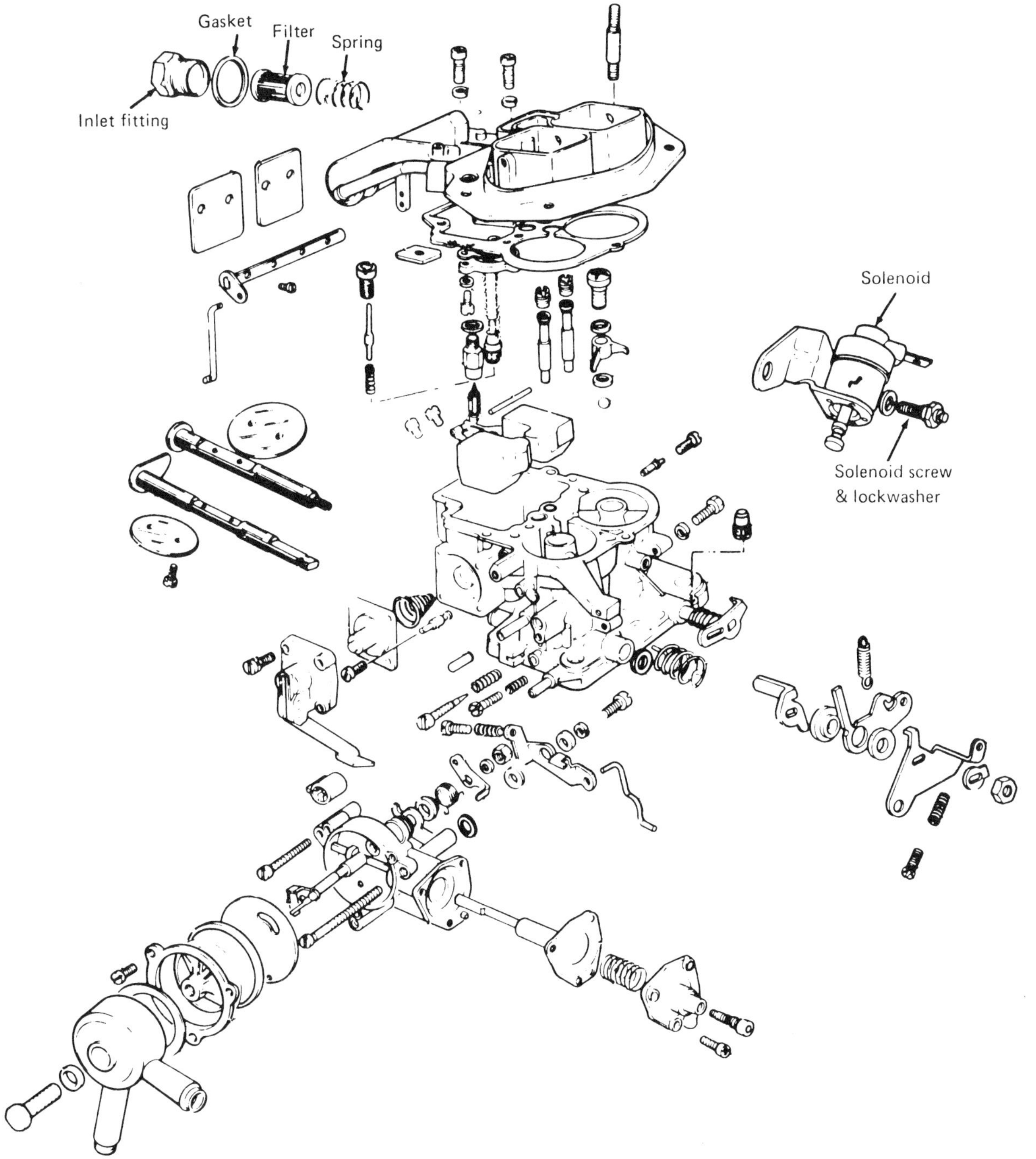

Gasket

Filter

Spring

Inlet fitting

Solenoid

Solenoid screw
& lockwasher

ALL BOLTS AND SCREWS ARE U.S. STANDARD, JETS ARE METRIC THREAD
PARTS NOT LABELED ARE ESSENTIALLY THE SAME AS FOR THE 5200 ON PREVIOUS PAGE.

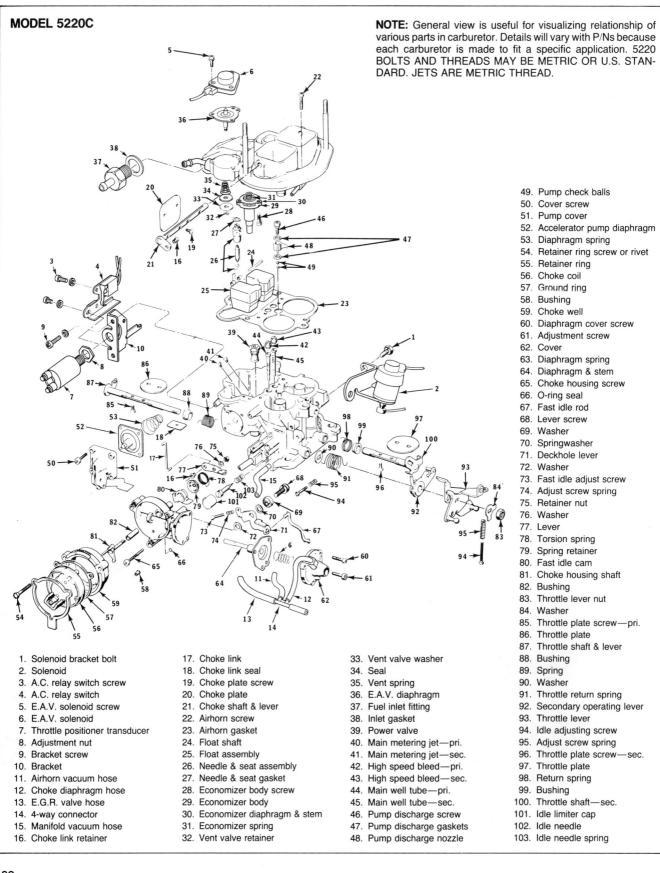

MODEL 5220C

NOTE: General view is useful for visualizing relationship of various parts in carburetor. Details will vary with P/Ns because each carburetor is made to fit a specific application. 5220 BOLTS AND THREADS MAY BE METRIC OR U.S. STANDARD. JETS ARE METRIC THREAD.

49. Pump check balls
50. Cover screw
51. Pump cover
52. Accelerator pump diaphragm
53. Diaphragm spring
54. Retainer ring screw or rivet
55. Retainer ring
56. Choke coil
57. Ground ring
58. Bushing
59. Choke well
60. Diaphragm cover screw
61. Adjustment screw
62. Cover
63. Diaphragm spring
64. Diaphragm & stem
65. Choke housing screw
66. O-ring seal
67. Fast idle rod
68. Lever screw
69. Washer
70. Springwasher
71. Deckhole lever
72. Washer
73. Fast idle adjust screw
74. Adjust screw spring
75. Retainer nut
76. Washer
77. Lever
78. Torsion spring
79. Spring retainer
80. Fast idle cam
81. Choke housing shaft
82. Bushing
83. Throttle lever nut
84. Washer
85. Throttle plate screw—pri.
86. Throttle plate
87. Throttle shaft & lever
88. Bushing
89. Spring
90. Washer
91. Throttle return spring
92. Secondary operating lever
93. Throttle lever
94. Idle adjusting screw
95. Adjust screw spring
96. Throttle plate screw—sec.
97. Throttle plate
98. Return spring
99. Bushing
100. Throttle shaft—sec.
101. Idle limiter cap
102. Idle needle
103. Idle needle spring

1. Solenoid bracket bolt
2. Solenoid
3. A.C. relay switch screw
4. A.C. relay switch
5. E.A.V. solenoid screw
6. E.A.V. solenoid
7. Throttle positioner transducer
8. Adjustment nut
9. Bracket screw
10. Bracket
11. Airhorn vacuum hose
12. Choke diaphragm hose
13. E.G.R. valve hose
14. 4-way connector
15. Manifold vacuum hose
16. Choke link retainer

17. Choke link
18. Choke link seal
19. Choke plate screw
20. Choke plate
21. Choke shaft & lever
22. Airhorn screw
23. Airhorn gasket
24. Float shaft
25. Float assembly
26. Needle & seat assembly
27. Needle & seat gasket
28. Economizer body screw
29. Economizer body
30. Economizer diaphragm & stem
31. Economizer spring
32. Vent valve retainer

33. Vent valve washer
34. Seal
35. Vent spring
36. E.A.V. diaphragm
37. Fuel inlet fitting
38. Inlet gasket
39. Power valve
40. Main metering jet—pri.
41. Main metering jet—sec.
42. High speed bleed—pri.
43. High speed bleed—sec.
44. Main well tube—pri.
45. Main well tube—sec.
46. Pump discharge screw
47. Pump discharge gaskets
48. Pump discharge nozzle

MODEL 6520

NOTE: Model 6520 is closed-loop version of 5220. Parts are similar except for circled assemblies. See 5220C view on previous page for part identification. Exploded view here is useful for visualizing relationship of various parts in carburetor. Details will vary with P/Ns because each carburetor is made to fit a specific application. 6520 BOLTS AND THREADS MAY BE METRIC OR U.S. STANDARD. JETS ARE METRIC THREAD.

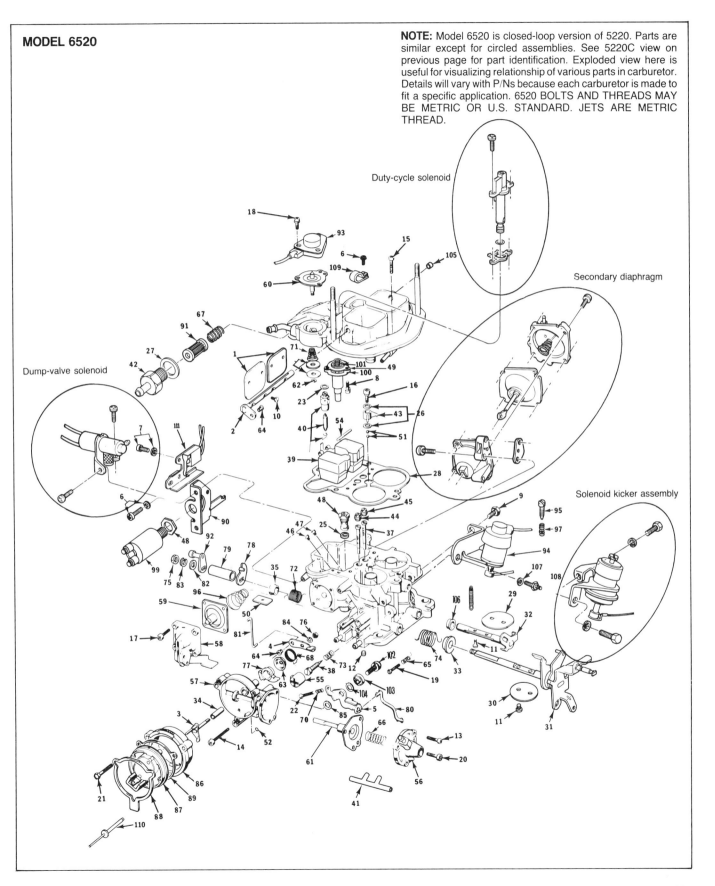

Duty-cycle solenoid

Secondary diaphragm

Dump-valve solenoid

Solenoid kicker assembly

183

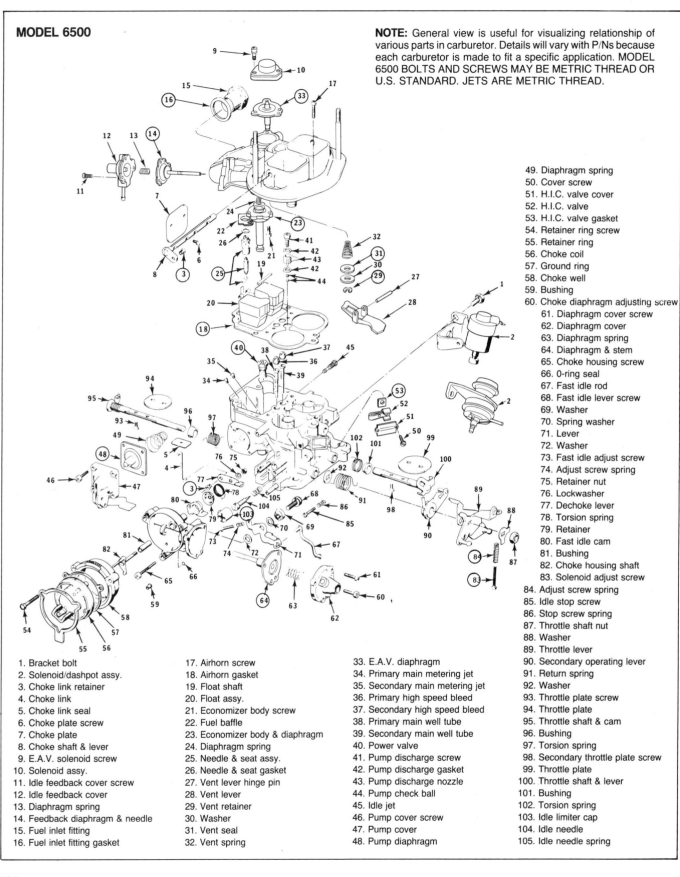

MODEL 6500

NOTE: General view is useful for visualizing relationship of various parts in carburetor. Details will vary with P/Ns because each carburetor is made to fit a specific application. MODEL 6500 BOLTS AND SCREWS MAY BE METRIC THREAD OR U.S. STANDARD. JETS ARE METRIC THREAD.

1. Bracket bolt
2. Solenoid/dashpot assy.
3. Choke link retainer
4. Choke link
5. Choke link seal
6. Choke plate screw
7. Choke plate
8. Choke shaft & lever
9. E.A.V. solenoid screw
10. Solenoid assy.
11. Idle feedback cover screw
12. Idle feedback cover
13. Diaphragm spring
14. Feedback diaphragm & needle
15. Fuel inlet fitting
16. Fuel inlet fitting gasket

17. Airhorn screw
18. Airhorn gasket
19. Float shaft
20. Float assy.
21. Economizer body screw
22. Fuel baffle
23. Economizer body & diaphragm
24. Diaphragm spring
25. Needle & seat assy.
26. Needle & seat gasket
27. Vent lever hinge pin
28. Vent lever
29. Vent retainer
30. Washer
31. Vent seal
32. Vent spring

33. E.A.V. diaphragm
34. Primary main metering jet
35. Secondary main metering jet
36. Primary high speed bleed
37. Secondary high speed bleed
38. Primary main well tube
39. Secondary main well tube
40. Power valve
41. Pump discharge screw
42. Pump discharge gasket
43. Pump discharge nozzle
44. Pump check ball
45. Idle jet
46. Pump cover screw
47. Pump cover
48. Pump diaphragm

49. Diaphragm spring
50. Cover screw
51. H.I.C. valve cover
52. H.I.C. valve
53. H.I.C. valve gasket
54. Retainer ring screw
55. Retainer ring
56. Choke coil
57. Ground ring
58. Choke well
59. Bushing
60. Choke diaphragm adjusting screw
61. Diaphragm cover screw
62. Diaphragm cover
63. Diaphragm spring
64. Diaphragm & stem
65. Choke housing screw
66. 0-ring seal
67. Fast idle rod
68. Fast idle lever screw
69. Washer
70. Spring washer
71. Lever
72. Washer
73. Fast idle adjust screw
74. Adjust screw spring
75. Retainer nut
76. Lockwasher
77. Dechoke lever
78. Torsion spring
79. Retainer
80. Fast idle cam
81. Bushing
82. Choke housing shaft
83. Solenoid adjust screw
84. Adjust screw spring
85. Idle stop screw
86. Stop screw spring
87. Throttle shaft nut
88. Washer
89. Throttle lever
90. Secondary operating lever
91. Return spring
92. Washer
93. Throttle plate screw
94. Throttle plate
95. Throttle shaft & cam
96. Bushing
97. Torsion spring
98. Secondary throttle plate screw
99. Throttle plate
100. Throttle shaft & lever
101. Bushing
102. Torsion spring
103. Idle limiter cap
104. Idle needle
105. Idle needle spring

184

Model 2360/6360 Repair & Adjustment

(1) Use a 1-inch wrench or socket to remove fuel-inlet fitting. Note spring behind pleated-paper filter. Nut immediately above fuel-inlet opening adjusts position of inlet valve and hence float level. Screw locks adjustment.

(2) Take one hairpin clip loose from lower choke link at lever behind bimetal housing. Leave link attached to choke lever on air horn.

(3) Remove cotter key (1) and take accelerator-pump link loose at upper end. Remove clip (2) from choke link in plastic lever on throttle side. For complete rebuild clip (3) can be removed to take off plastic lever. Then you can immerse main body in strong cleaner.

(4) Air horn is retained by 11 screws, including two under choke (arrows). Hold choke open to get these screws. They may be obscured by gasoline deposits or carbon. Screw sizes are: 7/8-in. (4 at back), 1/2-in. (2 inside airhorn) and 5/8-in. (5 at front). Accelerator-pump-linkage cover (1) has three screws. It is unlikely this dust cover needs to be removed.

2360/6360 CLEANING & REASSEMBLY

Carburetor is now ready for cleaning. Remember, don't put any plastic, rubber or electrical parts into strong cleaners—only metal parts! Clean all surfaces thoroughly and blow out all passages with compressed air.

Before reassembly inspect all parts to be reused for undue wear or damage. Pay particular attention to choke, throttle shafts and float. In most cases parts in Renew Kit, such as inlet and power valves, pump cup and all gaskets, are the only ones that will need replacing.

To reassemble carburetor simply reverse disassembly process. Screws attaching air horn and throttle body to main body require about 30 in-lb of torque for good retention. If you don't have a torque wrench, turn them down snugly.

Note the two dowels in throttle body which mate with corresponding holes in the main-body casting. And two dowels in main body mate with holes in air horn.

(5) Remove air horn, rotating it slightly to allow taking choke link out of plastic lever as air horn is removed. Don't lose two flat washers on back side of plastic arm. Float shaft retainer may jump out of its slot and and accelerator pump may fall out as air horn is lifted off. If power-valve piston doesn't move up and down freely, first squirt carburetor cleaner around stem and try to move piston up and down. If this fails, remove piston assembly. Because this requires removing staked material from around retainer and restaking upon reassembly, don't do it if you don't have to. A screwdriver and a few raps with a hammer can accomplish the restaking operation.

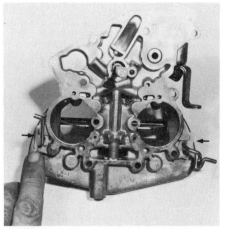 

(6) Note nylon guides on choke links (arrows). Leaving links attached avoids having to reinstall guides during assembly.

(7) Float hinge (shaft) is held by float-shaft retainer (in hand). Fuel-baffle legs straddle inlet valve

(8) There is usually no reason to take off throttle body because it doesn't reveal any passages likely to become plugged or need service. Throttle body is attached with seven screws.

(8a) With float removed, power valve and main jets are visible. Remove jets. Remove inlet valve.

(9) Float setting requires holding float tang against inlet valve so float is in up position. Be careful not to raise float hinge pin. Clearance between gasket surface and float is 0.150 in. (about 5/32-in.). Measure at float end farthest from pivot. Holley instructs doing this with bowl inverted, but with care it can be done right-side up. Adjust by bending float tang.

(10) Inlet valve is externally adjustable like those in Model 2300 and 4150 carburetors. Adjustment requires loosening lock screw. Use nut to turn inlet valve in or out for desired float setting. Retighten lock screw to secure adjustment. See Step (1) for lock screw and nut location.

(11) Install fuel baffle (1) and retainer (2) over float hinge pin. Insert accelerator pump and spring into cavity in main body.

(12) Put choke link into plastic lever, using two flat washers on backside and clip on front. Hold gasket onto underside of air horn with fingers. Position accelerator pump in its hole in air horn. Lower air horn into place, being careful not to dislodge retainer above float hinge. Take care to insert power-valve-operating stem between float legs and down onto top of power-valve pin. When air horn is against main-body casting, loosely insert two rear screws. Slightly lift front of air horn and peek at the float-hinge retainer to make sure it is in place. If it is OK, proceed with installing air horn screws. Install other choke link into lever behind bimetal housing; add hairpin clip.

(13) Dechoke setting. Keeping pressure against upper side of choke plate, open throttle. Choke should be forced open so you can measure 5/32-in. clearance between plate and air horn. Exception: 0-9978 has 1/4-in. dechoke clearance.

(14) Choke qualify. Check after carburetor is installed. idling engine should have at least 15 in.Hg manifold vacuum. Put fast-idle screw on top step of cam. With light closing pressure on choke lever, measure 0.120-in. (approximately 1/8 in.) between top of choke plate and air horn. As shown here, use 5/64-in. hex wrench to turn adjustment on choke housing. Manually operate throttle and choke mechanisms, checking for binding or other malfunctions. Any binding or interference could result in uncontrolled engine speed. Once carburetor is on car, check to be sure there are no leaks or flooding which might cause a fire.

MODEL 2360

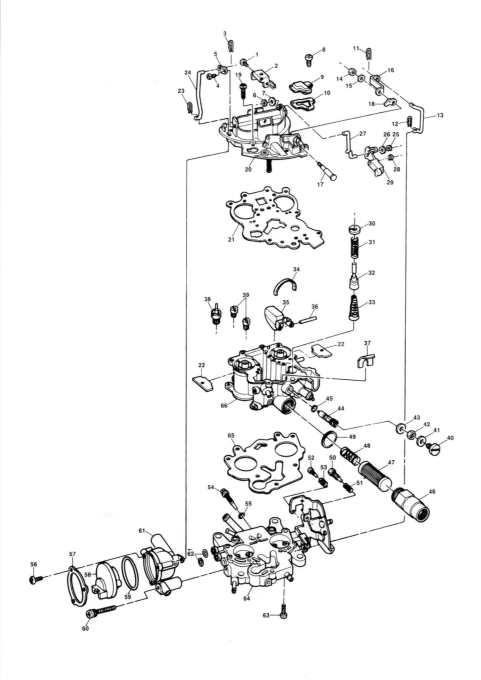

1. Bracket clamp screw
2. Air cleaner bracket
3. Choke rod retainer
4. Choke lever screw & l.w.
5. Choke rod lever
6. Fast idle cam link retainer
7. Washer
8. Pump cover screw
9. Pump lever cover
10. Pump lever cover gasket
11. Pump link retainer
12. Pump link retainer
13. Pump link
14. Hex nut
15. Lockwasher
16. Pump operating lever
17. Pump operating shaft
18. Pump lever
19. Airhorn screw
20. Airhorn assy.
21. Airhorn gasket
22. Choke rod seal
23. Choke rod retainer
24. Choke rod
25. Fast idle cam retainer
26. Washer
27. Fast idle cam link
28. Fast idle cam retainer
29. Fast idle cam
30. Pump spring retainer
31. Pump operating spring
32. Pump head and stem assy.
33. Pump return spring
34. Float shaft retainer
35. Float & hinge assy.
36. Float lever shaft
37. Fuel inlet baffle
38. Power valve assy.
39. Main jets
40. Needle & seat lock screw
41. Seat lock screw gasket
42. Needle & seat adjusting nut
43. Adjusting nut gasket
44. Fuel inlet needle & seat assy.
45. Fuel inlet O-ring
46. Fuel inlet fitting
47. Fuel inlet filter
48. Inlet filter spring
49. Fuel inlet fitting gasket
50. Curb idle adjusting screw
51. Curb idle adjust. screw spring
52. Fast idle adjusting screw
53. Fast idle adjust. screw spring
54. Idle adjust needle
55. O-ring seal
56. Thermostat cap retaining screw
57. Thermostat cap retaining ring
58. Thermostat & cap assy.
59. Thermostat housing gasket
60. Choke housing screw & l.w.
61. Choke housing assy.
62. Choke housing O-ring seals
63. Throttle body screw & l.w.
64. Throttle body assy
65. Throttle body gasket
66. Main body assy.

NOTE: General view is useful for visualizing relationship of various parts in the carburetor. Specific details will vary with Part Numbers because each carburetor is made to fit a specific application.

Model 2280/6280 Repair & Adjustment

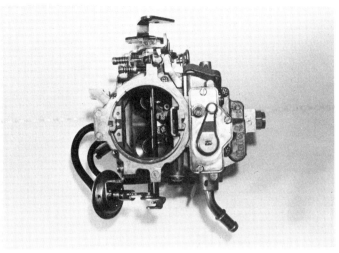

(1) Place carburetor on stand or 5/16-in. bolts and nuts to prevent throttle-plate damage. Disconnect any vacuum hoses. This is Model 2280 with divorced choke and throttle-position transducer. Model 6280 is very similar but uses duty-cylcle solenoid to control supplemental idle-air bleeds and main jets.

(2) Top view showing vent cover and seven air horn screws.

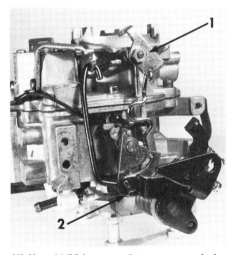

(3) Remove accelerator pump/vent-valve cover. Here is complete vent-actuating linkage. Vent valve levers are in place, showing spring that fits into installed cover.

(3a) Now one vent-valve lever is removed and other moved to one side so mechanically actuated power-valve stem (arrow) would show. 2280s with a mechanical power-valve override must be adjusted if accelerator-pump adjustment is changed. Here 5/64-in. hex wrench is used for adjustment. Throttle must be wide open as screw is turned clockwise to zero clearance (check by pushing down and releasing), then back off *one* full turn.

(4) Use 11/32-in. wrench to remove choke lever (1) from choke shaft. NOTE: Lever tab faces in. If it is installed *backward*, then throttle won't open. Remove fast-idle/choke link from throttle lever. Link is held between main body casting and throttle lever when air horn is installed. Remove cotter key from pump link (2), taking care not to lose flat washer if one is used. Keep track of hole pump link is installed in. Some 2280s have only one hole. Some links hook into pump lever, others have cotter keys at both ends.

(5 & 6) Remove six large screws in air horn/carburetor cover. Take off air horn with care. You may have to insert putty knife between the castings, destroying gasket. On Model 6280, rubber grommet holding duty-cycle solenoid wires must be removed from air horn. Carefully place air horn upside-down on workbench. Don't play with accelerator pump. It easily comes loose from its link in air-horn cavity. Reattaching pump stem, especially where there is a mechanical power valve, isn't easy. When putting link back into accelerator-pump stem, headed part goes in pump lever. If possible, don't take out pump stem; cut off old pump cup and new one will push on easily. NOTE: Some vent valves are electrically operated, simplifying the linkage.

Brass piston (1) on right is for vacuum-operated power valve. If power-valve-piston doesn't move up and down freely, first squirt carburetor cleaner around stem and try to move piston up and down. If this fails, remove piston assembly. Because this requires removing staked material from around retainer and restaking upon reassembly, don't do it if you don't have to. Screwdriver and few raps with hammer can accomplish restaking operation.

Plastic-tipped stem (2) on left mechanically actuates a second power valve as throttle nears wide open. Vent valve (3) is at left.

(8) Remove main jets and power valve/s. On Model 6280, remove feedback solenoid.

(9) Main jets and power valves. Because there's little to distinguish two types of power valve, these were marked (M) and (V), denoting mechanical- and vacuum-actuated. Mechanical power-valve stem is slightly longer (about 0.060-in.). Keep valve seats with their respective stems. Identify by scratching (M) on mechanical valve. Be sure to reinstall power valves in correct holes. Letters M and V may be cast into bottom of bowl. Some 2280s have vacuum-operated power valve only.

(10) Booster assembly is held by two screws. Under booster is accelerator pump check valve consisting of a ball and weight. Be careful not to lose these.

(7) Model 6280 solenoid-actuated valve fits in bowl where vacuum-operated power valve is on 2280s. Vacuum-operated power valve moves to other side of bowl on 6280.

(11) Remove inlet valve, then fuel baffle with float and its hinge pin.

(12) On Model 2280, remove limiter caps from idle-mixture screws with screwdriver or pliers. Turn mixture screws in gently, counting turns to seat. Record for reassembly. Remove mixture screws and springs. Here, Model 6280 mixture screws are sealed in throttle base. Removal is not recommended for cleaning/rebuilding.

2280/6280 CLEANING & ASSEMBLY

Remember, don't immerse any plastic, rubber or electrical parts into strong cleaners—only metal parts! In particular, don't submerge the duty-cycle solenoid in cleaner, a simple wiping will do. Clean all surfaces thoroughly and blow out all passages with compressed air.

Before reassembly inspect all parts to be reused for undue wear or damage. Pay particular attention to choke and throttle shafts and float. In most cases parts in Renew Kit, such as inlet and power valves, the pump cup and all gaskets, are the only ones that will need to be replaced.

Reverse the disassembly process to reassemble the carburetor. Screws attaching air horn and throttle body to main body require about 30 in-lb of torque for good retention. If you don't have a torque wrench, turn them down snugly.

(13) Float setting should measure 0.288-in. (approximately 9/32 in.) measured between gasket face and end of float farthest from pivot. Bowl can be inverted. Hold fuel baffle in place while making this measurement. Or, carefully hold float tang against inlet valve while making measurement. Don't apply pressure on Viton-tipped inlet valve. Adjust by bending float tang.

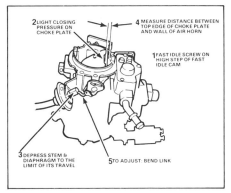

(14) Choke-qualifying dimension is in Renew Kit. It varies so widely that no typical dimension can be supplied here. With fast-idle cam on high step, depress vacuum-break stem. While applying light closing pressure on choke plate, measure qualifying dimension between top edge of choke plate and air horn. Adjust by bending link. Drawing courtesy Holley.

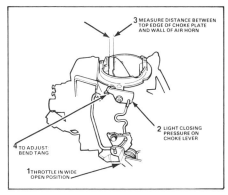

(15) Choke unloader (dechoke) adjustment is made at WOT with light closing pressure on choke. Measure unloader dimension between top edge of choke plate and air horn. Dimension is in Renew Kit instructions. No typical dimension can be supplied here. Drawing courtesy Holley. Other adjustments described in Renew Kit instructions include Throttle Position Transducer, Fast-Idle Cam Index and Bowl Vent. Manually operate throttle and choke mechanisms, checking for binding or other malfunctions. Any binding or interference could result in uncontrolled engine speed. Once carburetor is on car, check to be sure there are no leaks or flooding that might cause a fire. Drawing courtesy Holley.

MODEL 2280

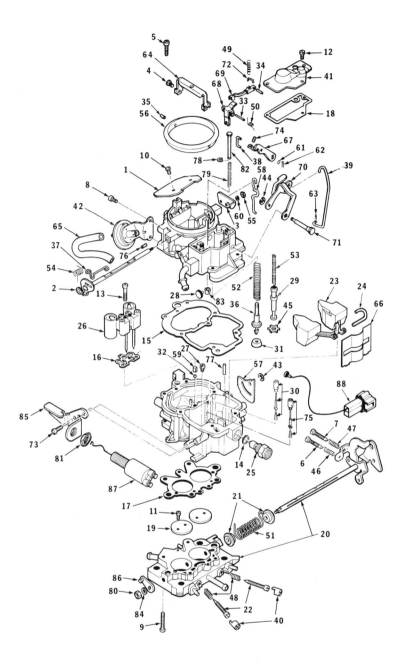

21. Throttle return spring bushings
22. Idle adjust needle
23. Float & hinge assy.
24. Float hinge & retainer
25. Fuel inlet needle & seat assy
26. Nozzle bar assy.
27. Main jet
28. Vent valve
29. Power valve piston
30. Power valve assy.
31. Pump cup
32. Pump discharge ball
33. Vent valve lever pin
34. Vent valve operating lever pin
35. Air cleaner ring retaining pin
36. Pump stem & head assy.
37. Choke diaphragm link
38. Pump stem link
39. Pump link
40. Idle needle limiter
41. Accelerator pump housing
42. Choke diaphragm assy.
43. Fast idle cam retainer
44. Pump operating lever retainer
45. Power valve piston retainer
46. Throttle stop screw spring
47. Fast idle adjusting screw spring
48. Idle adjust needle spring
49. Vent valve operating lever spring
50. Vent valve spring
51. Throttle return spring
52. Pump drive spring
53. Power valve piston spring
54. Choke shaft spring
55. Dechoke lever nut
56. Air cleaner ring
57. Fast idle cam
58. Fast idle rod
59. Pump discharge weight
60. Dechoke lever nut l.w.
63. Pump link retainer
64. Air cleaner bracket
65. Vacuum hose
66. Float baffle
67. Pump lever
68. Vent valve lever
69. Vent valve operating lever
70. Pump operating lever
71. Pump operating lever shaft
72. Vent valve retainer
73. T.P.T. bracket screw
74. Power valve adjusting screw
75. Power valve assy, (staged)
76. Choke diaphragm link pin
77. Roll pin
78. Power valve stem retainer
79. Power valve spring
80. T.P.T. lever nut
81. T.P.T. assy, locknut
82. Mechanical power valve stem
83. Mechanical. power valve stem cap
84. T.P.T. lever lockwasher
85. T.P.T. bracket
86. T.P.T. lever
87. T.P.T. assy.
88. T.P.T. wire assy.

1. Choke plate
2. Choke shaft & lever assy.
3. Dechoke lever
4. Air-cleaner bracket screw
5. Air horn to main body screw & l.w.
6. Throttle stop screw
7. Fast idle adjusting screw
8. Retaining bracket
9. Throttle body to main body screw & l.w.
10. Choke plate screw
11. Throttle plate screw
12. Cover screw
13. Nozzle bar screw
14. Fuel-inlet gasket
15. Main body gasket
16. Nozzle bar gasket
17. Throttle body gasket
18. Pump housing cover gasket
19. Throttle plate
20. Throttle body & shaft assy.

Model 2210/11/45 Repair & Adjustment

(1) These three models are very similar. Model 2210 was used for system descriptions; 2211 and 2245 are used for repair photos. Place carburetor on stand or 5/16-in. bolts and nuts to prevent throttle-plate damage. Note which slot the pump link is in. Mark slot so you can put it back correctly on reassembly. Remove nut and lock washer from accelerator-pump shaft (at box wrench). Remove lever. Remove pump link. Remove nut retaining choke lever to choke shaft (top arrow). Remove lever and link to fast-idle cam. Be careful with the fast-idle-cam retainer clip (bottom arrow), they're easy to lose. Remove hairpin attaching link to integral choke.

(2) On divorced-choke models, disconnect vacuum hose. Remove two screws holding vacuum-break to air horn. Remove vacuum break, including link to choke lever. Remove inlet fitting with its filter (GM models).

(3) If there is an external bowl vent, remove clip holding bowl-vent lever and slide lever from pivot pin, being careful not to lose spring mounted inside of lever.

(4) Remove 8 or 9 screws holding air horn to main body. Note: One screw is hidden in air horn. Less-obvious screw may be threaded as an air-cleaner mount. If used, it is in center of air-horn opening. Use pliers to get it out. A slight rap may be needed to separate the castings. If you insert a putty knife into bowl gasket, don't shove it in at screw holes. There are two dowels in air horn and well tubes extend below it. You don't want to cut these off.

(5) Lift air horn straight up, being careful not to damage main-well tubes.

(6) Remove fuel-inlet fitting, filter (GM models) and gasket from air horn. Remove fuel-inlet baffle from casting by removing retaining screw. Remove float hinge pin and float. With a wide-blade screwdriver, remove fuel-inlet seat and gasket. Push on accelerator-pump plunger while pushing in on shaft to allow disassembly of pump plunger, spring and retainer. On 2211 rotate cranked end of pump shaft to vertical and remove accelerator-pump stem from shaft.

Remove air-horn gasket and discard. If you have to scrape it off, be careful not to damage sealing surface. It's best to use spray-on gasket remover, then use plastic scraper or fingernail to get rid of gasket residue. Photo shows air horn completely disassembled except for power-valve piston.

(7) If power-valve-piston is sticking (doesn't move up and down freely), first squirt carburetor cleaner around stem and try to move piston up and down. If this fails, remove piston assembly. Because this requires removing staked material from around retainer and restaking upon reassembly, don't do it if you don't have to. A screwdriver and few raps with hammer can accomplish the restaking. Arrows indicate staking.

(8) Loosen screws holding vent-valve cover and remove cover, valve and spring. Don't immerse power-valve-piston assembly in strong carburetor cleaner. Check choke plate and shaft for binding or damage. If either exist, remove choke assembly. Don't do this if you don't have to because staking must be removed from attachment screws. Screws must be restaked on reassembly. Choke shaft must be supported to prevent bending during restaking.

(9) Model 2211 vent valve. Note spring that is captured by cover.

(10) Turn casting upside down and catch accelerator-pump discharge valve as it drops out.

(11) Disassemble main body. Use wide-blade screwdriver to remove power valve from bottom of fuel bowl, being careful not to bend power-valve stem. Remove main jets. Remove fast-idle-cam retainer and cam. Main body is completely disassembled and ready for cleaning.

(12) Remove five screws holding throttle body to main body.

(13) Turn idle-mixture screws clockwise (lean direction) until limiter caps reach stops. Photo shows idle limiter in lean position. Pry off idle-limiter caps with screwdriver or pliers, being careful not to turn or bend mixture screws. Turn screws in gently until seated, counting turns. Record this information and use it on reassembly if kit contains new limiter caps. Remove mixture screws.

(14) Photo shows throttle-body assembly with idle-mixture screws removed. Don't remove throttle plates from throttle body unless there is damage or wear. If you remove plates, staking must be removed from attachment screws. Screws must be restaked upon reassembly to prevent them from loosening and causing engine damage. Throttle shaft must be supported during restaking. Carburetor is ready for cleaning.

2210/11/45 CLEANING & ASSEMBLY

Remember, don't immerse any plastic, rubber or electrical parts into strong carburetor cleaner—only metal parts. Clean all surfaces thoroughly and blow out all passages with compressed air.

Before reassembly, inspect all parts to be reused for undue wear or damage. Pay particular attention to choke and throttle shafts and the float. In most cases parts supplied in Renew Kit, such as inlet and power valves, pump cup and all gaskets are only ones that need replacing.

When reassembling carburetor, simply follow the disassembly process in reverse. This carburetor is relatively easy to assemble. Screws attaching air horn and throttle body to main body require about 30 in-lb of torque for good retention. If you don't have a torque wrench, turn them down until they are snug.

Photographs of adjustments are also shown. These include float setting and drop, rough curb and fast-idle speed, choke vacuum-kick or qualify, dechoke or unloader setting, accelerator pump and vent-valve clearance.

(15) Measure dry float setting between float and casting with assembly inverted as shown. Specification is 0.180 in., about 3/16 in. Adjust by bending tang at inlet-valve end, being careful not to mar contact surface.

(16) Float drop is adjusted by bending back tang (arrow) so bottom surface of float parallels gasket surface.

(17) Normal or curb-idle adjustment. Adjust engine rpm later, but three turns from seating throttle plates bores is close.

(18) With fast-idle screw set on high step of cam . . .

(19) . . . adjust screw for 0.025-in. clearance between throttle plate and bore. This is good fast-idle-speed setting. If using tachometer, set speed at 1700 rpm with screw in same position and engine warm.

(20) Choke qualify (vacuum kick) is measured between choke plate and casting at high side. Use vacuum source (the engine) to activate vacuum break. Measure clearance with slight pressure on choke plate as shown. Specification is in Renew Kit instruction sheet. Adjust by bending link.

(21) Dechoke spec is checked between plate and casting with throttle wide-open. See Renew Kit instructions for correct dimension. Adjust by bending tang on throttle lever (arrow).

(23) Vent valve clearance over stem with throttle at normal or curb idle position varies. See Renew Kit instructions for specifications for your specific carburetor. Adjust by bending tang (arrow).

(22) Bend pump link until you get a 5/8-in. pump-stem-to-casting dimension as shown with link at inside or pump-lever position (1). Position (2) decreases pump capacity.

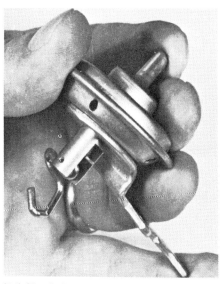

(24) Check divorced-choke vacuum break by pushing stem in and holding finger over end of vacuum tube. If stem moves more than 1/16-in. in 10 seconds, replace assembly. Integral-choke vacuum break requires applying a vacuum source to choke assembly and observing operation of choke lever

Manually operate throttle and choke mechanisms, checking for binding or other malfunctions. Any binding or interference could result in uncontrolled engine speed. Once carburetor is on car, check to be sure there are no leaks or flooding that might cause a fire.

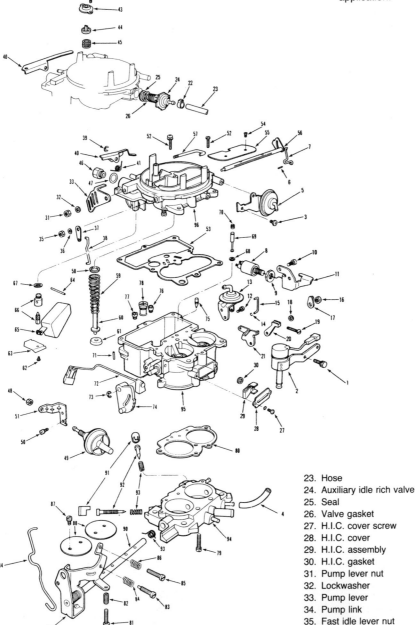

MODEL 2210/2245

NOTE: General view is useful for visualizing relationship of various parts in the carburetor. Specific details vary with P/Ns because each carburetor is manufactured to fit a specific application.

1. Solenoid bracket screw
2. Solenoid assembly
3. Choke diaphragm bracket screw
4. Choke diaphragm hose
5. Choke diaphragm assembly
6. Choke link pin
7. Choke link
8. Throttle position transducer
9. Transducer adjusting nut
10. Transducer bracket screw
11. Transducer bracket

12. Modulator bracket screw
13. Modulator-choke side
14. Link retainer
15. Link
16. Nut
17. Lever
18. Lockwasher
19. Adjusting screw
20. Pick-up lever
21. Modulator lever & bushing
22. Hose clamp

23. Hose
24. Auxiliary idle rich valve
25. Seal
26. Valve gasket
27. H.I.C. cover screw
28. H.I.C. cover
29. H.I.C. assembly
30. H.I.C. gasket
31. Pump lever nut
32. Lockwasher
33. Pump lever
34. Pump link
35. Fast idle lever nut
36. Lockwasher
37. Fast idle lever
38. Fast idle rod
39. Lever retainer
40. Vent valve lever
41. Spring
42. Screw
43. Vent clamp
44. Vent valve
45. Spring
46. Fuel inlet fitting
47. Inlet fitting gasket

48. Locknut
49. Dashpot
50. Bracket screw
51. Dashpot bracket
52. Airhorn to main body screw
    & lockwasher
53. Airhorn
54. Choke plate screw
55. Choke plate
56. Choke shaft & lever
57. Pump lever shaft
58. Drive spring washer
59. Pump drive spring
60. Pump stem
61. Pump piston cup
62. Baffle screw
63. Baffle
64. Float hinge pin
65. Float assembly
66. Needle & seat
67. Needle seat gasket
68. Power valve piston retainer
69. Power valve piston
70. Piston spring
71. Stop & cable pin
72. Stop & cable assembly
73. Fast idle cam retainer
74. Fast idle cam
75. Pump discharge valve
76. Main jet-choke side
77. Main jet-throttle side
78. Power valve
79. Throttle body to main body screw
    & lockwasher
80. Throttle body gasket
81. Solenoid adjusting screw
82. Spring
83. Fast idle screw
84. Spring
85. Throttle stop screw
86. Spring
87. Throttle plate screw
    & lockwasher
88. Throttle plate
89. Throttle shaft & lever
90. Redundancy spring
91. Idle limiter cap
92. Idle needle
93. Idle needle spring
94. Throttle body
95. Main body
96. Airhorn

MODEL 2211

NOTE—General view is useful for visualizing relationship of various parts in the carburetor. Specific details vary with P/Ns because each carburetor is manufactured to fit a specific application.

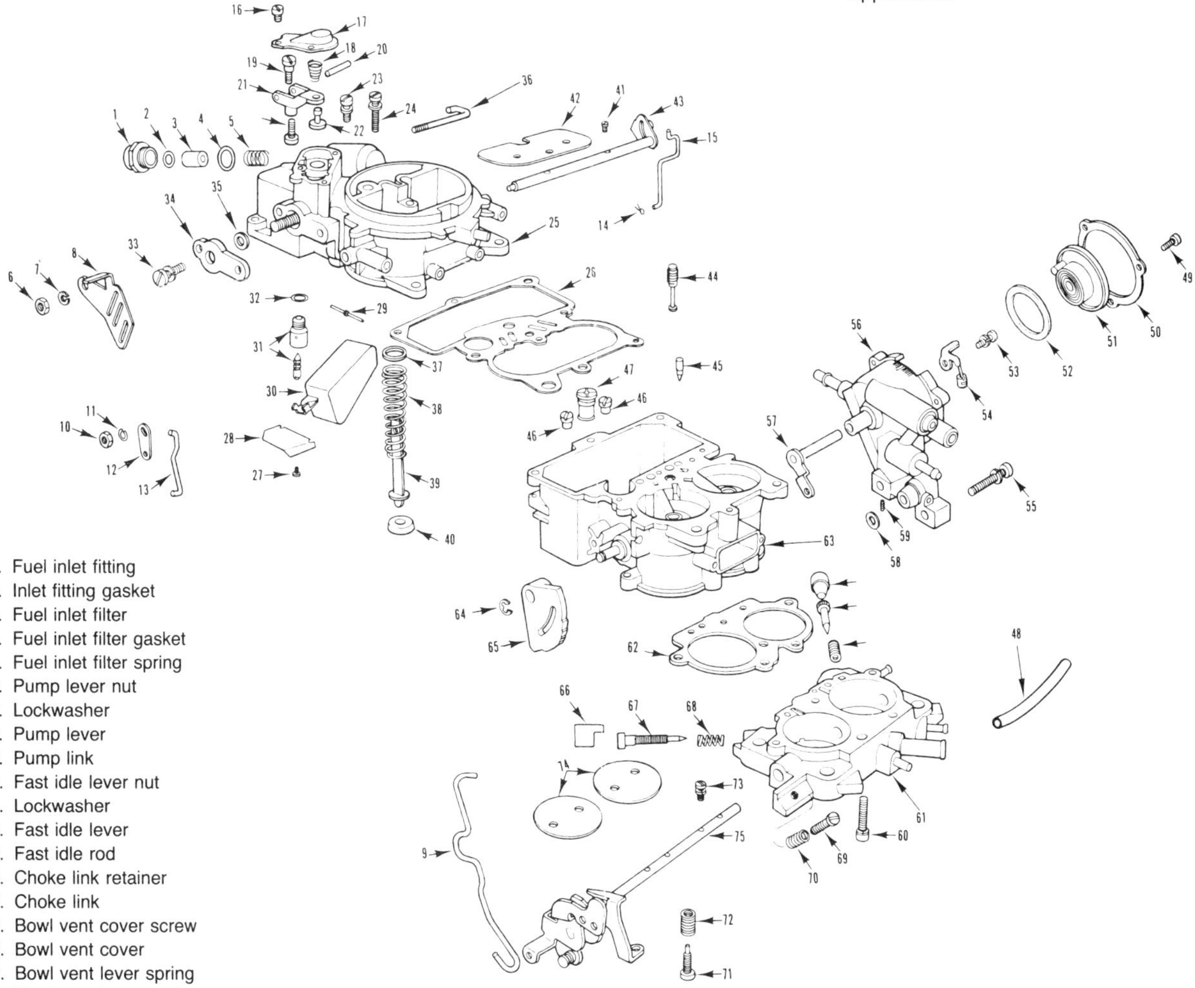

1. Fuel inlet fitting
2. Inlet fitting gasket
3. Fuel inlet filter
4. Fuel inlet filter gasket
5. Fuel inlet filter spring
6. Pump lever nut
7. Lockwasher
8. Pump lever
9. Pump link
10. Fast idle lever nut
11. Lockwasher
12. Fast idle lever
13. Fast idle rod
14. Choke link retainer
15. Choke link
16. Bowl vent cover screw
17. Bowl vent cover
18. Bowl vent lever spring
19. Bowl vent lever retainer screw
20. Bowl vent lever hinge pin
21. Bowl vent lever
22. Bowl vent seal
23. Air horn screw & lockwasher (short)
24. Air horn screw & lockwasher (long)
25. Air horn assembly
26. Air horn gasket
27. Fuel bowl baffle screw & lockwasher
28. Fuel bowl baffle
29. Float hinge pin
30. Float assembly
31. Needle & seat assembly
32. Needle seat gasket
33. Pump shaft retainer screw & lockwasher
34. Pump shaft retainer
35. Pump lever shaft washer
36. Pump lever shaft
37. Drive spring washer
38. Pump drive spring
39. Pump stem
40. Pump piston cup

41. Choke plate screw
42. Choke plate
43. Choke shaft & lever
44. Power valve piston
45. Pump discharge valve
46. Main meter jet
47. Power valve assembly
48. Choke diaphragm hose
49. Thermostat clamp screw
50. Thermostat cap retainer ring
51. Thermostat & cap assembly
52. Thermostat housing gasket
53. Choke lever screw & lockwasher
54. Choke thermostat lever & piston assembly
55. Choke housing screw & lockwasher
56. Choke housing assembly
57. Choke lever & shaft assy.
58. Choke housing gasket
59. Choke piston adj. screw
60. Throttle body to main body screw & lockwasher

61. Throttle body assembly
62. Throttle body gasket
63. Main body assembly
64. Fast idle cam retainer
65. Fast idle cam
66. Idle limiter cap
67. Idle adjusting needle
68. Idle adjusting needle spring
69. Throttle stop screw
70. Throttle stop screw spring
71. Fast idle screw
72. Fast idle screw spring
73. Throttle plate screw
74. Throttle plate
75. Throttle shaft & lever assy.

Metering block for Model 4150 alcohol carb has 1/8-in. hole above normal main jets. These holes connect into main well to supply addition fuel flow required when running alcohol. Jet changes are still made with the main jets. Fuel inlet valve has steel inlet needle, 0.130-in. inlet.

ALCOHOL STRUCTURE

Alcohols are a partial oxidation product of petroleum and are not found in basic crude oil. To get technical, from a chemistry point of view, the alcohol compound contains a basic paraffin hydrocarbon radical with a hydroxyl radical attached.

As an example, the formula for methane or natural gas is CH_4. This means there is one carbon molecule and four of hydrogen. The formula for methyl alcohol or methanol is CH_4O. You can see that we've added oxygen. That's what we mean by the partial oxidation of a paraffin hydrocarbon.

Ethane, also a gas, has a formula C_2H_6. Add oxygen and you get C_2H_6O or ethyl alcohol, known also as *ethanol*.

We could go on and on. Add oxygen to any of the paraffins and you get the corresponding alcohol. The last time we counted there were well over 20. But, for our purposes, let's limit our discussion to the first two: methanol and ethanol.

Ethanol—The chemistry for this type is explained above, now let's get to the nitty gritty. Ethanol or *grain alcohol* is so named because it is derived from the fermentation or distillation of fruits and grains. The alcohol in beer, wine and all types of distilled spirits is ethanol.

But ethanol can be used as a fuel. We won't write the combustion formula, but if ethanol is burned perfectly or stoichiometrically, the air fuel ratio is 9.0:1. This means there are 9 pounds of air consumed for every pound of ethanol. The stoichiometric mixture for gasoline is 14.7 pounds of air per pound of fuel. We must put in 1.63 the amount or 63% more ethanol than gasoline per pound of air. Consequently, fuel metering orifices will need to be larger, but only about 56% larger in cross sectional area since ethanol has a slightly higher *specific gravity* than gasoline.

The heating value of ethanol is about 12,800 Btu per pound. (*Btu* stands for British thermal unit, which is the amount of heat required to increase the temperature of one pound of water one degree Fahrenheit.) Which means that 12,800 Btu of energy are released when we burn one pound of fuel. When the engine burns one pound of air, 1422 Btu are released.

Now examine gasoline's values. It has a heating value of 20,700 Btu per pound. It releases 1408 Btu when the engine burns one pound of air. In this case, it is a wash. We gain no increase in energy when burning ethanol.

Ethanol has an octane rating of 106 while normal unleaded pump gasoline runs about 87, a definite plus for ethanol. The octane numbers we're using in this chapter are *research numbers*. Octane is also rated by *motor numbers,* which run about 10% lower. The advertised numbers have traditionally been the higher research numbers, of course. Recent legislation states that the number on the pump shall be an average of the two. Are you totally confused? Anyway, we'll use the higher research numbers in all cases so that we're comparing like values to like values.

During the past two crude oil shortages there was considerable interest in ethanol as a motor fuel. Our country has great capacity beyond our current output to produce grains of all types and so produce ethanol. The process is expensive and would only be practical if the price of crude increased many times over its value at the time of this writing.

Ethanol is excellent as a gasoline extender, that is, added to gasoline to conserve its usage. This product is called *gasohol* and is very successful in extending octane rating as well as gasoline usage. There are usually no adverse effects to the fuel system as long as the alcohol content is held to 10% or less. Gasohol has been used quite successfully since the mid-70s.

But there is one problem when using alcohol as a blend with gasoline. The alcohol in the mixture can absorb water, either vapor or liquid, from its surroundings. Unfortunately, after the water has reached a certain concentration, about 1/2 of 1%, the alcohol and water separate from the mixture with the gasoline. They become stratified, with the alcohol and water mixture forming the lower layer, because it is heavier.

You can picture what happens. The heavier water and alcohol mixture goes to the bottom of the carburetor fuel bowl. This causes a lean condition and the vehicle just won't run. This is not a hypothetical case. It actually happens, given the right concentration of water.

Methanol—Methyl alcohol or *methanol* is produced from natural gas, coal or practically any form of bio-mass, including forest products, agricultural or municipal waste. Gas and coal are in abundant domestic supply. And other feed stocks are renewable.

With perfect burning conditions, as described earlier, the air/fuel ratio for methanol is 6.4:1. Since gasoline requires 14.7:1, we need 2.30 times the amount of methanol or 130% more than gasoline for every pound of air.

The heating value of methanol is 9800 Btu

per pound. This means that 1530 Btu are released when the engine burns a pound of air. Remember, we said earlier that only 1408 Btu were released by gasoline when the engine burned one pound of air. This amounts to almost a 9% gain in energy at equal airflow rates, a definite advantage. Of course, we have to pay the price of adding 130% more fuel. Again, because methanol is a little heavier, metering orifices need only be 120% larger in cross-sectional area.

Methanol's octane rating is about 106, the same as ethanol. Like ethanol, it has been used as a gasoline extender in concentrations as high as 10%. We have to be careful with concentrations much higher than this, because corrosion and attacking of synthetic materials such as diaphragms and accelerator pump cups occurs.

Also, remember that the carburetor's orificies need to be much larger, so we can expect some degradation of vehicle driveability when using unmodified carburetors with concentrations of methanol as low as 10%. The stratification problem caused by absorption of water, as described above, is also true of methanol.

So what's methanol's primary advantage? It can be produced at about 1/3 the cost of ethanol.

METHANOL AS AN ALTERNATE FUEL

Methanol is probably the best bet as an alternate fuel if a crude shortage and high costs ever appear again. This is likely given that there is a finite amount of crude available in the world. You'll hear all kinds of opinions as to what that number is, but it is a finite quantity.

All of the major auto companies and a lot of others have programs evaluating the feasibility of running with "neat" or 100% methanol.

Advantages—Besides being the best candidate economically for mass production, methanol has some other advantages because of the characteristics stated above.

Because more energy can be attained per pound of air, greater power output can be attained with the same engine. And the increased octane opens several performance possibilities. Ignition timing can be advanced and compression ratios increased. This puts more "tune" back in the engine and increases efficiency.

Disadvantages—*Methanol is toxic: avoid breathing the fumes and contact with your skin* (use rubber gloves when handling it). Of course, you can't drink it either. It's also highly corrosive, especially in the presence of aluminum and brass. More expensive materials, such as stainless steel, have to be used in the fuel supply and delivery systems. In addition, castings must be nickel-plated. All this adds signif-

icantly to production costs.

Most of the lower cost elastomers and gaskets designed to be compatible with today's gasolines are attacked by methanol. They will have to be replaced with more exotic materials such as fluorocarbons, again adding cost.

Fuel flow capacity must be increased by 130%. This means larger metering orifices in carburetors and higher capacity injectors in fuel injection systems. Fuel pumps must have higher capacity. Fuel supply lines must be larger and fuel filters less restrictive. To attain the same cruising range, fuel tanks must be larger, which could be a problem with today's down-sized vehicles.

There are some operating problems at both cold and hot temperatures. Because the boiling point of methanol is 149F (65C), there is no vapor available at low temperatures, making cold starting very difficult. To overcome this problem, the fuel is "spiked" with 10% Isopentane, which has a much lower boiling point.

Another problem occurs at the other end of the thermometer—hot starting. Gasoline is a heterogeneous mixture of many different hydrocarbons, each having a unique boiling point. So, during shut-off, after running the engine in high ambient temperatures, the fuel in the tank and carburetor bowl boils or vaporizes gradually as temperature rises.

This is not so with methanol, which is a single homogeneous compound. There is virtually no vaporization until the fuel bowl reaches 149F (65C). At this point, all of the fuel will boil, causing percolation and vapor lock. A fuel bowl temperature of 149F is easily reached in Southern climates in the summer. These problems can be overcome by increased venting, vapor return lines and an in-tank electric fuel pump.

Methanol has poorer lubricative properties than gasoline, therefore an additive must be used to prevent excessive wear to valve seats and guides.

In summary, methanol is not a practical replacement for gasoline in existing production vehicles. It is, however, a viable fuel when used with a fuel supply, induction and exhaust system specifically designed for methanol. For methanol to work as an alternative to gasoline, commercial fuel handing systems have to be greatly changed. Vehicle costs increase because more expensive materials are used and special vapor handling mechanisms are employed. Nevertheless, it is a fuel that can be inexpensively manufactured if the supply of crude oil should dry up or become much more expensive.

RACING WITH METHANOL

Because of the low manufacturing cost com-

pared with the other alcohols, methanol is the only alcohol practical as a racing fuel. So, we will limit our discussion to it.

We stated before that methanol has greater output per pound of air and the octane rating is higher. Add to that the fact that methanol burns cooler and cleaner and we have a very popular racing fuel. A natural. In fact, the fuel has been widely used in circle track racing for quite some time, especially with fuel injection. Currently, the fuel sees use in grass roots drag racing and specialty events such as tractor pulls.

During the fuel crisis of 1981, various racing sanctioning bodies became concerned about the adverse publicity surrounding the use of gasoline in motor sports. Remember, this was when the average driver had to stand in long lines to get fuel, if he could get it at all. Never mind that the fuel used in racing was an insignificant amount compared with the total usage. Plus, some racers were having trouble obtaining the fuels they desired and costs were rocketing.

The opportunity existed to show the concern that the racing industry had for the problem and to prove that the use of alcohol in an engine was practical. A chance to take a leadership position was at hand.

Holley was encouraged by these sanctioning bodies to supply racing carburetors designed and calibrated to run on methanol. It responded with three new carburetors. The Model 2300 two barrel, list number 0-9647, flows 500 cfm. Two new Model 4150 four barrels were also released. List 0-9645, which flows 750 cfm and 0-9646 with 850-cfm capacity.

Carburetor Modifications—These are based on existing models with modifications made to adapt them to methanol. The main wells, metering body cross channels and booster IDs were opened up as much as possible while staying within the confines of their respective castings.

A supplemental drilling of 0.125-in. diameter was added from the fuel bowl to each main well. This drilling is just above each main jet. The purpose is to introduce more fuel into the main system without requiring larger main jets. Main jets couldn't be made larger without changing to a larger external size.

Needles and seats are steel with an opening of 0.130 in., the largest possible. Holley recommends a fuel pressure at idle of 9 psi to ensure maximum possible fuel flow into the bowl. Any higher pressure would be inviting fuel handling problems. Brass floats are used because Nitrophyl will not hold up in methanol. New hollow plastic floats were added in 1987.

All accelerator pumps are the 50cc variety with pump shooters in the 0.042-in. area.

No special plating was added to the castings and the pump diaphragm material was not changed. These items would have added considerable cost to the carburetors. Instead, racers should tear the carburetor down more often, clean it and change the diaphragms and gaskets. Holley recommends that after each use with alcohol, the fuel system be purged with gasoline.

Holley recommends using a 12-802 electric fuel pump with the external regulator. Two reasons here: the pump has few rubber parts and has the capability of providing the 9 psi needed. Clean the pump and install a new repair kit at frequent intervals.

There has been a problem with using this pump. The rubber gasket between the body and cover plate can swell. Use this gasket as a template to make one from a higher-grade material. A fluoro-silicone gasket material is best.

With multiple carburction use one pump and one regulator for each carburetor. Use 1/2-in. steel fuel lines, never rubber hose.

In summary, methanol is an excellent racing fuel. Anyone using it should be aware of its toxicity and the problems when using it, and be prepared to deal with them. All fuel-metering orifices must be larger and fuel supply capacity needs to be much greater than gasoline. Corrosion and incompatibility with some rubbers and plastics must be adapted to.

SHORT TRACK RACING WITH METHANOL

Norm Schenck of Competition Fuel Systems (3820 E. 44th St. Unit 410, Tucson, AZ 85713) has years of experience supplying and modifying Holley methanol carburetors for racers. The remaining text in this chapter was written by Norm. It's based on knowledge he has gained from being at races and his research and development in racing methanol carburetors.

"Because methanol carburetion applies itself best to oval short track racing, and because that is where the majority of methanol carbs are being used, most of my comments are about running methanol in short track racing engines.

Methanol Improvements—"When we compare gasoline to methyl alcohol (methanol), the most important factors to consider are improved torque and horsepower (HP), and cooler engine temperatures.

"When methanol is run in American wedge-chamber engines, we usually see a mid-range torque increase of 8—12% over gasoline, depending on compression ratio, valve timing, combustion chamber design and many other factors. Even with some of these being far from optimum, there will be, in most cases, a significant torque increase with methanol. At the majority of short tracks, 'off-the corner' torque is the most important factor of the engine's output, and this is the major reason for the popularity of methanol in this type of racing.

"Top-end HP increases with methanol range from moderate losses to increases around 10%.

The reason for this wide range is that high-rpm combustion efficiency varies widely from one engine to another. With methanol, good combustion efficiency is more difficult to achieve because methanol is a slower burning fuel. Compared with gasoline, methanol will usually require 3—5° more ignition advance and a higher energy spark to get combustion properly started and progressing.

"To allow the flame travel to progress across and around the combustion-chamber volume, combustion chamber and piston dome design must not impede the movement of the flame front any more than is necessary to achieve the desired static compression ratio. The higher the compression ratio, especially over 13:1, the more critical chamber and dome shapes become if good high-rpm flame travel is to be maintained.

"Generally, the faster the flame travel proceeds through the combustion volume, the more complete the combustion will be, thus making more cylinder pressure (during the power stroke) available to produce power at the flywheel.

"Higher compression ratios will nearly always increase mid-range torque because there is adequate *time* available for flame travel. But improvements in high-rpm HP *may be little or none* if high-rpm flame travel is slowed by a larger piston dome used to increase the compression ratio.

"The characteristics of methanol can be used to help cool the engine. Methanol's richer air/fuel ratio cools in two ways. First, the increased volume of fuel absorbs more heat energy from the intake system in the process of vaporizing, and second, the combustion temperatures with methanol are generally 100—150F (38—65C) lower than with gasoline.

"The price to get the power and cooling benefits from methanol is paid in the components (carb, fuel pump, fuel lines and so forth) necessary to deliver the larger volume of fuel to the engine. Compared with gasoline, methanol fuel flow will be from 2—2.5 times higher, depending on the combustion efficiency of the engine and cooling efficiency of the cooling system in the race car.

"A convenient term to describe fuel flow requirements is *Brake Specific Fuel Consumption* (BSFC). This is the fuel flow (in lb/hr) at a particular rpm divided by the observed HP at that rpm. It is stated as 'lb per HP-hr.' The BSFC of short track engines in track tune is usually around 1.0—1.2, but has been seen as good as 0.88 and as bad as 1.35. An engine with good combustion efficiency and cooled by an efficient cooling system can have a BSFC at the lower end of this range without having overheating or detonation problems.

"If combustion or cooling system efficiency falls off, more fuel will be needed to maintain the engine at a reasonable temperature. This

increases fuel consumption and lowers torque and HP, making the BSFC numbers rise quickly into the inefficient end of their range—over 1.15. This demonstrates that the myth about not needing a good cooling system when running methanol is false, particularly when you are running a track that will accept as much torque and HP as your engine can make.

ENGINE MODIFICATIONS

Norm continues: "There are other engine modifications, in addition to increased compression ratio and total ignition advance, that are needed to achieve all of the potential response and power improvements of methanol over gasoline.

Intake Manifold—"One of the most important considerations is the size and shape of intake manifold and cylinder head intake passages. Because methanol air mixtures are so rich with fuel, some potential airflow of the engine is being 'crowded out' by the fuel.

"To compensate for this requires an increase in the volume of intake plenum and ports. But this port volume increase must be approached carefully so that mixture velocity doesn't drop low enough to affect the volumetric efficiency (VE) of the intake stroke, or to allow some of fuel to 'drop out' of the mixture flow and 'puddle' in the bottom of the plenum.

"Another requirement to keep the fuel in the airflow is to keep the number of directional changes that the fuel/air mixture has to make on its way to the cylinders to a minimum. And make each of those changes as gentle as possible (i.e., largest radius curvatures possible). For this reason, most short-track engines will work better with a single-plane intake manifold, because the mixture flow has fewer and gentler turns compared with other manifolds.

"The temperature of the intake system needs to be higher with methanol for two reasons. First, a higher temperature encourages even mixture distribution, minimizes fuel 'drop out' problems (at lower engine speeds) and maximizes combustion efficiency. It is necessary to vaporize as much of the fuel (in the fuel/air mixture flowing through the intake system) as possible *before* it gets to the cylinders.

"A methanol/air mixture (at its proper fuel/air ratio) requires about 9 times more heat energy (compared with a gasoline/air mixture) to vaporize the fuel. Most of that heat energy must be provided by the intake system. The cooler the intake air temperature above the carburetor, the warmer the intake system needs to be to compensate.

"In weather where the air temperature is below 50F (10C), heating the area under the intake manifold plenum with engine coolant improves engine performance through the entire rpm range, particularly low speed driveability, and mid-range response and torque.

"The second reason for making the engine's

heat available to the fuel/air mixture is to take some of cooling load off of the cooling system by absorbing some of heat generated by the engine to vaporize the fuel in the intake system.

"The typical short-track V8 engine running methanol will run best when the engine coolant temperature is between 190—210F (88—99C). As stated before, the racer will be HP ahead by making the cooling system as efficient as possible. And, in many cases, you should use a thermostat to *regulate* engine temperature—rather than using excess fuel to absorb the heat the otherwise inefficient cooling system can't handle.

Ignition Advance— "Modifications to engine ignition advance must be done to compensate for the slow burning characteristics of methanol, especially at part-throttle conditions with engine speeds below 3000 rpm. To improve low speed driveability and response with methanol, I *decrease* the amount of mechanical (centrifugal) advance in the distributor so that I can *increase* the amount of initial advance at the engine's idle speed.

"For example, a typical *high-compression* short-track small-block Chevrolet V8 engine will require *at least* 20° initial advance at idle speed (to idle and respond properly), and around 36°—38° total advance (all in by 3000 rpm at the latest). Some engines respond better to completely *locked* timing (no mechanical advance at all) to get a smooth steady idle, and sharp low speed response and driveability.

"Generally, the smaller the engine displacement and/or the longer the intake duration of the camshaft, the more initial timing needed to get good idle and low speed characteristics.

Connecting Rods— "To extend the torque improvements of methanol, many engine builders are using longer-than-stock connecting rods to increase the rod length/stroke ratio of the engine. By increasing this ratio, engine torque above 3000 rpm can be improved because higher cylinder pressures are generated during the power stroke. When this 'rod ratio' is *properly matched* to the engine's application and to the other components (heads, camshaft), torque improvement will be achieved.

Camshaft— "Camshaft selection for a methanol engine, especially one with a higher rod ratio and larger intake port volumes, is one of the most critical component selections. The cam must work with everything else in the engine to make the intake and exhaust cycles of the engine as efficient as possible through the entire rpm range the engine will see on the track.

"When rod ratios are higher and port volumes are larger, it is much easier to 'overcam' the engine. In particular, a little too much intake duration can really limit mid-range torque. This is because increased duration, combined with larger ports and longer rods, can allow the fuel/air mixture velocity in the intake ports to drop below a certain level. Below this level the VE of the intake cycles of the engine drops quickly. When the proper intake profile is used, that torque comes back, but check too that there is no loss of top-end HP.

CARBURETOR MODIFICATIONS

"When all of the engine component selections and modifications are done, all *that* information and some 'at-the-track' data should be used to select and modify the proper carburetor for the engine. This is just as important as camshaft selection when trying to get all of the engine components to work together to produce as much power as possible.

"To enable the carburetor to meter the proper amount of fuel needed to produce that power, all fuel delivery components (pump/s, pressure controller/s, fuel lines, fittings, and so forth) must be sized for adequate fuel flow capacity under all racing conditions.

Metering Orifices— "The 'methanol modifications' I do to make a better running Holley methanol carburetor are all designed to allow it to meter the proper amount of fuel under all conditions. Because this amount is 2—2.5 times higher than when metering gasoline, all of the diameters of the metering orifices (jets) and passageways must be increased by about 1.5 times over the proper diameters for gasoline. In many cases, the new passageway diameters required in the metering blocks are very close to the physical limits of the block.

"Special techniques have been developed to increase the flow capacity of these passages, especially on the larger carbs, i.e., 850-cfm 4150s and 1050-cfm Dominators. The most important passage is the one in each venturi booster that carries fuel out to the middle of the venturi. Some boosters have the capability of tolerating a larger passage; others don't.

Booster Signal— "Once the passage has been adequately enlarged without compromising any physical aspects of the booster, then the *booster signal* must be checked to see if it is 'usable' with methanol. This signal is the vacuum draw the booster generates and uses to pull fuel up through the main metering circuits to the venturis (where it is mixed with the incoming air).

"To be a usable methanol booster, the signal range of the booster through the entire airflow range of the carb must satisfy two conditions: It must allow the carb to meter a fairly lean mid-range fuel/air ratio for sharper response and torque. And it must supply a rich enough top-end mixture to keep engine temperature under control, even with a poor cooling system.

Needle & Seat— "The inlet needle and seat assemblies for a methanol carburetor should be chosen to handle fuel pressure and the required flow. They must be matched to meet the pressure capability of the fuel pump at the maximum fuel flow required. And they have to handle the maximum allowable amount of fuel level drop (*float drop*) for the particular carb being used.

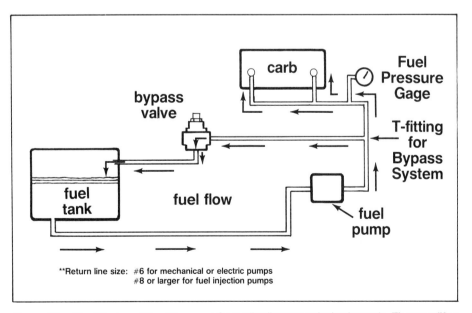

Competition Fuel Systems' Fuel Pressure Controller (bypass valve) schematic. They modify a Holley Hi-Pressure regulator to ensure steady fuel pressure to carburetor. Install valve as shown and ignore "IN" and "OUT" on side of bypass valve. These no longer apply. Connect fuel pressure gage to side of fuel distribution T-fitting at the carb. Set the fuel pressure with engine idling. Run in adjustment screw to increase pressure and back out to decrease. Then reset float levels in carb.

Holley 800-CFM carburetor modified for alcohol use by Competition Fuel Systems of Tucson, Arizona features annular-discharge boosters, removable air bleeds and idle adjustments for each barrel. Special throttle linkage allows adjusting secondary action to tune throttle response off the corners. Pro-Flow fuel line has provisions for fuel-pressure gauge and a bypass valve control circuit.

"Venturi booster signal characteristics, and needle-and-seat flow capacity are interdependent, i.e., one can partially compensate for inadequacies in the other. For example, in my experience, the Holley 4 bbl. methanol carb, 0-9645, tends to run too rich in the mid-range and too lean on the top end because of:

- The factory main jet calibration.
- Inadequate needle-and-seat flow capacity.
- Inadequate (too small) diameter in the venturi booster passage.

"Main jet calibration and needle-and-seat flow are easy to change. But the booster passage is much more difficult to change because of the booster's design. By using a needle-and-seat design with more flow capacity than would normally be needed in a carb this size, we can partially counteract the top-end lean-out tendency caused by the small booster passage size.

"By changing the main jets and needle/seat assemblies, we can get a fuel delivery curve that is safer and more competitive, even though it isn't as good as could be achieved if the booster passage were larger.

Fuel Delivery System—"Just as important as having proper passage sizing and flow capacity in the carb is the fuel flow capacity of the fuel delivery system: pump, line and pressure regulator. This system must deliver the correct amount of fuel to the carb *at the correct pressure.* This is the pressure needed to flow the correct amount of fuel through each needle/seat

assembly with a reasonable amount of float drop.

Fuel Pump—"The six-valve mechanical (pushrod) fuel pump, commonly called the 'NASCAR Pump,' has fuel flow capacity (at 7 psi fuel pressure) to safely handle about 550 HP with average maximum power BSFC of 1.15—1.20. If maximum power BSFC is lower, the *HP capacity* of the pump can be over 600 HP, but there is no safety factor. That is, no reserve capacity to compensate for any problems, such as a slightly clogged fuel filter.

"Engines in this HP range that must run this type of pump by rule, must be designed for maximum combustion efficiency to run safely. The entire fuel system must get daily and weekly maintenance, and the carb must not have *any* tendencies toward a top-end lean-out, which is the most common reason for engine damage.

"For those classes that don't specifically require a pushrod fuel pump, engines over 550 HP should use a belt-driven fuel-injection pump, i.e., the Hilborn 150-A. It's called the 'dash zero' pump. EVM, Enderle and Kinsler also make suitable pumps. The extra expense for this system should be viewed as a worthwhile insurance policy to protect the healthy investment already made to get the engine to this power level.

Fuel Line & Filters—"Fuel lines should be at least AN-10 size, including the pickup tube in the fuel tank (cell). Fuel filter/s should be of the highest flow capacity available. And filter ele-

ments should be cleaned or replaced at least once a week, particularly in the busiest part of the racing season.

Pressure Regulator—"This should not restrict fuel flow to the carb at full power. For this reason, many racers use a bypass valve system that controls fuel pressure by regulating the *flow* of fuel back to the fuel tank through a return line. This results in higher full power fuel pressure because there is no longer a flow restriction between the fuel pump and carb—a necessary design to help prevent top-end lean-out.

Fuel System Insulation—"Another very helpful, though less obvious modification to prevent lean-out and engine heating problems is to insulate the fuel lines, pump, and filter. By keeping the radiant heat of the engine, exhaust system, and air (from the radiator) away from the fuel in the delivery system, the temperature of fuel getting to the carb will be lower and more constant through the race.

"This lower fuel temperature keeps the specific gravity (density) of the fuel higher, and makes the carb's job of metering the proper amount (lb/hr) of fuel easier. Without insulation, a cycle of rising fuel temperature and engine coolant temperature can occur: Both temperatures keep rising during the race until the cooling system or the engine fails.

RACING PROBLEMS
Water In The Fuel—"Many problems racers have with running methanol are caused by the lack of regular fuel system maintenance. The characteristics of methanol make it harder on all fuel system components than gasoline. Methanol absorbs water moisture directly from the air, even through the fuel tank vent and carb bowl vents.

"The water content in the methanol, if allowed to get high enough, can cause fuel metering lean-out problems in the carb, flow restrictions in pleated-paper fuel filter elements, and severe corrosion of the metal parts in the fuel system.

"To prevent these problems, I recommend that the fuel remaining in the car's fuel cell, lines, pump, and carb fuel bowls should be drained out and put into an airtight container to minimize any further water contamination. This should be done as soon as possible after *each* day's racing is over, even if the car is to be raced the next day.

"A good way to analyze methanol for water contamination is to check the specific gravity of the fuel with a hydrometer. At 60F (16C) fuel temperature (standard checking temperature for fuels), pure methanol has a specific gravity of 0.792. If your methanol (at 60F) has a specific gravity over 0.800, discard it and obtain some new fuel—and check it too."

METRIC CUSTOMARY-UNIT EQUIVALENTS

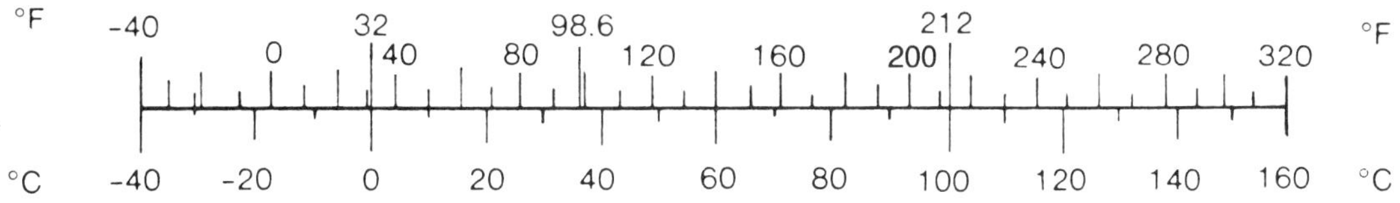

Multiply:		by:		to get:	Multiply:		by:		to get:
LINEAR									
inches	X	25.4	=	millimeters(mm)		X	0.03937	=	inches
miles	X	1.6093	=	kilometers (km)		X	0.6214	=	miles
inches	X	2.54	=	centimeters (cm)		X	0.3937	=	inches
AREA									
inches^2	X	645.16	=	millimeters^2(mm^2)		X	0.00155	=	inches^2
inches^2	X	6.452	=	centimeters^2(cm^2)		X	0.155	=	inches^2
VOLUME									
quarts	X	0.94635	=	liters (l)		X	1.0567	=	quarts
fluid oz	X	29.57	=	milliliters (ml)		X	0.03381	=	fluid oz
MASS									
pounds (av)	X	0.4536	=	kilograms (kg)		X	2.2046	=	pounds (av)
tons (2000 lb)	X	907.18	=	kilograms (kg)		X	0.001102	=	tons (2000 lb)
tons (2000 lb)	X	0.90718	=	metric tons (t)		X	1.1023	=	tons (2000 lb)
FORCE									
pounds−f(av)	X	4.448	=	newtons (N)		X	0.2248	=	pounds−f(av)
kilograms−f	X	9.807	=	newtons (N)		X	0.10197	=	kilograms−f

TEMPERATURE

Degrees Celsius (C) = 0.556 (F - 32)   Degree Fahrenheit (F) = (1.8C) + 32

```
°F   -40          32        98.6              212                   °F
           0    |40    80 | 120    160   200 |  240   280   320
         |  |  |  | |  |  |  |  |  | |  |  |  | |  |  |  |  |  |
°C   -40   -20    0     20    40    60    80   100   120   140   160   °C
```

ENERGY OR WORK

foot-pounds	X	1.3558	=	joules (J)		X	0.7376	=	foot-pounds

FUEL ECONOMY & FUEL CONSUMPTION

miles/gal	X	0.42514	=	kilometers/liter(km/l)		X	2.3522	=	miles/gal

Note:
235.2/(mi/gal) = liters/100km
235.2/(liters/100km) = mi/gal

PRESSURE OR STRESS

inches Hg (60F)	X	3.377	=	kilopascals (kPa)		X	0.2961	=	inches Hg
pounds/sq in.	X	6.895	=	kilopascals (kPa)		X	0.145	=	pounds/sq in
pounds/sq ft	X	47.88	=	pascals (Pa)		X	0.02088	=	pounds/sq ft

POWER

horsepower	X	0.746	=	kilowatts (kW)		X	1.34	=	horsepower

TORQUE

pound-inches	X	0.11298	=	newton-meters (N-m)		X	8.851	=	pound-inches
pound-feet	X	1.3558	=	newton-meters (N-m)		X	0.7376	=	pound-feet
pound-inches	X	0.0115	=	kilogram-meters (Kg-M)		X	87	=	pound-inches
pound-feet	X	0.138	=	kilogram-meters (Kg-M)		X	7.25	=	pound-feet

VELOCITY

miles/hour	X	1.6093	=	kilometers/hour(km/h)		X	0.6214	=	miles/hour

INDEX